GORHAM SILVER

GORHAM SILVER

Charles H. Carpenter, Jr.

Alan Wofsy Fine Arts

San Francisco

1997

Revised edition published 1997 by:

Alan Wofsy Fine Arts

P.O. Box 2210
San Francisco, CA 94126

Fax 415.512.0130

ISBN 1-55660-244-8

Printed in the U.S.A.

Table of Contents

Acknowledgments

Many people contributed to the making of this book. The help of the people at the Gorham Division of Textron was all that one could ask. There was a continuing cheerful willingness on their part to ferret out an incredible variety of records, to answer questions with patience and thoughtfulness, and to suggest interesting facts and ideas. At the same time they understood and agreed with the proposition that a book like this must be written completely independently of the present Gorham organization, that the decision of what was to be included in the book must be the decision of the author. Frank Grzelecki, Gorham's president, and his successor, James Thomas, have been most cooperative. Burr Sebring, Gorham's chief designer, with his knowledge of the company and his knowledge of silver making, was continually helpful. All the people in the Gorham design department were interested in the project; I particularly want to thank Eldred Adams, Richard Cragin, Jeff Elsbecker, Judith Lee, Edward Money, David Rogers, and Steven Wright.

A great many of the photographs in this book are by Richard Arling and his assistant Pat Del Toro. Their long experience in photographing silver is, I believe, evident in the superb quality of their work.

I also wish to thank many other people at Gorham for their help, including: Terre Boudreau, Elmer Caldwell, Leo Cardosi, Lorraine Devault, Karen Grady, Robert Gregg, Werner Leyh, Jack Madden, William Matthew, Roy Moffett, Lucien Sermon, Sidney Speed, George Tompkins, Douglas Ward, and Roy Wood.

A number of people were important in supplying information and helping in the evaluation of material in the book. The matter of style in Chapter I, "Introduction," was discussed at length with Kenneth Ames and Donald Fennimore at Winterthur and Milo Naeve at the Art Institute of Chicago. Their suggestions were carefully considered in writing the final draft of this chapter. Chapter 3, "Coin Silver Spoons," was reviewed by Deborah Waters of Christie's, New York, and Victor F. Hanson of the Winterthur Laboratories. Chapter 6, "Innovation and Fantasy," was reviewed in part by John Culme of Sotheby's Belgravia, London. Some of the Japanese material in Chapter 6 was suggested by Emil G. Schnorr of the George Walter Vincent Smith Art Museum, Springfield, Massachusetts. The basic ideas involved in Chapter 7, "Antoine Heller and the New Academy," were discussed with Richard Guy Wilson of the University of Virginia and Dianne H. Pilgrim of The Brooklyn Museum. Chapter 8, "The Bronzes," was reviewed by Sidney Speed, Robert Gregg, and Douglas Ward of the Bronze Division of Gorham and by Richard Cragin of the Gorham Design Department. Chapter 10, "Souvenir Spoons," was reviewed by Nancy Collins, Donna Felger, and Dorothy Rainwater.

The entire manuscript was critically read by Warren Thomas and Edward Money of Gorham. Warren Thomas's knowledge of Gorham history and the English language was most helpful. Ed Money was helpful in many ways throughout the writing of the book.

Finally, there are three former Gorham employees whom I particularly want to thank. Cheryl Greene's enthusiasm really got me started on the book. Her perception and knowledge of silver-making techniques was most valuable. Many, many of the facts in the book were obtained directly from Florence Rafuse. Her encyclopedic knowledge of the Gorham records made life much easier. Appendix II, "Gorham Sterling Flatware Patterns," simply could not have been written without Miss Rafuse's help. Thank you, Florence. F. Russell Woodward's memories of William Chistmas Codman were a wonderful link with the past. I also want to thank Jeff Elsbecker for his help with Appendix II and Roy Moffett for arranging the photography of the 313 flatware patterns.

I wish to thank the following individuals and organizations: Laurie-Ann Ackerman; American Numismatic Society: Alan Stahl; Art Institute of Chicago: Milo M. Neave; Anglo-American Art Museum, Baton Rouge, Louisiana: H. Parrott Bacot; The Battle Green Inn; Evelyn Bene; William Benedict; Mr. and Mrs. William C. Burt; Dr. Louis J. Camuti; Charles Chapin, Textron; Chicago Historical Society: Sharon Darling, Olivia Mahoney; Christie Munson & Woods, New York: Sheila Ainbinder, Deborah Waters; The Chrysler Museum, Norfolk: Mark A. Clark; Cleveland Museum of Art: Henry Hawley; Corning Museum of Glass: Jane Shadel Spillman; Kathleen S. Corrao; Department of the Navy: Commander G. P. Beamer, Jay Sinclair; Patrick Duggan; Mr. and Mrs. Michael E. Fitzgerald; Mr. Freeman and his associates at I. Freeman & Son, New York; Cheryl Gallagher; Wendell P. Garrett; J. Herbert Gebelein; Burrill Getman; Goldsmiths' Hall, London: Miss S. M. Hare; Charles and Roger Gorevic of F. Gorevic & Son, New York; Genia Graves; Robert Alan Green; Derick and Elisa Hamilton; Handy & Harmon: A. M. Reti; David Allen Hanks; The Henry Francis du Pont Winterthur Museum: Kenneth Ames, Bert Denker, Donald Fennimore, Victor F. Hanson, Maruta Skelton; The High Museum, Atlanta: Katharine G. Farnham; Donald C. Peirce; Harry Hilbert; Phillip Johnston; Allen Klots; Constantine Kollitus; Bard H. Langstaff, Nina Fletcher Little; Carey Mackie; MaryJean Madigan; Mrs. Ralph Major; Lawrence W. Marsh; Alfred Mayer; Hal and Jane McLane; Mead Art Museum, Amherst College: Judith A. Barter; Mathew J. Mitchell; Edgar W.

Morse; Morse Gallery of Art: Hugh F. McKean; Nancy C. Moore; Museum of Art, Rhode Island School of Design: Christopher Monkhouse; Museum of the City of New York: Margaret Stearns; Museum of Fine Arts, Boston: Wendy Cooper, Jonathan Fairbanks, Karen Guffey, Money L. Hickman, Naomi R. Remes; Museum of Fine Arts, Houston: Katherine S. Howe; Andrew Nelson; The New Canaan Library (many were helpful); The New-York Historical Society, New York City: Mary Black, Mary Alice Kennedy; The New York Yacht Club: Sohei Hohri; The Newark Museum: Ulysses G. Dietz; Richard Nixon; Office of the Architect of the Capitol, Washington: Florian Thayn; S. Phelps Platt; Francis J. Purcell II; Thomas P. Quinn; The Rhode Island Historical Society: Robert Emlin; Mona Sawyer; Eric Shrubsole; The Smithsonian Institution: Herbert R. Collins, Anne Golivan, Margaret Brown Klapthor, Harold B. Langley, Rodris Roth; Sotheby Parke Bernet: Sarah Coffin; Margaret Woodbury Strong Museum, Rochester: Susan Williams; The International Tennis Hall of Fame, Newport, Rhode Island: Robert S. Day; Victoria and Albert Museum, London: Shirley Bury; Arthur Vitols, Helga Photo Studios; L. D. Watrous; The White House, Washington: Betty Monkman; Erskine N. White, Jr.; Steward P. Witham; Yale University Art Gallery: Barbara McLean Ward.

Finally I want to thank my wife and toughest critic, Mary Grace Carpenter. With her knowledge and love of silver, her sense of proportion, her sharp eye, she has made countless contributions to this book.

Acknowledgments to the New Edition

I wish to thank Yvonne De Corte, Samuel J. Hough, Ed Money, David Rogers, Margarite Riel and Burr Sebring for their help, and particularly want to thank Fred Roy, Jr., Gorham's Director of Design, who supplied much of the new information included in the new preface.

Preface to the New Edition

A major reason for coming out with a new edition of GORHAM SILVER, first published in 1982 is to make available again a book that has become extremely scarce. This edition has new color plates, an updating of relevant sections of the book, and a brief review of the activities of Gorham in the 1980s and 1990s.

At a time when silver objects, such as flatware and hollow ware, have become a much less important part of everyday life than in the 19th and 20th centuries, the vigorous survival of Gorham as a manufacturer and purveyor of flatware is noteworthy. But one should add that the emphasis is on stainless steel flatware, rather than silver flatware.

The basic philosophy of the company has changed. In the last decade Gorham products have been coordinated into marketing strategies: the wedding, holiday gifts, and the coordination with other "table top" items such as glassware, china and lighting objects Interestingly enough, this late 20th century "look" includes objects designed in the last ten years, plus those made in the 19th century. "Chantilly" is still Gorham's most popular silver flatware pattern, a century after its introduction in 1895.

The design tradition, which dates from the 1870s, is still strong in Gorham. The sense of taste, and a thorough knowledge of the great designs of the past, still permeate the company's design decisions. There has been a policy of not making taste decisions solely on market research, which is a measure of current popularity. Gorham designers have traditionally striven to be taste leaders, rather than taste followers. This has sometimes led to designs that did not find wide acceptance, but it also led to real successes.

Even though many of Gorham's designers and craftsmen of the past have been Europeans, trained in Europe, their Gorham designs have always had an American feel and American look. This is not meant to be a chauvinistic statement, but one that has often been made by decorative arts historians. Silverwares, particularly flatware, from France, England, Germany, Austria, Italy, all have characteristic regional looks. French flatware has carefully designed backs to accommodate the French custom of setting a table with backs up.

In 1982 Gorham was owned by Textron Inc., a conglomerate based in Providence, Rhode Island. In 1989 Gorham was purchased by Dansk International Designs of Mt. Cisco, New York. In 1991 Brown Forman of Louisville, Kentucky (Jack Daniels) acquired Gorham and Dansk. Gorham's headquarters are now in Lawrence, New Jersey, where they are associated with Lenox and Kirk-Steif. The Gorham design and manufacturing facilities are in Smithfield, Rhode Island.

The Gorham Bronze Division was sold in 1989, and at a later date the employees made a "leveraged buy out", and as of November, 1996 is operating under the name Gorham Bronze at Aiken, South Carolina.

Flatware, both sterling silver and stainless steel, is today Gorham's principal product line. A number of variations of earlier silver patterns are offered, and two entirely new patterns have been introduced since 1982. "Sea Sculpture" (1985), designed by Ed Money, and "Townsend" (1987) designed by Fred Roy, Jr. Although the market for Gorhan's silver flatware is not increasing at a dramatic rate, there is a steady demand for their carefully crafted wares.

On the other hand, Gorham's heavy, well designed, stainless flatware is a growth business. There was so much cheap, light weight stainless flooding the market in the 1970s and 1980s, that Gorham's stainless found a ready market.

Gorham divides their stainless flatware in two groups: (1) the "Studio Design Collection" with fourteen different patterns, and (2) the "Elegance Collection," which includes ten different patterns.

Gorham first had their stainless flatware manufactured in Japan in the 1980s. Later, these wares were made in Korea and Indonesia. In 1995 the decision was made to produce their stainless patterns in the United States. Gorham purchased machinery from their Asian subcontractors and established a carefully engineered, cost-effective facility in Smithfield, Rhode Island.

Stainless steel is much harder than sterling silver, and high quality stainless wares require more energy in their manufacture. In simple terms, it is much easier to make and finish a silver spoon than one made of stainless steel It is now possible to have more rigorous quality control with fewer rejects. And since the market is primarily in the United States, inventories can be more carefully controlled and deliveries are easier and more prompt

We are living in a time when American businesses have been widely criticized for shipping jobs overseas or over the border. Gorham is bucking this trend, and they are doing it for logical mechanical and economic reasons.

Charles H. Carpenter, Jr
December, 1996

Notes on the Illustration Captions

Figure numbers of captions are indicated by the numbers set off to the left of the captions. Dimensions, when available, are given in inches (in.) and in centimeters (cm.). The mark numbers refer to the listing of the marks in Appendix I. The term "lion-anchor-G" represents the traditional Gorham mark of three separate symbols: a lion, an anchor, and an Old English G. The last line in the caption indicates the present owner or the origin of the photograph.

The names of the objects in this book are based, wherever possible, on the names used in the Gorham records. This procedure can at times be troublesome because some of the names used by Gorham appear to be imprecise and/or old-fashioned. For example, to designate many small bowls as "berry bowls" seems somewhat of a verbal impoverishment, but if that is the term used in contemporary Gorham records, it is the term used in this book. Today Webster uses the term coffeepot as one word. In the nineteenth century Gorham usually called it a "coffee." The term "black coffee" was used to describe a coffeepot for black after-dinner coffee. Another example of Gorham nomenclature is the pair of covered dishes in Figure 75, which they called "double dish" in 1881.

There are a few terms used in the captions that should be defined (see exemples):

Engraving. A mark or design made in the surface of the metal by the use of cutting tools. Metal is removed in engraving (Fig. 29).

Chasing. A mark or design made in the surface of the metal by the use of hammer and punches. No metal is removed in chasing (Fig. 37).

Repoussé chasing. Repoussé means "pushed out." The rough, pushed-out design is chased into the desired pattern (Fig. 128).

Die-rolled border. Decorated strips of metal made by passing the metal through small patterned steel rolls (Fig. 7).

Introduction

This book is a study of the silverware and related metalwares made by the Gorham Company and its predecessor companies of Providence, Rhode Island, from 1831 to the present (1981). My original intention had been to cover only the 1831–1915 era of Gorham (now the Gorham Division of Textron), because this seemed to be the period of most interest to collectors and art historians. During that time Gorham grew from a small, provincial maker of silver spoons to the largest maker of sterling silverwares in the world. However, after working on the book for some time I realized more and more that 1915 was altogether too arbitrary a cutoff date. Many interesting objects were made after that. It seems quite appropriate for this book to deal with the entire one–hundred–and–fifty–year history of this important American silver maker, with the principal emphasis remaining on the 1831–1915 period.

The book explores Gorham from several points of view:

1. A survey of the objects made by the company.
2. An outline history of Gorham, the men who moved the company, and the designers of the objects.
3. A study of the styles and stylistic currents of the time.
4. An account of how the objects were made, the new manufacturing techniques, and the continued devotion to the traditional craft disciplines.
5. A study of the social forces that led to the making and using of a vast variety of wares.
6. An aid for identification. Sections on sterling flat–ware patterns and marks are included in the appendices.

The main emphasis of the book is on the objects themselves. The story is told, where feasible, in a straight chronological fashion. However, from 1870 to 1915 Gorham silver developed along two parallel lines which will be described separately: the mainstream commercial lines that accounted for the bulk of their sales, and the Art lines which emphasized hand craftsmanship and which were, at times, truly avant-garde.

The first chapter, "Introduction," outlines the book itself and the main style currents of the time. Chapter 2, "The Beginnings," traces the traditions of silver making in Rhode Island, a background which furnished a solid foundation for Jabez Gorham's enterprises, first as a jewelry maker, then as a silver maker. Chapter 3, "Coin Silver Spoons," covering the period 1831 to 1850, tells of Jabez Gorham's entry into the silver spoon business in 1831, his retirement in 1848, and the beginnings of his son, John Gorham, in the company. Chapter 4, "John Gorham: The Expansionist," gives an account of Gorham's first hollow-ware pieces, made in 1850, and the expansion of the company from a small craft shop with fourteen employees in that year to a sizable corporation with four hundred employees after the Civil War.

Gorham continued to grow after the Civil War, and the

principal commercial lines of the company were sold to a wide and fastgrowing market. The number of people who could afford quality silverwares increased by leaps and bounds during much of the rest of the nineteenth century, and the demand for flatware services, silver tea sets, bowls, trophies, and a large variety of hollow ware seemed at times insatiable. Gorham silver became well known from Boston and New York in the East, to Mobile and Savannah in the South, and to San Francisco in the West. By 1870 Gorham had blanketed the United States with sales outlets. This mainstream Gorham silver after the Civil War is dealt with in Chapters 5, 7, and 11:

Chapter 5. "The Post-Civil War Years" (1865–1880)
Chapter 7. "Antoine Heller and the New Academy (1880–1890)
Chapter II. "Holbrook and Codman" (1890–1915)

About 1870 Gorham developed the first silverwares that could be designated Art silver, that is, objects made primarily as works of art. In most cases the forms were conventional and functional, but the point of view was different, the materials often unconventional, and the results were sometimes radically new. Chapter 6, "Innovation and Fantasy," which covers the period 1869 to 1885, describes works which reflect a return to the craft traditions of silversmithing, and a new aestheticism which looked to nature as a source of design ideas. These were the kinds of objects which were forerunners of both the Art Nouveau and Arts and Crafts movements of the turn of the century.

Chapter 12, "Martelé," parallels, in time, Chapter 11. It gives an account of Gorham's handmade Art Nouveau silver, a major expression of the movement in America.

Chapter 8, "The Bronzes," includes a brief survey of the bronze objects which were a direct outgrowth of Gorham's expansion in the ecclesiastical field.

Chapter 9, "Presentation Pieces," deals with presentation silver ranging from modest racing and yachting cups to the mammoth eight–foot–four–inch "loving cup" made for Admiral George Dewey in 1899 from 70,000 dimes, to the large and sometimes florid sterling services made for United States battleships and cruisers.

Chapter 10, "Souvenir Spoons," describes a phenomenon that started as a true craze in the 1890s, and that continues to fascinate collectors to this day. Gorham was the dominant factor in souvenir spoons in America, having designed and produced well over a thousand during the 1890–1910 period.

Chapter 13, "Art Deco," covers the 1915–1940 period. This chapter features the work of Erik Magnussen, a Danish silversmith who worked at Gorham from 1925 to 1929. Chapter 14, "After World War II," brings the story into our own time.

Styles

The styles of Victorian America have been both the joy and despair of the student of the decorative arts. Stylistic currents are complex and many objects do not fit neatly into any recognized style classification. A careful reading of recent literature on Victorian styles shows a considerable lack of agreement on style characteristics and style names.[1] Style names change with time. Few of those used today correspond exactly with those used in the nineteenth century.

In Owen Jones's great *Grammar of Ornament* (1856), a book used by generations of American and English designers, there are many more classifications for past styles than are usually used today, and some of Jones's styles, such as those of India and China, are vague and imprecise by modern standards.

There were a number of other stylebooks published in the last half of the nineteenth century, but Jones's *Grammar of Ornament* appears to have been a major source of design ideas for the Gorham silversmiths.[2] However, one must be careful in using such design books for naming the style of a particular piece of nineteenth–century silver. For example, very similar strapwork designs could have been inspired by at least five different styles in Jones's book: Moresque (pl. XXXIX), Celtic (pl. LXIII), Byzantine (pl. XXVIII), Arabian (pl. XXXIII), or Elizabethan (pls. LXXXIII and LXXXIV). Today, a number of the strapwork designs are called Renaissance Revival.

Gorham never confined its efforts at any one period to a particular style. Style was not their first consideration. They were first and foremost a commercial firm They made salable objects for a variety of customers with a wide variety of tastes and pocketbooks. The only part of the market they never tried to supply was the mass market for cheap wares. With this one exception, they consciously made, throughout the period covered by this book, objects for different tastes, in different styles, in different price ranges.

Silver not only derives its look from the style currents of its time, it also derives from other silver objects; from contemporary silverwares and from silverwares of the past. Silversmiths have always been influenced by other silversmiths. This point is emphasized because silver styles are not always too closely related to the styles of other arts of a time—the architecture, the painting, and the furniture.

Twentieth–century art historians have often been preoccupied with style and style classifications. They have made us very conscious that the study of style is important for an understanding of an object and its relationship to its time. The classification of Victorian silver objects into neat style categories is often a diffficult task, and possibly an inappropriate one as well. So many objects are exceptions, or borderline examples, that the law of diminishing returns sets in if too much emphasis is put on style. Such a preoccupation can also lead to a distorted picture of what really happened in the history of the art form. Nikolaus Pevsner, in writing about the 1851 London Exposition in the Crystal Palace, noted: "One is so used to defining Victorian architecture and design in terms of what style of the past is imitated that not enough attention is generally given to the fact how rarely the real date of a piece of 1850 is not written all over its period disguise."[3]

All art objects have roots in the past. Ad Reinhardt, the great abstract painter and Orientalist, said it well: "All art comes out of art."[4]

The following chart is an outline summary of the principal styles and style currents used by Gorham designers in the period 1850–1950. The time period (noted by the bars on the chart) indicates the heyday of the style, that is, the time when it was most used. Style ideas tend to linger on and a few objects were often made in an earlier style over a considerable period of time. Styles also have a way of coming back, of being revived. In fact, over a long period, silver styles tend to be quite cyclical.

Although the chart was specifically based on a study of Gorham silver, other American silverwares of the period generally fit into the style categories.

Rococo Revival

The dominant style at the beginning of the 1850s was at the time called variously Louis Quatorze, Louis Quinze (even contemporaries had diffficulty distinguishing the difference between these two), French, French Modern, French Antique, or French Rococo. It made use of stylized C– and S–scrolls, and naturalistic ornaments such as flowers, leaves, and fruit— usually grapes. A favorite ornamentation was repoussé ("pushed out") chasing. Some of the chasing was decidedly three–dimensional. Often the flowers and fruits were pushed out a quarter of an inch or more from the surface of the

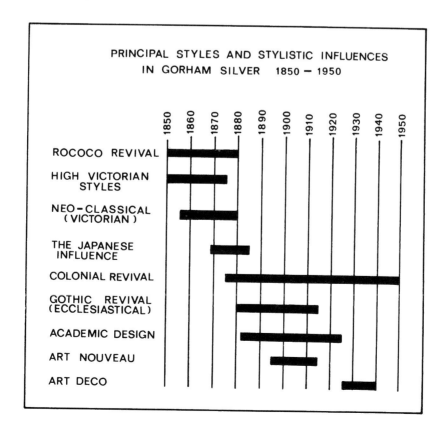

1 Advertisement in the *American Advertiser,* Boston, Massachussets, 1853.

silver. Repoussé chasing continued throughout the nineteenth century, but later chased works are usually flatter and more uniform in their ornamentation. Rococo had somewhat of a resurgence in the 1880s and 1890s.

The early Gorham advertisement in Figure 1 shows two of the main stylistic currents of the 1850s: At the top and bottom are pictured pieces of Rococo Revival silver and in the middle are naturalistic examples of High Victorian. The advertisement itself is Rococo Revival–High Victorian.

High Victorian

The term High Victorian has been used by Nikolaus Pevsner and others to describe that amalgam of style names, including Renaissance or Elizabethan Revival (classical and animal heads, strapwork), naturalism or rustication (branches, twigs, leaves, animals, icicles), Neo-Grec[5] (palmetto decorations, anthemia, flat chasing), eclectic, and so on, that flourished in the third quarter of the nineteenth century.

High Victorian is not a standard art historian's style term although it has often been used in a general way to describe the ultimate kind of Victorian object, the kind of fancy, intensively decorated, eclectic piece that we so often associate with the 1850–1876 era. The term is used in a more specific sense in this book to define a style or mixture of styles that flourished in England, France, and America from the 1850s to the 1870s. For Gorham, High Victorian reached a kind of crescendo in the ambitious and sometimes wild pieces the company made for the 1876 Philadelphia Centennial Exposition.

High Victorian is a particularly apt style designation for much of Gorham's silver of the 1850–1876 period since few of these objects are pure Renaissance Revival (which itself is a very imprecise term, representing as it does a complex mixture of styles and substyles which, in turn, were, in the Renaissance, revival styles from classical Rome and Greece), or pure Neo-Grec, or pure anything else. The Gorham High Victorian pieces are joyous, often flamboyant, *mixtures* of styles—potpourris (Figs. 2 and 3).

Since George Wilkinson, Gorham's first chief designer, and many of the company's skilled craftsmen came to America and to Gorham from England in the 1850s and 1860s, it is only natural to find that mid–nineteenth–century English design ideas dominate Gorham silver of this period. However, the English designs were almost always changed and simplified when adapted by Gorham silver makers. It was the kind of

2 High Victorian coffeepot made about 1860. Neo–Grec designs on the body, Classical beading around the top and the base of the spout, Rococo flourishes between the spout and the body, on the handle and lid wispy curls of metal that seem to fly off into space. Height: 12 1/2 in. (31.8 cm.). Mark: JACCGARD & co/140/lion-anchor-G. Jaccgard & Co. of St. Louis was the retailer. *(Photograph courtesy C. Kollitus).*

3 High Victorian centerpiece exhibited at the 1876 Philadelphia
Centennial Exposition. *(Gorham collection)*.

style change that had been going on in American silver
for two hundred years. The American-made pieces acquired an American look. A comparison between
Gorham silver of the 1850s and 1860s with English silver of the same and slightly earlier period makes this
point very clear.[6]

Examples of Gorham's High Victorian pieces include
the coffeepot in Figure 2, the centerpiece in Figure 3,
the Lincoln tea and coffee service in Figure 43, and the
ice bucket shown on the front jacket cover of the book.

The Exposition Style

One style, closely related to High Victorian, which is
not included in the style chart, could be dubbed the
Exposition style. The great international expositions
of the last half of the nineteenth century attracted thousands of exhibitors and millions of visitors. It all started
in London in 1851 (the Crystal Palace), New York in
1853, and Paris in 1855. They were held in London in
1862, Paris in 1867, 1878, and 1889 (the latter featu-

red the Eiffel Tower), Philadelphia in 1876 (the Centennial), and the world's Columbian Exposition in
Chicago in 1893. The old century went out and the
new was ushered in by the Paris Exposition of 1900,
which attracted thirty–nine million visitors.

The decorative arts objects made for the different
international expositions have a family "look," and, if
we factor out minor style notes, have more of a resemblance to each other than they do to the common run
of commercial objects made by these same firms. These
wondrous exposition objects were usually bigger than
life—large and flamboyant. They were meant to arrest,
interest, and astonish those thousands of visitors who
shuffled through the miles of exhibition halls. Many of
these objects were shown by their makers in more than
one fair. The four–by–five–foot, 140–pound Century
Vase was the centerpiece of Gorham exhibits at three:
Philadelphia in 1876, Paris in 1889, and Chicago in
1893.

If I describe the Exposition style with, perhaps,
tongue in cheek, I would nevertheless suggest it was

very real. It may well have been the most influential style of its time. The 1851 London Exposition launched the style. Although many critics bemoaned these showy, too-large, highly decorated objects, these were the very objects that established the trend for the rest of the century. From 1851 onward almost every maker felt he had to outdo himself and his competitors for each succeeding occasion.

The same mentality that produced the Exposition style persists today. "Blockbuster" museum exhibitions are built around "showstoppers," pieces that are meant to arrest, interest, and astonish. The level of today's taste may be judged higher than that of the nineteenth–century manufacturers, but the motive is similar.

Neoclassical (Victorian)

The classical Greek and Roman styles that had been in vogue since the beginning of the nineteenth century linger on in Gorham silver into the 1870s, and indeed remnants of the style were made throughout the last half of the nineteenth century. There was a resurgence of Neoclassicism in the 1870s silver which corresponded to the beginning of the second period in American Empire furniture. The silver featured strong, simple forms decorated with classic borders and friezes, and classic sculptured figures (Fig. 4).

Neoclassicism made use of helmet and urn shapes, die-rolled borders with Greek key and bead motifs, and undecorated surfaces. Tureens were often bulging and elongated.

4 The Travers Race Prize (1877) in the Neoclassical style. Height: 21 in. (53.3 cm.). Length: 24 in. (61 cm.). Weight: 212 ounces. *(Gorham photograph).*

Such classic devices as medallions and cast heads and the like are classified under High Victorian styles since, as noted earlier, they are characteristic of Renaissance styles that had already been recycled by the time the Victorians adopted them.

The Japanese Influence

In about 1870 an entirely new influence began to exert itself on Gorham silver, the influence of Japanese art. This resulted in a new line of Art silver and mixed–metal objects that were radically different from what had gone before them in American silver. Japanese art influenced Gorham silver in two ways: Japanese decorative designs and Japanese shapes were adapted to Western use (Fig. 5), and Japanese metalworking techniques were adapted to Western practices. The most important of the techniques was the hand–hammered finish. The idea of an object *looking* as if it were handmade came out of Japanese art (Fig. 6).

5 Silver teapot in the Japanese style, made about 1875. *(Gorham photograph).*

6 Water pitcher in the Japanese style, hammered body, cast handle, applied cast lizards, crab, and scroll. Engraved under handle: SDW/FROM/CSP/1878. Height: 8 1/2 in. (21.6 cm.). Mark: lion–anchor–G/STERLING/1200/P (1883). *(Private collection).*

7 "Turkish" black coffee, hand–hammered copper body, applied cast silver bird, moth, and flowers, silver die-rolled bands on body and top, ivory insulators on handle. Height: 13 in. (33 cm.). Mark: anchor/GORHAM CO/E40. *(Courtesy R. O. Cragin).*

6

7

The other related influence that was important to Gorham was that of Near Eastern or Islamic art. This was mainly felt in certain shapes, such as the tall, slim, graceful coffeepots. However, the Japanese influence was by far the most pervasive. Even Islamic shapes were often decorated with Japanese motifs (Fig 7)

The Japanese influence and its relationship to the Art Nouveau and Arts and Crafts movements of the 1895–1910 period is discussed in Chapter 6, "Innovation and Fantasy."

Colonial Revival

In the 1870s America "discovered" its past. Old houses were studied and new "colonial" houses began to be built. Old furniture was collected and reproductions of old furniture became popular. Silver makers made adaptations of American and English eighteenth–and early nineteenth–century silver.

Gorham made their first pieces of silver in this new style in the 1870s. In flatware they resurrected the simple fiddle handle flatware design of the first half of the nineteenth century, calling it *Old English Tipt*. In hollow ware they made pared-down, undecorated adaptations of earlier forms.

After about 1885 Colonial Revival became increasingly popular, and by the beginning of the twentieth century it was the dominant style in Gorham silver (Fig. 8). The style has retained its popularity right up to the present.

John S. Holbrook, son of Edward Holbrook, Gorham's president, described the style in an address before the School of Applied Design for Women in New York in about 1910. He called it the Colonial style:

> We take up now our Colonial style and show in a few examples its relationship to the period of George III. The same beauty of line is evident, the same restraint of decoration, and in the revival of taste today the demand for Colonial examples

and Colonial reproductions is one of the most hopeful signs we see, in my opinion, for the development of a sincere, pure, and true style of American art....

> The chief characteristics of the Colonial style, as evidenced by the examples, are a careful study of form, and the shapes showing classical tendencies and a marked repression of ornament. The ornament used is largely engraved or flat chased, or if any relief, it is extremely low. Simple forms of saw-piercing were used as in porringers but as a rule articles of this style depend but little upon decoration for their effect, and indeed many of them are severely plain.[7]

Gothic Revival

Gothic was one of the great revival styles of the nineteenth century. Thomas J. Pairpoint, one of Gorham's designers of the 1870s, defined the style this way:

> The Gothic is peculiarly a geometric and pointed style, with all the symbolism of the Byzantine contained in it. The chief characteristic is an elaboration of geometric tracery, circles, trifoils, quatrefoils, etc., with the pointed arch, which was also an element of the Saracenic style. Vertical and diagonal lines are preferred to all others in the tracery, and sometimes we find flowers mingled with it.[8]

Although it was a fairly popular style in American architecture and was occasionally used in American furniture, Gothic was used only in ecclesiastical work by Gorham (Fig. 9). They started making silver and bronze objects for religious use in the late 1870s and by the 1880s it had become an important part of their business.

Academic Design

In the latter part of the nineteenth century a traditional, scholarly strain of design began to appear in Gorham silver which was a counterpart to the academic painting and the Beaux Arts architecture of the time. Seven

8 Sauceboat with stand in the Colonial Revival style, made in 1908. Engraved AMW for Alice Motley Woodbury. Height: 4 5/16 in. (11 cm.). *(Margaret Woodbury Strong Museum, Rochester, New York).*

9 Gothic cross, ca. 1890. (Gorham photograph).

Art Nouveau

Gorham's silver in the Art Nouveau style made use of motifs characteristic of this turn-of-the-century movement: flowing, whiplash lines, restless curves, female forms with long undulating hair, often emerging out of waves, flowers, and nature forms. Most of the silver was handmade in the Arts and Crafts tradition. Figure 12 shows a typical high Art Nouveau piece of Martelé. This represents one extreme of the style discussed in Chapter 12, "Martelé." The other extreme is represented by simple, unadorned pieces with gentle curves and restrained forms (Fig. 13).

Art Deco

The term Art Deco was not used in the 1920s and 1930s when it was very much in fashion. It was called Art Moderne or the modernist style to distinguish it from the severe International style which made no use of ornament as such. The term Art Deco, first applied to the style in the 1960s, is from the Exposition des Arts Decoratifs et Industriels Modernes held in Paris in 1925 where the style was codified for the first time. The style was successful from the beginning, and was most influential during the 1925–1940 period, although Gorham made items with an Art Deco look well into the 1950s.

As a style, Art Deco was a modern adaptation of various ornamental styles of the past, particularly classical. It has been said of Art Deco that "It created the last ornamental style known to Western Art by marrying the machine with the old handicraft tradition."[9]

The handcrafted pitcher in Figure 14 made by Erik Magnussen in 1928 has a machine–made look. Magnussen's designs are discussed in Chapter 13, "Art Deco."

teenth-, eighteenth-, and early nineteenth-century English and French silver designs were carefully copied and adapted. Great emphasis was placed on authentic-looking detail and careful craftsmanship.

Academic design first came to Gorham in the flatware patterns of F. Antoine Heller, a brilliant silversmith and die cutter who came from Paris to Providence in 1881 (Chapter 7, "Antoine Heller and the New Academy"). Heller's designs were crisp, minutely detailed adaptations of traditional French motifs (Fig. 10).

The making of Academic hollow ware dates from the late 1880s (Fig. 11). William C. Codman, who joined Gorham in 1891, ably carried on the style. Even after his retirement in 1914, his son, William Codman, who followed his father as Gorham's chief designer, was a great devotee of Academic design. The trend continued into the 1920s.

10 Flatware handle designs of the *Fontainebleau* pattern designed by Antoine Heller (1882). From an engraving by Russell and Richardson

11 Tureen and stand in an Academic design Gorham called Louis XVI, made in 1888. Capacity: 9 quarts. *(Gorham photograph).*

10

11

12

12 Martelé rosewater ewer dish made in 1900. *(Gorham photograph).*

13 Martelé child's cup made in 1907. Height: 3 in. (7.6 cm.). *(Gorham photograph).*

13

14 Art Deco silver pitcher with Bakelite handle, designed by Erik Magnussen, made in 1928. Height: 8 1/2 in. (21.6 cm.). *(Gorham photograph)*.

Craftsmanship and Connoisseurship

A theme that threads through this book is the changing ways of making silver in the last half of the nineteenth century, and the relationship between these manufacturing methods and craftsmanship.[10] From the late 1840s, when John Gorham substituted steam power for horsepower to drive his rolling mill and polishing wheels, the company placed considerable emphasis on mechanization. In certain operations great strides were made in replacing labor–intensive hand operations with machine–powered manufacturing methods. These technological advances will be documented in the proper places in this book.

One of the simplistic views of silver of the Victorian era is that it was entirely machine–made and, therefore, was not entitled to quite as much attention and respect as the old handmade pieces. However, mechanization was a very selective matter in nineteenth–century silver making, and, although power–assisted operations were introduced wherever feasible, many operations continued to be performed by hand.

The greatest use of mechanization was in the making of flatware. The advances in flatware manufacturing were spectacular—from the early 1840s, when spoons were essentially handmade, to the 1860s, when great steam–powered drop presses stamped out a spoon with

a single blow. But even in flatware manufacture many hand operations remained. The presses were fed by hand, and finishing methods changed little from 1840 to 1860.

The one great *increase* in hand labor in flatware manufacture was the making of the steel dies used in the drop presses. The designing and hand carving of steel dies was an expensive and time-consuming operation that required a high order of skill. The cost of these dies could only be justified by volume production. Surprisingly, perhaps, this mechanization of flatware manufacture was accompanied by a marked increase in the quality of the product. Instead of the plain, often flimsy silver spoons of the 1840s, much sturdier, more uniform, and, for many people's tastes, more interestingly designed spoons were made in the 1860s. Prices were comparable. Pattern flatware, which became enormously popular in the 1860s, and whose popularity continues to this day, could not have been economically made by the old hand method.

This preview of flatware silver-making processes indicates that changes in manufacturing methods were not quite as simple as they might first appear, and suggests that mechanization does not necessarily mean a loss of quality.

The changes in hollow–ware manufacturing methods in the nineteenth century did not always result in *any* time–saving in the making of any one piece. This, of course, is due primarily to the changes of taste toward more ornamented and more complicated pieces of silverware. For example, a simple form such as a bowl, which could be made on a spinning lathe in an hour or two, would have taken many hours of patient hammering by the older handraising methods. But the elaboration of the piece of Victorian silver—the chasing, the engraving, the casting of applied parts, and the applying of new kinds of finishes—was often enormously time-consuming. The time needed to make a highly decorated Victorian bowl could have been considerably greater than the time involved in making a plain hand-raised bowl.

Whether or not a handmade hollow-ware form is necessarily better than a lathe-spun form is a moot question. It depends on the individual piece. A simple hand-raised shape by a great silversmith can be a very wonderful object. But when it comes to comparing a hollow-ware form made by a first-rate spinner with a similar form hand raised by a second-rate, plodder of a silversmith, it may be a different story. A piece of silver must be judged by what it is rather than how it was made.

Much handwork was involved in the ornamentation of hollow ware. With the exception of engine-turned engraving patterns and die-rolled borders, most of the silver-making operations were hand crafts demanding trained and highly skilled workmen: engravers, lost-wax casters, finishers, and chasers. The last half of the nineteenth century was truly the golden age of the chaser. Many of those at Gorham were, incidentally, trained in England or on the Continent. Even in the regular commercial lines, chasing, particularly repoussé chasing, was a hand operation. Nineteenth-century photographs of the Gorham plant show large rooms with dozens of chasers at work. Parenthetically, it should be noted that chasing seems to be a dying art. At the time of this writing (1981) there are probably less than a dozen chasers working in commercial silver-making plants in the United States.

Gorham's use of handmade ornamentation was quite pragmatic, and it reflected the taste of the time. I would imagine Gorham's workmen (and Gorham's designers, for that matter) would have been a bit incredulous if they had read John Ruskin's statement in the *Seven Lamps of Architecture*. "The right question to ask regarding all ornament is simply this: Was it done with enjoyment, was the carver happy when he did it?"[11] Even though, as will be pointed out in Chapter 12, the ideas of John Ruskin, William Morris, and others no doubt influenced Gorham's silver, the company was motivated by

more mundane considerations. Possibly there was not as much emphasis in the nineteenth century on the bottomline philosophy that so permeates business today. Nevertheless, Gorham was very much involved in profitability and growth. They were also involved in what now might be called responsibility. Gorham truly believed that making objects of the highest quality was good business.

The relationship between the men who ran Gorham and the men who designed the company's products is explored at some length in this book. It is a fascinating series of relationships. There is no question that the understanding and enlightened support of Gorham's designers by its top executives is one of the important reasons why the company' was able to grow to such a position of eminence. Both John Gorham, who was Gorham's president and driving force between 1848 and 1878, and Edward Holbrook, who became Gorham's president and chief stockholder in 1894, were men who were quite knowledgeable in the arts. They were men who really *cared* about art. William Crins, who was president from 1878 to 1894 was primarily a professional manager, but his tenure marked a period of remarkable expansion of sales and a period of considerable innovation. He was obviously a man who could create a climate favorable for good design.

Although this book is primarily concerned with the objects made by Gorham as artifacts, their "look" and their style, the problem of function should never be forgotten. The practical-minded Victorian insisted on objects which worked well; spouts that poured without dribbling; pieces that were well balanced, and convenient to the hand, easy to clean; and designs that fitted their functions. The twentieth-century dictum of "form follows function" was carried to some lengths in the plethora of specialized serving pieces. The making of dozens of different kinds of spoons can be criticized as being absurd from today's point of view, but many of these specialized objects *do* function superbly in their appointed tasks. Ice cream spoons do function beautifully. Grapefruit spoons work much better on a grapefruit than a teaspoon!

The sensual pleasures of a fine piece of silver should not be underestimated. It is both a matter of the tactile quality of silver and the *weight* of a piece. A certain heaviness is necessary; when a piece of silver is substantially lighter than it appears, we somehow feel cheated. Then there is the matter of changing lights when a piece of silver is handled and turned in the hand. Victorians usually avoided plain, mirror-finished surfaces. They preferred a surface that glowed rather than flashed; they liked chased or engraved surfaces and mat finishes—from frosty whites to dusty oxidized blacks.

Finally, we can't help but evaluate art objects by considering what happened to the history of art after the object was made. Gorham made a number of objects in the 1870s and 1880s that today appear quite avant–garde. There are pieces made in that period that look as if they should have been made in 1900, and there are a couple of remarkable objects which have a pure Bauhaus, 1930s, look. These objects *seem* to forecast the future and have a considerable fascination. One somehow thinks they are more important than objects that appear to look back in time. But new styles and new ways of making familiar objects change our ideas of the past. Jorge Luis Borges in writing on Kafka said, "The fact is that every writer *creates* his own precursors. His work modifies our conception of the past, as it will modify the future."[12] One can paraphrase Borges and say: *Every new and revolutionary art object creates its own precursors. These objects modify our conception of the past, as they will modify the future.*

Webster defines a connoisseur as "one who understands the details, technique or principles of an art and who is competent to act as a critical judge." In other words, connoisseurship involves both knowledge and a critical faculty. And an open mind.

The Value of Money in the Nineteenth Century

The American dollar in the last part of the nineteenth century was a very different dollar from today's (1981) dollar. One should multiply a nineteenth-century dollar figure by a factor of perhaps ten to twelve times to bring it up–todate.

There was comparatively little inflation in the United States from 1870 to 1910. In fact, the panics of 1873 and 1893 resulted in deflationary periods. The average factory wage in those four decades was about $400 per year.[13] The highest paid workers at Gorham, the silversmiths and chasers, made from $1200 to $1500 per year. The annual salaries of the top executives were from about $5000 to $10,000. The price of silver declined from $1.32 in 1850 to sixty–one cents per ounce in 1900.[14] There were no income taxes, no social security, and no unemployment benefits.

In the context of the time we can see that $1200 for a silver tea and coffee service, or $4000 for an epergne, were substantial amounts of money.

CHAPTER 2

The Beginnings

Silver making in Rhode Island was well over a century old when the Gorham Company made their first silverwares in 1831. Highly competent silversmiths had been working in Newport, R.I., since the 1690s.[1]

In the late seventeenth and early eighteenth centuries Newport was one of the few towns in colonial New England outside of Boston with the necessary wealth and culture to support the craft of silversmithing. Newport, a rich and cosmopolitan town with its lucrative sea trade with the West Indies, privateering, and yes, slave trading, had, by the middle of the eighteenth century, silversmiths and cabinetmakers of the first rank. Members of the Townsend–Goddard families made some of the finest and most important furniture ever made in America, and such silversmiths as Samuel Vernon (1683–1737), Arnold Collins (?–1735), and others of Newport made silver tankards, canns, creamers, porringers, and spoons of a quality comparable to similar pieces being made in Boston, New York, and Philadelphia.[2]

Newport was the most important and affluent town in Rhode Island during the first half of the eighteenth century, much more so than Providence, the town at the head of Narragansett Bay. Next to Newport in wealth from about 1725 almost to the Revolutionary War was the semirural town of Little Rest (its name was changed to Kingston in 1825), which was in the heart of a fertile farm area owned by the so–called Narragansett

Planters. This settlement of dairymen and stockmen, with their black slaves, had some of the flavor of southern plantation life. The farms were large by New England standards. Thomas Hazard owned twelve thousand acres of land. Thomas Stanton had a "lordship" four and a half miles long and two miles wide.[3]

Little Rest supported a half dozen silversmiths at one time or another during the eighteenth century.[4] One of these men, Samuel Casey, achieved a kind of fame in the annals of American silversmithing that would suggest that silversmiths had difficulty making a living at their profession in such rural areas as Little Rest. Casey, who was born in 1724, was a master craftsman who made porringers and teapots which are excellent examples of colonial silversmithing. The Garvan collection at Yale contains a tankard made by Casey for Ezra Stiles in 1755,[5] and the Museum of Fine Arts in Boston owns a well–known cream pot by Casey beautifully decorated with chased, scrolled initials.[6]

In the 1760s Samuel Casey was beset with Job–like troubles. Business was bad, and his house, considered one of the finest in town, burned. "It was entirely consumed with a quantity of rich furniture."[7] Later Casey took to counterfeiting Spanish milled dollars and other coins. He was caught, convicted, and sentenced to be hanged. On November 3, 1770 (traditionally the night before the date set for Casey's execution), "A consider–

able Number of People riotously assembled in King's County, and with their Faces black'd proceeded to his Majesty's Gaol there, the outer Door of which they broke open with Iron Bars and Pick Axes; they then violently entered the Gaol, broke every Lock therein and set at Liberty sundry Criminals, lately convicted of Money making, one of whom (Samuel Casey) was under sentence of Death."[8]

Casey fled and nothing more is known of him, except the fact that his wife, Martha, was able to obtain a pardon for him in 1779, presumably after his death.[9] Providence, with its somewhat isolated position at the head of the bay, its frequently unsettled political conditions, and its lack of wealth, did not, early in the eighteenth century, appear to be an attractive place for silversmiths. However, at least one "goldsmith," Joshua Doane, who died in 1753, made silver tankards and church plate which survive today.[10]

The steady growth of Providence in the last half of the eighteenth century and the British occupation of Newport during the Revolutionary War changed the patterns of trade more and more in favor of Providence, and by the 1790s Providence completely dominated Rhode Island.

Retail trade expanded. In addition to the general–store variety, there was an increasing number of shops selling clocks, watches, jewelry, books, and, for the seafarers, compasses and sextants. It is clear from the newspaper advertisements of the time that almost everyone in the retail trade in Providence sold a variety of goods. The silversmiths were no exception. Nehemiah Dodge and Stephen Williams, advertising in 1799, stated they could supply goods and services from jewelry to silverwares, to clocks and watches. They also bought scrap silver, gold, and copper (Fig. 15).[11]

Nehemiah Dodge opened his first shop in Providence in 1794 on Main Street, near St. John's Church. His sign styled him "Goldsmith and Jeweler, Clock and Watch Maker." In 1798 he moved his business to a better location, "a few doors north of the Baptist Meeting House, directly opposite Mr. Barker's Inn." Here he manufactured "gold necklaces, knobs and twists, gold rings, miniature cases and fancy jewelry."[12] At first his gold jewelry was 18–karat fine but he soon introduced a cheaper grade. Then, as now, price was a factor and mass markets demanded cheap goods. The cheaper goods made use of plated gold—thin sheets of gold plated onto copper by means of silver solder. (The process for making this plated ware may have been "invented" by Nehemiah Dodge's uncle, Seril Dodge, who opened a shop in downtown Providence in 1784.[13]) Early in the nineteenth century

The Subscribers having entered into Co-partnership, under the Firm of

DODGE and WILLIAMS,

BEG Leave to solicit the Patronage of the Public in their Professions.—They offer their Services in the GOLD-SMITH and JEWELLERY Line, in all its Branches; also HAIR-WORK executed in the neatest Stile.—The CLOCK and WATCHMAKING Business likewise attended to faithfully, and with Dispatch.

They have on Hand for Sale, a Variety of new Clocks and Watches, plated and Silver mounted Hangers, &c.

Pray call at their Shop, opposite Mr. Haws' Inn, main Street. The smallest Favours will be gratefully acknowledged, by the Public's obedient Servants,

NEHEMIAH DODGE,
STEPHEN WILLIAMS.

N. B. Cash and the highest Prices given for old Gold, Silver, Copper and Brass.

Providence, August 16, 1799.   t.f.

15

15 Advertisement for Dodge and Williams from the *Providence Gazette,* September 7, 1799, front page.

16 Coffin-handled tablespoon made by Nehemiah Dodge, Providence, Rhode Island, ca. 1810.

16

Dodge added silver spoons to his line. The coffin–handled spoon in Figure 16 by Nehemiah Dodge was probably made about 1810.

In 1799, Nehemiah Dodge took a partner, Stephen Williams. Dodge continued in business with various partners until 1826, when he retired. By then he had accumulated $70,000, which was considered a princely sum in those days.

Nehemiah Dodge is not only important as one of the founders of the jewelry and silverware industry in Rhode Island, he will also be remembered as the mentor of the founder of the Gorham Company, Jabez Gorham.

Jabez Gorham was a fifth-generation New Englander. The first of his family to come to America, John Gorham, was born in Benefield, England in 1621. He came to America, probably around 1640, and in 1643 married Desire Howland, born in Plymouth in 1623, daughter of John Howland and Elizabeth Tilley of the *Mayflower*. John Gorham's grandson, Benjamin, moved to Providence from Bristol, Rhode Island, early in the eighteenth century. Benjamin was a prosperous tanner and currier. When he died in 1771 his will mentions leaving to a grandson "a pair of silver buckles that were his uncle's, Samuel Gorham."

Jabez (pronounced Ja'bez) Gorham was born on February 18, 1792, the fifth of eight children. (The Gorham family genealogy is complicated by the fact that Jabez's father, grandfather, and great–great-grandfather were named Jabez, as were assorted uncles and cousins.)[14] Jabez was raised in a 1793 house (Fig. 17) still standing at 56 Benefit Street in Providence. The house was restored by Gorham and Company in the 1960s. It is now a private residence. The Gorham homestead is a two-story, center-chimney New England town house, very typical of its period. Its formal central doorway is framed with Ionic pilasters and surmounted with an arched pediment. The window caps, made of wood, are cut with molded key blocks to look like stone.

Jabez had the usual three Rs elementary education of the time. His father died in 1802 when he was ten years old, and when he was fourteen he was apprenticed to the above–mentioned Nehemiah Dodge to learn jewelry making. He served the standard seven–year apprenticeship in a shop that employed some eight or ten hands.

The apprenticeship indenture contract signed by Jabez, his mother, Caty Gorham (the document also spells it Katy), and Nehemiah Dodge was a standard form that had changed little since the seventeenth century. The stilted legal language of the contract spells out the high level of conduct expected of the young apprentice (plus some restrictions which appear amusing in our changed times):

THIS INDENTURE WITNESSETH

That Jabez Gorham Son of Jabez Gorham late of Providence in the County of Providence, deceased hath put himself and by these Presents doth voluntarily, and of his own free Will and Accord and with the Consent of his Mother, Katy Gorham of said Providence, Widow, put and bind himself Apprentice to Nehemiah Dodge of said Providence, Gold, Silver Smith and Jeweller to learn his Art, Trade or Mystery, and, after the Manner of an Apprentice, to serve from the fourteenth Day of February last for and during the Term of Seven Years next ensuing, to be complete and

17 Jabez Gorham house, Benefit Street, Providence, Rhode Island, built about 1793. Photographed in 1980 by Richard Arling.

ended. During all of which said Term, the said Apprentice his said Master faithfully shall serve, his Secrets keep, his lawful Commands gladly obey: he shall do no Damage to his said Master nor see it done by others, without letting or giving Notice thereof to his said Master. He shall not waste his said Master's Goods, nor lend them unlawfully to any: he shall not commit Fornication, or contract Matrimony, within the said Term. At Cards, Dice, or any other unlawful Game, he shall not play, whereby his said Master may have Damage. With his own Goods, or the Goods of others, without License from his said master he shall neither buy nor sell: he shall not absent himself by Day or by Night, from his said Master's Service, without Leave; or haunt Ale-Houses, Taverns, or Play-Houses; but in all Things behave himself as a good and faithful Apprentice ought to do towards his said Master . . . during the said Term. And the said Nehemiah Dodge doth hereby promise to teach and instruct, or cause the said Apprentice to be taught and instructed, in the Art, Trade or Calling, of a Gold, Silver Smith and Jeweller by the best Ways and Means he can. And to find and allow unto his said Apprentice good and sufficient Meat, Drink, Washing and Lodging and also to provide him Ten Dollars worth of Clothing for each and every year during said Term and shall put him to School the Evenings of three Winters to be instructed in Reading, Writing, and Arithmetick.

IN TESTIMONY whereof the Parties to these Presents have hereunto interchangeably set their Hands and Seals, the Second Day of April *Anno Domini* 1806 and in the 30th Year of *American* Independence.

Signed, Sealed and Delivered
in the Presence of Nehemiah Dodge

Alexr Rogers   Jabez Gorham
Benjamin Gorham   Caty Gorham

The only account we have of Jabez's experience as an apprentice is one by his son, John Gorham, written long after the fact in 1894:

Father commenced business as a maker of fine gold jewelry. He had learned the trade of Nehemiah Dodge, serving from the age of fourteen to twenty one, living during that period with the other apprentices in the master's family, as was the custom of the day. He attained but little knowledge of his trade the first year, the youngest apprentice being obliged to be errand-boy for both shop and family.

Father always spoke of Mr. Dodge as a good master, kind and indulgent to the boys.

I do not know where the workshop was situated but his dwelling house was on the site of Mr. Bailey Evans' present residence on Benefit Street, Providence; R.I. When Father, some years later, bought the estate on the north cor-

ner of Benefit and Star Sts., the house built by his father, he became a neighbor of Mr. Dodge with whom pleasant neighborly relations existed as long as he lived.[15]

When Jabez completed his apprenticeship (in 1813) he formed a partnership with four other men, Christopher Burr, William Hadwin, George C. Clark, and Henry Mumford, to manufacture jewelry, their location being on the second floor of a building on the corner of North Main and Steeple streets in Providence. Each of the five partners in "The Firm" invested $300 in the business. According to one account, business was good enough from the beginning to enable the partners to recover their investment in a relatively short time.[16] That a luxury business could have prospered then is somewhat surprising. After all, it was in the midst of the War of 1812, and the British sea blockade was seriously affecting the economic climate of all New England port cities.

The Firm's business continued for five years, when, in 1818, in very dull times, the business fell off to the point where the partnership was dissolved and Jabez continued alone under the name Jabez Gorham, Jeweler, the four partners forming other business connections. Christopher Burr, a member of the Burr Family of silversmiths, made jewelry and coin silver spoons. Burr died in 1824. George C. Clark also became a spoon maker. Henry Mumford made spoons, dealt in grain and hay, and from 1831 to 1845 worked for the City of Providence as Sheriff, Surveyor of Highways, and City Marshall. He died in 1859.[17] The only one of Jabez Gorham's partners to achieve much of a worldly success was William Hadwin, who moved to Nantucket in 1820. In 1822 he married Eunice Starbuck, daughter of Captain Joseph Starbuck, one of the richest men in Massachusetts. After a few years in the jewelry business on Nantucket, Hadwin went into an association with Nathaniel Barney of Nantucket in the whale-oil business and became a wealthy man.[18] Today, the white-columned Hadwin mansion on Main Street on Nantucket, opposite the famous Starbuck "Three Bricks," still has on its front door the silver doorknob made by William Hadwin.

In the 1820s Gorham moved his business to a house at No. 12 Steeple Street, between Canal and North Main. It was a two-story, gambrel-roof wood house which had been moved to the location. The first floor was converted into a store and rented to two brothers, druggists, named Taylor. The second story and attic were fitted into workshops and the old sign JABEZ GORHAM JEWELER was moved to the new location (Fig. 18).

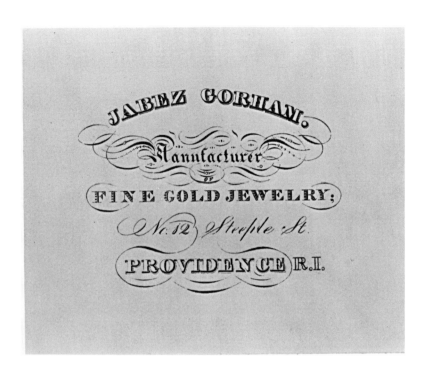

18 Jabez Gorham's trade card.

This general location was to be the home of the Gorham companies for over sixty years. The operations on Steeple Street expanded time and again until, in 1890, bursting at the seams, the company moved to a spacious new plant in the Elmwood section of Providence.

In the 1818–1831 era Jabez Gorham and his half–dozen or so employees made such items as gold beads, earrings, breast pins, and finger rings. He was one of the first to manufacture "French Filigree" jewelry, competing successfully with similar imported goods. Gorham also designed a special kind of gold chain which became known as the Gorham chain (John Gorham called it Gadroon chain). Unfortunately, at this writing (1981) no examples of Gorham jewelry of the 1818–1831 period have been identified.

Gorham sold his goods from his shop, and through peddlers, who regularly stocked up from Providence manufacturers. In those days peddlers were recognized as an important class of tradesmen. Each usually had his own circuit, going the rounds at stated and regular intervals. They often carried quite a rich stock of jewelry with their miscellaneous wares. Almost every habitable part of New England was serviced by these energetic men.

Jabez Gorham also traveled widely selling his wares. He not only regularly visited Boston and New York, he also traveled to towns and cities in New England. A graphic account of one of these sales trips (in 1819) is given in a packet of old letters which a great–grand–daughter of Jabez Gorham gave to the Gorham Company in 1967. The letters (five are from Jabez to his wife, Amey Gorham, and one is from Amey to her husband) are dated from October 21, 1819, to November 4, 1819. The letters cover a selling trip to Hartford, Connecticut, up the Connecticut River to Springfield, Northampton, and Greenfield in Massachusetts, then to Brattleboro and Chester, Vermont. In the two letters below, Jabez's erratic spelling and punctuation are quoted verbatim:

Hartford Oct 21 th 1819
half past 8 eving

Dear wife I arrived at this place at l/2 past seven last evening I did not have a very good night rest for there was a continual pasing through the long entry. there was someone going to bed until perhaps 1 oclock and about 2 oclock the stages began to start. there is perhaps 20 bedrooms joining. there was some one pasing my room all night by the dore. this morning after brakefast I began to look for market for my work without success. I have ben buisey amoust all day and all I could make out to sell was 39 dollars. hard work to do that I am allmost discouraged allredey. there is a great meny pepol in the tavern. I concluded if they disliked to leave home as bad as I doe, the tavern keeper would not get so much custom however I shall go up to Springfield tomorrow I shall have to wait untill tomorrow 2 oclock for the stage, time passes heavy. if my work sold as it did 2 years ago I should not have so much time to think about home and perhaps be more content. if I go up the river I am afraid I am spending my money to no purpos if I do not sell any of my goods in springfield I expect I shall return emedeady If I go further I shall write you. I hope you are all well. you cannot write so that I can get a letter if I should go up into Vermont state I shall tel you ware to direct a letter

your loving husband
Jabez Gorham
do not tell anyone what I have done— except Farther

Northhampton Oct 25th Tuesday
2 Oclock 1819

Dear Wife I wrought you friday last in order to pass off dull hours I pass the time in wrighting to you again I have been in this place sens friday 3 oclock all my trade in this place amounts to 89 dollars the whole amount sens I left is 131 dollars of witch I have about twelve dollars in old gold. my expenses up to the time I arrived here amount to 15 dollars I wrought you before from this place I expect to go to brattlebourough tomorrow there is so much difficulty in geting along I think I shall not stop at greenfield the stage comes up tomorrow and pases to brattlebourough a tuesday it comes down and Wednesday up again. of course if I stoped at Greenfield I could not go to Brattlebourough until Wednesday I am in hopes of selling a little in Brattleb and Walpole that will be the last town of note untill I get to my Ants I sell so little I do not think it will prudent to go further and not very prudent to go there but I shall have got so nigh when I am at Walpole I think I shall go there I shall have to hire a private convaance to Walpole witch will cost perhaps $3.50 stage fare $125. I cannot arrive untill thursday next. I attended meeting this forenon. a very handsome house mahogany pulpit and the preaching about as good as opertune. I should be glad to here from home if you have not wrought I hope you will attend to it when you get this letter Direct your letter to Chester and there will be no doubt that I shall get it if I am well tell farther of my determination of not going any further and let him wright a few lynes in your letter—if you have wrote if you write again when you get this it will be time enough for me to get it. as my time is not very valuble if I do here from home and you are all well I think I shall stay to my ants 5 or 6 days as when I get there I shall not be upon expence but if I do not here from you I shall not stay so long. tel farther if he is anxous for me to go to the town we talk of I will go. doe not fail to let him wright in your letter tell him the only objecttion is the exspenc I am afraid I shall not sell enough to make it an object if he has wroght tell him what further I say about it and if you wright hee may wish to wright again tell me how you get along for water as the well was so low when I left.
Wipe Amandas nose with a soft handkerchif so as not to make it sore tell Jabez to be a good boy If he does not I shall give the cowhide when I get back

DO NOT FAIL TO WRIGHT WHEN YOU GET THIS LETTER

tell Amanda farther will be home in about 12 days

From your loving husband Jabez Gorham [See Fig. 19.]

19 Jabez Gorham's signature, October 25, 1819 letter.

The other three letters from Jabez to his wife are in much the same vein. The October 27 letter had a postscript "take good care of my pig and little babe" which elicited a wry remark from his wife, Amey Gorham, in her letter of November 1. "Lucy was here last evening she said she supposed you wanted to see the Hog more than any one else."

Jabez sold a total of $131 worth of goods on the whole trip—barely enough to cover his costs and traveling expenses.

These letters tell a story of boredom and hard work and frustration. In later years Jabez remembered the past through rosier-colored glasses. In 1867 he gave a writer from the *Atlantic Monthly* an account of an early sales trip which is at a remarkable variance with the story told by the letters. This account of a sales trip to Boston makes it sound as if his customers were fighting to buy his goods:

The old gentleman Jabez Gorham gives an amusing account of the simple manner in which business was done in those days. When he had manufactured a trunkful of jewelry, he would jog away with it to Boston, where, after depositing the trunk in his room, he would go round to all the jewelers in the city to inform them of his arrival, and to say that his jewelry would be ready for inspection on the following morning at ten o'clock, and not before. Before the appointed hour every jeweller in the town would be at his door; but as it was a point of honor to give them all an equal chance, no one was admitted till the clock struck, when all pushed in in a body. The jewelry was spread out on the bed, around which all the jewellers of Boston, in 1820, could gather without crowding. Each man began by placing his hat in some convenient place, and it was in his hat that he deposited the articles selected by him for purchase. When the whole stock had been transferred from the bed to the several hats, Mr. Gorham took a list of the contents of each; whereupon the jewelers packed their purchases and carried them home. In the course of the day, the bills were made out; and the next morning Mr. Gorham went his rounds and collected the money. The business being thus happily concluded, he returned to Providence, to work uninterruptedly for another six months. In this manner, Jabez Gorham conducted business for sixteen years, before he even thought of attempting silverware.[19]

This account of Jabez's Boston sales trip was quoted in an abridged version in an "official" company history written by W. R. Bagnall in 1878 titled, *Historical and Bibliographic Sketch of the Gorham Manufacturing Co.*[20] Bagnall's story has often been quoted and has become part of the folklore of Gorham history. But the October 25, 1819, letter with "I sell so little I do not think it will be prudent to go further...." and "wipe Amanda's nose with a soft handkerchif so as not to make it sore...." has the true ring of the real world.

The salesman's life on the road has never been easy!

CHAPTER 3

Coin Silver Spoons

In 1831 Jabez Gorham added coin silver spoons to his line. He knew from his own experience and the experience of his peddlers that the sale of silver spoons was a growing business throughout New England, a business with a promising future.[1]

Jabez Gorham was late in getting into spoon making. Coin silver spoons were being made all over the eastern part of the United States in 1831. They were replacing pewter spoons for "Sunday best." Even though silver was an expensive commodity, labor was cheap, and by making very *thin* spoons the makers were able to keep the price down. One of the striking characteristics of many American coin silver spoons of the 1830–1850 period is their light weight and their flimsiness. It is amazing that so many have survived today in relatively good condition.

A measure of how light these coin silver spoons sometimes are is indicated by comparing them with later spoons. The teaspoon in Figure 22–1, made in the 1840s, weighs 0.38 troy ounces, while a regular Gorham *Chantilly* teaspoon weighs about 1.0 ounce. The *Chantilly* spoon (an average–weight spoon in the Gorham line) is two and a half times heavier than the coin silver spoon. Coin silver spoons had been made in Providence since the beginning of the nineteenth century. The coffin-handle spoon in Figure 16 was made in Nehemiah Dodge's shop about 1810, at the very time when Jabez Gorham was an apprentice there.

Whether or not Jabez Gorham learned spoon making during his apprenticeship is unknown, but when he decided to go into the spoon business he went to Boston for his expertise. There he made an agreement with Henry L. Webster, a young silversmith, who had had a long apprenticeship in the shop of Lewis Cary of Boston, after which he started his own business as a maker of silver spoons.[2] He had only been in business a short time when he made the agreement with Gorham to come to Providence to form the partnership of Gorham & Webster, with Jabez Gorham in charge of the jewelry department and Henry Webster the silver making.

The partnership prospered. In 1837 William G. Price, a jeweler, was admitted to the company. The name was changed to Gorham, Webster & Price. Price died in 1839, but the company name apparently continued unchanged until about 1840 or early 1841, when Jabez sold his entire interest in the partnership to Peter Church and Whitney Metcalf, manufacturing jewelers of Providence. The silver branch of the business was continued by Henry Webster under the name H. L. Webster & Co.

Jabez Gorham's retirement didn't last long. In 1841 Henry Webster offered to sell his silver business to him. Webster had been proposed a partnership in N. Harding of Boston, the largest spoon maker in New England, and he wanted to sell his Providence company. Jabez, who was financially comfortable, was not particularly anxious to resume an active business career. He decided he would do so on one basis, that is, if his son John would enter the business with him. John was interested. He later wrote of his father's offer:

> The opportunity was peculiarly attractive. It was not only a mechanical operation but one which seemed to me to possess unusual opportunities for development. I eagerly accepted my father's proposition, putting in one thousand dollars, all the money I had, and early in August the partnership was formed for the making of silver, under the name J. Gorham & Son.[3]

Henry Webster remained in Boston until the late 1840s when he returned to J. Gorham & Son as spoon foreman. In 1852 he left Gorham to form a partnership with Joseph B. Knowles of Providence. Their firm on Meeting Street was named H. L. Webster & Co. In about 1859, Samuel J. Ladd joined the firm, at which time the name became Knowles & Ladd. Webster retired in 1864 and died a year later.[4]

John Gorham was the third child of Jabez and Amey (Thurber) Gorham. Their first child, Benjamin, died a few days after his birth in 1817. Their second, Amanda, was born on December 11, 1818. John was born on November 18, 1820 and his mother died eight days later.[5]

John Gorham's beginnings in the family business were rather inauspicious. The plan was for him to serve an apprenticeship in his father's shop to learn the trade of manufacturing jewelry, and he embarked on this course in 1837. However, after only a few months, he found himself unable to get along with the shop foreman and so, with the consent of his father, he left home to try something else. For a year or so he worked on a farm in Smithfield, Rhode Island, and for the next three years he worked as a clerk in various businesses in Providence, New York, and Boston. When his father offered him a partnership in the silver business he was ready and willing to return home.

When J. Gorham & Son was formed in 1841 the business was relatively small, with total annual sales in the $10,000 to $12,000 range. The main business of the company was spoons. In addition, they made, on order, forks, sugar tongs, silver and steel–tipped thimbles, nursing tubes, simple styles of ladies' belt buckles, and silver combs.

At first Jabez Gorham was active in the business with his son, but as the decade went along he gradually withdrew, leaving John to run the business. John was mechanically minded and the manufacturing side of the business got most of his attention. In 1846 John took on his cousin, Henry Owen Gorham, to keep the books

and take charge of the office. John ran the workshop and made occasional sales trips to New York and Boston. Henry Gorham continued with the firm until the early part of 1850, when bad health forced him to leave. In an attempt to recoup his failing health he sailed with a friend on a small schooner from Providence to the Sandwich Islands (Hawaii), where he stayed for a few months. He returned to Providence, where he died in October, 1852.

The expansion of the business of J. Gorham & Son in the late 1840s was due to the increased sales of spoons and other products mentioned earlier, and to new items added to the line: fruit knives, napkin rings, more highly ornamented combs set with glass stones, and two new spoon patterns, *Threaded* and *Prince Albert*.

By 1847 the company had completely outgrown their small quarters in the old house at No. 12 Steeple Street (Fig. 20). The premises at that time consisted of the basement, a room on the first floor of about thirty by thirty-five feet, and half the attic. The second floor of No. 12 was occupied by the jewelry business of Church & Metcalf. The power for both Gorham and the jewelry manufacturing on the second floor was furnished by a horse–driven shaft from the basement where a horse traveled around in a circle. Whenever they needed extra speed they called through a speaking tube, "Get up, Dick."[6]

The working quarters of the firm were cramped and old Dick, the horse, was overworked. More power was needed. John Gorham decided he must install a steam engine. But there was a problem— there wasn't enough room in the basement for the kind of steam engine John felt he needed. After a long study John came up with a bold plan. He proposed to his father that a 100–foot lot contiguous to No. 12 Steeple Street be bought and that a four–story brick building be built to house manufac-

20 Building at No. 12 Steeple Street which housed the Gorham operations in the 1830s and 1840s.

turing space and a fifty–horsepower steam engine. He was not only thinking about his present needs, he was planning for the future. His idea for the first phase was that J. Gorham & Son would occupy all of the old building at No. 12, with power being supplied from the new engine in the new building. Church & Metcalf would move into the new building. The remaining space there would be rented to manufacturers who could utilize the power from the new steam engine on a rental basis. The new building would also provide space for the future expansion for which John was planning. It was an ambitious plan, one that required considerable capital and faith in the future.

Jabez Gorham went along with John's idea, apparently with some reluctance. He put some money into the venture, but most of the money, $17,000, was borrowed from Richmond Bullock of Providence, a financier, on six–month notes at 6 percent interest.

As the work progressed Jabez became more and more nervous about the project. Neighbors were complaining about the dangers of a steam boiler in so congested a city neighborhood, and the magnitude of the financial investment worried him. So early in 1848 Jabez decided to get out.

He sold his entire interest in J. Gorham & Son to his son, John. The wording of the bill of sale makes it abundantly clear that the indebtedness of the partnership was Jabez's chief worry. He wanted to make *very* sure he was getting out from under this yoke of responsibility:

> It is agreed, that the Copartnership existing between Jabez Gorham and John Gorham 2nd both of the city and county Providence state of Rhode Island, heretofore known under the name J. Gorham & Son, is this day dissolved.
>
> Now therefore, in pursuance of said agreement, and in consideration of Eight Thousand Dollars paid and secured to the said Jabez Gorham, he the said Jabez Gorham doth grant, sell, assign and set over to the said John Gorham 2nd, all his interest and right in all the goods on hand, stock, tools and fixtures, together with all the books, debts and demands due said partnership, of whatever kind or nature, with full powers to collect the same by writs at law or equity, and for his own use and benefit, and to hold the same free from all claims by the said Jabez Gorham, his administrators, executors or assigns.
>
> And these presents further witness; that the said John Gorham 2nd for himself, his executors, administrators and assigns, doth covenant with the said Jabez Gorham his executors and administrators, that he will pay all the debts and demands which are now due and owing by the said firm to any person or persons, whomsoever, and save him the said Jabez Gorham harmless from all actions, costs, or expenses concerning the said debts and liabilities. In wit-

ness where of, we have here unto set our hands and seal the first day of February one Thousand Eight–Hundred and Forty Eight

In Presence of   Jabez Gorham
Henry C. Gorham   John Gorham 2nd

Jabez agreed to allow the use of his name in the business, which continued as J. Gorham & Son until 1850.

The new brick building, which was started early in 1847, was finished in 1848. Good tenants were found and the business of J. Gorham & Son continued to grow. But the mere expansion of the business brought on new problems. John Gorham struggled to pay back the Bullock notes and at the same time he needed more money for working capital. He needed financial help and he needed help in running the business.

The next chapter deals with the remarkable fifteen-year period when John Gorham and his associates expanded the company from a small craft shop making mainly silver spoons to a large, highly mechanized plant—one of the largest silverworks in the world.

It would be easy to criticize Jabez Gorham (Fig. 21) for his lack of vision. If the Gorham story were to end in 1848, Jabez would be remembered only as one of the dozens and dozens of small spoon makers who flourished all over the eastern United States during the 1830s

21 Daguerreotype of Jabez Gorham, ca. 1850. *(Gorham collection).*

and 1840s. His whole thinking was that of a craftsman trained in the traditions of the eighteenth century. He was conservative. He made familiar objects and he was no innovator. He made a good living and his cautious style enabled him to survive the Panic of 1837, which ruined so many of his competitors. He gave his son, John Gorham, a good start in life. Jabez Gorham deserves the honored place as founder of the Gorham Company.

Spoon Styles of the 1830s and 1840s

The silver spoons made by the various Gorham companies in the 1831–1850 period were in the simple, plain styles of the era. The earliest of the spoons, marked Gorham & Webster (1831–1837) has a plain fiddle handle with only a slight taper (Fig. 22–1). The top is gently rounded and curves down. The shoulders of this particular spoon are pointed. This handle form continued through the Gorham, Webster & Price period (1837–1841) (Figs. 22–2 and 22–3), and on into the middle of the 1840s (Figs. 22–4 and 22–5). The handles of some of the later spoons are slightly wider and the straight sides of the handles taper a bit more. In the last half of the 1840s the spoon handles tended to be wider.

The two *Tipt* (or *Tip*) patterns, plain *Tipt* (Fig. 23–1), and *French Tipt* (Fig. 23–2) with its wavy fiddle handle, were the beginnings of a trend toward decorated flatware handles which flowered a decade later into patterned flatware.

The *Threaded* pattern (also called *English Threaded* or *Old English Threaded*) was a traditional pattern with a thread outline on the handle. This pattern, introduced about 1846, is now often called *Fiddle and Thread*. It had been a popular pattern in both England and America since the eighteenth century.

The *Prince Albert* (or *Albert*) pattern (Fig. 24) used by Gorham was designed by Michael Gibney, a New York silversmith, in 1845.[7] Gibney's *Prince Albert* was a copy of an English flatware pattern named after Queen Victoria's Prince Consort. Gorham used a cumbersome and inefficient means of obtaining pieces in this pattern. Flatware blanks were roughly hammered out in the shop in Providence and sent to Gibney in New York who passed them through his die rolls and returned them to Gorham in Providence where they were finished. John Gorham complained: "For this service we paid him a larger price per dozen than we charged ten years later for the whole work complete."[8]

Based on surviving examples and bills of sale, most of the Gorham output in the 1831–1850 period was

spoons. Ladles are often found and occasionally forks, butter knives (Fig. 25), sugar spoons, sugar tongs, and sugar sifters. The *French Tipt* sugar sifter in Figure 26 is simply a small ladle with holes drilled in the bowl. An 1848 invoice indicates some of the typical items sold by Gorham & Son. This particular sale was made to Amey Thurber, four days before she married John Gorham:

1848 BILL OF SALE

Miss Amey Thurber
  Bot of J. Gorham & Son

1/2 Set Tip Tables (Large)		9.91
1 " (Small)		15.26
3 " Teas		22.61
1 " Tip Oyster Laddle		11.47
1 " Cream "		2.53
1 pr Tip Salts		1.57
1 Tip Mustard		1.25
1 pr Pearl B★ Knife		6.00
1" " Knife & Fork		5.50
1 Pearl Cake knife		6.00
1/2 pr. Ex. Heavy B★ Knife		2.50
		$84.41

Providence Sept. 1/48
Recd. Pyt. J. Gorham & Son

★(Bread or Butter)

Coin Silver

In her excellent paper, "From Pure Coin. The Manufacture of American Silver Flatware 1800–1860," Deborah Dependahl Waters defines coin silver:

"Coin" as applied to American silver flatware manufactured before the Civil War has two distinct, but not mutually exclusive, meanings. First, it identifies a common source of raw material. Second, it specifies a quality standard for alloy employed in such products....
The American silversmith long had relied on silver coin or wrought objects out moded in style for his material. Coins, particularly Spanish milled dollars, French crowns and five-franc pieces, and American dollars and half dollars remained the principal source for silver in the early nineteenth century. The standards to which these coins were minted largely determined the quality of alloy employed by the craftsman.[10]

Gorham's coin silver flatware falls into two separate and distinct periods. First, the 1831–1850 period when most of the spoons were handmade from common stock

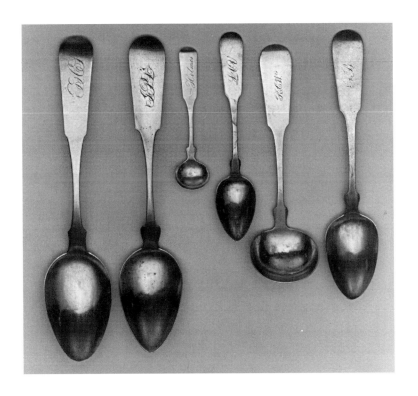

22 *Left to right: (1)* Tablespoon, 1831–1837, Length: 8 9/ 16 in. (21.7 cm.). Mark: GORHAM & WEBSTER. (2) Tablespoon, 1837–1841. Length: 8 5/16 in. (21.1 cm.). Mark: PROVIDENCE, RI/GORHAM, WEBSTER & PRICE. (3) Salt spoon, 1837–1841. Length: 3 3/4 in. (9.5 cm.). Mark: GORHAM, WEBSTER & PRICE. (4) Teaspoon, 1841–1850. Length: 5 1/2 in. (14 cm.). Mark: J.G. & SON. (5) Ladle, 1841–1850. Length: 6 3/16 in. (15.7 cm.). Mark: PROVIDENCE, RI/J. GORHAM & SON. (6) Small tablespoon (dessert), 1845–1850. Length: 7 1/16 in.(17.8 cm.). Mark: J.GORHAM & SON/ PROVIDENCE, RI. (*1, courtesy George Tompkins, 2–6, Gorham collection*).

23 (1) Teaspoon, plain *Tipt* pattern, 1850–1852. Length: 6 3/16 in. (15.7 cm.). Mark: GORHAM & THURBER/PROVIDENCE, RI. (2) Teaspoon, *French Tipt* pattern, 1845–1850. Length: 6 3/16 in. (15.7 cm.). Mark: J. GORHAM & SON/PROVIDENCE, RI. *(Gorham collection).*

24 Small serving spoon in the *Prince Albert* pattern, designed by Michael Gibney, New York, in 1845. Length: 6 7/8 in. (17.5 cm.). *(Courtesy Gebelein Silversmiths).*

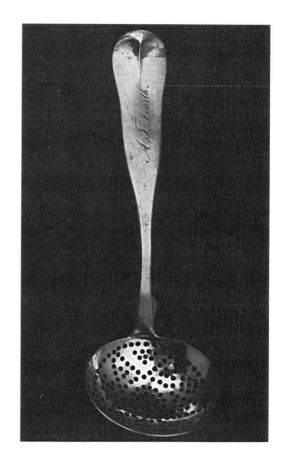

25 Butter knife, engraved "J. M. & S. G. Bunker," for James
M. and Sarah G. Bunker of Nantucket, who were married
February 10, 1848.[9] Length: 6 7/8 in. (17.5 cm.). Mark: No.
6. *(Private collection).*

26 Sugar sifter, *French Tipt* pattern, 1845–1849. Length: 7 1/16
in. (17.8 cm.). Mark: J. GORHAM & SON/ PROVIDENCE, R.I. *(The
National Museum of American History, Smithsonian Institution).*

of 0.800 fine silver. Second is the 1850–1868 period
when the coin stock was 0.900 fine. (In 1868 Gorham
adopted the English sterling standard of 0.925 fine.) In
the second period the old hand methods of manufacture were replaced by the drop press. The 0.900 fine
coin silver stock was first used in about 1846 in the
making of the *Threaded* and *Prince Albert* patterns.

We have three firsthand accounts of the type of silver
raw material used in the 1845–1868 period. The first of
these accounts is by Henry Bushnell who had been familiar with Gorham's operations before joining the company in 1850. (As an independent craftsman Bushnell
made dies for Gorham as early as 1843):

> Mr. Gorham melted all the silver in the morning that was
> to be used through the day, mostly half dollars, melting
> them on the forge, in the crucible placed inside of an iron
> ring, filled with charcoal, and blown with bellows. He
> poured one bar of common stock weighing about 80 ounces
> and two bars of coin stock weighing about 60 ounces,
> making altogether about 140 ounces a day. The amount
> used gradually increased in proportion to orders received.[11]

The second of these accounts was in an 1867 *Atlantic
Monthly* article, "Among the Workers in Silver":

> The first operation is to buy silver coin in Wall Street. In a
> bag of dollars there are always some bad pieces, and as the
> Company embark their reputation in every silver vessel
> that leaves the factory, and are always responsible for its
> purity, each dollar is wrenched asunder and its goodness
> positively ascertained before it is thrown into the crucible.
> The subsequent operations, by which these spoiled dollars

> are converted into objects of brilliant and enduring beauty,
> can better be imagined than described.[12]

The third of these accounts is from *Harper's New
Monthly Magazine,* September 1868:

> In the manufacture of silver–ware the first operation is, of
> course, to buy the silver. Wall Street is the usual source of
> supply. Occasionally, however, a longhoarded treasure will
> find its way to the melting–pot from remote and unex-
> pected quarters. The vicissitudes of life sometimes consign
> to the crucible a quantity of the clumsy "old plate" which
> people used to cherish with so much pride; and many
> persons now deliberately exchange their ancient imple-
> ments and vessels for the elegant creations of modern taste.
> Recently, the Gorham Company received from
> Ogdensburg, in the State of New York, a bag of silver coins
> for melting, which had been the secret hoard of a miser
> for forty years, and was found to contain three thousand

dollars' worth of the precious metal. There were coins of every country and every denomination, a few of which were of considerable value as specimens. The poor man had counted these rough, dull coins, no doubt, a thousand times, and hugged them to his heart as his dear treasure and sure resource in time of need. Useless to him, they found their way at last to the meltingroom, to be converted into forms of beauty, and adorn the tables of more generous spirits. Generally, however, it is to Wall Street or its vicinity that the makers of silver–ware resort for their daily supply of the precious metals.[13]

From these contemporary descriptions it is clear that although Gorham used a mixture of many kinds of silver coins to make their wares, United States coins were their main raw material. The composition of the United States coins would have depended on the dates when they were minted. Coins minted before 1837 had a slightly lower silver content than those minted after 1837. United States coins from 1792 to January 18, 1837, had a composition of 0.8924 silver (89.24 percent). The remainder was copper. After the act of January 18, 1837, United States silver coins were 0.900 fine, or 90 percent silver and 10 percent copper.

Foreign coins were circulated as legal tender in the United States until 1857. Congress stipulated that all such foreign currency must be assayed annually. One such analysis found French crowns to be 0.915 fine, French five–franc coins 0.896 percent fine, and Spanish dollars 0.897 fine.[14]

Did Gorham actually conform to their avowed standards of 0.800 fine for common stock and 0.900 fine for coin stock? Modern chemical analyses were made to check this point. Several of the Gorham spoons of the 1831–1852 period were analyzed at the Winterthur laboratories, using nondestructive energy dispersive x-ray

fluorescence spectroscopy.[15] Those spoons which were supposed to have been made from common stock, 0.800 fine, varied from 0.711 to 0.848 fine. Based on these results one can be pretty sure that John Gorham was not very precise in his metallurgy. Gorham's coin spoons of the 1850–1868 period tend to be fairly near the 0.900 fine standard.

The tabulation below shows the silver and copper content of spoons in Figures 22 and 23–1. Also shown are two of the significant trace elements in the silver—gold and tin.

The amount of gold in a silver alloy is an indication of age. Silver objects made before the 1860s usually contain significant amounts of gold. Refining processes were crude. After the 1860s recovery methods improved to the point where the gold content of silver was practically zero.

The amount of tin in a silver spoon is a clue to the method of manufacture. Tin is not normally present in silver and when it is found it suggests that a tin die or "force" was used in the making of handles and/or bowls of spoons. Spoons made entirely by hand hammering or in a drop press using steel dies contain little or no tin.

A study of the tin content of the spoons in the above table helps explain how the spoons were probably made:

Figure 22–1 Entirely handmade
Figure 22–4 Handle handmade, bowl made with tin die
Figure 22–5 Handle made with tin die, bowl handmade
Figure 22–6 and 23–1 Both handles and bowls made with tin dies

Analyses of Gorham Spoons of the 1831–1852 Era[16]

Composition of Handle (%)

Figure No.	Silver	Copper	Gold	Tin
22–1	80.7	18.9	.10	0
22–2	80.6	18.7	.09	.16
22–3	83.7	15.8	.07	.10
22–4	78.8	20.7	.06	0
22–5	82.0	17.0	.08	.35
22–6	75.0	22.8	.09	1.30
23–1	71.1	27.0	.06	.99

Composition of Bowl (%)[17]

Silver	Copper	Gold	Tin
79.6	20.0	.09	0
80.2	19.1	.07	.26
84.8	14.5	.06	.22
78.1	20.9	.09	.48
81.3	18.1	.08	0
74.8	23.6	.10	.72
72.3	26.2	.07	.67

The Making of Coin Silver Spoons

The making of coin silver spoons at Gorham went through three phases:

1830s Entirely handmade
1840s Handmade with tin dies
1850s Stamped in drop press using steel dies

The changing methods of making flatware at Gorham can be documented from historical records and from modern chemical analyses.[18]

The raw materials and the melting process have already been described. Melting was a key operation. In the 1830s melting was performed by Joshua Godfrey, an old–timer who had been an apprentice to Nehemiah Dodge along with Jabez Gorham. In the 1840s John Gorham himself took over the melting job.

The hot liquid silver was cast into bars. After the bars cooled and were surface cleaned, they were rolled into thin strips a half-inch wide and cut into spoonlength blanks. By the use of an oval–faced peening hammer the bowl end of the blank was pounded into a leaf shape, and the other end into a handle shape. The bowl of the spoon was shaped in one of two ways. It could have been shaped by hammering the leaf shape over an appropriate steel stake, or it could have been shaped with the aid of a hand–carved wood mold or die. Metal dies were apparently not used by Jabez Gorham and his partners in the 1830s.

Steel punches and tin (or pewter) dies for shaping handles and spoon bowls were introduced in the 1840s. The steel punch is used to hammer the silver spoon blank into the relatively soft tin die. The tin die holds its shape by conforming to the shape of the punch. Figure 27 shows a steel punch and die for making spoon bowls. (This particular punch and die are slightly earlier, ca. 1820, than those used by Gorham, but they illustrate the principle). Figures 23–1 and 23–2 show spoons whose tipt handles are poorly formed, suggesting that the dies used to make these handles were rather crude.

By 1850 new dies resulted in crisp, well–defined tipt-handle ends (Fig. 26). Unusual shapes such as ladle bowls were entirely handmade until the early 1850s.
Silver becomes hard on working and must be reheated to red heat (annealed), to regain its malleability. It was necessary, on average, for Gorham to anneal their coin silver spoons nine times during the making process.

In 1852 John Gorham ordered the first steam–powered press ever made to stamp flatware (see Chapter 4). It was probably installed in 1853 or 1854, in time to produce the new flatware patterns *Josephine* and *Roman*.

Although great strides were made in the forming of flatware in the 1831–1855 period, finishing methods changed very little during this time. The main change was the introduction of power–driven polishing wheels.

Finishing was set up as an assembly operation of the type that had been common in the larger silversmithing shops since the eighteenth century. First, the filer trimmed the spoon and filed off the rough edges. Next,

27 Steel punch and tin die for making spoon bowls. In the center is a steel die for forming tipped handle ends. *(Courtesy Gebelein Silversmiths).*

the edges were smoothed–first by hand, and later, on a lathe–mounted scouring wheel with Scotch stone and oil. The spoons were then polished with fine brick dust and oil. The last typical step was burnishing. This gave a smooth, glossy, and quite durable surface to the metal.

Burnishing is a process whereby the surface of the silver is rubbed with a polished–steel hand–burnishing tool which is lubricated with soap and water. Burnishing produces a polished, mirrorlike surface of good luster; it removes marks left by polishing compounds and produces a darker surface than other modes of finishing.

Spoon making was a slow, laborious process before the introduction of the drop presses: "Two men by exceedingly hard work and sometimes violent exertion, could make in a day two dozen of their rough tea–spoons, no two of which were alike in shape or weight."[19]

Working Conditions

Silverworkers had a long workday and a six–day work-week in the nineteenth century. In the 1840s the eleven–hour day was standard at J. Gorham & Son. In the summer the day started at 5:00 A.M. Breakfast was from seven to eight, dinner, twelve to one. The day ended at six in the evening. In winter the hours were from seven to twelve in the morning and one to seven in the afternoon.

Vacations were unheard of. There were four regular holidays in the year: Thanksgiving, Christmas, the Fourth of July, and Commencement Day at Brown University.

Henry Bushnell recorded an early labor dispute:

Soon after 1850 we discussed the question of a ten hour day. At that time the company was working eleven hours.

Consequently we called a meeting in the old barber shop on the corner of the lane, organized, and appointed a committee of three to wait upon the Company and present a petition for a ten hour day. The committee consisted of Henry L. Webster, James Salisbury and Giles Manchester.

About three days after the petition had been presented, James Salisbury inquired if it was not about time to hear from the Company. He was advised to call upon Mr. Gorham, which he did; his reply was: "If you want an answer now, it will be no. If you wait a week, we will see." Then Mr. Salisbury advised with me what would be best to do, and we agreed to wait. At the expiration of the week, a notice was posted stating that: Hereafter, ten hours would constitute a day's work; the time to be taken by the hour and quarter hour; three minutes would be counted as five, and the loss of two minutes, nothing.[20]

The End of Handmade Spoons

The year 1852 marked the end of an era for Gorham. At about that time the company ceased making spoons of common, 0.800 fine, silver, and started making all their spoons of true coin silver, 0.900 fine. Also, in 1852 John Gorham ordered the steam–powered drop press which would mean the end of handmade spoons.

Styles lingered on. In 1871 the company reintroduced their original flatware pattern, *Fiddle,* under the name *Old English Tipt.* As late as 1881 the Gorham fall catalog shows the old *Tipt* and *French Tipt* patterns. These old patterns were no longer made in common silver as they were in the 1840s, or in coin as they were in the 1850s and 1860s, but in sterling. Names were changed. *French Tipt* was now called *Fiddle.* (The changing of flatware names seems to have been a neverending process since the 1850s.)

CHAPTER 4

John Gorham: The Expansionist

The year 1850 was a crucial year in Gorham history. The company was at a crossroads. It was doing well, in spite of the shortage of working capital. The annual sales volume of the business, which had averaged $15,000 to $20,000 per year during the early 1840s, had begun to creep up to nearly $30,000 in 1848 and 1849. A comfortable growth pattern could be seen for the company—just by continuing the business the way it was.

But John Gorham (Fig. 28) wasn't thinking of comfortable growth. He had something quite different in mind. He had plans that would revolutionize Gorham, and in doing so would revolutionize the silver–making industry. In two decades, wares of solid silver, which had been the precious possessions of a relatively few families of wealth, would become almost commonplace. Many middle–class Americans would set their tables with sterling by the 1870s.

One should not overdramatize John Gorham's role, but it *was* remarkable. A mere review of the facts will suggest the intelligence, energy, and vision (an old–fashioned word!) he must have had.

At the beginning of 1850 the company, J. Gorham & Son, consisted of John Gorham, his cousin Henry Gorham, who was dying, and fourteen employees. We even know the names of all the employees.[1] The company made silver flatware, thimbles, combs, and a child's cup or two—all by hand with the simplest of hand tools. Most of the company's products were sold to stores in Providence and Boston and distributed to various parts of New England by the celebrated Yankee peddlers.

John Gorham planned to change the whole setup. First, he decided he must make all kinds of silverwares—not just spoons. He wanted to make tea sets, pitchers, and bowls, in other words, to make hollow ware. He set his sights high. He would make only the best wares, in the latest fashion. He would mechanize his operations, using machinery wherever possible. He also meant to mechanize flatware production. He dreamed of power–driven presses where one man could produce dozens of spoons per hour with a machine, instead of one spoon per hour by the old hand methods. Finally, he would revolutionize the concept of marketing his goods. Instead of depending on peddlers and occasional sales calls by himself, the company would have its own salesmen, selling anywhere and everywhere in the United States that silverwares could be sold. The salesmen would be supported by a vigorous advertising campaign.

These are familiar precepts of twentieth–century industrial management. But they were new to businessmen of the mid–nineteenth century, and absolutely revolutionary to the makers of fine silverwares. Silversmiths had always been the aristocrats of the crafts world, and their methods of doing business in America had changed little since the seventeenth century. Small shops supplied, usually on order, the needs and wants of a relatively small, affluent clientele.

28 John Gorham, from a photograph of about 1865.

In the 1850s Gorham Company sales increased fourteen times—from $29,000 in 1850 to $397,000 in 1859. The number of employees went from fourteen to two hundred. In the next decade (the 1860s the number of employees would again double—to four hundred—sales would approach a million dollars, and Gorham would be recognized as the largest maker of fine silverwares in the world.

Gorham and Thurber

John Gorham solved the problem of additional capital and manpower in one bold action. He made a partnership with his twenty–five–year–old cousin, Gorham Thurber. Gorham Thurber not only brought fresh capital to the company, he also brought nine years' experience as the bookkeeper for the Franklin Foundry and Machine Company.

John Gorham wrote of the event this way:

I struggled along till the later part of 1849 when, needing capital to carry the business onto advantage, I arranged for a partnership with Gorham Thurber, son of Dexter Thurber, to commence on Jan. 1, 1850. But during the week previous to this date a very serious fire occurred on the premises which deferred the actual beginning of the partnership for some two or three months, when the business took the name Gorham & Thurber, he taking an equal interest in the business, thus doubling its capital. Mr. Thurber took

charge of the financial part, the books and the selling of the goods, as I wished to give more attention and thought to the processes of manufacture and the improvement of our machinery and tools, and especially to the introduction of Hollow Ware, as Dinner and Tea Services, etc.[2]

Early Hollow Ware

John Gorham was conscious that if he were to make hollow ware he would have to look outside the company for craftsmen. He hired an experienced silversmith in New York and began to acquire the necessary tools and machinery.

It is not known what was made first. The 1868 *Harper's New Monthly Magazine* article (see Note 12, Chapter 3) stated that the first hollow ware made by Gorham was a Chinese tea set, made from designs commissioned in New York. However, it appears that the Chinese tea set was actually made in 1851. It will be discussed later.

The only pieces that we can say with some certainty were made in 1850 are the child's cup in Figure 29 and a tea set, the teapot of which is illustrated in Figure 30.

It was a common practice to give silver cups (or mugs) to children soon after their birth. The D.M.T. of the cup in Figure 29 was presumably born on November 25, 1849. The mug, which is marked Gorham & Thurber, was probably made in 1850. The Rococo engraving on the cup is somewhat crude and the silversmithing is a bit amateurish.

29 Child's cup, ca. 1850. Mark: GORHAM & THURBER/ PROVIDENCE, RI/PURE COIN. *(Gorham photograph).*

30 Teapot made in 1850. Height 8 1/2 in. (21.6 cm.). Mark: GORHAM & THURBER/ PROVIDENCE, RI/PURE COIN. *(The Art Institute of Chicago).*

The teapot in Figure 30 is more important and more ambitious. It is part of a large tea and coffee service. Pieces of the service are dated 1850, and it is known that it was purchased in that year.[3] This highly decorated pot, with its naturalistic spout, handle, finial, and feet is of a design that was very popular at mid–century. At least a half–dozen other makers at this time used very similar design elements: Tiffany, Young & Ellis in New York,[4] J. E. Caldwell and P. L. Krider in Philadelphia,[5] Hayden & Wheldon, Charleston, South Carolina, La Forme Brothers, Boston,[6] and Adolph Himmel, New Orleans.[7] The Gorham & Thurber pot is somewhat less successful than the best of these designs. The workmanship is pedestrian, the shape dumpy, and the overall design not well organized.

The reporter for the *Providence Journal* was much less critical of the Gorham & Thurber wares when they were shown for the first time in Providence in September 1850:

> The Fair of the Society for the Encouragement of Domestic Industry, and the Rhode Island Horticultural Society, was opened yesterday morning at Howard Hall. This is the first time that the societies have held their show in conjunction in Providence, and, as might have been anticipated, the exhibition is very much more attractive than in former years....
>
> At the center of the east side are several cases of silver ware by Gorham & Thurber. The tea and coffee sets are

superbly elegant, perfect in design and execution and reflect the highest credit upon the manufacturers. They are fully equal to the best specimens of Jones, Ball & Poor. The wealth of our city will see that it need not go abroad for the most luxurious ornaments for the table. Providence has long been distinguished by its manufacture of jewelry and some descriptions of silver ware; but hollow ware of silver has not, we believe, been before attempted here.[8]

The Chinese service mentioned previously was the most ambitious and most publicized of Gorham's early tea sets. It was featured in the Gorham & Thurber exhibit at the 1851 Rhode Island State Fair. John Gorham stated in his 1894 notebook that the set created quite a stir when it was shown at the fair "just after it was finished."

In the early 1850s Gorham used the Rhode Island fairs, which were held in September, as a major showcase for their wares. The company made particularly great efforts to exhibit their very best things in 1851 and 1852, when they were just getting started in the hollow–ware business. Pieces were made with the fair in mind and were set aside for the fair. Gorham apparently felt they were getting their money's worth in these exhibitions. They continued to have major showings at the Rhode Island fairs throughout the 1850s.

The 1851 fair was particularly important for the company. It was the first large showing of their work. The *Providence Journal* devoted a lot of space to the Gorham

& Thurber exhibit:

THE GRACEFUL ARTS

We continue our notes of observations made in this attractive department of the Exhibition. From their extreme elegance of design, and finished workmanship, the principal articles in Messrs. Gorham & Thurber's collection claim the first place and the fullest description. An illustration has been prepared by which, with the addition of a few words, a tolerable idea may be had of the quality of these productions [Fig. 31]. The value of the silverwares in the Exhibition will probably not fall short of ten thousand dollars. The various manufactures of gold are undoubtedly worth an equal sum.

The centre and chief piece grouped in the cut is a large and heavy water kettle of new and elegant model, and style of decoration. It is fully chased, the body being surrounded by a succession of scenes peculiar to China, which are exquisitely rendered. The feet, spout, etc., are formed of the tea plant, bearing leaves, buds and blossoms. The stand is

supported on the shoulders of four Chinamen, who rest on rich scroll and shell work, based on the backs of dolphins. The lid, covered with rich chasing, is surmounted by the image of a Chinaman holding a parrot. The parts are intended to harmonize, and the effect of the whole is in the highest degree ornate and graceful. The value of this piece is not much less than $100.

The next object to the left, in the group, is a water pitcher; also, as we are assured by the maker, of an entirely new design. It is supported on a foot composed of the leaves, flowers and stem of the waterlilly. The handle is formed of aquatic plants, and dolphin. The body is elegantly chased representing fruits and flowers with scrolls. The form of the pitcher is peculiar, and of great beauty. Of its value we are not informed.

The object to the right is a teapot. It is one of a service, consisting of six pieces made to order for a gentleman of this city. It is chased very beautifully, and the mountings are highly ornamental. In the foreground are goblets, cups, pie knives, napkin rings, etc., all elaborately engraved.

Among the larger pieces not represented in the cut, are a plain octagon kettle, designed to match the tea service of a lady of this city, by whose order it was made; a claret jug, in a unique style, the handle and foot composed of grape

31 Drawing of Gorham silver exhibited at the Rhode Island State Fair, 1851. *Providence Journal,* September 13, 1851, p. 2.

vine, the body covered with its tendrils, foliage and fruit, intermingled with bacchanalian figures; card receivers, bread plates, etc., . will be noticed;

We have given space to a particular account of only part of this collection. To describe, or even catalogue the whole, would be a labor, however pleasant at another time, certainly not to be coveted in a hot day.[9]

The silverwares pictured in the woodcut in Figure 31 are in the Rococo style that prevailed for several years in American silver at mid–century. The pieces shown have naturalistic, High Victorian elements, such as the spouts and handles of the teapot and the water kettle. The hot water kettle (center) is a wildly eclectic High Victorian creation. The flatware serving pieces in the foreground are all of the *Albert* pattern which Gorham now made themselves. They no longer depended on Michael Gibney of New York to make the pattern for them. The teapot on the right is similar in shape to the pot in Figure 30, but the body is chased with a naturalistic wreath of twigs and leaves and flowers. The advertisement in Figure 32 shows the variety of wares *sold* by Gorham & Thurber in 1851 or 1852. The word *sold* is emphasized since some of the items in this advertisement were not made by Gorham & Thurber. For example, "Plated Ware" was not actually made by Gorham until about 1865. We know from John Gorham's diaries that he purchased many kinds of silver items in England and France for resale in the United States. This of course can create problems of identification for us today. For example, do we know for sure which pieces of silver marked only Gorham & Thurber were actually made by the company? This question cannot always be answered with complete confidence, but it seems many or most of the pieces so marked *were* made by the company. English sterling pieces would have had the usual English marks. The only reason this matter is brought up is that it is somewhat hard to conceive that the company could have added *all* the items noted in Figure 32 to their line in the two–year period of Gorham & Thurber's existence. The Gorham & Thurber years were a time of great personal growth for John Gorham. The company's expansion into the hollow–ware business must have been continually challenging. Silversmiths, chasers, modelers, and engravers had to be hired. New equipment had to be purchased or built. Probably a spinning lathe to make hollow–ware forms would have been acquired almost immediately. The old hand–raising method of making hollow–ware forms would have been too slow and too costly for John Gorham. A good spinner could make a simple form such as a small bowl in an hour or so that would have taken many hours by the old hand–ham–

32 Gorham & Thurber advertisement in *The Rhode Island Almanac for the Year 1852*. (Providence: H. H. Brown, 1852).

mering method of raising.

The fact that John Gorham was not a trained silversmith was a weakness, but it was also his greatest strength. The lack of traditional training in the craft meant there were many facts of silversmithing of which he was ignorant. However, it also meant that he was not strapped with "the right way" of doing things. He was far more innovative than his better–trained competitors. He had an intensive interest in machinery and he knew instinctively that progress in silversmithing must depend on mechanization.

In the first months of 1852, after the company had been making hollow ware for about two years, John Gorham decided he should go to Europe. He wanted to study English and French silverworking methods and, most of all, he wanted to find skilled workers to bring back to Providence. By the middle of the nineteenth century the traditional seven–year craft apprenticeships had begun to disappear in America. This meant there were not enough trained men in any of the silverworking crafts to fill the needs of a fast–growing company like Gorham. They would have to come from Europe.

This philosophy of using Europe as a major source of silversmiths and chasers and modelers and designers was practiced by Gorham right up to World War I. John Gorham and his American associates felt fully capable of inventing and adapting machinery to cut the costs of making fine silverware, but they depended heavily on Europe for their craftsmen and designers.

Gorham & Company

In 1852 John Gorham and Gorham Thurber invited another cousin, Lewis Dexter, Jr., to join the firm. At that time the name of the company was changed again, to Gorham & Company. Dexter remained with Gorham for nine years, retiring in 1861.

Trip to Europe—1852

John Gorham made a three–month trip to England and the Continent in May–July of 1852. He kept a diary of the trip which documents an extraordinarily high level of physical and mental activity. His diary records a wide range of interests. He was of course interested in every-thing to do with silverwares. Going over on the steam-ship *Arctic* he noted: "This steamer has a very large set of dining and dessert forks; table, dessert and tea spoons, Olive pattern, besides soups, ladles, fish knives, etc., fur-nished by Ball, Tompkins & Black. Her plated cutlery are Sheffffield, all handsomely marked" [May 7].

Gorham came to know London, Birmingham, Manchester, and Sheffield well. He called on all kinds of silver–making shops—large and small. Sometimes they wouldn't let him in: "Called on Thomas Walstenhone at James Dixon & Sons. Was treated very politely but couldn't get in shop" [May 21]. He looked at equip-ment and talked to die cutters, stampers, piercers, chas-ers, and other silverworkers about coming to work for Gorham & Co. in America.

John Gorham was also a tourist in Europe. He visited cathedrals, castles, and museums. He often dined in the best restaurants. He went to the theater and the races at Ascot. Once, at Covent Garden, he saw the Queen: "At 9:15 Queen arrived, Prince Albert, Lord Grafton (?) and Maj. Genl. Buckley. Very common looking but ani-mated. Viewed her at leisure with glass" June 19]. Gorham often talked to strangers on the streets. One evening he had a long conversation with a derelict who

had lived eight years in the London sewers.

Taking a bath was not an everyday affair. When he had one—usually on Sunday—it rated an entry in his diary: "Sunday June 6, 1852. This morning took a bath which place was found after quite a hunt. Bath lined with tiles, large tub and large room. Table. Carpeted. Three towels and plenty of brushes and soap. Light room with marble mantle in it. Price 1/2, cheap."

On June 11 Gorham met an experienced silver caster. "Had a long confab with a caster about learning his art and all the mysteries." He made an agreement with the caster, Charles Martin, who, for a fee of fifty dollars plus expenses, agreed to give him an intensive three–weeks training course in "core work, etc." It was hard, dirty work but Gorham seemed to enjoy it. He learned the "mysteries" of casting such things as spouts, handles, and finials. In the evenings he wrote letters or attended the theater.

John Gorham was very much impressed with his teacher Charles Martin; calling him a "little master." When they parted he invited Martin to come to America to work for Gorham & Company.

The Steam–Powered Drop Press

One of the major objectives of John Gorham's 1852 trip was to buy a drop press for the making of flatware. In 1852 all of Gorham's spoons were still handmade with the simplest of dies and hand tools. Michael Gibney and others in New York had begun, in the middle 1840s, to make flatware by the use of roll dies. A flat silver blank was drawn between two steel rolls on which a flatware pattern design had been engraved. This method of roll-ing patterns had one disadvantage. The lengths of the finished spoons or forks varied from piece to piece, de-pending on the thickness of the blanks.[10] (There is no record of Gorham using the die–roll method of making flatware.)

Gorham had decided that they needed a drop press to make flatware. Hand–operated drop presses had been used in England for several years, but they did not make efficient use of labor. Two or three men were required to lift the hammerheads of these presses. John Gorham, investigating the situation in England, described it this way:

> Previous to leaving home I had felt the necessity of a drop press for the embellishment of forks and spoons between dies. Soon after coming to Birmingham I called Mr. Nasmyth [on June 5, 1852], the inventor of the steam ham-mer, explaining my needs. What I wished was a press where the heavy weight should be lifted by the direct action of

the steam upon the piston rod in the cylinder above. He looked at me for a moment with some astonishment, and then asked me if I had crossed the Adantic to get such a machine. I replied that I knew of no place to procure such a tool except from its inventor. He said he had never built one, though he had been trying for several years to get the manufacturers in Sheffield and Birmingham to adopt such a machine. He would be very glad to build it for me and would make no charge whatever for the cost of the patents, but would take his chances on remuneration by its ultimate adoption in those cities after he had built one for America.[11]

In a subsequent visit with Mr. Nasmyth at his works some distance from the city, John Gorham noted:

When examining the drawings for the machine I was introduced to a gentleman whom I afterwards learned was Mr. Nasmyth's partner in the business and the great land owner of the district. I was introduced with the remark: I have been trying for years to get our manufacturers to adopt the steam press without success, and here comes a Yankee across the water expressly to have one built, and our people still use the hand drop press with several men to each machine." It led to remarks of one American who was economizing labor.[12]

James Nasmyth (1808–1890) was the greatest English maker and inventor of tools of his time. His best–known invention, the steam hammer, delivered great and rapid power with precision. The heavy hammer could even descend—as the 1851 Exposition catalog pointed out —"with power only sufficient to break an egg shell." [13] It was characteristic of John Gorham to go directly to James Nasmyth, the most famous man in his field, to obtain a steam–powered drop press. The cost was to be £165 to £170 "delivered on board canal boat." The date of installation of the new drop press in the Gorham plant in Providence is not known, but it was presumably in 1853 or 1854.

The mechanization of flatware manufacture was a major factor in the success of the Gorham Company. The steam drop press was so superior to other methods that it enabled Gorham to obtain, in little more than a de-

cade, a dominant position in solid silver flatware in America. English– and French–born designers and die–cutters produced a line of new and highly salable flatware patterns. John Gorham's visit to James Nasmyth in Birmingham, England, in June 1852 was an important part of this success.

Patterned Flatware

In 1855 three new flatware patterns were introduced, *Josephine, Roman,* and *Saxon Stag.* The first of these, *Josephine,* was patented by John Gorham. The design patent number 699 was issued on April 10, 1855. The spoon in Figure 33, in the *Josephine* pattern, is of unusual interest because it belonged to Abraham Lincoln and his wife, with Mary Todd Lincoln's initials engraved on the handle. The *Saxon Stag* pattern (see Appendix II), with its applied staghead, was the most expensive of the three 1855 patterns. It seems to have been used more for serving pieces than for regular spoons and forks.

The newer, more ornamented flatware patterns supplemented and began to displace the old plain *Fiddle* and *French Tipt* patterns of the 1840s. The growing popularity of patterned flatware is indicated by the drawing in Figure 31, which shows only *Prince Albert* pattern serving pieces. Incidentally, Michael Gibney, the New York silversmith who patented *Prince Albert* in 1845, appears to have been one of the first, if not the first, American silversmith to specialize in patterned flatware.

Machinery made the difference. The die–cut rolls of Michael Gibney and others and the steam–operated drop press of Gorham produced quality spoons in such quantities that the handmaking of spoons quickly became obsolete. The old hand methods were too costly and too slow.

Figured flatware had been made since the eighteenth century but the high cost of making such wares by hand limited their usage. It was the combination of the new techniques of rolling and stamping plus a fundamental change of taste in the 1850s that brought on the rather abrupt change to patterned flatwares. The die–cut rolls and the drop presses made the making of patterns on

33 Teaspoon in the *Josephine* pattern, engraved MTL for Mary Todd Lincoln. Length: 4 3/4 in. (12.1 cm.). Mark: Pat 55 COIN plus pseudomark. *(The National Museum of American History, Smithsonian Institution).*

flatware handles economically feasible. The change in taste from simple classical forms toward Victorian ornamentation assured their widespread acceptance. John Gorham's steam–operated drop press came along at the right time.

In 1861 three new flatware patterns were introduced— *Cottage, Beaded,* and *Grecian.* The *Cottage* butter knife in Figure 34 has an engraved and engine turned blade. In 1864 Gorham introduced *Medallion,* a highly successful and widely admired pattern (Fig. 35). Gorham's *Medallion* pattern was retailed by several companies including Tiffany & Co. of New York.

The designer of *Medallion* was George Wilkinson. Wilkinson, who was to become a very important force in the Gorham organization, was born in Birmingham, England, in 1819. He was early apprenticed to learn the trade of silversmith. He worked as a silversmith for some years before coming to America in 1854 to join the Ames Company of Chicopee, Massachusetts. In 1857 Wilkinson joined the Gorham Company, where his ability as a designer and die–cutter was immediately appreciated. In January 1860 Wilkinson left Gorham and went to New York to join a firm whose name became Rogers, Wendt & Wilkinson. They made silverwares for Ball, Black & Co., then an important New York firm. The copartnership was not of long duration, for on the eighth of August it was dissolved. Wilkinson returned to the Gorham Company in Providence where he was to stay until his death in 1894.

The design of the *Medallion* pattern, with round medallions on the handles picturing a series of classical heads, was possibly suggested to Wilkinson by Wood & Hughes's *Medallion* pattern which had been patented in 1863. The Wood & Hughes pattern made use of oval medallions. It was not as successful as Gorham's *Medallion* pattern, either from an artistic or commercial point of view.

A number of other American firms sold variations on the *Medallion* pattern during the 1860s, including Ball, Black & Co., New York; R. Hardwig, Boston; Peter Krider, Philadelphia; and Palmer & Bathelder, Boston. Reed & Barton, Taunton, Massachusetts, made a silver–plated *Medallion.*

34 Butter knife in the *Cottage* pattern, owned during the Civil War by a member of the Dearth family of Rhode Island. Length: 7 5/8 in. (19.4 cm.). Mark: PATENT 1861 COIN GORHAM & CO. *(The Museum of American History, Smithsonian Institution).*

35 Serving pieces in the *Medallion* pattern (1864). *Left to right:* Ladle with a pierced, fluted, engraved bowl. Length: 10 1/2 in. (26.7 cm.). Mark: lion–anchor–G/ PAT 1864 STERLING. Ice cream knife. Length: 10 3/4 in. (27.3 cm.). Mark: STERLING/PAT 1864/lion–anchor–G. Stuffing spoon. Length: 12 3/8 in. (31.4 cm.). Mark: lion–anchor–G/PAT 1864 plus TIFFANY & CO/STERLING. *(Burt collection).*

35

34

Right after the Civil War the Gorham Company introduced six more flatware patterns. It was during this period that Gorham gained a dominant position in solid silver flatware, a position they were to maintain for 125 years. In Appendix II all of the Gorham sterling flatware designs are identified by name of pattern and date of introduction. A total of 313 patterns were made in the first 150 years of the company, a remarkable record.

Hollow Ware in the Latest Taste

By the middle of the 1850s there was a marked increase in the quality of hollow ware made by Gorham. The individual pieces were well made and the designs were quite up–to–date. The lovely goblet in Figure 36 is a far more sophisticated and elegant object than the silver in Figures 29 and 30.

John Gorham was a fast learner. His trip to Europe had paid off. His use of the best of English and French silverwares as models and the influx of experienced craftsmen from England and France enabled the company to make great strides in a comparatively short period of time. This is reflected not only in the quality of the objects made by the company but also in the actual sales volume of the firm during the 1850s:

Gorham Sales 1850–1859

Year	$ x 1000
1850	29
1851	33
1852	38
1853	50
1854	91
1855	113
1856	189
1857	171
1858	215
1859	397

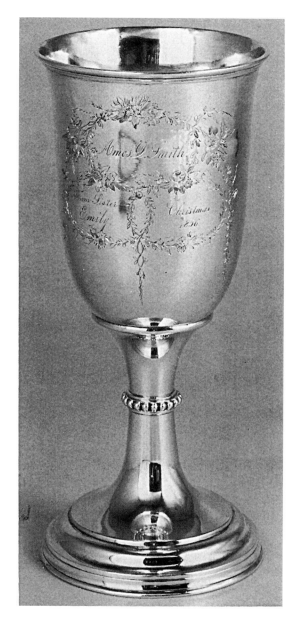

36 Goblet engraved "Amos D. Smith/From Sister Emily/ Christmas 1856." Mark: No. *13*. *(Photograph courtesy Francis J. Purcell II).*

37 Four salts made about 1855. Height: 1 5/8 in. (4.1 cm.). Mark: No. *12*. *(Private collection).*

The Rococo influence waned in the late 1850s. However, Rococo tea sets, pitchers, and small items, such as the salts in Figure 37, were made throughout the 1850s and 1860s. Individual open salts were popular. Those in Figure 37 are repoussé chased. Three have the Greek key border and one has a beaded border, although all four have the same pattern number. The quality of the chasing seems different on each of the four salts, suggesting different craftsmen may have worked on them.

The Neo–Classical style was a continuing influence in Gorham silver throughout the third quarter of the nineteenth century. This could perhaps be ascribed to a lingering New England conservatism even at a time when the fanciest and most fanciful of nineteenth–century styles, High Victorian, was coming into popularity. The simple, sturdy sauceboat in Figure 38 has palm–front handle parts as practically its only decoration. The charming tête–à–tête set in Figure 39 has bands of beading, cast handles, and cast bird finials on the lids. The large serving dish or centerpiece in Figure 40 is much more ambitious. The cast winged caryatids on the base and the masks on the handles and on the two sides of the bowls are skillfully integrated into the overall design. The undecorated base and the plain surfaces of the bowl work well with the classical elements of the design.

38 Neo–Classical sauceboat made about 1855. Length: 9 3/4 in. (24.8 cm.). Mark: No. 13/COIN/ 10. (*Burt collection*).

39 Three–piece black–coffee set made about 1860, cast handles and bird finials, beaded borders. Height of coffeepot 5 1/4 in. (13.3 cm.). Mark: No. 13/ 510. (*Courtesy Mrs. Michael E. Fitzgerald*).

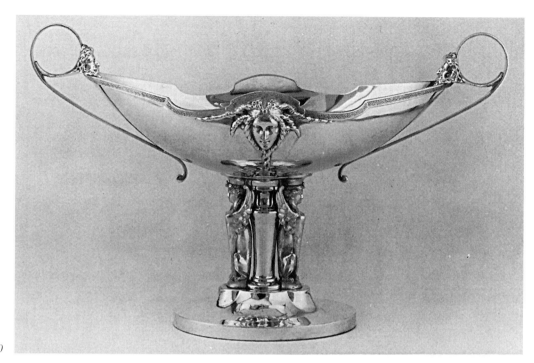

40

41

The robust tureen in Figure 41, with ram's–head handles and stag finial, represents a popular Gorham design of the 1860s and 1870s. The castings are vigorously modeled, giving a distinctiveness to the overblown form. Several variations of this design were made. Fruit dishes of the kind shown in Figure 42 were used as centerpieces or on sideboards. This form is often called a tazza today but no mention of this term has been found in early Gorham records. Stylistically this piece has classical elements, but its overall design is High Victorian.

The Lincoln Tea and Coffee Services

When Abraham Lincoln and his wife, Mary, moved into the White House in March 1861 the mansion was in a dilapidated, sad state of repairs. Politicians, tourists, and office seekers roamed the building at will. Mrs. Lincoln felt that the place was disgraceful and decided to do something about it. The White House must be rehabilitated, refurbished, and refurnished in a style befitting the dwelling place of the leader of a great nation. Congress agreed and appropriated twenty thousand dollars for the project.

Soon after the inauguration Mrs. Lincoln tackled the job of rejuvenating her new home. The spending spree she went on during the next six months acquiring things for the White House (and herself) is justly celebrated. Her many buying trips to New York, Boston, and Philadelphia were avidly reported in the newspapers of the time and brought on considerable condemnation. She spent far more than her budget. Lincoln was furious.

Even in the best of times Mrs. Lincoln's buying spree would have caused lifted eyebrows, but when we remember that the Civil War was under way (Fort Sumter had been fired on on April 12, 1861), her actions were inappropriate, to say the least. Even Mrs. Lincoln's most articulate and sympathetic biographers, such as Justin and Linda Levitt Turner, seem aghast at her actions during this period.[14]

One of the things Mary Lincoln acquired in 1861 was the large and impressive tea and coffee service made by the Gorham Company (Fig. 43). Later, Mrs. Lincoln said the service was given to her "by New York friends."[15]

42 Centerpiece or fruit dish made about 1865. Height: 12 3/4 in. (32.4 cm.). Diameter of bowl: 13 3/8 in. (34 cm.). Mark: lion–anchor–G. *(Chrysler Museum at Norfolk).*

40 Compote or centerpiece made about 1865. Height: 10 in. (25.4 cm.). Length: 17 in. (43.2 cm.). Mark: lion–anchor–G/201. *(Photograph courtesy Richard McGeehan).*

41 Tureen made in 1871. Width: 14 1/2 in. (36.9 cm.). *(Yale University Art Gallery).*

43

43 Tea and coffee service presented to Mrs. Abraham Lincoln when she was First Lady. Mark: No. 14. Mark on tray: J. MARQUAND. *(The National Museum of American History, Smithsonian Institution).*

44 Kettle and stand from Lincoln tea and coffee service in Figure 43. Height: 17 7/8 in. (45.4 cm.)

45 Todd coat of arms and initials MTL for Mary Todd Lincoln on tray of Lincoln service in Figure 43.

45

The service was possibly acquired from Haughwont & Company, a New York firm where Mrs. Lincoln had purchased for the White House a Haviland dinner service decorated with the arms of the United States.[16]

The Lincoln service is typical of the so–called complete tea services. These large sets became fashionable in the 1850s and maintained their popularity throughout the rest of the nineteenth century. The service consists of a hot water kettle (Fig. 44), teapot and coffeepot (the coffeepot is the taller of the two), a hot milk pot (in this case the hot milk pot is indistinguishable from the teapot), creamer and sugar, and a slop bowl. This latter object, inelegantly named, was used to receive the cold dregs from a cup before receiving more fresh, hot beverage. All of these pieces have the Gorham mark stamped on the bottom along with the pattern number 30 and the word COIN. There were other sets made of this same pattern. There is every indication that the set was an off–the–shelf item, that is, it was not specifically made for Mrs. Lincoln.

44

46 Mrs. Abraham Lincoln's "chicken–leg" tête–à–tête set, made about 1860. Height of black coffeepot: 5 1/2 in. (14 cm.). Mark: 0110/lion–anchor–G/COIN. *(The National Museum of American History, Smithsonian Institution).*

The tray was not made by Gorham. The mark on the tray is badly rubbed, but it appears to read J. MARQUAND. Josiah P. Marquand was at one time a partner in the New York firm of Marquand & Company, a predecessor of Ball, Tompkins & Black.

The style of the Lincoln service is High Victorian. It has elements of Renaissance Revival such as the engraved strapwork and the cast satyr–head handles of the hot water kettle (Fig. 44), vignettes of repoussé–chased Rococo flowers, classical beading, and naturalistic leaf forms on the stand of the hot water kettle. In other words, the service has all of the joyous eclecticism of High Victorian, yet the various style notes are so skillfully and unselfconsciously blended that a kind of stylistic unity is achieved. Such silver designs have been out of favor in almost all of the twentieth century. It is only since the mid–1970s that such High Victorian pieces have again been given consideration as objects worthy of study and even admiration.

The craftsmanship of the Lincoln service is first–rate. The quality of the chasing, engraving, and casting is light–years better than the relatively crude and awkward first pieces of hollow ware made by Gorham & Thurber in 1850. The workmen John Gorham had lured to Providence from England and France had transformed the company's wares.

The individual pieces of the Lincoln tea and coffee service are engraved with the crest and initials MTL of Mary Todd Lincoln. The tray has the full coat of arms plus the initials (Fig. 45).

The tête–à–tête set in Figure 46, made about 1860, was referred to in Mr. Lincoln Isham's will as "Mrs. Abraham Lincoln's chicken–leg coffee set." The engine–turned, globular pieces are engraved with the Todd family crest and MTL for Mary Todd Lincoln.

The horror of Abraham Lincoln's assassination and the deeply unsettling years after the Civil War turned Mrs. Lincoln's mind to other things than her possessions. Her large tea and coffee service and her tête–à–tête set were in her house at 375 West Washington Street, Chicago. A letter written to Mary Harlan Lincoln, Robert Todd Lincoln's wife, from Frankfort, Germany, on March 22, 1869, made it quite clear that her daughter–in–law was to have anything of hers that she wanted. This of course included her silver services. The letter said in part:

Do oblige me by considering me as a mother for you are very dear to me as a daughter. *Anything* and *everything* is yours—if you will consider them worth an acceptance. My mind was so distracted with grief in that house, 375, I cannot remember where anything was put. It will be such a relief to me to know that articles can be used and enjoyed by you… Remember everything is yours and feeling so fully assured as you must of my love, will you now, my dear girl, consider them as such ?[17]

In the 1870s Mrs. Lincoln, who had for several years shown signs of instability, became increasingly erratic in her behavior. She became more and more obsessed with the idea that she was poor although she carried thousands of dollars in securities in her skirt pocket. In 1875 her behavior had become so alarming that Robert, her only living son, had her declared legally insane and confined to Bellevue Place, a private sanitarium for women in Batavia, Illinois.[18] There seems to be considerable doubt whether Mrs. Lincoln would have been judged insane by modern standards.

When she was released as sane a year later she vented her pent–up fury on her son, who clearly felt he had done the right thing for his mother. Three days after she was released she wrote Robert a searing letter demanding the return of her belongings—which she had "given" to Robert's wife seven years earlier. High on the list were the Gorham tea and coffee service and tête–à–tête set:

Springfield, Illinois.
Junc 19–1876

Robert T. Lincoln

Do not fail to send me without *the least* delay, *all* my paintings, Moses in the bullrushes included—also the fruit picture, which hung in your dining room—my silver set with large silver waiter presented me by New York friends, my silver tête–à–tête set also other articles your wife appropriated & which are *well known* to you, must be sent, without a day's delay. Two lawyers and myself, have just been together and their list, coincides with my own & will be published in a few days. Trust not to the belief, that Mrs. Edward's tongue, has not been *rancorous* against you all winter & she has maintained to the very last, that you dared not venture into her house & our presence. Send me my laces, my diamonds, my jewelry—My unmade silks, white lace dress—double lace shawl & flounce, lace scarf—2 blk lace shawls— one blk lace deep flounce, white lace sets 1/2 yd in width & eleven yards in length. I am now in constant receipt of letters, from my friends denouncing you in the bitterest terms, six letters from prominent, *respectable,* Chicago people such as you do not associate with. No John Forsythe's & such samps, including Scamman [sic]. As to Mr. Harlan—you are not worthy to wipe the dust, from his feet. Two prominent clergy men, have written me, since I saw you— and mention in their letters, that they think it advisable to offer up prayers for you in Church, on account of your wickedness against me and High Heaven. In reference to Chicago you have the enemies, & I chance to have the friends there. Send me all that I have written for, you have tried your game of robbery long enough. On yesterday, I received two telegrams from prominent East-

ern lawyers. You have injured yourself, not me, by your wicked conduct.

Mrs. A. Lincoln

My engravings too send me. M.L. Send me Whittier Pope, Agnes Strickland's Queens of England, other books, you have of mine—[19]

The Lincoln tea and coffee service was given to the Smithsonian Institution in 1957 by Mr. Lincoln Isham, who was the great–grandson of President and Mrs. Lincoln. Mrs. Lincoln's tête–à–tête service was a gift from the Estate of Lincoln Isham in 1972.

Trip to Europe–1860

John Gorham made a second trip to Europe, in 1860. This time he was looking for craftsmen, and particularly for a designer. As noted earlier, George Wilkinson, who had become Gorham's chief designer, left the company for awhile in 1860, leaving a serious gap in the organization. Gorham visited the Kensington Museum School and other art schools in London, Manchester, Stoke, Birmingham, and Shefffield looking for designers—without any luck. He even tried, unsuccessfully, to hire designers away from Hunt & Roskell. It was not until he got to Paris that he had any success. The first man he talked to was a M. Leveleeth, on July 31. He noted in his diary that "His designs are not good." On August 14 he signed an agreement with a designer named Thabard. Nothing is known of Thabard's work at Gorham.

John Gorham was more successful in hiring (in London *and* Paris) chasers, modelers, and other workers for the plant. He was careful whom he hired. On June 14 in London he noted, "Met a young man at room in hotel and had some hours interview. He is not quite up to the mark."

He bought some goods for Gorham & Company, including plated wares from Dixon & Sons in London and a "shaping planer and grindstone" in Manchester (June 16). The main purchases were for Gorham, Co. & Brown, the store located at No. 60 Westminster Street in Providence. Gorham, Co. & Brown, the predecessor to the present day Tilden–Thurber, was founded in 1856 by John Gorham and Gorham Thurber with a man named Henry T. Brown. Brown ran the store, which was an outlet for Gorham & Company silverwares, plus other luxury items.

John Gorham spent August in Paris where he bought a great variety of items for the store: "Fine gilt ware, Shell mirrors, Ivories, Fans" (August 3); "Plated ware, laces" (August 4); "Porcelains, Bisquit and Parian figures" (August 6). On August 7, "Purchasing nicknacks all day"; August 8, "Selecting bronzes all day, also some clocks"; August 19, "Selected some prints for shop." On August 20 he bought "Bronzes, Opera glasses and Telescopes," and had an interview with a chaser. The next day he bought "Microscopes and Microscope objects" [slides]. He also had "Interview with chaser and saw two others who would not go." On Saturday, August 25, "Finished buying goods. Arranged with fine arts chaser."

John Gorham's 1860–trip diary is much more sketchy and telegraphic than the 1852 diary of his trip to Europe. He seemed to have much less time for the theater and sightseeing. However, on May 24 he spent all day at the Crystal Palace in London: "Wonderful, Wonderful, Wonderful!" He visited the Kensington Museum (now the Victoria and Albert) several times.

The Gorham Library

John Gorham's diaries of his 1852 and 1860 trips contain several notes about buying books for the use of Gorham designers. The *Harper's* article mentioned earlier tells us that the Gorham library was well established in 1868:

> Upon being shown into the Designing Room of this establishment, the visitor is surprised to find himself in an apartment which has the appearance of a library. It is indeed well stored with books, and with illustrated works of the costliest description. All beauty is akin. A designer may get from an arch of the Cologne Cathedral an idea for the handle of a mustard–spoon, and infuse the spirit of a gorgeous mosque into the design for a caster. He may borrow from the gnarled hands of a brave old oak and crook for a pitcher–handle, and imitate the droop of a vine in the bend of its spout. Antiques vases, the Elgin marbles, and all other accumulations of grace and beauty, may be useful to those whose business it is to cover with grace and beauty the tables of mankind.[20]

The Gorham library today contains a large, extensive, and catholic collection of books, many of which were acquired in the nineteenth century. The elephant folio *Grammar of Ornament* by Owen Jones was discussed in the Introduction. A sampling of the fine folio– and elephant–folio–sized books in the library include such works as:

H. Roux Arne, *Herculanum et Pomper* (6 vols.) (Paris: Dedat Freres, 1840)

John Britton, *The History and Antiquities of the Cathedral Church of Exeter* (London, M.A. Nattali, 1836)

Kindergruppen gizeichnet und auf Stein radirt von Gugenklissch (Frankfurt: Kleimsch & Co., no date)

Knight's Unique Fancy Ornaments (London: J. Williams, no date)

Rodolphe Pfnor, *Ornementation* (Paris: A la Librairie Artistique de E. Devienne et Cie, Editeurs, 1866)

T.H. King, *Orfèvrerie et Ouvrages en Métal* (1854) (Bruges: 1854)

Museum Worsleyanum, or a Collection of Antique Basso Relievos, Bustos, Statues and Gems (London, 1794)

There are books on flowers, architecture, antiquities, gems, old silver, birds, ceramics, furniture, costume, Indians, and the Vikings. There are catalogs of museum collections in England and the Continent, and catalogs of almost all of the great international expositions. In addition to encyclopedias and histories, there are long runs of such publications as: *Paris Salon, Studio, Magazine of Art, L'Art Pour Tous, Harper's New Monthly Magazine, American Architect, Art et Décoration,* and the *Illustrated London News.*

Japanese books acquired in the 1860s and 1870s are listed in Chapter 6.

All in all, the Gorham library was, and is, an excellent collection of books on the decorative arts that have been used by generations of the company's designers and silversmiths.

Opening Up California

Preserved in the present–day Gorham files with the 1852 and 1860 diaries are packets of letters sent *to* John Gorham from various people in the Gorham Company while he was in Europe. At the time of the writing of this book John Gorham's own letters to the company have not been located. Most of the letters deal with everyday matters of plant operation. However, one letter from C. C. Adams, the company's agent (today he would be called sales manager), of his visit to California is worth quoting in full:

Providence July 3rd, 1860

Mr. Gorham,
Dear Sir

The long talked of California trip has been made and I am again safely at home. I cannot write you the particulars as fully as I could relate them to you but knowing from experience that anything from home is acceptable to one so far away I will just scribble off what items I think will interest you most. Nothing of any particular interest occurred in the voyage which, by the way, was the most uncomfortable twenty three days I ever passed. The goods arrived there in first order and when I got them open made a fine display. Mr. Lovett and myself took two rooms together at the International Hotel at $20 per week each. A very reasonable price. At first I could not interest Mr. Tucker,[21] and in fact held off from him two or three days until I was afraid of giving offence to the others, then concluded to bring him through the others. I sold all the stock I carried with me and got 5% advance on prices, which is 1% more than the cost of getting the goods there. I also took orders for about $15,000 which makes the present trip rising $25,000, so that I think it is a paying trip. I am confident that we shall do splendid business in the future, as the population becomes more permanent. The demand for our rich goods will increase.

Wood & Hughes [New York] have been sending a large amount of goods there which were but 840/1000 fine. Farrington & Hunnewell [Boston] have also been selling Forks & Spoons to Geo. C. Shreve & Co.[22] for coin which were but 880/1000 fine. Of course it stirred up quite an excitement, which was very favorable for us. I presume that both W. & H. and F. & H. will consider us at the bottom of it. In fact, one of Wood & Hughes' clerks said to Gilbert a few days ago, "Town folks have been kicking up a d—l of a stink lately." Geo. C. Shreve sent on by me part of a spoon which he had assayed—to his brother being of S. Brown & Co. I took it to him and he said he would cut it open, give one half to F. & H. to assay and the other assayed himself without letting them know it. So you can see that it places them in an awkard position. I did not stir this matter up. Tucker was the one. He got an assay on all the silver sold in San Francisco, and his own came out much the worse.

I got well acquainted with all the trade and made some new customers up the country. Upon the whole I feel very well satisfied with the trip myself from a business point of view.

Cannot write more now as I am going down to Newburyport in the next train. Wishing you a prosperous and successful journey and safe return. I remain very respectively yours

C.C. Adams

A letter to John Gorham from H. E. Lathrop of July 31, 1860, noted:

Business a general thing is quiet, although we have been hurried up for two or three weeks on a part of Mr. Adams' California orders that will be shipped on August 11th. We shall ship about $7000 worth of goods, part of which will be a Railroad set.

The Civil War

The rumblings of the coming Civil War that were be

ginning to be felt in 1860 had an adverse effect on Gorham's business. Eighteen sixty–one was a bad year. Sales in that year were only about one–quarter of what they had been in 1859. Employees had to be laid off. Lewis Dexter, the partner of John Gorham and Gorham Thurber, decided to leave the business. Obviously he was worried about the future.

With silver sales off so dramatically the company looked for other things to manufacture. They started making small bronzes. The company was apparently experimenting with bronze manufacture as early as 1860. In a letter dated July 17, 1860, to John Gorham in Paris, Gorham Thurber wrote: "Mr. Black finished the first half dozen bronze candlesticks today. They are now ready for bronzing. Can you tell us how to do it the most effective way, and with the least trouble and expense."

Business picked up in 1862 and went to a new high in 1863. The following sales figures for the first half of the 1860s suggest that the Civil War had little effect on Gorham's business after 1862. On the contrary, the last years of the war were a boom time for the company:

Gorham Sales 1860–1865

Year	$ x 1000
1860	286
1861	109
1862	218
1863	415
1864	603
1865	759

Incorporation

In 1863 the decision was made to incorporate the Gorham Company as the Gorham Manufacturing Company. A charter was granted by the General Assembly of the State of Rhode Island during the May 1863 session, authorizing three hundred shares of stock with a par value of $1000 per share. The actual formation of the Gorham Manufacturing Company took place on January 2, 1865. The offficers and their shareholdings were:

John Gorham	President 113 shares
Gorham Thurber	Treasurer 113 shares
C. C. Adams	Agent 25 shares
J. F. Lawton	Secretary 5 shares

Other shareholders were George Wilkinson (25 shares) and H. E. Lathrop (20 shares), making, incidentally, a total of 301 shares, one more than was authorized.

John Gorham and Gorham Thurber's combined stockholdings (75 percent of the total) gave them joint control of the company. At the time this was obviously a satisfactory arrangement for the two men. Control was in the Gorham family. However, neither man alone could control the company.

All the evidence suggests that the matter of control was not important to John Gorham. This contrasts with his main competitor in the silverwares business, Charles L. Tiffany, who maintained control of Tiffany & Co. throughout the last half of the nineteenth century. John Gorham probably could not have maintained complete control of his company, even if he had wanted to. The capital requirements were too great. This was the reason he formed a partnership with Gorham Thurber in the first place.

This matter of control was to become critically important in the late 1870s.

Contrasts

In the 1860s there was a proliferation both flatware and hollow–ware designs. Figures 47 and 48 show two pieces made by Gorham in the 1865–1868 period which are dramatically different in their design approach. The water pitcher in Figure 47 has a provincial, rather squat form with an awkward handle. The engraving on the pitcher has a primitive, almost folk–art quality. The house in the landscape, with the festoon of posies hung above it, is related to nineteenth–century textiles. The contrast with the elegant chafing dish in Figure 48 is sharp indeed. The shallow dish is decorated only with four applied masks wearing tricorn hats and bow ties and is supported by four classical caryatid figures, all of which are part of the beautifully integrated design. The classical drapery festoons tie the design together.

The *Medallion* pattern which was so popular in flatware was also widely used by Gorham in hollow ware, particularly in tea and coffee services. The coffeepot in Figure 49 has classical medallions on both sides of the body (surrounded with strapwork engraving), on the handle, at the base, and atop the tip of the spout—five medallions in all. This pot illustrates the Gorham designer's careful use of plain surfaces to emphasize and show off the decorative details. The cast figure on the lid sits on a plain, flat area. The medallions and engraved areas on the body are well placed in relation to the plain areas, emphasizing the height of the piece.

Figure 50 shows a silver decanter stand with two cut–glass bottles that was given to Cyrus W. Field on the completion of the laying of the Atlantic cable in 1866.

47 Water pitcher, 1865–1868. Height: 9 1/4 in. (23.4 cm.). *(Photograph courtesy Sotheby Parke Bernet).*

48

48 Chafing dish, 1865–1868. Diameter: 10 1/2 in. (26.7 cm.). *(The High Museum of Art, Atlanta, Georgia).*

49 Coffeepot in the *Medallion* pattern. Height: 7 3/4 in. (19.7 cm.). Mark: lion–anchor–G/261/GORHAM & CO. *(Private collection).*

50 Decanter stand with cut–glass decanters. Die–rolled borders, cast satyrs, medallion of George Peabody. Engraved: "George Peabody to Cyrus W. Field." Height: 13 1/2 in. (34.3 cm.). Mark: S&M (Starr & Marcus)/ lion–anchor–G/60. *(Museum of the City of New York).*

49

50

Other pieces of this presentation set are illustrated in Chapter 9. The reason for showing the decanter stand here is that its handles are decorated with cast medallions. In this case the medallions picture Cyrus Field and George Peabody, the donor, instead of the usual classical heads. This Renaissance device was only occasionally used on presentation pieces of the 1860s.

Death of Jabez Gorham

Jabez Gorham lived out his retirement in the old family house on Benefit Street. He could easily have afforded a larger and showier house, but he preferred his familiar surroundings. He died on March 24, 1869, leaving a substantial estate. (His "properties and effects" were valued at $317,930.08 on August 1, 1867.) His will mentioned several pieces of silver which were left to his grandchildren, including two goblets and "my silver salver," and "I give and bequeath to my youngest grandson, living at the time of my decease, to and for his own use, the silver water jug, presented to me by the Gorham Manufacturing Company" (Fig. 51)

51 Water jug presented to Jabez Gorham in 1867. Engraved on front: "Jabez Gorham/ from the/Gorham Manufacturing Co./In appreciation of past favors/1867/Born Feb. 18th 1792/ Died March 24th 1869./ Bequeathed to his grandson/Jabez Gorham." Height: 13 1/4 in. (33.7 cm.). Mark: No. 17. *(Gorham collection).*

Chapter 5

The Post–Civil
War Years

The ending of the Civil War unleashed great energies in the decorative arts in America, particularly in silver. The two–decade period from 1865 to 1885 saw American silver really coming into its own. For the first time in over two hundred years of silver making in America, new and original designs began to emerge which gave this country an acknowledged leadership over Europe. The history of American silver up to this time had always been a study of derivations and influences. American silversmiths were either copying or adapting the latest fashion from Europe. There was a continuing influx of silversmiths from England and the Continent who often brought elements of their styles with them.

To say that most early American silver is derivative in style is not of course to denigrate it. Many wonderful pieces of silver were made in the Colonial period and the early years of the Republic, but they were made in styles that originated in England, or Holland, or France, or occasionally Spain and Italy. American silver of this period never had any influence on European silver.

Most early American silver has a characteristic "look." Forms were usually simplified and there was usually less decoration than was used on comparable English and French objects. This preponderance of simpler forms in American silver was no doubt due to two quite different factors. Certainly taste was involved. The Puritan influ-

ence in New England, and the Quaker influence in Philadelphia, led to strong, simple forms, and objects that were not too showy. The other influence for simplicity was cost. Decorated objects were more expensive than simple, plain objects. We know that, almost from the beginning, there were silversmiths in America capable of making highly ornamented silverwares, but they obviously did not have as much chance to display the full range of their skills as did their contemporaries in England and France.

In the years following the Civil War the growing sophistication of American silver was quite marked, both from the point of view of craftsmanship and originality of design. Strangely enough, the renaissance in American silver was matched by a decline in English silver. John Culme, in his book Nineteenth–Century Silver writes: "The truth was that in England after the late 1860s, the silver industry was in decline,"[1] and, "while the plate industry in England was in decline, the same was not true in other countries where fine work continued to be made for the exhibitions. In the United States of America, particularly, great strides had been made since the 1860s."[2] Nikolaus Pevsner in his great essay "High Victorian Design," writing about the 1851 Crystal Palace Exposition in London said:

The exhibition in this respect only continued a line of undaunted progressiveness for which Britain at the time was still famous, but which has since become chiefly connected with the United States and Germany. Today indeed Britain is regarded as a bulwark of conservatism and solid tradition, a complete *volte face* of distressing effect on industrial prosperity. The change began as early as the seventies, when German and American competition was first felt as a nuisance.[3]

This and the next chapter document two sides of Gorham's part in the American silver renaissance. This chapter describes the commerical silverwares and the High Victorian styles that culminated in Gorham's exhibition at the 1876 Centennial Exposition in Philadelphia. Chapter 6, "Innovation and Fantasy," documents the wave of new ideas that came out of Japanese art, ideas that were to be one of the main sources of Art Nouveau.

George Wilkinson and the New Designers

George Wilkinson (Fig. 52) was the driving force behind Gorham's growth after the Civil War. In the 1850s John Gorham directed the design efforts of the company, even though he was not primarily a designer. His name appears on several of the flatware design patents of the time. Wilkinson was the company's chief designer from the time he returned to the company in 1860 until 1891, when William Christmas Codman was given the title.

Gorham's design department expanded considerably during the post–war years. We have already learned from John Gorham's diary of his search for designers in England and France during his 1860 trip. In 1868 Thomas Pairpoint, who had been with the English firm Lambert & Rawlings, joined Gorham as a designer under Wilkinson. A. J. Barrett, formerly employed by Hunt & Roskell, came to Gorham about the same time.

This tradition of European designers joining Gorham was to continue well into the twentieth century. The work of Antoine Heller, the French designer who joined Gorham in 1881, is described in Chapter 7. William C. Codman, Gorham's chief designer from 1891 to 1914, came to Gorham from England in 1891. His son, William Codman, who became Gorham's chief designer in 1914 on the retirement of his father, had already come to Gorham from England in 1887. All of these men became true American designers, but their roots were in Europe.

High Victorian

That amalgam of styles making up High Victorian, which

52 George Wilkinson (1819–1894), from a drawing made in 1892 by F. Antoine Heller.

was popular in England during the *middle* of the nineteenth century, reached its zenith in Gorham silver in the 1870s. It was not only a "top–of–the–line" popular style, it was a style preeminently suited for public display. Gorham made the most of it in pieces designed specifically for the 1876 Centennial Exposition. As the decade went along the designs became more complex, more complicated, more flamboyant. To our modern eyes, conditioned by modern design, some of the Gorham High Victorian pieces of the 1870–1876 period are wild, sometimes bizarre, and often overblown. Nevertheless, it was part of the taste of the time. It was also a taste that seemed to have both peaked and ended with the centennial showing. Many of these High Victorian objects are amusing; some are fascinating, and, from a silver maker's point of view, remarkatble tours de force. However, for the long run, Americans preferred simpler, more solid and conservative forms. Gorham made very little High Victorian silver after 1876.

Thomas J. Pairpoint is given credit for designing most of Gorham's High Victorian pieces. Pairpoint served his apprenticeship in Paris before joining the London firm of Lambert & Rawlings. He was a designer and modeler for Gorham from 1868 to 1877 when he left to join the Meriden Britannia Company, Meriden, Connecticut. No doubt Pairpoint's departure in 1877 accounts for

53 Large fruit stand or centerpiece made about 1870. Height: 16 3/4 in. (42.5 cm.). Mark: lion–anchor–G/380/STERLING. (*Burt collection*).

54 Pair of small candlesticks, with cast phoenix birds and cherubs, made in 1869. Engraved S. Mark: lion–anchor–G/ 960/B. Height: 8 1/4 in. (21 cm.). (*Burt collection*).

53

the ending of Gorham's High Victorian designs. In the 1880s he helped form the Pairpoint Manufacturing Co.[4]

The dozen or so High Victorian pieces in this section show a shift in emphasis from the simpler, chunky objects related to styles of the 1850s, to the more complicated, airy pieces of the seventies.

The large, relatively chaste fruit stand in Figure 53 should be classified as Renaissance Revival rather than High Victorian, although the breaking up of the stem into separate decorative elements already points to the more eclectic, open pieces of the seventies.

The small candlesticks in Figure 54, with the cast phoenix–bird decorations above and the putti on the base, are typical examples of Victorian whimsy.

Although there is no indication in the Gorham records as to who might have designed either of the pieces in Figures 53 and 54, all of the pieces in Figures 55–58, 60, 62, 64, and 65 can be attributed to Thomas Pairpoint. Several of the pieces, such as the Century Vase in Figure 65, are known to have been designed by Pairpoint. Others are so related in style as to make such attributions reasonably firm.

54

55 Waiter or dish made in 1875. (*Gorham collection*).

The lovely waiter in Figure 55, with its classical and Renaissance style notes, shows the superb quality both of Pairpoint's draftsmanship and the skill of the Gorham silversmith who executed the design so flawlessly.

The waiter is part of what has become known as the Furber collection. In 1873 Colonel Henry J. Furber, the thirty–three–year–old president of the Universal Life Insurance Co. of New York, placed his first order for a dinner service at the Gorham showrooms at No. 1 Bond Street, New York. The service, which was ordered over a six–year period, numbered at least 740 pieces. In size and quality it rivaled that other great American silver service of the 1870s, the Mackay service made by Tiffany & Co.[5]

Colonel Furber's calling card read:

Colonel Henry Jewett Furber

Docteur en Philosophie

Officier de la Légion d'Honneur

Pieces of the Furber collection are monogrammed EIF for Colonel Furber's wife, Elvira Irwine Furber. The last time the service was used by the Furbers was at a Chicago dinner party given at the turn of the century in honor of the actress Lillian Russell.

The collection now consists of 606 pieces of flatware, serving pieces and cutlery, and 132 pieces of hollow ware, all beautifully fitted into eighteen walnut and oak chests. Each piece of flatware is individually engraved and chased. Many of the pieces are gilt or parcel gilt. Most of the hollow ware is in the High Victorian style, but much of the flatware is decorated with Japanese motifs. The butter plates in Plate I are pure Japanese. The craftsmanship of the entire service is of the highest order.

In 1949 Furber's son, Colonel Henry J. Furber, Jr., sold the collection back to the Gorham Company. The collection was accompanied by a number of the original bills of sale.[6] It is often diffficult to identify specific items from these bills of sale, particularly if there is more than one such item in the collection. For example, the waiter in Figure 55 may be either the one listed in a bill of sale dated April 30, 1875, "1 round waiter $90," or it may be the waiter in an 1879 bill listing the following items (the year is on the bill but not the day and month):

12 Oyster Forks	52.74
24 Pie Forks	120.00
48 Ice Cream Spoons	270.20
24 Egg Spoons	81.64
12 Dessert Knives	75.50
48 Ice Cream Plates	960.00
1 Soup Ladle	35.00
1 Round Waiter	125.00
1 Butter Dish	188.00
3 Plateaux	2,250.00
1 Epergne	4,000.00
Pr. Candelabra 10 light	2,800.00
7 Oak Chests	525.00
Refinishing all silver in vault	100.00

$11.634.08

The salver or serving tray in Figure 56 made in 1873 was described as being in the style of Benvenuto Cellini when a drawing of it was published in the *Jeweler's Circular* in 1874. In the nineteenth century Cellini's name was often invoked by silversmiths and critics as being the preeminent master of the craft. There was even a time earlier when almost any well–made and fancy piece of sixteenth- or seventeenth–century silver was liable to be attributed to Cellini when it came on the market— no matter what its actual country of origin.[7]

Although the border of the tray in Figure 56 is of Renaissance origin the beading around the handles and the border surrounding the bottom are pure Neo–Classical touches.

The pitcher and goblets in Figure 57, in a style similar to the salver in Figure 56, are part of the Furber collection. The goblet in the middle of the photograph shows the decoratively chased initials EIF of Mrs. Furber.

In the 1874 *Jeweler's Circular* article mentioned above, entitled "The Silver Age," a drawing of the pitcher in Figure 57 was published with the caption:

SILVER PITCHER. DESIGNED AND EXECUTED BY THE GORHAM COMPANY. The placques are allegorical half reliefs, indeed silver, *repoussé*. The obverse represents Venus lighting of the torches of Loves. On the reverse she is catching and confining them in a net, "for better or for worse." The oval border or frame of the placque is gold: The concave surfaces burnished, and the convex satin finished.[8]

The plaques (in the nineteenth century it was spelled with a c) of the pitcher in Figure 57 were probably designed by Thomas Pairpoint. On the next page of the *Jeweler's Circular* article was pictured a very similar classically derived figural group with the caption:

BAS–RELIEF PLACQUE, FOR THE SIDE OF A VASE. Designed and wrought in silver by Pairpoint, one of the Gorham Company's artists. A delicate and lifelike texture of the skin in this figure is one of the effects peculiar to Silver Art.[9]

The best pieces Pairpoint designed for Gorham have a wonderful sense of lightness and airiness. The epergne in Figure 58 is an example of how carefully and thoughtfully these qualities were achieved. The pierced bowl forming the base sets pertly on the four scrolled feet. The buoyant angels seem to float around the stem. The candles set in glass bobeches, and the four small plain fruit holder trays are held by unobtrusive, square-sectioned arms. This candelabrum–epergne is in contrast to far more ornamented English and American epergnes of the same period.

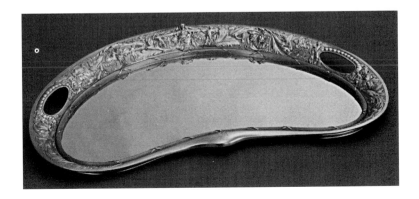

56 Salver or serving tray made in 1874. The fluted column border, wound with ribbons, is gold plated. Length: 32 1/2 in. (82.6 cm.). Mark: lion–anchor–G/STERLING/ G/GORHAM MFG./1 BOND ST. N.Y. (*Gorham collection*).

57

57 Pitcher made in 1874 and goblets made in 1875, repoussé chased. Plain surfaces are frosted. Height of goblets: 6 1/2 in. (16.5 cm.). Mark: GORHAM & CO./ lion–anchor–G/STERLING/H. Height of pitcher: 11 in. (27.9 cm.). Mark: 885/lion–anchor–G/STERLING/G. (*Gorham collection*).

58 Parcel–gilt epergne made in 1871. Weight: 175 ounces. Mark: lion–anchor–G/5/D. (*Gorham collection*).

58

The cake basket in Figure 59 is very much involved with Victorian naturalism. The decorative elements, the morning lilies, and the handle modeled after an adjustable leather strap, are nicely balanced with the unadorned parts of the basket and the base.

The festive punch bowl in Figure 60 has all the exuberance of the best of High Victorian design. The vigorously modeled bacchanalian figures, the Renaissance lion heads on the feet of the bowl, the medallion on the handle of the ladle, the naturalistic grapes and grape leaves and winding tendrils on the handles, give, in spite of their eclectic complexity, a joyous quality to the piece. The majestic three–foot–high candelabrum in Figure 61 (one of a pair) from the Furber collection, is more conservative than the punch bowl, and more classical in its design approach.

Possibly the most interesting of all of Gorham's High Victorian pieces is the large centerpiece in Figure 62, called "Hiawatha's Boat," which has been in the White House in Washington since 1876. The piece was acquired from the Philadelphia Centennial Exposition. Mrs. Ulysses S. Grant, in her *Memoirs*, tells of the piece coming to the White House:

59 Cake basket made in 1874. Length: 11 1/2 in. (29.2 cm.). Mark: lion–anchor–G/STERLING/647/G. (*Peale Museum, Baltimore*).

60 Parcel–gilt punch bowl and ladle made in 1872. Height: 14 1/2 in. (36.8 cm.). Width over handles: 20 1/2 in. (52 cm.). Mark: STERLING/lion–anchor–G/80/E. Length of ladle: 14 3/4 in. (37.5 cm.). (*Gorham collection*).

59

60

59

61 Candelabrum made in 1879. Engraved with monogram EIF
on column. Height: 35 in. (88.9 cm.). Weight: 300 ounces.
Mark: lion–anchor–G/B 92/L. (*Gorham collection*).

At the centennial opening, the General and I were the guests of Mr. G[eorge] W. Childs, who took much pleasure in giving several magnificent entertainments to the many distinguished visitors then in the city. All of these we enjoyed. We were at our cottage at Long Branch during the latter part of the summer and enjoyed many trips to this wonderful and most instructive exhibition. I took much pleasure in selecting a piece of silver for the Executive Mansion and was happy in securing a piece entirely American in history, ideal, skill, and material. In that centerpiece I found something all our own. The artist had exquisitely wrought in American silver the beautiful story of Hiawatha. The piece consisted of a lake of mirrored glass surrounded by a border of grasses, rushes, and water lilies. Upon this lake, which was about twenty–four inches wide and thirty–six inches long, rested a light and graceful Indian canoe with a sail set, and in this canoe Hiawatha was reclining on robes of fur, all wrought in native silver. You can imagine the effect. I also had the pleasure of selecting for the Executive Mansion a magnificent bronze shield on which was wrought in honor of Milton some of the scenes from *Paradise Lost*. It was very beautiful and called the Milton Shield. These articles are still at the White House and are universally admired.[10]

In the 1880s and 1890s the Hiawatha centerpiece seems to have been kept on a sideboard in the private dining room in the White House (Fig. 63). It was used on the dining table in a dinner party given by President Chester Arthur:

The President gave a large dinner party on March 8th, 1882, to personal friends.

It was his choice not to use the State Dining-room. In the refurnishing of the house last Fall, special attention was given to this room in which the President regularly dines and breakfasts. The walls were covered with heavy gold paper in large designs, and the windows and mantelpiece draped with hangings of pomegranate plush. Another sideboard was made to match the elaborate one ordered by Mrs. Hayes, and on these pieces are displayed specimens of the Limoges china set designed by Theodore Davis. The open fireplace and side lights of crimson glass were suggested by President Arthur. The floral decorations were elaborate, and the room was almost surrounded with large azaleas in full bloom. The Hiawatha boat of silver in the centre of the table was filled with Bonsilene and Jacqueminot roses, and large vases at each end were filled with roses. Compotiers, decanters, and candelabra of wax–lights were ranged around these. At each lady's plate were corsage bouquets tied with long blue satin ribbons.[11]

Apparently the Hiawatha centerpiece disappeared into storage during much of the twentieth century. There

62 Centerpiece, "Hiawatha's Boat," made by Gorham in 1871. Inscribed with a quote from Longfellow's poem *Hiawatha*: "Swift or slow at will he glided, veered to right or left at pleasure" and "All alone went Hiawatha through the clear, transparent water." Height: 34 in. (83.4 cm.), Length: 44 1/2 in. (113 cm.). Width: 19 in. (48.3 cm.). Mark: lion–anchor–G/STERLING/D. (*White House Collection*).

63 Private dining room, the White House, 1889. "Hiawatha's Boat" on sideboard at left. (*Photograph courtesy Library of Congress*).

was an account that Richard Nixon turned it down as a White House decoration saying that he didn't want such a wishywashy representation of the ship of state around. When I wrote Mr. Nixon to verify this story he replied, "I cannot recall the incident with regard to the Hiawatha centerpiece."[12]

The little sauceboat in Figure 64, a reproduction of a High Victorian design of the 1870s made by Gorham in

the 1940s, was given to the White House by the National Society of Interior Decorators in 1961. The present–day White House table silver was also made by Gorham. The 130 place settings of the Gorham pattern *King Charles* totaling 3,434 pieces were ordered in May 1974 "after many consultations between Mrs. Nixon, Rex Scouten, the Chief Usher, and Clement Conger, the Curator, with officials of the Gorham Company."[13]

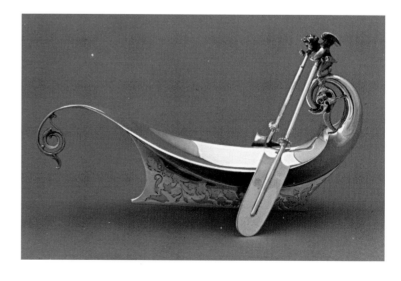

64 Sauceboat, a reproduction of an 1870 piece made in the 1940s. Length: 8 3/8 in. (21.3 cm.). Mark: lion–anchor–G/STERLING 115/REPRODUCTION 1870. (*White House Collection*).

The flatware arrived in September 1974 with additional table items from the order received in February 1975

The Century Vase

The most important piece of Gorham silver made in the 1870s was that immense object which Gorham named the Century Vase (Fig. 65). It was made specifically for the 1876 Philadelphia Centennial Exposition and was the centerpiece of Gorham's exhibit. The vase was four–feet–two–inches high and five–feet–two–inches long. It contained 2000 ounces of silver and was valued at $25,000. The Gorham records indicate some 17,900 man–hours were spent in the making of the piece.

The ambition of the makers of the Century Vase was to summarize the whole story of the Republic in silver. The piece was jammed with symbolism, and, in its way, was just as storytelling a device as one of Longfellow's or Tennyson's narrative poems.

Gorham published a booklet for the Centennial Exposition, entitled "The Story of the Century Vase," by Alexander Farnum, which explained in minute detail the meaning of the vase. Some of the symbolism is obvious. The Indian with his lance and the pioneer with his long rifle were clichés of the time. Other references are more obscure. For example, resting on the lower member of the base was a granite slab "signifying the unity and solidity of the government on which rest the thirty-eight States, symbolized in a threaded band running around the top of the base, bearing thirty-eight golden stars, thirteen of which are directly in front."[14] On opposite sides of the base were sculptural groups representing the Peaceable Kingdom and the horrors of war.

65 The Century Vase. Height: 50 in. (127 cm.). Length: 62 in. (157.5 cm.). *(Gorham photograph).*

The cover of the vase was topped with a group which was considered its culmination:

America, as the presiding genius, a female figure elegantly and most gracefully draped, stands on a globe, with symbols of literature, science, and art at her feet, with outstretched arms, and holding branches of palm and laurel, emblems of success, and welcome, inviting Europe, Asia, and Africa to join with her in celebrating the triumphs of her Centennial year.

Europe comes with pen and palette, Asia and Arab in appropriate costume, and Africa with its ivory—all generously contributing to adorn the natal festivities of their sister, the youngest in the family of nations.[15]

It would be easy to poke fun at the Century Vase. That is not my intent. There *is* a heroic quality about the piece, and when we read Alexander Farnum's long and obviously sincere account we feel a sense of lost innocence, a sense of wonder and pride and patriotism that has become a rare quality in our cynical age.

The Century Vase was shown at two other international expositions, Paris in 1889 and Chicago in 1893.

In 1875 Thomas Pairpoint was involved in a highly publicized design competition, the results of which must have been disappointing to him. Gorham was one of five leading firms (the others were Black, Starr & Frost; Starr & Marcus; Tiffany & Co.; and the Whiting Manufacturing Co.) that submitted designs for a trophy to be given to the poet and editor, William Cullen Bryant, on his eightieth birthday. Pairpoint's design for Gorham stressed Bryant's poetry. A tall vase form was topped with a winged figure. Bryant's portrait was centered on the vase. Around the pedestal base were six groups in high relief illustrating well–known Bryant poems: "Thanatopsis," "The Death of Slavery," "Waiting at the Gate," "The Conqueror's Grave," "A Day Dream," and "Odyssey of Homer."

Tiffany & Co., with a design by James H. Whitehouse, won the competition.[16]

The Philadelphia Centennial Exposition

The Gorham pavilion at Philadelphia consisted of a series of glass cases displaying silver. In the middle of the exhibit was a glass case containing the Century Vase. The company showed the largest and the fanciest of its High Victorian designs, including "Hiawatha's Boat," plus huge three–drawer chests of flatware. Millions of people saw the exhibit. The critical comments were favorable and the company received a gold and other medals.

Classical Designs

At the very time when Gorham was making the most elaborate of its High Victorian designs it was also making simple, almost plain silver hollow–ware forms. A couple of these pieces, completely without ornament, are, because of their innovative design, shown in the next chapter.

Most of these plain wares were derived from classical forms of the first part of the nineteenth century. The bowl in Figure 66 is another matter. It is a pure product

66 Small bowl with fluted body and die-rolled border, made about 1875. (*Gorham photograph*).

of the machine. The plain body was made on a spinning lathe. The die–rolled border was extended (almost appearing to be stretched) on the two sides to form the handles.

The goblets in Figure 67 have classical die–rolled borders as their principal ornament. The goblets, along with a water pitcher marked Bigelow Bros. & Kennard, Boston (not illustrated), were given in 1875 to commemorate the one-hundreth anniversary of the American Revolution. They were presented to Thomas Whittemore, a great–grandson of Samuel Whittemore, the patriot soldier of Arlington, Massachusetts.

The footed tray in Figure 68, made in 1877, with the raised lettering GIVE US THIS DAY OUR DAILY BREAD, has almost an Art Deco quality. The strong and vigorous bands of "stringing" and the geometric inner band are a far cry indeed from the mercurial qualities of Pairpoint's High Victorian pieces.

The superb tea and coffee service in Figure 69 is a restrained example of the Neo-Classical style. The straightforward, plain, squared surfaces and the rolled, gilt borders around the bases are carefully balanced. The

67 Goblets made in 1874. Presented in 1875 to Thorndike Whittemore (TW). (*Gebelein Silversmiths*).

68 Footed salver made in 1877. Diameter: 12 in. (30.5 cm.). Mark: lion–anchor–G/STERLING/J. (*Courtesy Nancy C. Moore*).

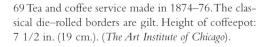

69 Tea and coffee service made in 1874–76. The classical die–rolled borders are gilt. Height of coffeepot: 7 1/2 in. (19 cm.). (*The Art Institute of Chicago*).

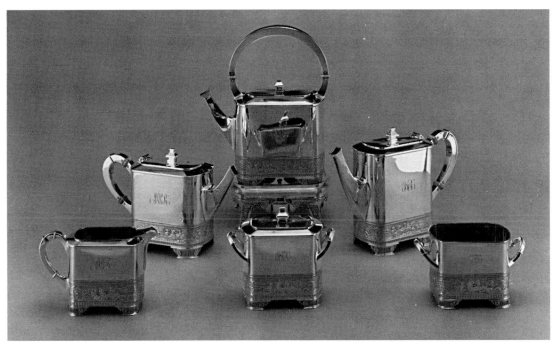

fixed arc handle of the hot water kettle in the center is a characteristic Gorham form (see Fig. 74) that may have derived from Japanese teapots. The service in Figure 69 is the standard size tea and coffee service of the 1870s insofar as the number of pieces is concerned. Occasionally a seventh piece was added, the hot milk pot.

The butter dish in Figure 70, made in 1877, is a utilitarian form that was popular throughout the last half of the nineteenth century. Both the top and base of this butter dish were hand raised. Ice is placed in the bottom, which is fitted with a pierced tray to hold the butter (Fig. 71). The stylized applied flowers below the molding are strikingly similar to drawings of flowers in Plate 21 of F. Edward Hulme's *A Series of Sketches from Nature of Plant Forms* (London: Day & Son Ltd., 1863), a book that has been in the Gorham library since the 1860s.

70

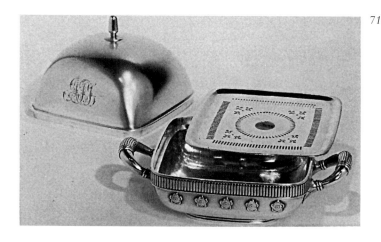

71

70 Butter dish made in 1877, with bottom and top hand raised, cast handles and finial, stylized flowers applied to base, rolled border. Top, in form related to Tibetan stupa, has a mat satin finish. Engraved APT. Height: 4 1/2 in. (11.4 cm.). Mark: 660/lion–anchor–G/STERLING/J. (*Private collection*).

71 Butter dish in Figure showing drain tray.

72 Claret jug made about 1875. Height: 8 5/16 in. (21.1cm.). (*Photograph courtesy Henry Francis duPont Winterthur Libraries*).

The claret jug with hinged lid in Figure 72, with its cast naturalistic handle, is another fine example of Gorham's restrained classical pieces. The vegetable dish in Figure 73, with its vigorous cast lion finials and "feet" on the lid, was a favorite form of the 1860s and 1870s. The turnkey lion finial can be removed and the top used as a separate serving dish. Many of the vegetable dishes of the period were made with this convertibility.

72

73 Neo–Classical vegetable dish with cover, made in 1871. The turn–key finial with lion can be removed so that the cover can be turned over and used as a serving dish. Height: 7 1/4 in. (18.4 cm.). Length: 11 1/2 in. (29.2 cm.). Mark: GORHAM CO./lion–anchor–G/STERLING/D/ 60/★. *(Burt collection).*

The decorations on the hot water kettle in Figure 74 show the same restraint of decoration, which is limited to the die–rolled borders with holly and the fluting on the spout. The strong simple feet of the kettle stand harmonize with the plain square–sectioned circular handle of the kettle. One feels that all of these reticently decorated, classically derived pieces were catering to a very sophisticated taste, a taste we do not usually associate with the mid–Victorian era.

The classical pieces in Figures 75 and 76 are more monumental. The classical friezes are prominent. We are much more conscious of the decorative elements, particularly with the double dish in Figure 75. The stately centerpiece in Figure 76 has an architectural quality with its careful balance of plain, undecorated forms and the classical decorations.

After mentally coping with the great centerpiece in Figure 76 it is almost a relief to consider some interesting small objects made by Gorham in this period. Figure 77 shows a silver buttonhook and two silver fruit knives with silver blades.

Many elaborate serving pieces were made by Gorham in the sixties and seventies. These ranged from the High Victorian whimsies such as the *Lady's* pattern which made use of a ladies hand on the handle to hold the bowl (Fig. 78) to pieces in the Egyptian style (Fig. 79). The Egyptian style (see also Fig. 80) had a brief period of revival in the late 1860s and early 1870s.

74 Kettle and stand made about 1870. *(Gorham photograph).*

75

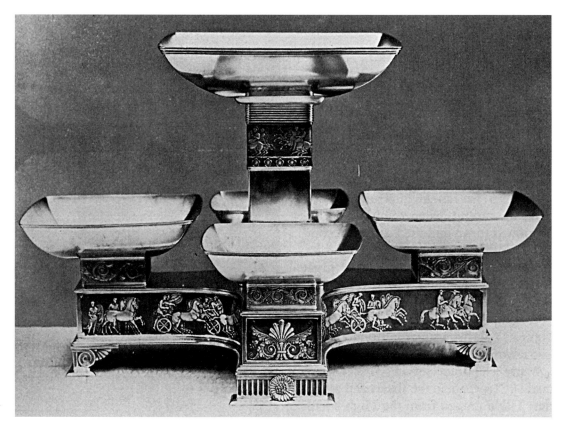

76

75 Double dish made in 1881. Size: 8 in. (20.3 cm.) square. *(Gorham photograph)*.

76 Centerpiece made in 1881. Weight: 236 ounces. Height: 14 in. (35.6 cm.). *(Gorham photograph)*.

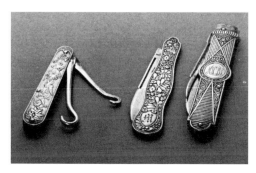

77

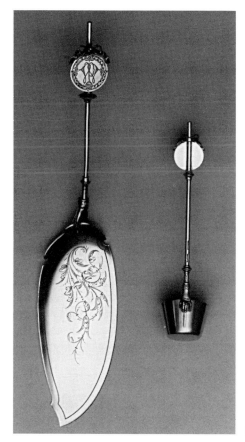

78

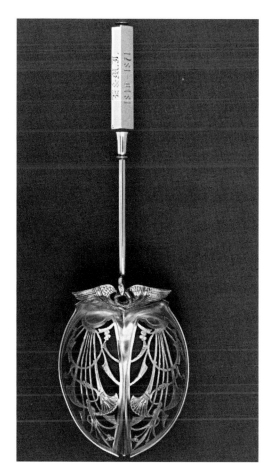

79

80

77 Buttonhook and fruit knives with silver blades, ca. 1880. (Courtesy George Tompkins).

78 Front and back of serving pieces in the *Lady's* pattern. Length of pie server: 12 13/16 in. (32.5 cm.). Mark: lion–anchor–G/PATENT 1868 STARR & MARCUS STERLING. Length of small ladle: 65/8 in. (16.8 cm.). Mark: lion–anchor–G/PAT. 68 STERLING. *(Private collection).*

79 Serving piece in the *Isis* pattern, ca. 1871. Length: 11 in. (27.9 cm.). (*Yale University Art Gallery*).

80 Small bowl made in 1869. Height: 3 3/4 in. (9.5 cm.). Mark: STERLING/lion–anchor–G/690/B. *(Courtesy Donald L. Fennimore).*

Electroplated Wares

Gorham was late in getting into electroplating. Rogers and others had started electroplating spoons in the 1840s and by the 1850s electroplated hollow ware was flooding the American market.[17] John Gorham visited a number of plating shops on his 1852 trip to England and was undoubtedly familiar, at least in a general way, with the technical aspects of electroplating.

The idea of electrolytically depositing a coating of silver on a cheap base metal had fascinated chemists and metalsmiths for several decades in the early part of the nineteenth century. The introduction of what is now called old Shefffield plate in the eighteenth century had greatly broadened the market for silversmith's goods, since these new "plated" wares were cheaper than those made of sterling. The old Shefffield plate consisted of a sandwich made of a thin sheet of silver laminated onto a thicker sheet of copper, or a three-component laminate made from thin sheets of silver laid on both sides of a sheet of copper. Objects were fabricated from these laminates in the usual manner.

In about 1840 the Birmingham, England, firm of G. R. & H. Elkington developed a practical process for electrolytically depositing a thin coating of pure silver directly onto a fabricated object. The new process soon replaced the old Sheffield plate. Electroplated wares were cheaper and easier to make. The object to be plated was placed in a solution ("bath") containing the proper chemicals, usually cyanides. The object was attached to an electrical circuit which included a power source (first a battery and then a dynamo), and another electrode, usually pure silver. In the solution the silver metal electrode acts as the anode and the electrical current causes atoms of silver to leave the anode and migrate to the cathode, which is the object being plated. The amount of silver deposited on a piece is a function of the amount of electrical current, the composition of the solution, and the plating time.

There are probably two reasons why John Gorham took his time in getting into electroplating. Quality was a problem. The manufacturers of electroplated wares in the 1850s were either unwilling or unable to produce pieces that could stand up very long. After a very few years of use, the silver surfaces of these early pieces became worn and the undermetal showed through. The main problem was simply that not enough silver was being deposited on the electroplated wares. The silver-plated coating was too thin. Part of the reason was that objects were not kept long enough in the plating bath. However, technology was undoubtedly a factor. Process

improvements were continually being made in the early years of electroplating.

The other factor was profitability. There was almost as much labor involved in making a fine electroplated tea and coffee service as there was in making one of coin silver or sterling. This created a problem in pricing. Electroplated tea and coffee services were sold for as little as a hundred dollars by some makers in the 1850s, while Gorham was making coin-silver services that sold in the $400 to $1200 range. Even if we take into account the difference in the silver value used in the coin silver services, it is clear that the profit margins were greater for those sets made in solid silver. Of course

81 Gorham broadside advertisement, ca. 1868.

very high volumes of cheaper electroplated wares would no doubt have been profitable, but Gorham was not set up for that kind of business.

It was not until 1863, when the Civil War had made silver harder to obtain, that Gorham started to develop their own electroplating process. By that time the basic electroplating patents of Elkington had expired. In 1865, after two years of development, Gorham started producing a line of electroplated wares.

The Gorham advertisement in Figure 81 puts great emphasis on the quality of their plated wares. These claims seem to be justified. The 1868 *Harper's* article mentioned previously states that "It was found by actual experiment . . . that the Gorham ware had upon its surface four and a half times as much silver as the English plate commonly sold in this market."[18]

The *Harper's* article says that Gorham's plated wares had completely supplanted English wares:

Five years ago all the really serviceable plated ware—all that was good economy to buy for household use—was brought here from Sheffield and Birmingham. The importation of such ware has now ceased, and nothing is imported except the cheaper kinds, which are only cheap in

the imagination of the purchaser. The Gorham plated ware blocks the way, making it impossible for the foreign article of equals merit to be imported at a profit.[19]

Gorham sold their plated wares through retailers, including Tiffany & Co. of New York. One of Gorham's large services created considerable interest when it was displayed in Tiffany's windows in the 1860s:

This new plated ware played a part in the "flurry" excited some time ago by the Bears of Wall Street in Pacific Mail Stock. Complete services of the Gorham plated goods were ordered for the new steamer Japan, belonging to this Company, and now plying between San Francisco and China. Before sending away the goods, Messrs. Tiffany and Co., through which they were supplied, exhibited them in the windows of their store in Broadway, and a truly superb appearance they presented, filling all the four windows. This ware, indeed, is so exactly like solid plate in appearance that no silver–smith can perceive any difference. Soon one of the Agents of the Pacific Mail Company came up town to beg Messrs. Tiffany to remove the gorgeous show from their windows, because the Bears, among other means of depressing the stock, were circulating the rumor that the Company was guilty of "the most reckless extravagance"

82 Electroplated tea and coffee service made in 1882. Mark: No. 28. (*Courtesy of Mrs. Ralph Major*).

in fitting up the new steamship, even going so far as to furnish the tables with solid silver plate. The services were accordingly removed, to the serious loss of the passersby, who had much enjoyed the brilliant spectacle. The Bears were signally mistaken in supposing the purchase of this ware to be an extravagant outlay. On the contrary, it was the result of a closely calculating economy. China services would, indeed, have been reckless extravagance, and still more reckless would it have been to provide for a steamship the brazen trash usually styled plated ware, that would have worn into shabbiness in one voyage.[20]

The present–day condition of some of Gorham's early plated wares suggests that they were indeed well made. The superb tea and coffee service in Figure 82 is in as pristine condition today as it was when it was made over a hundred years ago. When this service was brought to the Gorham plant for photographing it was examined by designers and silversmiths and pronounced to be of the highest quality of workmanship. The simple, chaste forms are carefully and beautifully hand chased (Fig. 83). The design is comparable to Gorham's best sterling wares of the time.

83 Coffeepot from service in Figure 82.

84 Electroplated tureen and stand made in 1875. Length: 15 3/4 in. (40 cm.). Mark: No. 27. (*Museum of the City of New York*)

The prices of Gorham plated wares were higher than their competition, sometimes double. Tea and coffee services sold as high as $175 to $250. Gorham's sales of plated wares never reached a very high percentage of their total sales, probably because of their comparatively higher prices.

Large serving pieces in electroplate are often found today, such as the tureen in Figure 84. This fine piece is indistinguishable to the eye from Gorham's best sterling pieces of the same time. One must examine the mark to tell the difference.

In 1880 Gorham enlarged their plant facilities for plated wares and introduced a lower-priced line. Tea services were offered in the $75 to $100 range.

Plated Items Listed in the Fall 1881 Gorham Catalog

Tea Sets,	Pitchers,	Communion Ware,	Peppers,
Kettles,	Fruit Stands,	Bread Trays,	Salts,
Waiters,	Berry Bowls,	Crumb Trays,	Butter Plates,
Tureens,	Cake Baskets,	Warmers,	Knife Rests,
Double Dishes,	Ice Bowls,	Wine Coolers,	Grape Scissors,
Meat Dishes,	Spoon Cups,	Scallop Shells,	Syrup Pitchers,
Vegetable Dishes,	Candlesticks,	Bells,	Flasks,
Salad Dishes,	Candelabra,	Napkin Rings,	Match Boxes,
Butter Dishes,	Cutlery,	Fruit Knives,	Tobacco Boxes,
Pudding Dishes,	Black Coffee,	Cups,	Soap Boxes,
Casters,	Bottle Stands,	Mustards,	Goblets.
Tea Spoons,	Salad Spoons,	Salad Forks,	Soup Ladles,
Dessert Spoons,	Ice Cream Spoons,	Tea Knives,	Oyster Ladles,
Table Spoons,	Jelly Spoons,	Dessert Knives,	Gravy Ladles,
Salt Spoons,	Preserve Spoons,	Butter Knives,	Cream Ladles,
Mustard Spoons,	Tea Forks,	Cake Knives,	Punch Ladles,
Coffee Spoons,	Dessert Forks,	Pie Knives,	Ice Tongs,
Egg Spoons,	Table Forks,	Ice Cream Knives,	Asparagus Tongs,
Sugar Spoons,	Pickle Forks,	Pickle Knives,	Sugar Tongs,
Berry Spoons,	Oyster Forks,	Crumb Knives,	Salad Tongs,
Gravy Spoons,	Fish Forks,	Fish Knives,	Nut Picks,
Nut Spoons,	Pastry Forks,	Sugar Sifters,	Cheese Scoops.

The Sterling Standard

In 1868 the Gorham Company adopted the English sterling standard of .925 fine silver for all of their solid silverwares. The company, along with many other American silver makers, had continued to use the coin silver standard of .900 fine up to that time, in spite of the fact that Tiffany & Co. in New York had adopted the sterling standard in the early 1850s. When Gorham went over to sterling in 1868, the rest of the silver industry, with only a few exceptions, followed suit. By the 1870s sterling was the American standard.

Sterling had been the standard in England since 1300. The fact that Gorham aspired to sell wares in England may have been a factor in their going to sterling.

The Depression of the Seventies

Gorham sales, from a peak of $1,024,000 in 1872, fell off considerably during the next six years, declining to a low of $521,000 in 1878. The Panic of 1873 (the "Jay Gould Failure") started a down trend that caused a very difficult period in the Gorham Company. Profits declined rapidly.

Salaries were cut. At the beginning of 1873 the annual salaries of the officers, Messrs. Gorham, Thurber, Wilkinson, and Adams (the agent) were all set at $10,000. In 1877 the salaries of Gorham, Thurber, and Wilkinson were cut to $5,000. Mr. Adams had been fired in 1875. The new agent, the bright young head of the New York showrooms, Edward Holbrook, received $7,500. One of the first things Holbrook did in 1876, when he became agent, was to acquire the fifty–eight shares of Gorham stock formerly held by Adams. The purchase of these shares was accomplished with money borrowed from the company. Holbrook took several years to repay the debt.

These were difficult times for all American silver makers. In 1877 the Whiting Manufacturing Co. of New York approached Gorham about a possible merger, but nothing came of it. In that same year Gorham made the decision to get out of the retail business in New York. (The No. 1 Bond Street warehouse of Gorham, which was formerly exclusive to the trade, was opened as a retail store in 1873. In the 1860s Gorham did extensive retail trade in New York through Tiffany & Co.). A proposal was made to deal with Starr & Marcus, a well-known New York retailer. These negotiations dragged on for many months before a tentative agreement was made to deal only with B. F. Starr in New York.

John Gorharm's Departure from Gorham

A sad and troubling event of Gorham history was discovered in digging through old "secret" records of the company. This was the personal bankruptcy of John Gorham and his subsequent ouster from the Gorham Manufacturing Co., the company he founded. Bankruptcy was a dirty word in the nineteenth century, and for a man of John Gorham's standing, it was almost a disgrace.

Some of the facts of the case are obscure. After the Civil War John Gorham became involved in business operations other than the Gorham Co. and the Gorham Co. & Brown store. The new venture (or ventures) obviously involved considerable capital and *time*. For example, the minutes of the February 14, 1870, Gorham board meeting noted that "John Gorham said he expected to be absent for a considerable portion of the year." His salary as president of Gorham was set at a nominal $3,000 for the year 1870. It is not known what or where the outside business interest was.

In 1874 and 1875 the records indicate several transfers of John Gorham's stock shares in the company. One cryptic note of September 10, 1875, stated: "100 shares— Marcy Gorham collateral for indebtedness of J. Gorham. " John Gorham lost all his shares in the Gorham Manufacturing Co., apparently by the end of 1875. At the beginning of 1878 Gorham was relieved of his duties with the company and was dropped from the board of directors.

The other members of the Gorham board obviously felt that none of them should assume the Gorham presidency. For this job they turned to a complete outsider, William H. Crins, a well–known and highly respected Providence businessman.

The 1878 annual meeting of the company was held on February 13. Mr. Gorham was present. It must have been an awkward situation. No one of the board group had any ill feelings toward John Gorham. However, he had lost his stock, he had gone into personal bankruptcy, and there seems to have been feeling that he had neglected his duties at Gorham for several years. Apparently they felt they had no other choice.

John Gorham felt otherwise. He was deeply hurt. Even the dry minutes of the 1878 annual meeting convey some of the drama that must have been felt by those present:

> Mr. Gorham presented a letter addressed to the "Stockholders of the Gorham Mfg. Co." and retired. At the request of the Chairman it was read by the Secretary. Remarks were made by Mr. Barstow, Mr. Thurber and Mr. Crins and in response to the question what action should be taken. Motion was made, seconded, and it was That Mr. Gorham's letter be received and referred to a committee with instruction to recommend such action as they deem advisable.

John Gorham's letter read:

Providence, February 13 th, 1878

To the Stockholders of the
Gorham Mfg Co—

> My connection with this business dates from 1841 under the name of J. Gorham & Son, my father retiring in 1847. I formed afterwards a growing business that demanded an accession of capital, which I obtained with the services of Mr. Gorham Thurber in 1850, he furnishing an equal amount of capital & financial accommodations and attending to the books and finances. In 1852 Mr. Dexter became an associate retiring at the panic of 1861 with his capital & accommodations.
>
> The present organization dates from 1865. From the period of 1841 to the panic of 1873 there was done a profitable and constantly increasing business with but slight exceptions common to all businesses.
>
> With all other manufacturing enterprises this company felt the depression & decrease in values consequent upon the disastrous times we have had since 1873.
>
> Outside operations with which I had become connected during the years of prosperity found me unprepared for the reverses consequent upon the panic and in 1875 I was forced to an assignment, the Company being in no way

directly associated with my embarrassments. I received my discharge in Voluntary Bankruptcy in March of last year and was in condition to again give the company my undivided services, but found the influence which I had heretofore exerted lost, and my advice and council unheeded.

The important actions the company have taken the past year in regard to its retail interests has not met my approval. Neither has the important connection made with Mr. J.B. Starr although I advocated at an earlier period an effort to form a closer connection with Messrs. Starr & Marcus on a *different* basis.

I am conscious during the whole period of 36 years that I have been connected with this business (employing at first but fourteen hands to its present status) I have hesitated at no personal sacrifice whereby I felt the prosperity of the business could be advanced.

For a long period of time it has been my aim, so to place the cares and responsibilities upon my junior associates that in the event of my decease, or withdrawal from my position, the least possible interruption of the business would occur. Believing the best interest of the Co. justified that course, little heeding the admonitions of friends that my position by so doing might be used to my disadvantage.

I feel that the course pursued by the present action of the company to be an injustice to me, unwarranted in consideration of the years of service given to its best interest in the building up of this business, with the assistance of those whom I have been chiefly instrumental in associating with me, leaving me at this period of a life's work with nothing to show of its results.

I most respectfully request this paper may be accepted and placed on file.

Yours truly
John Gorham

The committee came through with a terse and cautiously worded report on John Gorham's letter at the March 1878 meeting of the board:

The Communication presented of Mr. Gorham to the Company at its last meeting which was referred to a special Committee, has been carefully considered by said Committee and they would present the following report:
Whilst they recommend that according to Mr. Gorham's request, his communication be placed on file, and which they would express their most heartfelt sympathy for his present financial condition, for which the Company is not in the slightest degree responsible, at the same time they feel it to be a duty to enter their disclaimer to the imputations in the paper and to express their confidence in the justice of the Company's action.

J.C. Hartshorn
Geo. Wilkinson
J.F.P. Lawton

Providence March 4th 1878

For a hundred years after these events took place there was no mention of any kind in any of the several published and unpublished histories of Gorham as to what really happened to John Gorham in 1878. It was usual to speak of his "retirement" in that year.

The unhappy annual meeting of February 13, 1878, was obviously a shattering event for John Gorham. As he said in his letter, he had nothing to show for his thirty–seven years at Gorham. Not even a job.

CHAPTER 6

Innovation and Fantasy

It is a curious fact that the two greatest silver makers of Victorian America, Gorham and Tiffany, both made some of their first hollow–ware pieces about the same time, 1850–1851, and in the same style, chinoiserie. Gorham's Chinese tea set, discussed in Chapter 4, didn't represent any particular interest of John Gorham in Oriental art. From the point of view of style the brief interest in Chinese motifs by American silversmiths in the middle of the nineteenth century was one of those revivals of interest in things Chinese that has affected Western decorative arts periodically ever since the first wave of chinoiserie in the seventeenth century. It could be classified as another example of Victorian historicism, along with other revivals of the mid–nineteenth century.

Japanese art was a different matter. It was clearly not treated as a revival by the artists and craftsmen who first came into contact with it in the 1860s and 1870s[1]. Japanese art, particularly the wood–block prints, opened up a new way of seeing; a flat, wonderfully decorative vision. The Japanese metalwares demonstrated subtle ways of handling a variety of metals that were entirely new to Western silversmiths. Japanese art brought an excitement and sense of renewal to Western art. It suggested fresh new approaches and new ways of looking at nature that captivated silversmiths and painters alike.

Although small quantities of Japanese ceramics and lacquer wares had been exported to the West since the sixteenth century, little was known of Japanese metalwares. The first large showing of Japanese art in the West, after Admiral Perry's 1854 treaty, was at the London Exposition of 1862, which aroused great interest. The American Civil War, and the bleak business outlook of the time, no doubt prevented John Gorham from attending the 1862 exposition.

Metalwork in Japan in the Edo period (1600–1868) reached great heights. The principal customers were the shogun and his wealthy feudal lords or daimyo. Craftsmen were often part of a household. Swords, the emblem of the ruling samurai class, were magnificently adorned. Scabbards, hilts, and guards were decorated in delicate designs in silver, gold, and alloys. This same kind of ornamentation was carried into household wares, flower vases, and figurines.

By the 1860s Japan was undergoing disruptive unrest and political change. The civil war in Japan in 1868 and the abolition of feudalism in 1871 marked a profound change in Japanese society. The samurai were no longer allowed to wear swords and the shogun and his daimyo became powerless. One of the results of this turmoil in Japan was the availability in the marketplace of first–rate pieces of metalware such as sword guards (*tsubas*). These objects found a ready market in the West; first in London and Paris, then by the late 1860s, in New York.

Japanese Design Sources

We know that the Gorham designers were influenced by Japanese metalworks in the 1870s and 1880s, but some of the very earliest Japanese influences probably came from wood–block prints rather than metal objects. The Gorham library has today a number of Japanese books that were acquired as early as the 1860s and 1870s. Included are the following:[2]

1. *Temmangu Godenki Ryakuja* (1820), 2 vols. An abbreviated history, with illustrations, of the Temmangu, a famous Shinto shrine in Kyoto. 8 7/8 in. x 5 7/8 in.
2. *Manga* by Katsushika Hokusai, 6 volumes, one of which has Gorham date stamp of Oct. 16, 1871. 9 x 6 in.[3]
3. *Kasho Gaden* by K. Hokusai, vol. 2 only, no date. Prints of birds and flowers. 9 x 6 in.
4. Album with fourteen hand–painted double–paged watercolors. No date or identification of any kind other than two owner's seals. Gorham date stamp of Oct. 16, 1871, in front and back of book. 11 3/4 in. x 6 3/4 in.
5. Book of forty–two photographs of album paintings of birds and flowers. No identification or tide. One painting is dated (in the original) 1873. 9 in. x 9 in.
6. A book of architectural details (1876). 5 1/16 in. x 7 1/4 in.
7. Pattern book of designs, *Musa Koeki Mohcha,* compiled by Murakami, 1885. 4 7/15 in. x 6 1/4 in.

There are also books in English and French in the Gorham library on Japanese art, such as Louis Gonse, *L'Art Japonais,* 2 vols. (Paris: A. Quantin, 1883).

These books show signs of having been well used by generations of Gorham designers. They are still consulted today.

Some examples of how Gorham designers of the nineteenth century used the Japanese wood–block prints are illustrated on the following pages.

The Gorham casting pattern in Figure 85 was copied from the upper part of the Hokusai print in Figure 86. It is obvious that, although the Gorham designers got Hokusai's facts straight, his figures became Westernized in the translation. These casting patterns were made by hand in lead or white metal. The pattern would then have been copied in silver or other metal, either by the use of sand casting or the lost–wax process. The silver plaque, known as a mount, would then have been soldered onto the metal object for which it was intended. Gorham often spoke of these mounts as appliqués. Figure 86a shows a small silver tray (ca. 1880) using a mount

85 White–metal casting pattern. Width: about 4 in. (10.2 cm.). *(Gorham collection).*

86a Tray with silver mounts. *(Photograph courtesy Gebelein Silversmiths).*

made from the casting pattern in Figure 85.

The silver bird, with the long, flowing tail, mounted on the ivory cup in Figure 87 is closely related to the *howo* (or *hoho*) birds in the Hokusai print in Figure 88. The bird mount in Figure 87 is not soldered, but is held in place by metal pins attached to the back which fit into holes in the ivory.

The dragon in Figure 89 is much tamer than Hokusai's vibrant dragon in Figure 90. This is not meant to suggest that this particular Hokusai dragon was the model for the Gorham dragon in Figure 89. It indicates the kind of prototype available to the Gorham designers in the 1870s and 1880s.

86 Print from Hokusai's *Magnum*. Page size: 9 x 6 in.
(22.9 x 15.2 cm.).

87

89

88

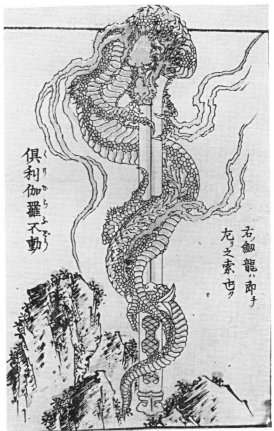

90

87 Three–handled ivory cup shown in color Plate II.

88 Print from Hokusai's *Magnum*. Page size: 9 x 6 in. (22.9 x 15.2 cm.).

89 Three–handled ivory cup shown in Plate II. The incised inscription at upper right corner of shield may be a pseudomark.

90 Print from Hokusai's *Magnum*. Page size: 9 x 6 in. (22.9 x 15.2 cm.)

91 Iron and silver tea caddy, made in 1883, the fabricated iron body of cylindrical form and fluted at the base, the sides applied with a silver dragon, fan, and the initials A. R., further inset with a silver panel depicting a sculptor carving a demon mask, the slip-on cover topped with an applied silver crab and with wavy borders of chased scrolls. Height: 6 1/4 in. (15.9 cm.). Mark: anchor/GORHAM & CO/W27 P/STERLING/ & IRON/15. *(Private collection)*. See Plate II.

The third side of the three–handled cup shown in Figures 87 and 89, made in 1883, is illustrated in color in Plate II. Each of the three sides of the cup are decorated with quite different kinds of Japanese motifs: bamboo and a spider; an exotic bird; and a dragon. The irregularly shaped, flanged silver base band supports the bottom of the three handles as well as the glass bottom of the cup. The tops of the ivory handles have silver mounts which are fastened by pins into the ivory. One of the handle mounts has a cast silver fly appliquéd on it. All three of the handles have different thicknesses, and all are much thicker than the ivory body of the cup itself, which is no more than an eighth–inch thick in places.

This remarkable ivory cup is somewhat atypical of Gorham's Art objects of the 1870s and early 1880s, most of which were made of silver or copper, in combination with other metals. Although the decorative motifs of the cup clearly derive from Japanese art, the Gorham design has an integrity of its own. The designer and the maker created an original object of great strength and beauty. Time has added the additional dividend of a lovely, burnished, bronzelike patina to the ivory.

Gorham designers of the 1870s and 1880s showed a continuing willingness to try new materials such as copper and ivory, and new combinations of materials. A few pieces made use of iron, a diffficult and intractable art material (Fig. 91).

The silver coffeepot in Figure 92 is entirely Japanese in its decoration, although its shape is Islamic. The Gorham records call it a Turkish Coffee. The word Turkish was used loosely by Gorham, since Turkish coffeepots are usually shaped quite differently, more like an Erlen meyer flask with a handle on it. The Gorham pot in Figure 92 is modeled after a water vessel—more Persian in design than Turkish. The Japanese–type finial on top is of the kind frequently found on Satsuma vases. The chased depiction of the two men in the driving rain illustrates a Japanese version of the story of Pandora's box. The man on the left, on opening the box, has unleashed a wild storm sent down by Raden, the God of Thunder. This coffeepot was part of a tea and coffee service made in 1880 that was pictured in a number of Gorham advertisements of the time. The pot alone had a retail value of $500. The plant records indicate there were over 150 hours involved in its making, 110 hours of which were for the chasing.

The exuberant punch bowl in Figure 93 features a dragon or sea serpent in turbulent, thrashing waves. Realistically encrusted shells are used on the cast ladle and as handles of the punch bowl.

92 Turkish coffee made in 1880. (*Gorham photograph*).

81

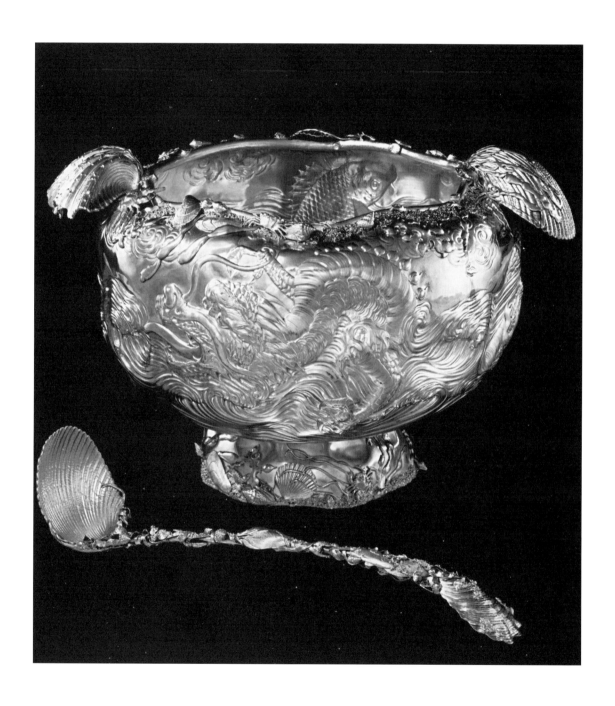

93 Punch bowl, repoussé chased, cast handles. Height 9 1/2 in. (24.5 cm.). Mark: lion–anchor–G/STERLING/1880 plus date mark for 1885. Length of ladle: 14 in. (35.6 cm.). Mark: STERLING. (*Museum of Fine Arts, Boston*).

Figure 94 shows two Gorham fruit knives with silver blades with bright–cut engraving in the Japanese style. The handles are bronze. The front and back parts of the handles are cast separately and soldered together. The silver blades are pinned into the handles. There seems to have been at least twenty–four different patterns used by Gorham in these handles. By altering the combinations of front and back patterns a very large number of different knife (or fork) designs were theoretically possible.

These Japanese fruit knives were sold in sets of six and twelve, and in sets of six and twelve each of knives and forks. They were gift sets, usually attractively packaged in silk–lined boxes.

The cast bronze handles are found in a variety of finishes: plain, parcel gilt, gilt, and with variously colored "gold" washes.

The Japanese prototypes for Gorham's Japanese fruit knives were the small *ko–gatama* knives with removable push–on handles called *kodzuka*.[4] These knives have been erroneously called hara–kiri knives. It was not, however, the *ko–gatama* knives that were used in the gruesome hara–kiri suicide ritual, but rather a samurai sword blade, wrapped in a towel.[5]

The Japanese *kodzuka* handles of the type shown in Figure 95 were copied rather literally by the Gorham craftsmen, but the latter's designs were simpler and coarser than the Japanese models. The *kodzukas* are more varied in their techniques and designs, and, frankly, the best of

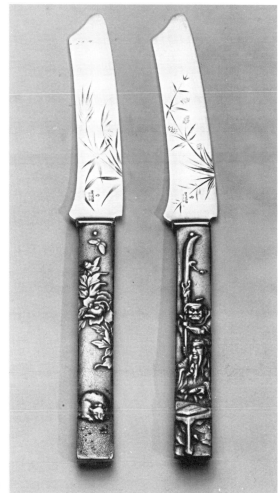

94

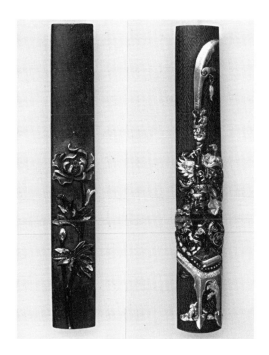

95

94 Gorham fruit knives, handles cast bronze, sterling blades with bright–cut engraving, made ca. 1880. Length: 7 3/4 in. (18.7 cm.). Mark on blade: lion–anchor–G/STERLING/5. *(Private collection)*.

95 Japanese *shakudo kodzukas,* handles for *ko–gatama* knives, ca. 1710. The *kodzuka* on the left has an applied silver and gold peony. The one on the right depicts Kwanyu sitting on a chair, with a scroll in front of him. At his back one of his warrior attendants holds his famous halberd *(Seiryuto)*. The mount is in yellow and green gold, shakudo, copper, and silver. It is signed on the reverse: *Hisanori, Kakihan.* Length: 4 in. (10.2 cm.). *(The George Walter Vincent Smith Museum, Springfield, Massachusetts)*

the Japanese *kodzukas* of the Edo period are far superior to the Gorham products. The restrained, exquisite use of gold and silver inlays on marvelously detailed backgrounds of the Japanese *kodzukas* represent one of the peaks of Japanese metal art. The Gorham craftsmen used the Japanese knives as models, making their own free, simplified translations. From a practical, commercial point of view Gorham *had* to do this. It would not have been commercially feasible, at that time, for Gorham to have their handles made in Japan; nor would it have been practical for them to have brought Japanese workmen to Providence.

Early Pieces in the Japanese Style

At the beginning of this chapter it was pointed out that Gorham and Tiffany introduced their hollow–ware lines at about the same time, 1850–1851, and in the same style, chinoiserie. In addition, the silversmiths of both companies became involved in Japanese art at about the same time, at the end of the 1860s. However, it seems clear that Gorham was first. The four shallow bowls in Figure 96, bearing the Gorham date–letter B for the

year 1869, have Japanese motifs that are related to Gorham's *Japanese* flatware pattern (Fig. 97), which was introduced about 1870. The parcel–gilt bowls are engraved with Westernized versions of Japanese motifs. The butterflies, bamboo, and the fans are Japanese, copied from such sources as Babiyu screens, woodblock prints, or textiles such as obies. The borders are Western or Westernized interpretations of Japanese designs.

The kettle and lampstand in Figure 98, with the date–letter D for 1871, and the cup in Figure 99, made in 1872, are both earlier than the first piece of hollow ware in the Japanese style made by Tiffany & Co. in 1873.[6] Gorham's *Japanese* flatware had five different handle designs, one of which is shown in Figure 97.

The melon–shaped kettle in Figure 98 was probably copied from a Japanese iron pot with a basketry handle. Two of the panels are engraved with Japanese figures. The round, flattened panels are soldered onto the body of the pot. The stylized geometric borders are engraved. The cup in Figure 99 has a stylized Chinese good–luck border around the top and an Oriental landscape border around the bottom. The strange, seemingly too–large handle was apparently designed for the cup, to give it an

96 Four small shallow bowls engraved with Japanese decorations, parcel gilt, made in 1869. Diameter: 4 in. (10.2 cm.). Mark: 10/lion–anchor–G/STERLING/B. *(Courtesy Patrick Duggan).*

97 Serving spoon in the *Japanese* pattern, pierced bowl. Length: 10 in. (25.4 cm.). Mark: lion–anchor–G/STERLING. *(Private collection).*

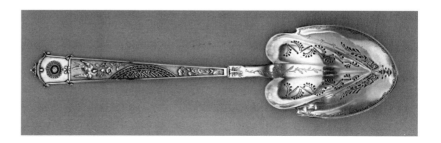

98

99

98 Kettle and lampstand made in 1871. Engraved panels are set into the body of the kettle. Height: 10 7/8 in. (27.6 cm.). Mark: T. KIRKPATRICK/10/lion–anchor–G/STER-LING/D/5 1/2 PINTS. (*Museum of Art, Rhode Island School of Design*).

99 Cup made in 1872. Applied die–rolled borders, cast handle. Height: 4 7/16 in. (11.3 cm.). Mark: lion–an-chor–G/STERLING/1065/E. (*Private collection*)

exotic, Oriental look.

The two silver serving spoons in Figure 100 were made about 1880. The one on the left is a cast pattern called *Hizen*. Hizen, the Japanese province in the north-western part of the island of Kyushu, is famous for the city– and kiln–sites of Areta, Imari, and Karatsu. The dragon on the handle of the *Hizen* spoon is a modified version of a Japanese *menuki* or similar–type ornament. The design on the spoon bowl is a fantasy, showing Japa-nese–patterned clouds and a birdlike figure with an ar-row tongue. The spoon on the right of Figure 100 is a pattern called *Cairo*, with speckles of copper, brass, and bronze on the handle. The floral decoration is Islamic which may account for the name *Cairo*.

There are similar speckled Japanese mixed–metalwares. Gorham may have "reinvented" a Japanese method, or developed their own process. There do not seem to be any records on what process Gorham actually used to make *Cairo*. A suggested method involves placing drop-lets of metal on a silver surface which is hot enough to

allow the different metals to fuse. The metal is then rolled, formed into the desired shape, and polished. Another possible method would be to pour the molten brass, copper, and bronze into water, which would form small irregular droplets of the metals. The solid droplets could then be sprinkled onto a molten bar of silver which was just fluid, not overheated, but fluid enough to receive these metals, after which it was quenched. The silver, containing specks of these metals, could be formed and finished in the usual way.

Art Silver

In the middle 1870s Gorham began to develop the concept of a line of Art silver, pieces that were con-ceived as works of art rather than as utilitarian objects. Part of the concept developed naturally out of their de-signers' interest in Japanese art.

The idea of a line of Art crafts was in the air. In En-gland it was labeled the Aesthetic Movement. There was

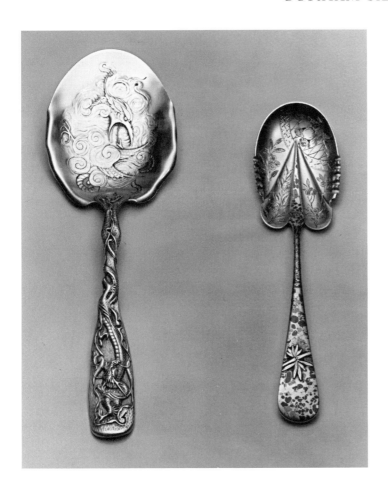

100 *Left: Hizen* tomato server, cast handle, bowl chased and engraved. Length: 9 in. (22.9 cm.). Mark: lion–anchor–G/ STERLING. *Right*: Serving spoon in *Cairo* pattern. Applied flower on handle, engraved bowl. Engraved on back, LTK.

101 Gorham broadside advertisement, ca. 1880.

much talk in the English and American art journals of the seventies of Art furniture and Art pottery, objects made for the "artistic interior."

Gorham's concept of Art silver (Fig. 101), particularly in the 1869–1876 period, seems not to have been confined to any one style. It included Japanese–derived designs and Thomas Pairpoint's High Victorian pieces. Neither Pairpoint's work or his writings indicated any interest or knowledge of Japanese art.[7]

After 1877 Gorham's Art line was primarily based on Japanese art. Although many of the objects no longer had an Oriental look, the concepts, the design ideas, and some of the techniques derived from the Japanese. The luncheon set in Figure 102, made up of two each of salts, peppers, and butter dishes, is, along with the similarly decorated parcel-gilt butter dishes in Plate I, an example of what Gorham would have designated Art silver. The gilding beautifully sets off the silver color of the bright–cut engraving. The six–piece luncheon set was packaged in a red silk–lined box in which was printed the name of the retailer, T. W. Whitney, Binghamton, New York.

THE Gorham Co., Silversmiths, at their new warerooms on Broadway (cor. 19th St.), are exhibiting choice examples of Art Work in Silver and in different combinations of silver with other metals. The constant accession of new products from original designs is a feature which gives to their stock, at all seasons, a distinctive character, evincing an air of incomparable completeness and elegance. With each recurring season, the advance, judged from the most critical stand-point, is readily apparent, and the recognition of the merits of their wares abroad is evidenced by the recent shipment of orders, in sterling silver, to the Royal Family of Portugal.

GORHAM M'F'G CO.
SILVERSMITHS,
Broadway & 19th St. New-York, N.Y.

Hammered Finishes

A hammered metal surface, with hammer marks left in, automatically conveys, or is meant to convey, the feeling that a piece was handmade, even when such marks are stamped onto the surface of an object with a steel die. Hammering, particularly on silver and copper, has become almost standard for handmade wares of the twentieth century.

Hammered metals were one of the principal techniques used by Arts and Crafts artisans in the early 1900s to achieve the feeling of being made and finished only with a hammer. The hammered bronze hinges, door- and drawerhandles of Stickley and other American Mission furniture were meant to suggest that the pieces were handmade, even though they were mostly machine-made in factories. The Roycroft Copper Shop of East Aurora, New York, made a whole line of hammered copper wares.

When we realize how commonplace hammered surfaces are in late nineteenth- and twentieth-century metalwares, it comes as a surprise to realize that the idea of a hammered surface was almost certainly the " invention" of an unknown American craftsman in the nineteenth century. In fact, the date can be pinpointed fairly closely to about 1876. Although both Gorham and Tiffany made hammered wares in 1877, the evidence, as discussed below, indicates that the idea of hammering came from a silversmith working at Tiffany & Co. in New York in 1876. This same silversmith later worked for Gorham, joining the Providence company in about 1883.

What *is* hammering? It is a metal surface covered with a maze of indentations which *seem* to be the result of forming the surface of an object with a hammer. The word "seem" was italicized in the previous sentence because hammered surfaces can be achieved in two ways—by the use of a silversmith's hammer, or by the use of chasing tools. Of course chasing tools are driven by a hammer, but, strictly speaking, such work should be called chasing rather than hammering.

There is a simple test to tell which method was used to obtain a hammered surface. If the marks show through clearly on the *back* of the surface, the hammering was probably achieved by the use of chasing tools (Fig. 103). When such objects are chased they are filled with pitch which "gives" when struck by a tool, allowing the metal to indent into the pitch. Hammering, with a hammer, is done on a hard, resistant, steel surface; on a stake or anvil, for example. The indentations on the metal surface are not carried through to the back (b in Fig. 103).

102 Luncheon set, parcel gilt; open salts, peppers, and butter dishes; made in 1880. Height of peppers: 3 1/4 in. (8.3 cm.). Mark: lion–anchor–G/STERLING/1530/M. *(Private collection).*

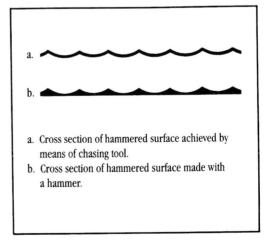

a. Cross section of hammered surface achieved by means of chasing tool.
b. Cross section of hammered surface made with a hammer.

103 Hammered surfaces.

On a thin piece of metal there may be indications of the marks on the back surface, but they do not mirror the surface marks as exactly as with chasing (a in Fig. 103).

In the 1870s and 1880s Gorham (and Tiffany) used both methods, sometimes on the same piece. Chasing was generally used to indicate large marks (up to, say, 3/8–inch in diameter), and precise, honeycomb surfaces. Silversmiths say that the precision of hammering on some pieces, such as the bowl in Plate I, could only be achieved with chasing tools. Hammering marks of carefully graduated sizes, such as those on the pitcher in Figure 6 in the Introduction, are mostly chased. Uneven, rough hammering (see copper coffeepot in Fig. 109) was achieved with a hammer.

The above–mentioned silversmith who worked for both Tiffany and Gorham kept a diary of his Tiffany years from 1876 to 1883.[8] Two entries in this diary suggest that he or one of his colleagues at Tiffany actually came up with the idea of hammering in 1876, and that by the end of 1877 it had become an established silver–making technique:

Oct. 13th, 1876

A very fine ground effect is produced by finishing the article first, then peaning it (not planishing) in regular courses and then chasing devices in the rough surface, smoothing the chased parts. The effect has a remarkably fine appearance. The old English work was planished in regular courses giving it a hammered look.

The second diary entry, a year later, records that hammering had been successfully introduced, but that the public was misreading the technique:

Dec. 7th, 1877

Hammered work has proved a success; at present the coarse hammering is the favorite style as it is asserted that it looks as if left so, from the silversmiths' hand in raising the work. The morocco style (peaning) and all others giving the idea of decoration only. Sawyer Barlow gives his opinion as such. I merely note this to show the effect upon the public. Clerks represent it as being the result of the hammer in forming the work. "Beating it up out of a sheet of metal into shape" as the clerk tells the buyer.

The idea of leaving a hammered surface on a piece of silverware is a complete reversal of the traditional idea of smoothing out hammer marks in the finished object. Hammer marks of various kinds have been left on silverwares since the beginnings of the craft, but it was usually thought that such marks were an indication that the piece had not been quite finished. Certainly English and American silver was so judged. Although early nineteenth–century American silversmiths were usually more careful to remove all traces of hammering than smiths of the seventeenth and eighteenth centuries, almost none of them left much more than a hint of the hammer marks resulting from the raising in the finished object.

The use of hammering spread quickly after 1877. It was introduced to Europe in the 1878 Paris Exposition where Tiffany's hammered pieces in the Japanese style created a sensation. The French critics and the buying public alike were entranced with the *martelé* (hammered or hand–hammered) surfaces of the Tiffany pieces. The silversmiths who visited the exposition were impressed. Elkingtons of England bought a number of the Tiffany pieces for study purposes. The hammered surfaces were not only beautiful in the way they broke up light into glittering reflections, they were also practical. Hammered silver didn't show finger marks as easily as plain, highly polished silver.

Gorham did not participate in the 1878 Paris Exposition, so their hammered pieces were almost unknown in Europe at the time. From the beginning Gorham's use of hammering was different from Tiffany's. It was more varied, and, perhaps, more innovative. At Tiffany the procedure of hammering was quickly systematized. Detailed hammering and mounting drawings were made of each piece which indicated the size and shape of the hammer marks.[9] The Tiffany pieces had the same size and kind of hammer marks uniformly over the entire surface of a piece. Usually the smaller pieces had smaller hammer marks, and the larger pieces larger ones, marks of 3/8–inch or more in diameter.

The working drawings of the Gorham pieces gave no indication of hammering sizes. The silversmith followed his own artistic instincts. Hammering patterns varied from the graduated marks on the pitcher in Figure 6 in the Introduction, which was chased by a whole series of different–sized punches, to the bowl in Plate I whose beautifully crafted surface was realized by the use of a single–sized chasing tool.

The intent of hammering in the 1870s and early 1880s was to achieve a decorative (and useful) surface. The idea that a hammered surface should suggest that the piece was handmade came later, in the Arts and Crafts period.

In the 1880s hammered surfaces began to be used by many American silversmiths, and by the early 1900s such surfaces became almost de rigueur for Arts and Crafts metalsmiths. English Arts and Crafts silver of the turn of the century often made use of hammered surfaces. The makers included C. R. Ashbee, and pieces Alexander Knox designed for Liberty of London.[10]

The idea of hammering was suggested by Japanese metalwares of the nineteenth and earlier centuries. The Japanese often used a textured background to set off mounts applied to the surface. They used a variety of grounds for their surface designs. The most important of these include: *nanako* ("fish roe"), a series of raised dots produced by a cupped punch; *ishme*, a rough surface tooled with a punch or chisel; *tsuchime*, an *ishmi* surface produced by the side of a hammer; *yasurime*, file marks used for such purposes as imitation of rain; *amida yasurime*, or *amida tangane*, radiating lines made with a file or chisel; *neko–yake* ("cat scratches"), chisel marks in which the burr is left in place and flattened with a hammer.[11]

Although the Japanese had a number of techniques for texturing metals, hammering as a decorative ground was apparently not used, or at most seldom used.

In the 1920s and 1930s Tiffany & Co. put hammering marks on lathe–spun pieces and marked them SPECIAL HAND WORK. Apparently the firm of Georg Jensen used the same kind of technique for many of their regular stock pieces after World War II. Even today Gorham's stainless steel pattern *Baluster*, designed by Burr Sebring, has hammered handles (die–stamped) which give it a handmade look.

Hammering, first used by Gorham and Tiffany in the late 1870s, is still popular today. It was an innovation that has become a basic silversmithing technique.

104 Tête–à–tête set, hammered and appliquéd, made in 1880. Size: 5 1/8 x 9 in. (13 x 22.9 cm.). *(Gorham photograph).*

Hammered Wares

The bowl in Plate I has a hammered body appliquéd with stylized silver leaf sprays with flower buds. Some of the buds are sheathed in gold. The die–rolled border around the top is made up of miniature wave–forms and rising suns. A gilt–silver rod (with unevenly spaced rings of solder spatter) wraps around the base of the bowl and loops up on the two sides to form handles. It is this odd and unexpected combination of an elegantly hammered and decorated bowl with the rough, almost casual bent–rod handles, a combination of restrained good taste and virtuoso flair, that makes this bowl such an interesting and innovative object. It certainly must have looked avant–garde when it was made in 1879. Even today it is unexpected to find that such an object was made in Victorian America.

The regularity of the evenly sized and spaced, chased hammer marks of the bowl in Plate I show the precise control of a master craftsman. The hammering functions visually in different ways on the outside and inside of the bowl. On the outside it looks like a hammered surface. The gilt inside looks like a golden honeycomb. The gilt interior plays off against the gilt handles and the touches of gold on the flower buds, giving a warm glow to the object. Incidentally, this use of a gilt hammered surface is a very practical solution to the problem of decorating the inside of a bowl. Plain bowl surfaces tend to get rough and scratched, a detracting visual element. The gilt hammered surface is more durable.

The little tête–à–tête set in Figure 104, with its copper appliqués, has triangular–shaped pot, creamer, and sugar perched on a small oval tray.

105 Five–piece tea and coffee service made in 1881. Height of coffeepot: 6 in. (15.2 cm.). Mark: lion–anchor–G/STERLING/1540/ N.(*Photograph courtesy Washburn Gallery*).

The five–piece tea and coffee service in Figure 105 uses chased hammering to simulate cracked ice, with flowers and Japanese decorative motifs showing through the holes in the ice. The squat, round bodies with square tops represent a form that was used a number of times by Gorham on the tea and coffee services of the 1870s and 1880s. The flared collar on the tops of the handles of the service in Figure 105 are related to the one on the handle of the cup in Figure 99.

The ice–cream slicer in Figure 106, made in 1883, has a trompe l'oeil bamboo handle fastened casually to a large hammered bowl.

The loving cup in Figure 107 is notable for the realistically chased carp leaping out of the water, and for the daring handle design. The two plain handle forms soar out of the sides and almost seem to whip around the top of the cup. Again we see the Gorham designers combining odd, abstract elements, such as these handles, with realistic, decorative elements—the bug, the carp, and the water.

The large punch bowl in Figure 108 and the small bowl in Plate IV are typical examples of a group of objects made in the early 1880s by Gorham. Most were bowls, usually with chased hammering, and appliquéd with copper branches, silver and copper leaves, and clus–

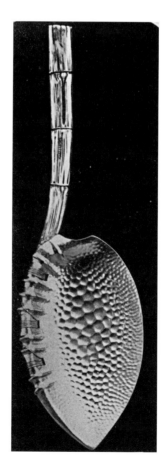

106 Ice–cream slicer made in 1883. (*Gorham photograph*).

107

108

107 Loving cup made in 1882, No. D.39. Weight: 26 ounces. (*Gorham photograph*)

108 Punch bowl, applied–copper grape clusters, applied branches and leaves, hand–hammered body and base. This trophy was "The First Lawn Tennis Singles Challenge Bowl." It was won in 1885 by Richard D. Sears. Width: 18 in. (45.7 cm.). Depth: 11 in. (27.9 cm.). Height: 9 1/4 in. (23.5 cm.). (*The International Tennis Hall of Fame, Newport, R.I.*).

ters of copper grapes. Flat cast bronze– and silver–appliqués depict flowers, plants, moths, and birds. Some of the decorations are decidedly three dimensional.

The honeycomb hammering appears to be more casual on these objects than on those pieces described above. The pieces are colorful, flamboyant and more adventuresome than the comparatively reticent and conservative hammered and applied bowls made by Tiffany & Co. during the same period.

Copper

In 1881 Gorham introduced a line of copper wares. This was truly an Art line of objects, usually with silver appliqués or silver decorations and/or silver fittings. The copper pieces were handmade by silversmiths. In no way was copper treated as a cheap, nonprecious metal. The pieces were beautifully designed and made. They were finished with all the care of the finest silverwares.

The copper wares have the bonus of color. The polished finishes, often hammered, range in color from warm reds to tans to deep chocolate browns.

The autumn 1882 Gorham catalog described the line in some detail:

COPPER

Our introduction of this line of wares during the past season was greeted by the Trade with the most hearty sense of appreciation; and so well have our efforts been sustained that the variety originally confined to a few specific articles has been increased from time to time, until we are now enabled to offer a list of suffficient moment to constitute a distinct department of our business.

The dealer unaided by actual inspection and misled by the term Copper would doubtless fail to comprehend the real beauty and true merits of these goods. The skill displayed by the designer in producing the varied tones of color has given to them an indescribable charm, and the appliqué and other forms of ornamentation used to a large extent enriches them materially, and renders them choice examples of an art kindred to that of the precious metals.

The following excerpt describing Gorham's new copper line is from *The Jewelers' Circular and Horological Review*, January 1882:

Copper predominates, and is very fashionable; in hammered designs the colors are dark warm reds of finest polish, mellowing into yellowish browns; scales and shadings, like shapeless lichens, wine-tinted. This is seen in beautiful gas standard lamps; some have silver decorations applied. Some tea–caddies of this metal are hammered; the colors as described above, barred with thin silver cords, a lizard on the lid. Some exquisite small pieces show a pot for black after–dinner coffee of silver in purest Persian shape.

A wreath of leaves and berries rises from the base on one side the other shows water, and the figure of a man and birds. This is in copper applied. On the sugar bowl is a branch, leaves, a huge spider, and an owl of copper. The little square tray, in warmest red tints, has the highest polish. The reverse of this is a tea–caddy of silver, in satin finish, hammered surface, over which trails a branch of cherries and foliage in dark copper; a snail decorates the lid. A similar caddy oxidized has copper decoration of strawberry vines. A magnificent punch bowl defies pen description. The base is copper, wrought into a branch of a pear tree gnarled and twisted. Another branch, also of copper, droops gracefully from the edge of the brim over the outside, with exquisitely carved and burnished leaves, and three natural–sized pears of golden green with a tint of red; one is slightly specked. Over the other side of the bowl droops

109 Copper Turkish coffee made in 1883, hammered surface with a deep reddishbrown glaze, die–rolled silver band around middle, silver band around top, ivory insulators on handle. Height: 13 in. (33 cm.). Mark: anchor/GORHAM CO/E40/P (*Private collection*).

a bough of cherries, natural size, deepest red, one or two apparently worm–eaten, and in some of the dark veined leaves insects seem to have left signs of depredation. Among tobacco sets is a superb specimen of copper, with silver applied. In the cigar stand, the decoration is in silver, a strawberry vine drifting about the top; on the side is another vine and a grasshopper. This is on the ground of softest warm–hued shadings of rosy copper.

The little cigar lamp for alcohol is hammered. A dragon forms the handle; the silver decoration is of water–fowls and fish. The tray has the effect of water: a sanded beach, shells, fish, and birds, in decoration of silver on the rich, dark–red copper ground.

Some cigarette cases are similar in workmanship.

A copper tea caddy, similar to the one described above, with a silver lizard on its lid, is shown in Plate IV right. The appliquéd silver leaves, flowers, bird, and moth are heavily oxidized, blending well with the warm brown surface of the copper.

A favorite Gorham form was a tall, slim Turkish coffeepot, with a long, graceful spout. Figure 109 shows a hammered example made of copper with a rich, deep reddish–brown glazed finish. A similar copper pot, appliqued with silver mounts, is shown in Figure 7 in the Introduction. These Turkish pots were also made in plain copper finishes, some with silver mounts, and in solid silver.

The copper tea service in Figure 110, made in 1882, has elaborate, oxidized silver mounts on all three pieces. The creamer and sugar have cast dragon handles. Although the teapot in Figure 110 has a Western–shaped body and spout, it was probably modeled after a Japanese prototype. The *karakane* metal body of the Japanese pot in Figure 111 has a coppery look similiar to the Gorham pot. The massing of the floral work, and the moth and the curve of the handle are related. The applied decoration is much more complex on the Japanese pot, being made of *taka niki bori iroye,* which means that yellow and green gold, *shakudo,* copper, and silver were used.

The copper lamp in Figure 112, made in 1882, has a glass globe painted with Japanese motifs, and an elaborately hammered and chased base depicting a carp and Imari wave pattern. The lamp was a comparatively ex–

110 Copper tea service with silver mounts made in 1882, enameled red and applied with cherry or plum blossoms, flowering foliage, insects, and birds. Height of teapot and stand: 10 in. (25.4 cm.). *(Photograph courtesy Christie, Manson & Woods International).*

111 Japanese teapot made of *karakane*, with overlay decorations of *taki niki bori iroye,* malakite knob on lid. The inside of the lid and body are silver. Height through handle: 7 7/8 in. (20 cm.). Signed in a circle on bottom: "Jomi of Kyoto 1876." *(The George Walter Vincent Smith Art Museum, Springfield, Massachusetts).*

112 Chased copper lamp with painted glass globe, made in 1882. *(Gorham photograph).*

pensive item, retailing at $200. Almost a hundred hours were involved in the making of the lamp, sixty hours for the chasing alone.

The copper ale mug in Figure 119a, made in 1883, with a silver–mounted elephant–ivory handle, has a hammered surface of marks that are graduated in size. The Gorham photographic records show that a similar ale mug was made in 1882 with large, uniformly sized markings over the whole body of the piece. The mug in Figure 119a is the more successful of the two. The graduation of smaller hammer marks toward the top and bottom of the sloping cylinder is much more visually satisfying than the use of large, uniformly sized marks.

The surfaces of Gorham's copper pieces made in the 1880s can be described as lacquerlike glazes. However, they are chemically more like ceramic glazes than organic lacquers. It is not known what process Gorham used to obtain these colored surfaces, but it was no doubt a version of standard procedures. There are many such procedures recorded in the literature, such as simply heating the copper to produce a thin film of red–to–brown cuprous oxide (Cu_2O) on the surface, which is then polished until an enamellike, lustrous glaze is obtained. Many formulas are recorded using such chemicals as copper sulfate, copper nitrate, barium sulfide, ar–senic, iron oxide, ammonium sulfide, etc.[12] In general, solutions of these materials work quicker and more efficiently when hot.

Although these glazed copper finishes are quite durable, they cannot survive rough scouring or the use of a buffing wheel. The best method of cleaning these glazed copper pieces is with mild soap and warm water. After the piece is thoroughly rinsed and dried, a thin coating of clear, polishing wax helps preserve the surface.

The 1882 Gorham catalog listed the following copper pieces, which range in size from matchboxes to umbrella stands:

LIST OF ARTICLES MADE IN COPPER

Smokers' Sets

a Cigar Vase and Lighter
b Match Vase, Cigar and Ash Tray
c Match Vase and Tray
d Match Vase, Cigar Vase, and Tray
e Cigar Vase, Lamp, and Tray
f Cigar Lighter and Tray
g Cigar Lighter and Cigarette Case
h Cigar Lighter and Vase
i Match Box and Cigarette Case
j Cigar Lighter, Tray, and Cigar Case
k Match Box and Cigar Case
l Cigarette Vase, Tray, and Cigar Lighter

Match Boxes	Tea Caddies
Trays	Stands
Ash Trays	Liquor Flasks
Cigar Trays	Kettle and Stand
Pen Trays	Coffees
Cigar Vases	Sugars and Creams
Cigarette Vases	Inkstands
Cigar Lighters	Match Vases
Love Cups	Ale Mugs
Soap Boxes	Stand and Lamp
Peppers	Cracker Jars
Lamps	Umbrella Stands
Drop Lights	Candlesticks

The heyday of Gorham's handmade copper line was relatively short. Most pieces were made in the 1881–1885 period. The production was relatively small.

One could speculate that the line was not a commercial success. The pieces were expensive to make because of the amount of hand labor involved. Possibly the kind of public that could afford and appreciate a luxury cop-

per line preferred to put their money into more expensive solid silver objects

Gorham made copper wares again in the early twentieth century. Most of these pieces were in the *Athenic* line (Chapter 11)

Whimsy and Fantasy

The Gorham records of the 1870s and 1880s contain photographs of a series of fascinating objects that can probably best be classified as whimsy and fantasy. Occasionally the objects border on kitsch, only being saved by a high order of craftsmanship. This whole matter of whether one should take kitsch or "camp" seriously is beyond—well beyond—the scope of this book. Perhaps it is best to show a sampling of these pieces and let the readers make their own value judgments.

Figure 113 shows a silver camp kettle supported by three rustic silver sticks. The price was $160. Figures 114 through 117 illustrate a group of trompe l'oeil objects where silver is used to imitate basketry, cloth, leaves and insects, straw and crackers.

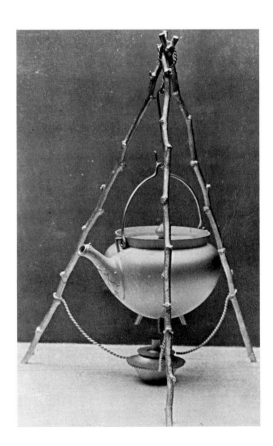

113 Silver camp kettle and support, made in 1874. *(Gorham photograph).*

114 Silver fruit plate, No. Z.312, made in 1880. Diameter: 10 in. (25.4 cm.). *(Gorham photograph)*. See Plate III

117 Silver cracker jar, No. C.92, made in 1880. *(Gorham photograph)*.

115 Silver pitcher, No. D.56, made in 1880. Weight: 32 ounces. *(Gorham photograph)*.

116 Silver cracker jar, No. D.10, made in 1880. *(Gorham photograph)*.

Figure 114 and Plate III show two views of a silver basket–weave plate on which is placed a white fringed napkin of frosted silver. An 1885 *Silversmith's Handbook* gives several methods for whitening silver for such surfaces as the napkin:

> One of the oldest methods of producing a snowy whiteness upon articles of silver was as follows: Take an iron or copper annealing pan (the latter is much preferred), place the work upon it in proper order, so that it may be heated all over alike. It should, previous to this, be immersed in a thick solution of borax, or otherwise brushed over with it. After the work has been properly arranged upon the pan for annealing, it must be sprinkled over with fine charcoal dust; the pan is then placed in the muffle upon a bright clear fire without blaze, and when the work has assumed a degree of heat approaching to cherry redness, it is withdrawn and allowed to cool.
>
> When this has taken place, it is removed and boiled out in a very weak solution of sulphuric acid, commonly called oil of vitriol. If the right color was not then produced, the process was repeated as many times as circumstances permitted, though usually two or three times was found to be amply sufficient.[13]

The extraordinary pitcher in Figure 115, made in 1880, has a silver handle in the form of a twisted white silk shawl with black fringe. This four–pint pitcher was priced at $350. It involved seventy–seven hours of chasing.

There were a number of small, whimsical silver cracker jars made in the year 1880, two of which are shown in Figures 116 and 117. The mouse nibbling the crackers on the lid of the jar in Figure 117 was a device used a

115

116

117

118 Silver swing kettle with lamp, No. 1090, made in 1874. *(Gorham photograph).*

119 Silver coffeepot, No. 0826, made in 1875. *(Gorham photograph).*

number of times by Gorham. Another example (not il–lustrated) has a cast mouse perched on the edge of a cheese plate. However, probably the most interesting thing about the jar in Figure 117 is the deliberately crushed, damaged effect on the upper part of the jar. One wonders whether such jars have survived unscathed. The impulse to knock out the bumps must have oc–curred to more than one later owner!

These little cracker jars were not cheap. The one in Fig–ure 117 retailed at $140.

Forecasts of the Future

Gorham made a few objects in the 1870s that seem re–markably avant–garde, objects that look as if they were made in the twentieth century. (This matter of "precur–sors" was discussed in the Introduction). Although we have seen in the previous chapter that Gorham, in the 1870s, made a whole line of simple, classically derived wares, it is still fascinating to come onto photographs of objects which look quite up–to–date, even today, a cen–tury later. Figures 118 and 119 show simple, strong, undecorated pieces that seem out of place in Victorian America.

The swing kettle in Figure 118 was part of a six–piece tea and coffee service. The kettle was entered in the Gorham records on September 15, 1874. The retail price was $360. A kettle is always the most expensive piece of a tea and coffee service. The next most expen–sive piece of the service, the coffeepot, retailed at $165. This sturdy and chunky kettle (56 ounces) derives from Japanese prototypes, but the influences have been ab–sorbed.

The elegantly simple coffeepot in Figure 119, made

119a Ale mug made in 1883, hammered copper, gilt interior, sterling-mounted elephant-ivory handle. Height: 6 1/2 in. (15.3 cm.). Mark: Anchor/GORHAM CO/437/P

in 1875, is quite remarkable. It could easily be a mid–twentieth century pot with a Bakelite handle. There is nothing to give it away. It has a sleek, machine–made appearance which completely belies its age. Even though it is based on earlier American and English forms (it could be classified Colonial Revival), its whole look is away from the past, toward the future.

The brilliant, contemporary–looking objects in Figures 118 and 119 probably had no affect whatsoever on twentieth–century design. The designers didn't know about them. They were too far ahead of time. They have only *become* precursors as a result of similarly designed objects made in the twentieth century.

The Japanese–influenced wares of Gorham (and Tiffany) *did* influence the future. Stylistically, the Japanese wares were one of the true precursors of Art Nouveau. They led to a new love of nature. Flowers, branches and leaves, birds, animals, fish, and swirling depictions of water began to become commonplace in the decorative arts. These themes have their origins in the wood–block prints and decorative arts of Japan. The love of color, the preference for asymmetry, the preference for curving, sensuous lines—all Japanese ideas developed in the 1870s and 1880s—became part of Art Nouveau.

There were, in the decorative arts of the 1870s and 1880s, parallels in furniture, ceramics, wallpaper, and textiles. In England the Japanese influence (the Aesthetic Movement) was particularly strong in the decorative arts *other* than silver.[14] The use of mixed metals created an almost insurmountable difficulty for English silver makers—the pieces could not be hallmarked as sterling.[15]

The Japanese–influenced wares of Gorham were primarily handmade. Gorham's Art wares, by their very nature, necessitated a high level of craftsmanship. This meant one–at–a–time, handmade objects which were, in a way, antimachine. They represented a philosophy which was later codified by the leaders of the Arts and Crafts movement (see Chapter 12).

Interest in things Japanese led to great experimentation; to new forms, new materials, and new finishes. The hammered surface, which later was so widely used by Arts and Crafts metalworkers, has become almost a standard finish for handmade silverwares of the twentieth century.

The 1870–1885 period was certainly one of the most interesting and creative periods in Gorham history. It was a period when a considerable number of fascinating and memorable objects were made, ranging from Thomas Pairpoint's flamboyant High Victorian concoctions at the beginning, to the beautifully crafted silver and copper mixed–metal objects at the end of the period.

CHAPTER 7

Antoine Heller
and the New Academy

In the 1880s a traditional, scholarly strain of design began to appear in Gorham silver which was a counterpart to the academic painting and Beaux Arts architecture of the time. The origins of the style at Gorham were the results of one man's ideas, F. Antoine Heller, the brilliant French silversmith and die–cutter who joined the company late in 1881 (Fig. 120).

Antoine Heller, who was born and trained in France, was steeped in the tradition of the Ecole des Beaux–Arts, the great Parisian art and architectural school.[1] Generations of Americans were trained at the Ecole, including Augustus Saint–Gaudens, Richard Morris Hunt, John Singer Sargent, H. H. Richardson, and Charles F. McKim. McKim was one of the founders of the most famous American architectural firm of the time, McKim, Mead & White. This firm designed a fine building for the Gorham Company on Fifth Avenue at Thirty–third Street in New York which was finished in 1905 (Chapter 11). McKim, Mead & White worked in a manner that Richard Guy Wilson has labeled "scientific eclecticism,"[2] using motifs from the past, particularly those of the Italian Renaissance, with a clear, rational sense of order.

Heller's approach to silver design was very much in the Beaux Arts tradition. His silver designs were precise, rational, and academic. However, the origin of his designs, particularly the hollow–ware pieces, came more from eighteenth– and early nineteenth–century European silver rather than from the Italian Renaissance directly.

Antoine Heller, an Alsatian, was born in Saverne, France, about 1845. He was apprenticed to a M. Chaplain, a well–known engraver. In 1864, through the recommendation of Baron de Bouilheres, he obtained a scholarship from his native town to study in Paris. He received a gold medal from the Paris Salon in 1870.[3]

Heller first came to America in the late 1870s to work for the New York firm of Tiffany & Co. It seems reasonably certain that he came to Tiffany to help design and cut the dies for Tiffany's flatware pattern *Olympian*, which was patented by Edward C. Moore on August 12, 1879. The *Olympian* pattern made use of a *series* of intricately designed, elaborate flatware handles of classical mythological scenes.[4] The *Olympian* designs are radically different from any previous flatware patterns of Tiffany, and reflect Heller's French sensibilities.

It would appear that Gorham hired Heller away from Tiffany & Co. It was probably the work of Edward Holbrook, the energetic agent for Gorham in New York. Holbrook would have heard about Heller's work for Tiffany and he would have been quite conscious of the excellent reception Tiffany's *Olympian* pattern had received.

In 1880 Heller left Tiffany and returned to Paris. Tif–

120 Photograph of F. Antoine Heller in his studio in 1892.
His drawing of George Wilkinson is on the wall, upper right.
(Gorham photograph).

fany made a very strong (and unsuccessful) attempt to lure Heller back to New York. A series of entries in the diary of the unknown Tiffany silversmith, mentioned in the previous chapter, documents the events:

October 27, 1880. E.C.M. [Edward C. Moore] report receipt of letter from his son Charley [in Paris] stating that Mr. Heller has returned dies for coffee spoons saying he cannot cut it for T & Co. as he is about returning to America having been engaged by Gorham & Co. E.C.M. is willing, if able to intercept him, to offer $1000 more than Gorham & Co. for his services, yet he does not know what steamer he is coming on.

October 28, 1880. Mr. Heller sails on 23rd October French steamer.

October 29, 1880. T & Co. propose offering Mr. Heller $75 per week or $1.25 per hour payable as follows: $50 per week cash, $1200 at the expiration. For 2 years.

January 20, 1881. Mr. Heller answers letter and states he cannot work for us as he has no bench at home etc. Writes at the same time to Mr. Soligay stating his getting better

pay than while here and only 8 hours.

Heller must have been paid well by Gorham. The above diary entries suggest he probably received four to five thousand dollars per year, a very high salary for the time.

Antoine Heller's first work for Gorham was announced with considerable fanfare in their autumn 1882 catalog. It was the meticulously detailed flatware pattern *Fontainebleau* (Fig. 10 in the Introduction). *Fontainebleau* was also featured on the cover of the 1882 catalog.

The catalog contained a rambling six–page account, "The Story of the Fontainebleau," which described Francis I and his court in great detail. It was only in the last two paragraphs of the account that the author mentions the actual silver:

Much of the silver spoon work of the present day is crude in workmanship and thoroughly inconsistent, often entirely meaningless, in design. Our leading silversmiths, however, have of late been giving to us, in a rapid succession of artistic productions, a nearly endless series of chaste and elegant designs. A study of the latest design by the

Gorham Company, which they have appropriately named the Fontainebleau, has suggested to the writer the above reminiscences of the famous French court of the period of Francis the First.

The artist who designed the decorations of the set is a Frenchman, and has very few rivals as a workman. He entered upon the task with enthusiasm, and spent many months in the execution of it. The diffficulties in the way of expressing conceptions on such a common–place article as a spoon or a fork may be imagined, and when we see it successfully, artistically done, we are not slow to recognize the merit of it. Heretofore designers have still further limited their field by making every handle alike, which limitation was probably dictated by mechanical diffficulties, and has now been set aside in order to make room for the variety and extent of expression which good taste demands. Since there are in every pattern over ninety different articles, such as spoons, knives, and forks for various special purposes, ladles and a host of similar pieces, the artist is required to exercise his fancy and ingenuity to a considerable extent in order to depict appropriate scenes. He has taken his cue in "The Fontainebleau" from the feast or dinner service and, as may be seen in the illustration, on the principal pieces he depicts the host and hostess in court dress. On another is the cook with lobster in hand; on another a waiter and soup tureen; another with guitar, typifying music; on another a waiter bearing the roast turkey, and on another a companion bearing a tray of coffee cups, all in the costume of the period. The designing has been done in a truly artistic spirit, and in every detail is faithful to the facts. The execution of the designs is in keeping with their beauty and elegance.

The 1832 catalog also illustrated a three–piece knife, fork, and spoon set in the *Piper* pattern, a child's version of *Fontainebleau*.

Oxidized Backgrounds

Pictorial flatware patterns were always oxidized to bring out the details of the design. The importance of these darkened backgrounds should not be underestimated. One has only to compare *Fontainebleau* pieces with and without the dark oxidized backgrounds to see how much is lost in the latter. Pieces that have had their oxidation removed by too much polishing lose much of their detail.

An 1888 Gorham catalog contained a section on oxidizing:

THE MERITS OF OXIDIZING

The idea which prevails to a certain extent, that oxidizing is a modern invention and one of questionable taste, is

a mistaken one.

The remarkable productions of Cellini and Vechti, and of other eminent chasers, exhibit nothing but oxidized work. Such work must necessarily be oxidized to properly express the intended artistic feeling. The exquisite effects of the chasing tool would be lifeless without it. There must be light and shade, and that is the whole intent and meaning of the process. It must not, however, be applied unintelligently: and hence it is generally done by the chaser, who best knows what degree of light and shade is required to express his thoughts. Any person of ordinary intelligence who will indulge in but a brief examination of some perfectly finished articles oxidized, and then observe the same with the oxidizing removed and the article polished, can scarcely fail to be convinced of the necessity for oxidizing.

We have spoken of its effect on chased work. It is equally applicable to any work which simulates chasing. In spoon ware, for instance, it would, comparatively speaking, be enormously expensive to chase by hand each individual spoon or fork or ladle; and for such work, where many thousands of the same piece must be made, the design is wrought in a die, which in itself is expensive if the design be especially elaborate; but as it is capable of producing in

121 *Medici* (now often called *Old Medici*) serving knife. Length: 10 13/16 in. (27.5 c.). (*The National Museum of American History, Smithsonian Institution*).

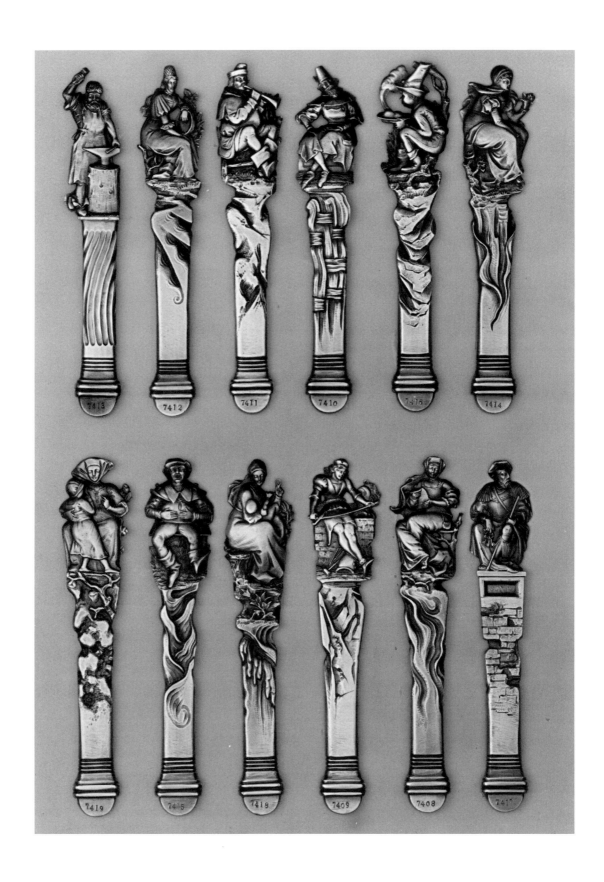

122 Casting patterns for handles of *Nuremburg* dessert knives, ca. 1884. *(Gorham photograph)*

exact facsimile duplicates to any required extent, expense is never spared upon the original, though more than thirty pairs of dies are required for each pattern, in order to make the tea spoons, dessert spoons, table spoons, forks, ladles, knives, etc.

The introduction of the Fontainebleau pattern was a verification of the truth of this assertion. This pattern embraced a series of delicately wrought figures in the costumes of the French court of Fontainebleau. It was immediately followed by the Medici, the figures therein being shown in the Italian court costumes during the time of Lorenzo the Magnificent. These patterns are veritable pictures in silver. Each figure, picturesquely costumed, is enclosed in a panel, while here and there a charming bit of background is shown, making a most effective setting to the original design.

There can be no question about the requisite method of finish. If the artist be instructed to bright finish instead of oxidize, his interest in the work is gone. As well might one ask for a steel engraving of one uniform tint. The result would be an attempt at a picture, not a picture. Light and shade are indispensable to any picture, and equally so in the best examples of chased work.

Oxidizing is also as essential to the best class of cast or molded work. In this respect, the Old Masters pattern is an excellent example. Unlike the Medici, the Fontainebleau, or Cluny, each handle is surmounted with an exquisitely wrought bust of one of the old masters in art, either Michael Angelo, Da Vinci, Raphael, Titian, Rubens, Rembrandt or others, some twenty-five in all.

Another style of decoration, other than chasing or molding, is that of etching. The design is "thrown up," technically speaking, in bas relief, not by embossing, but by action of acid upon the background. The effect is exquisite. Oxidizing is absolutely indispensable to this method of decoration. There would be no life, no spirit, to the work without it.

In conclusion we may add that the process is neither a complicated nor an expensive one. In reality it adds nothing to the cost of the article, and it may be worth noting that table ware oxidized requires little or no labor to keep in order.

About 1883 Gorham came out with two new Heller patterns, *Medici*, inspired by Renaissance Italy (Fig. 121), and *Cluny*, a floral pattern named for the Hotel de Cluny, a museum on the Boulevard St. Germain in Paris. There were different handle designs for the different kinds of flatware pieces for both *Medici* and *Cluny*.

In 1884 and 1885 two more Heller designs were introduced. They were the cast patterns *Old Masters* and *Nuremburg*. Figure 122 shows the original casting patterns for a set of twelve *Nuremburg* dessert knives. The animated and lively sculptured figures are good examples

of Heller's virtuosity. There is even a hint of Art Nouveau in the handle work below some of the figures.

In 1886 *St. Cloud* (Fig. 123) was introduced, *Versailles* in 1888, *Coligni* in 1889 and *Marie Antoinette* in 1891, all of which were deservedly popular patterns.

Possibly Heller's most famous flatware design was *Mythologique,* issued in 1894. *Mythologique* (Fig. 124) featured twenty-four different subjects from mythology. In 1896 the Luxembourg Museum in Paris acquired a set of *Mythologique* flatware. Gorham gave this event wide publicity, saying it was "the only design and execution of a silver flatware pattern that has ever been recognized by any government."[5]

123 St. Cloud ladle, engraved MBW. Length: 13 1/2 in. (34.3 cm.). Mark: lion–anchor–G/STERLING/PAT.1885. *(Burt collection).*

124 Asparagus server, *Mythologique* pattern. Length: 9 1/2 in. (24.1 cm.). Mark: lion–anchor–G/STERLING/COPYRIGHTED 1895. *(Museum of the City of New York)*.

125 Tureen made in 1887 for the 1889 Paris Exposition. No. A185 3. *(Gorham photograph)*.

Academic Hollow Ware

In the late 1880s Heller's academic flatware designs inspired a line of beautifully crafted hollow–ware pieces. The tureen in Figure 125 has its origins in late eighteenth– and early nineteenth–century French and English silver. The details are well orchestrated and the proportions are carefully thought out. The design of this piece involved exactly the same kind of thought processes that were used by McKim, Mead & White when they designed the Henry Villard Houses on Madison Avenue in New York (1882–1886), basing their designs on the Palazzo Cancelleria in Rome. Details were varied, forms adapted, but close attention was paid to the original, whether it involved a building or a piece of silver. This was the true Beaux Arts tradition.

The oyster tureen in Figure 126 is more flamboyant, more exotic than the tureen in Figure 125. It looks both backward and forward in time. One sees some of the energy and wildness of High Victorian, and the undulating forms have in them the seeds of Art Nouveau.

The large terrapin tureen in Figure 127, made in 1890, has precedents in English and French silver, although it is not a common form.[6]

The rococo, repoussé–chased teapot in Figure 128 is related to the silver of the 1850s, particularly with its rustic handle and spout. The crisply chased daisies and

126 Oyster tureen made in 1888. Length: 13 1/2 in. (34.3 cm.). *(Gorham photograph).*

127

127 Terrapin tureen made in 1890. Cast finial, head, and feet. Length: 14 1/2 in. (36.8 cm.). Mark: lion–anchor–G/STERLING/455. *(Private collection).*

128 Teapot, repoussé chased, with the date mark for 1889. Engraved on bottom MLN. Height: 3 1/2 in. (8.9 cm.). Mark: lion–anchor–G/2805. *(The Chrysler Museum in Norfolk).*

128

129 Waiter with repoussé–chased border, made in 1896. Length: 18 in. (45.7 cm.). Mark: No. 21. *(Private collection).*

130 Olive dish, made in 1883. *(Gorham photograph).*

131 Brass kettle and lamp, with iron crane, made in 1886. *(Gorham photograph).*

132 Covered vegetable dish, ca. 1885. *(Gorham photograph).*

roses on the border of the tray in Figure 129 remind us that Rococo was one of the sources of Art Nouveau. The olive dish in Figure 130, made in 1883, is an odd mixture of a classical motif on a chased, Japanese inspired background.

133 Black coffee made in 1888. No. 2846. (*Gorham photograph*).

The Beginnings of Art Nouveau and Modernism

In the 1880s a few simple, geometric objects were beginning to be made in strong contrast with the more highly decorated mainstream wares. The fluted brass kettle with a plain spout in Figure 131, made in 1886, is not related in any way to the Academic designs of Heller.

The wonderful twisting iron crane certainly is in tune with later Art Nouveau objects. The covered vegetable dish in Figure 132 also makes use of fluting as its main decorative device. The clarity and simplicity of the design forecasts the twentieth century.

The black coffee in Figure 133, made in 1888, has a form derived from earlier American and English silver. This type of Colonial Revival silver—using old forms with new decorations—continued a trend that started in the 1870s.

The matchbox in Figure 134, also made in 1888, seems almost pure Art Nouveau with its stylized curves and coils.

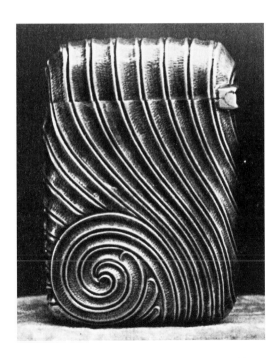

134 Matchbox made in 1888. *(Gorham photograph).*

107

Nicholas Heinzelmarn

One of the interesting sidelights of Gorham history of the 1880s is the story of Nicholas Heinzelman, the ragged tramp who turned out to be a *brilliant silver chaser* (Fig. 135). Heinzelman, without any introduction, was able to get to see Edward Holbrook and pique his interest with some plaster models of his work. Holbrook gave Heinzelman money for clothes and later hired him. Apparently though, the silversmith had been a wanderer too long. He would work for a period and then disappear. After a few years of on–again, off–again, work periods Heinzelman left Gorham for good. He died in New York in 1900.

The romantic story of the eccentric Heinzelman obviously appealed to Edward Holbrook. Later, in 1918, he privately published a lovely little twenty–page monograph on the silversmith, with handmade paper and

135 Shield mounted with chasing tools, hammers, drawing tool, examples of chasing on copper, and photograph of Nicholas Heinzelman. Inscription on plaque: "Nicholas Heinzelman/ silverware chaser/ Born in Switzerland/ April 3, 1837/ came to America/ 1849/ Died/ in New York City/ March 20, 1900 12 30 A.M." Height of shield: 19 in. (48.3 cm.). (*Gorham collection*).

tipped-in illustrations. The account was written by Horace Townsend:

NICHOLAS HEINZELMAN

The Man and The Artist

Somewhat too apt are we to imagine that the fever and the unrest of latter–day business conditions have stifled the free breath of that artistic temperament which seemed so well–nigh universal a heritage when the world was younger and more leisurely. Speaking generally, that is, perhaps, an approximation to the truth, but every once in a while there appears among us some individual spirit who traces back as it were to his predecessors of the Middle Ages.

Such a one was Nicholas Heinzelman, who, born in Switzerland in 1833,[7] journeyed to this country in 1849, and, following his natural bent, developed under the most untoward circumstances into one of the most individually distinguished chasers and modelers this country has ever known.

Of his earlier life in this country but little is known beyond the fact that he learned his trade as a silverchaser in New Orleans and worked for many years in St. Louis. It was not until he had reached his grand climacteric that, in 1885, he attracted the attention of Mr. Edward Holbrook of The Gorham Company.

It was a piece of good fortune for Heinzelman to arouse the interest of one to whom the silversmiths of the United States owe so large a debt of gratitude for consistent encouragement and support. Doubtless it would have been more to the advantage of Heinzelman had this meeting taken place long years before, since, when he did finally make an unforeseen appearance at the Gorham offfices, he had reached a time of life when his habits were formed, and were hardly of a nature to commend the craftsman to the confidence of an average community.

It is therefore to the credit of Mr. Holbrook's perspicacity that, when this unkempt, unshorn and starved–looking foreigner burst upon his privacy one fine late Spring morning more than thirty years ago, he should have recognized the ability that lay beneath so unpromising an exterior. Heinzelman, in lieu of any letter of introduction, presented as his credentials some half dozen models in plaster of Paris, comprising leaves, twigs and spring fruits quite evidently studied direct from nature. Enquiry elicited, not only the fact that the modeler of these exquisite woodland fancies had, as was usually his habit, been spending the spring months in the very heart of the woods, until sheer hunger drove him closer to the haunts of men, but that he was a silverchaser by trade and longed to meet with the opportunity of translating into silver the subtleties of his work in plaster.

Upon that opportunity he had unwittingly stumbled. So impressed was Mr. Holbrook with the possibilities dis–

played in this rare work, that he provided for his caller the means whereby he could obtain the suitable clothing and proper food that were necessary to so build him up that he could undertake some work in silversmithing.

Further than this, some minor articles requiring ornamentation were given to him and he disappeared for a while, to return a new man in outward respects, and bearing with him the fruits of his labours.

So technically admirable were these, so unusual in conception and so beautiful in result that no man having a knowledge as intimate as Mr. Holbrook's of the actual workings of the silversmith's trade could have failed to be impressed. Now The Gorham Company even then was one of the largest and most effficiently administered silver–making establishments in the world, but it had never been allowed to forget, as is supposed to be the case with all great corporations, that it had a soul. This soul, personified by the President, was so stirred by Heinzelman's artistry, it was felt that in the Company's interest his services should be permanently secured. The attention of Mr. George Wilkinson, who was then the Superintendent of the Gorham works, was directed to the unusual quality of Heinzelman's work and talent, and Mr. Wilkinson was requested by Mr. Holbrook to find a place for the craftsman at Providence.

With a man so eccentric and so alien to the world at large as Heinzelman, this was no easy task, but after more than one essay he was finally induced to occupy a room that was set apart for him at the Providence factory and to devote himself to the chasing and decoration of silverware in his own inimitable and individual style.

Here for some years he worked under what appeared to be ideal conditions. Practically unfettered, he was allowed to come and go as he pleased, and for weeks at a time he would disappear from his atelier and wander through the woods of Rhode Island and nearby States. Anything like sustained effort was foreign to his nature, and it is not surprising therefore that his output was exceedingly limited. Occasionally, it is true, he kept at work long enough to finish the chased decoration of a complete tea–service or some ecclesiastical silverware of importance, but as a rule his fits of industry were short, and after the completion of a single small piece he would wander off to saturate himself, as it were, with nature.

Even an appearance of restraint rendered him restive, and so there was but scant opportunity for wonderment when he finally broke away from any settled connection with the firm that had done so much to further his aims, and came to New York to live after his own fashion. For two or three years, The Gorham Company provided him with the means for his modest existence, but of actual accomplishment the remainder of his life was practically barren, and when, in 1890 [sic], the end came, it was found that since his departure from Providence he had done nothing which even approached importance.

Such few examples of Heinzelman's art as are today in existence show that his talent was peculiar to himself and curiously expressive of the man and his pathetic love for the beauties of nature [Fig. 136]. Technically his work as a chaser is unrivalled, while artistically it is of singular merit. So low in relief that it almost falls under the definition of "flat chasing," his intimate knowledge of all growing things enabled him so to define each vein and serration, so to model the swelling curves of his leaves, that they seem to burgeon before our eyes and to carry with them the perfume and savour of the Spring and Summer woods in which he spent so much of his time.

While personally Nicholas Heinzelman was an artist, he was more of a Bohemian in the truest sense of that much abused word. He loved rather to live with nature than to produce the beautiful things of which his inborn talent rendered him capable. What would have been the outcome had he met with Mr. Holbrook and The Gorham Company earlier in his life it is impossible to say, since, as we have seen, that meeting took place when his mode of living was irretrievably settled and his errant tendencies had become an integral part of his nature.

Perhaps for the man himself it was better that this should be so; perhaps he was happier moulding his life in his own way; working not for money but for the love of his art, and, for the rest, living as it best suited him and enjoying the world and nature in his own Bohemian fashion.[8]

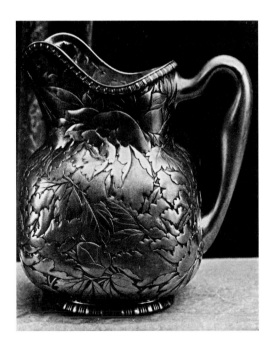

136 Pitcher, chased by Nicholas Heinzelman, made in 1887. No. 1535. Height: 7 7/16 in. (18.9 cm.). (*Gorham photograph*).

Gorham Catalogs and Books

In the 1880s, under the aegis of Edward Holbrook, Gorham embarked on an extensive publication program of annual catalogs and, later, books.

The earliest catalog in the present–day Gorham library is dated autumn 1881. This catalog refers to a spring 1881 edition. There are suggestions that Gorham may have published catalog literature as early as the 1860s but copies have not been located.

The sumptuous, beautifully illustrated catalogs of the 1880s and 1890s were available in paperback editions plus leather–bound copies for special customers. The catalogs did not contain price lists, which were available separately. These catalogs became annual events of some importance, which were fully reviewed in such trade publications as *The Jewelers' Circular*.

In the latter part of the nineteenth and first part of the twentieth century the Gorham Company sponsored the first of a series of scholarly and popular books and booklets on silver and related subjects. The first of these was *Old Plate, Ecclesiastical, Decorative and Domestic; Its Makers and Marks* by J. H. Buck, published by Gorham in 1888, a true landmark in the history of American silver. The 268–page book was the first serious attempt to classify American silver forms, their makers and the marks. In 1903 an expanded second edition of *Old Plate* was published.

The two editions of Buck's *Old Plate* were pioneering efforts which were true predecessors of the whole literature of American silver. Buck, a sound scholar working virtually alone, gave form and substance to the study of American silver. That Gorham should have sponsored such a scholarly work is most interesting, suggesting a remarkably enlightened point of view for the time.

The size, subject matter, and intent of the Gorham publications other than catalogs varied considerably in the late nineteenth and early twentieth centuries. Two books on souvenir spoons, published in 1891, are among the best of the primary sources in that field: *Souvenir Spoons of America* and *Souvenir Spoons*, the latter compiled by George B. James (see Chapter 10),

Several pamphlets with photographs celebrated the new Gorham plant in Elmwood which was finished in 1890. Elaborate brochures were printed for the international expositions in which Gorham participated, particularly for Chicago in 1893 and Paris in 1900.

A charming book, bound in soft, velvety fawn–colored suede leather published in the 1890s is titled *Woman's Work at the Gorham Manufacturing Company* (no date). The first paragraph reads:

Employment adapted to women in the silverware establishment of the Gorham Manufacturing Co., at Providence, R.I., is confined to a comparatively few of the numerous departments of the works; such as the Case Room, where in their work consists in lining the cases with satin or other suitable material, or blocking, or other incidental operations: in the Etching Department, and also in the Photograph rooms. It is believed that a much better idea of the several processes can be obtained from the series of photographic illustrations, than any mere word description could convey (see Fig. 231).

A sampling of the dozens of pamphlets published include the following titles:

The Story of Columbus in Pictures of Silver, 1893
Bronzes and Bronze Castings, 1899
The Art of the Silversmith and Its Development (ca. 1910)
Some Famous Silversmiths and Their Marks, 1915
Nicholas Heinzelman, The Man and the Artist, 1918

Gorham published a number of miniature books (average size 4 1/2 x 3 inches), most of which were illustrated:

Cocktails—How to Make Them, 1898
The Bumper Book, A Collection of Toasts, 1899
The Art of Carving, 1899
The Gorham Golf Book, 1903
The Gorham Chafing Dish Book, 1905
An Elementary Manual of Heraldry, 1905
Sterling Silver Toys—What They Are, 1907
The Gorham Sandwich Book, 1908
The Gorham Book of Salads, 1917
The Gorham Book of Beverages, 1919

The Rise of Edward Holbrook

Edward Holbrook, who was born in 1849, joined Gorham in New York in 1870. He was elected agent of the company in charge of New York sales, in 1876, at the age of twenty–seven. At twenty–eight, as noted in Chapter 5, Holbrook was the highest paid man in the company, making more than the president and the veteran George Wilkinson who was in charge of the plant and design.

Holbrook, who became known for his salesmanship and brilliant sense of business, was a young man in a hurry. One of his first moves on becoming agent in 1876 was to go deeply in debt to the company to buy stock. To have committed himself to buy stock valued at $59,000 when his salary was $7500 per year was indeed an act of faith. By 1880 he had paid off his debt and had begun to acquire more stock. It is not known how he financed these stock purchases, but by the end of 1882 there were 341 shares of stock registered in his name. By 1888 he had absolute control of Gorham.

Holbrook was elected a director of the company in 1882. In 1888 he was elected treasurer. It was not until 1894, when William Crins was seventy–five, that Holbrook finally took on the presidency.

Holbrook continued to live in New York throughout his long career with Gorham. He was quite satisfied to have others run the day–to–day operations of the company in Providence.

The man he depended on most during the eighties and nineties was William Crins, the Providence businessman who was brought in as president in 1878 to replace John Gorham.

The decade of the eighties was one of great expansion for Gorham. Sales rebounded from the 1878 low of $521,000 and grew steadily to almost three million dollars by 1890. In the late 1880s it became obvious that a new manufacturing facility would have to be built. Property was purchased in the Elmwood section of Providence and plans were made to build the largest and most modern plant in the world for fine silverwares.

A few years before the company had moved into a new headquarters building in New York at Broadway and Nineteenth Street. The 1884 Gorham catalog quoted a description of the building from *The New York Mail*:

Ranking among the palatial business houses that have been erected in this city within the past year is the edifice of the GORHAM Mf'g COMPANY, situated at the north–west corner of Broadway and Nineteenth Street. The building, which is brick and terra–cotta trimmings, is built in the Old Dutch style of architecture. It stands very high and has a frontage of 55 feet on Broadway and 120 feet on Nineteenth Street. Seen from Union Square, with its oddly–shaped tower of clay, casting long shadows on the buildings beneath, the scene is highly suggestive of old Antwerp. There are eight stories in the building, three of which are devoted to the business of the Gorham Company alone.

The Gorham building was owned by Robert Goelet, the New York financier.

The Diaries of William Crins

Personal diaries kept by William Crins (Fig. 137) during his later years give a series of fascinating insights into the Gorham Company in the late 1880s and the 1890s.[9] The daily entries are brief, usually starting with a note

on the weather, in the maritime, ship–log tradition. He records mainly business events, with an occasional mention of his family. It is a very private diary. It gives a view of the inner workings of top management of a great nineteenth–century company that sounds surprisingly contemporary.

In the diaries Mr. Crins comes through as a sincere, orderly, and well–organized, hardworking, demanding executive. It is the diary of a professional manager, a generalist, who seemed little involved with the actual products made by the company. He never mentions silver once in the diaries.

Mr. Crins was sixty–nine years old in 1888 when Edward Holbrook gained control of Gorham. Crins thought it was only a matter of time before Holbrook would take over the president's job:

Feb. 6, 1888: Mr. Holbrook here from New York. The Annual Company Meeting takes place on the 8th. The slate is being made up and it remains to be seen whether I resign or serve another year.

Mr. Crins was not only renamed president of Gorham for 1888, he was to hold the position for six more years. Holbrook took on the job of treasurer in 1888 but he was quite content to have Mr. Crins continue as president.

Crins and Holbrook were close. They saw each other almost on a weekly basis and they carried on an extensive correspondence. Holbrook continued to live in New York and he needed Crins in Providence. Plans for the new plant at Elmwood were under way and Holbrook wanted Crins to be in charge of its construction. Perhaps the obvious choice for this job would have been George Wilkinson, the plant superintendent, but Holbrook picked Crins. We have no record of Holbrook's candid opinion of Wilkinson as an executive, but from Crin's diaries we have a very clear idea of what he thought of Wilkinson.

After a May visit of Holbrook, Crins wrote: "GW has been stirred up with a sharp stick by Holbrook" [May 2, 1888].

On May 19, 1888, the board decided to go ahead with the construction of the new plant:

Board Meeting in the forenoon and after a full discussion on the plans for a new building. Plan #14 was adopted. It was voted to put them in train for construction and empowering me to make contracts which means much hard work for me.

137 William Crins, president of Gorham 1878–1894. From a photograph of about 1900.

The next week Crins and his wife went to New York to see the Holbrook family off to Europe. The complex job of building a new plant was a major undertaking. The plant was to be by far the largest operation in the world for making fine silverwares. In addition to the facilities for making sterling flatware, hollow ware, and electroplated wares, there was to be a large bronze foundry.

The new plant was not Crins's only responsibility. He still had to deal with the antiquated facilities on Steeple Street (Fig. 138) and George Wilkinson. If we are to believe Crins, Wilkinson was neglecting his job. He felt Wilkinson was "goofing off." He documents his case often in 1888 and 1889:

Wilkinson left for a pleasure trip of as I understand some two weeks [May 26, 1888—three days after Holbrook left for Europe].

Letter from Mr. Houghton saying Wilkinson had arrived in New York and would be here Thursday. Hard time this Englishman has of it [June 13, 1888].

Crins felt he was carrying the whole burden of the company on his shoulders:

Uncommonly quiet at the office today. Nothing doing. All away. Myself being the only one to remain on duty [Saturday, July 14, 1888].

Wilkinson's frequent absences irked Crins:

Mr. W. not in this afternoon [August 1, 1888]. Mr. W. not in much today. Not at all in afternoon [August 2, 1888]. Mr. Wilkinson out most of day [August 8, 1888]. Holbrook

138 The Gorham plant on Steeple Street in Providence, Rhode Island. From a photograph of about 1885.

here. Wilkinson put in an appearance this morning after an absence of 7 days on a lark [Oct. 4, 1888]. Wilkinson went to New York on 11 AM train ostensibly for business but really for a good time generally. How this man humbugs the Corporation and hoodwinks Holbrook [Jan. 11, 1889].

Feb. 14, 1839: Reception at Art Club this evening. Gorham Mfg. Co. display of art bric a brac. Feb. 15, 1889: Wilkinson would make people think the Exhibit at the Gallery was the emination of his own efforts which is all bosh, Bosh. March 28, 1889: Went to the Corliss Engine Works and completed contract for engine and boiler for new works which involves a large amount of money. This man Wilkinson has annoyed me excessively today by his devilishness. At times it becomes unbearable.

This is only a sampling of Crins complaints about Wilkinson. The responsibilities and pressures of building the new plant weighed heavily on Crins and his tolerance level was very low for anyone such as Wilkinson who he thought was not working as hard as he did. Holbrook's liberal use of money for promotional purposes ran against the grain of the careful William Crins:

At the Board Meeting it was voted to exhibit our wares at the 1889 Paris Exposition at the expense of some thirty thousand dollars which I should think was ample [Dec. 14, 1888].

The 1890–1893 diaries are missing. By 1894 Crins, who was seventy–five, was ready to retire. Wilkinson was not well. There was a recession going on and men had been laid off at the plant.

January 14, 1894: Pleasant and moderate Down street a short time this AM. Called on another destitute family, one of our employees who was laid off in August.

The next day Crins "visited another destitute family."

January 18, 1894: Have written my resignation today and shall present it to the Board of Directors next week when they meet.

Holbrook was named president on January 25, 1894. He continued to commute from New York. Crins stayed on until December doing what he had done for the last

113

fifteen years. On December 5 he left:

> This is the last day I shall be here for a long time. This afternoon has been rather trying although pleasant. The expressions from the men at the factory of the regard they had for me and the feeling of esteem.

For the next four months Mr. Crins was in California. Soon after he left for California, on December 28th, 1894, George Wilkinson, his old foe, died. The Providence Telegram featured the story on page one with the headlines:

> "SILVER KING"
>
> SUDDEN DEATH OF THE WORLD'S
> GREATEST SILVER WORKER
> THIS MORNING.
> GORHAM SUPERINTENDENT,
> GEORGE WILKINSON, WAS TO
> THE SILVER INDUSTRY WHAT
> WEDGEWOOD WAS TO POTERY

On April 10, 1895, William Crins returned from his California visit. He was back in his office at Gorham the next day. He seems to have gone back to work as if nothing had happened. He was still Edward Holbrook's man in Providence. They consulted often and carried on a regular correspondence, but the schedule was more relaxed and each year Crins spent less time in the plant.

William Crins died on May 20, 1904, at the age of eighty–five.

Scattered entries in the diaries of William Crins mention John Gorham. These entries suggest Gorham was in real financial need in the last years of his life:

> October 26, 1895: Letter this morning from Mr Holbrook in regard to Mr. Gorham's condition financially.

> October 28, 1895: Wrote Mr. Holbrook regarding Mr. Gorham.

> October 29, 1895: William Thurber was in to see me about Mr. Gorham.

> October 31, 1895: Mr. Holbrook here today. A long talk with him regarding Mr. Gorham's necessities.

> January 25, 1896: Wrote Mr. Gorham at New York.

> June 27, 1898: News of John Gorham's death. He died the 26th in southern Pennsylvania where he had lived this winter.

On the next day, June 28, 1898, Mr. Crins's old friend, Charles Carpenter (no relation to the author) died. Carpenter had originally owned the Elmwood property on which the Gorham plant was built. His name is mentioned many times in Crins's diaries. On July 1, 1898, Mr. Crins attended the funerals of both John Gorham and Charles Carpenter.

CHAPTER 8

The Bronzes

Small bronzes were made by Gorham as early as 1860 (see Chapter 4). However, at the time of this writing none of these early bronzes have been identified. The real birth of the bronze business at Gorham came in the 1880s. It developed naturally out of their ecclesiastical line. The making and selling of silver chalices, patens, cups, and crosses opened up a whole new field for the company. It was a logical next step to make bronze objects for churches: lecterns, altar rails, doors, crucifixes, and sculptures of Christ and the saints. Technically, bronze casting is not too different from silver casting, except, of course, in the matter of scale. Incidentally, it is said that Gorham's first bronze casters came from France, where the state of the art had reached a high level in the nineteenth century. French bronzes were widely famed for their quality. Edward Holbrook may well have made arrangements to hire French foundrymen on one or more of his annual European trips.

A separate ecclesiastical department was organized in about 1885 to make objects in silver, gold, bronze, stone, and wood for churches and related institutions. This department saw a rapid expansion in the 1890s and the early part of the twentieth century. This was one of the great church–building eras in the United States, and there was a continuing demand for high quality ecclesiastical objects.

The founding of the new department created the demand for a designer. Gothic was *the* style for ecclesiastical wares, and the obvious place to look for a designer was in England, where the Gothic Revival had been in full swing for several decades. In 1887 Edward Holbrook, on his annual European tour, met William C. Codman, who was touted as a "master of the Gothic," and his son, William Codman, who was working in the ecclesiastical field. Holbrook hired young Codman to come to Gorham to head up the ecclesiastical department of the company. His father, William C. Codman, came to Gorham four years later, in 1891 (Chapter 11).

In 1885 Gorham made their first large, nonecclesiastical sculpture. The sculptor Frederick Kohlhagen had been commissioned to create a Civil War memorial for the battlefield at Gettysburg, Pennsylvania. When his model, *The Skirmisher* (not illustrated), was finished, Kohlhagen approached Gorham to see if they were interested in casting it in bronze. Up until that time it had been standard practice to have large bronzes, "heroics," cast in Europe. Gorham successfully tackled the job.

When the bronze was unveiled and dedicated at Gettysburg it created widespread interest. Years had passed since the Civil War had ended but the unveiling of *The Skirmisher*, which became known as "Johnny Stoneface," set off a chain reaction. Suddenly, towns and

139 Gorham bronzes, about 1892. *(Gorham photograph).*

villages began ordering "Johnny Stonefaces" and other Civil War bronze statuary.

Figure 139 is a photograph taken about 1892 of a Gorham storage room. Most of the bronzes, with the exception of the two plaques (center and left–center), are ecclesiastical pieces. The plaque in the center of Figure 139 is now at the entrance of the Gorham Company plant office in Providence. On the plaque is a symbolic figure of the Arts and the lion–anchor–G house mark of Gorham. It is thought to have been designed and modeled by Antoine Heller. Three large bronze lecterns are visible in Figure 139. In the center, between the two eagle lecterns, is a large lectern of a winged angel holding a Bible on her shoulders. Replicas of this seven–foot–eight–inch angel lectern are in the Church of All Angels in New York, and the Trinity Episcopal Church in Chicago. The Trinity replica was in Gorham's exhibit at the 1893 Columbian Exposition. This lectern was a popular item for several decades. The 1916 Gorham

catalog listed its price at $2000.

In addition to the large bronzes, Gorham also sold a variety of small ecclesiastical items such as the hexagonal altar vase in Figure 140 made about 1906.

The Making of Bronzes

The making of bronzes at Gorham, even today, is a process that has changed little in its essential features since ancient times. There have, of course, been technological improvements, but bronzes are still made in a one–at–a–time, nonassembly line fashion.

There are three main steps in the making of a bronze:

1. The casting. This may involve either sand casting or the traditional lost–wax process.
2. Finishing the bronze casting. The bronze, as it comes from the foundry, bears little resemblence to what it will look like in its finished state. Attached to the

about 1800° F. The metal is heated to 2050° to 2200° F. for pouring. The higher temperatures are used to make small pieces, and lower temperatures are used in the pouring of large bronzes. The heavier the bronze, the cooler the temperature.

Two principal methods are employed in the actual casting of bronzes. The oldest, known as the cire perdue or lost–wax process, may be thus briefly described: A central and removable core, composed generally of clay, is built up to the rude outline of the work to be cast, but somewhat smaller than the cast. This core, carefully dried and baked, is overlaid with modeling wax, which is then worked by the sculptor to the form desired in the finished sculpture. Molds can also be used to shape the wax form. On this wax model another mold of clay or plaster (or both mixed together) is laid, and the whole is dried and heated, which melts the wax. The melted wax runs out from between the core and the outer mold, which are attached to each other by rods, through suitable channels provided at the bottom for the purpose. The cavity left by the wax then is filled with molten bronze. After cooling the mold is taken away and extraneous metal is then removed from the sculpture, the surface cleaned and chased to sharpen details, and finally the surface is chemically colored.

In the second method the mold is made from a well–packed, fine, claylike sand enclosed in a form called a flask. Originally, French sand, a natural product imported from France, was used. Today synthetic sands are used. The form is divided into as many parts as may be necessary for removal of the pattern. Usually two forms, or flasks, are sufficient. The top half of the mold is called a cope. The bottom half of the mold is called a drag. For large pieces a middle mold, or cheek, is sometimes required. After the original pattern is packed with sand on all sides, the molds are separated and the pattern removed. The hollow space left is in the exact shape of the sculpture to be made. However, the mold is not ready for casting unless a *solid* casting is desired. A core is needed to produce a hollow sculpture which is desired because a solid statue would be too heavy.

A core is made by ramming sand into the newly made mold after the pattern has been removed. The mold is once more taken apart, the core removed, and a thickness of sand corresponding to the thickness of metal required in the finished casting is shaved from the surface of the core. The core is then returned to place, where it is supported on suitable bronze bars. The remaining parts of the mold are assembled in place surrounding the core, leaving perhaps a space of a quarter of an inch. Molten bronze is then poured into the free spaces, forming the

140 Altar vase made in 1906. Engraved on the bottom: "Gift of St. Margaret's Society/ Easter 1906." Height: 10 in. (25.4 cm.). Mark: No. *33*. *(The Margaret Woodbury Strong Museum, Rochester, N. Y.)*.

bronze is the gating system and vents and risers used in the making through which the molten metal has been poured.[1] This extraneous metal must be trimmed off. The casting is then chased to make it look as much as possible like the original

3. Coloring or patination, the making of an oxidized, colored, decorative surface on the bronze. Patinas range from blacks and browns to greens and blues.

There are a number of copper–based alloys which can be classified as bronzes. These range from bell metal with 80 percent copper and 20 percent tin, to statuary bronzes of 88 percent copper, 8 percent tin and 4 percent zinc, to more complex silicon bronzes and manganese bronzes. Brass is also a copper alloy, with zinc being the principal alloying element.

The 88–8–4 statuary bronze has a melting point of

141 Chasers finishing the bronze casting of the *Marquette Memorial* by Herman Atkins MacNeil. *(Gorham photograph).*

sculpture. After cooling the mold is removed and the casting is cleaned and finished in the same manner as in the lost–wax process.

Part of the core is frequently left inside the finished sculpture, it not being possible to get it all out. This is one of the reasons why different castings of a duplicate series will vary in weight. The other reason for variances in weight is the wall thickness of the casting. For example, a series of castings of Dallin's twenty–two–inch *The Protest* averaged around forty–five pounds per cast, although the weights of the individual castings ranged from 37 1/4 pounds to 52 3/4 pounds. Of course all the castings look identical.

The first part of the second phase of the making process of a bronze, the trimming off of the gates and risers, begins to reveal the true form of the sculpture. The second part of this phase, the chasing, requires a considerable level of skill. Figure 141 shows chasers at work cleaning the surface and sharpening the details of a huge bronze casting, the *Marquette Memorial* by Herman A. MacNeil.

The natural patinas, the greens, the blues, and the browns and blacks, are oxide films that are achieved only after several decades of outdoor exposure.

Artificial patinas can be produced by treating the surface of the bronze with acids and other chemicals, either cold or with a flame, thus the names *patine à froid* and *patine au feu*.

The making of artificial patinas is definitely an art. The color and quality of the final finish of a bronze is very much a function of the knowledge and skill of the craftsman. The quality of the bronze metal is also important. For a good patina, a good, sound, homogeneous bronze casting is essential.

The cold process, *patine à froid,* involves wetting the surface many times with such chemicals as copper sulfate, ferrous sulfate, copper carbonate, salt, ammonia, etc. Sometimes the treated bronze is buried in humid soil for ten to fifteen days.

In the fire process, *patine au feu,* the solutions of chemicals are applied with a brush and caused to react with the base bronze, typically with the flame of a gas torch. The operation may have to be repeated several times before the desired color and finish is obtained. The fire process can produce shiny surfaces; those by the cold process do not shine on completion. The latter can be left mat or given a gloss if so desired.[2]

The Bronze of Houdon's George Washington

Since Frederick Kohlhagen's "Johnny Stoneface" was unveiled at Gettysburg, Gorham has seen hundreds of their large bronze statues installed in public places— all over the United States, and in foreign countries from Iceland to Argentina. Some of these bronzes are truly heroic in size, such as the *Marquette Memorial* group in Figure 141, now in Chicago. A list of some of the better–known bronze sculptures cast by Gorham is shown in Appendix III.

One of the most visible of all of the Gorham bronzes is the cast of *George Washington* in the Rotunda of the Capitol of the United States in Washington (Fig. 142). This cast is a copy of the celebrated marble sculpture by Jean Antoine Houdon (1741–1828) which has been in the quadrangle or rotunda of the statehouse in Richmond, Virginia, since 1796. This sculpture is not only one of the true icons of American history, it is also one of the great art masterpieces in America.

The story of the original sculpting of Houdon's *Washington* and its several copies is worth recounting.

In 1784, soon after the close of the American Revolution, the State of Virginia decreed a statue of George Washington, authorizing Thomas Jefferson, who was then in Paris, to secure the artist and arrange for a statue "to be of the finest marble and the best workmanship."[3] Jefferson was able to interest Houdon, the leading sculptor in France, to consider the job. Arrangements were made for the artist and three assistants to come to America and visit Washington at Mr. Vernon. Houdon crossed the Atlantic in the company of Benjamin Franklin. Houdon arrived at Mt. Vernon on October 3, 1785, and remained with Washington a fortnight. He took a plaster cast of Washington's face, head, and upper parts of his body, and made minute measurements. As an additional help to Houdon, Governor Harrison of Virginia had Charles Willson Peale paint for him "a full length picture."

Washington was consulted about the costume. It was an age when the great were cloaked in Roman garb in their public statues. In a letter to Mr. Jefferson he stated his preference *(very* diplomatically): "I shall be perfectly satisfied with whatever may be judged decent and proper. I should even scarcely have ventured to suggest that perhaps a servile adherence to the garb of antiquity might not be altogether so expedient as some little deviation

142 Bronze cast of *George Washington* made in 1909 by the Gorham Company, in the United States Capitol Rotunda. Height of statue: 74 1/2 in. (189 cm.). Height of pedestal: 51 in. (130 cm.). *(Photograph courtesy the Architect of the Capitol)*

in favor of the modern costume, if I had not heard from Colonel Humpherys that this was a circumstance hinted in conversation by Mr. West to Mr. Houdon."

It was more than ten years later that Houdon's *Washington* was unveiled, in 1796, three years before the great patriot's death.

A word about the symbolism of the sculpture: The erect column of thirteen rods, one for each of the original states, has Washington's military cloak thrown over its top, and his left hand resting thereon, while the column itself stands on the moldboard of a plow. The Roman fasces was a bundle of rods with an ax in its midst, carried by the lectors in front of the chief magistrate as symbolizing the administrative power of the state. The sword hangs on this column, now put aside after serving its purpose. The plow supporting the column means not only that Washington was a farmer, but that agriculture is the source of our national strength. The epaulets are reminders of Washington as commander in chief of the armies of the Revolution. The cane, instead of the sword, in his right hand asserts civil authority over the military in times of peace.

In 1853 William J. Hubard, a Richmond, Virginia, sculptor, was allowed to make casts of the Houdon statue of Washington. Six bronzes and one whitewashed plaster were cast. The molds made by Hubard were destroyed during the Civil War. There was apparently some discoloration of the original marble resulting from Hubard's work. At any rate, the State of Virginia gave no more permissions to copy the Houdon marble during the remainder of the nineteenth century.

In 1909, in order to make a bronze copy of Houdon's *Washington* for the Rotunda of the Capitol in Washington D.C., the Gorham Company was authorized to make a cast.

The bronze of Washington was delivered in 1901, but it was not until May, 1932, that the United States Congress finally got around to accepting it officially. It was unveiled in the Capitol Rotunda on May 18, 1934.

At the time of this writing Gorham has made fourteen casts of Houdon's *Washington*.

Abraham Lincoln was the subject of many sculptures. Gutzon Borglum's *Seated Lincoln* (Fig. 143) is certainly one of the best. It is a quiet, introspective Lincoln that we are shown, a Lincoln of great strength and character. Figure 143 is a smaller version of a life-sized sculpture in Newark, New Jersey.

Gutzon Borglum, who is no doubt best known for his giant Mt. Rushmore carvings in South Dakota of Washington, Jefferson, Lincoln, and Theodore Roosevelt,

cast a number of bronzes at Gorham. When one of the largest, the equestrian statue of General Philip Sheridan, now in Washington, D.C., was finished, Borglum gave a dinner for the Gorham workmen. The invitation read:

YOU ARE INVITED TO ATTEND A DINNER
IN THE GORHAM CASINO
ON THURSDAY, DECEMBER 17TH, 1908,
AT 8 O'CLOCK
COMPLIMENTS OF MR. GUTZON
BORGLUM
TO THE EMPLOYEES OF
THE STATUARY FOUNDRY
IN RECOGNITION OF THE
FAITHFUL SERVICES IN CASTING AND
FINISHING THE SHERIDAN STATUE

The Independent Man

A sculpture well known in Rhode Island is the twelve-foot figure atop the statehouse in Providence. It was commissioned by the architects of the new statehouse building, McKim, Mead & White. The sculptor, George T. Brewster, modeled a young man clad only in a loincloth with a spear in his right hand, and holding in his left hand an anchor, the symbol of Rhode Island since 1647 (Fig. 144). Gorham cast the 900-pound sculpture in the summer of 1899, and it was installed without fanfare the same year. The sculpture was raised to its 100-foot perch atop the statehouse dome by a huge derrick supported by platforms located around the dome. At the top of the dome was a platform of heavy timbers

143 Bronze of *Seated Lincoln* by Gutzon Borglum (1871–1941). Dimensions: 22 x 28 3/4 x 16 3/4 in. (55.9 x 71.1 x 42.5 cm.). *(The Newark Museum)*.

144 The "Independent Man" atop the statehouse, Providence, Rhode Island. *(Photograth courtesy Rhode Island Department of Economic Development).*

until stopped by a court order against its being displayed in such a commercial manner. It was put on display in the statehouse rotunda and more than 60,000 people came to see it during a six–month period.

The Independent Man was put back in place by a helicopter. The first attempt failed because of high winds, but on July 19, 1976, it arrived safely back home.[4]

One of the more dramatic of the Gorham bronzes is the *Gloucester Fisherman* now set in a public square in Gloucester, Massachussetts (Fig. 145). With the ship's wheel gripped fast in his competent hands, feet spread apart to take the roll and heave of a straining deck, and a watchful eye, presumably on the mainsheet hauled to its limit, the bronze fisherman typifies those hardy men who go down to the sea in ships. One can almost hear the shriek of the wind.

The *Gloucester Fisherman* was sculpted by Leonard Craske about 1923. When Craske was modeling the sta-

145 The *Gloucester Fisherman,* Gloucester, Massachusetts.

supported by a trestle work of hard pine. The uprights stood on the gallery at the base of the dome, and the derrick boom was fastened to one of these uprights. When the sculpture reached its perch it was bolted in place through a hole in the top of the dome.

Brewster had given the sculpture the Rhode Island name of *Hope,* but it soon became known as the "Independent Man." The sculptor was paid $3000 for his work and the Gorham Company received $2000 for casting the statue in bronze.

In 1927, the "Independent Man" was struck by lightning (in his "stomach") and nearly knocked off its perch. Forty–two small metal "stitches" were required to close the wound. These repairs were rather unsightly, but were not noticeable on top the statehouse. Although the statue had a lightning arrester attached to it, it was damaged again in 1953, and had to be welded.

In 1975 the statue was taken down from its perch on the dome for a general refurbishing. The old "stitches" were removed, the break welded, and the figure was re–gilded. It was shown for two weeks in the Warwick Mall

tue he had a young assistant whose ambition was to be a sculptor. Craske let him help. Behind the wheelhousing there are two small–letter lines of doggerel:

This being a place no one can see
Was modeled by Jimmy and not by me[5]

The Gloucester Fisherman monument is the site of an annual memorial service for fishermen lost at sea. The service in 1925, the year the monument was dedicated, was particularly poignant. Two Gloucester fishing schooners had been sunk by ocean liners and thirty seamen had been lost. After the memorial services at the monument flowers were carried to the nearby Blyman bridge and cast in the waters where they were carried out to sea.

Art Bronzes

In the period from about 1915 to 1940 Gorham produced a considerable number of bronzes, ranging in size from a few inches to five or six feet, which were designed for the home and the garden. A handsome book published by Gorham in 1928, *Famous Small Bronzes,* illustrates forty–eight sculptures with brief descriptions. Most of the artists in the group were conservative, academic sculptors. A number were quite well known, such as Gutzon Borglum, Cyrus Dallin, Harriet Frishmuth, Emil Fuchs, Anna Hyatt Huntington, Alexander Procter, and Mahonri Young. In addition to larger bronzes, there were small coffee–table sculptures, flower holders, fountains, bookends, and automobile hood ornaments.

Figure 146 shows a casting of Cyrus E. Dallin's *Appeal to the Great Spirit,* which is part of a series of four equestrian statues depicting the saga of the American Indian, sometimes called the Epic Series, a group of sculptures that gave Dallin a permanent place in the history of the art of the American West. Dallin is often grouped with Frederic Remington and Charles M. Russell as pioneers of Western sculpture. Russell, and particularly Remington, were more concerned with action and drama, and their sculptures were more detailed and naturalistic. Dallin's sculptures were simpler, more monumental, more introspective. They were also fiercely partisan on the side of the Indians.

Dallin was born in 1861 in a log cabin in the newly founded settlement of Springville, Utah, about fifty milessouth of Salt Lake City. Young Dallin grew up near a tribe of friendly Ute Indians. He grew to respect and love the Indians:

Those Indians whom I knew were not reservation Indians, by the way. They were a free people, proud of their heritage and their race, at liberty to come and go as they chose....

They had a culture and refinement that was lacking in our settlement inside the adobe wall—as a matter of fact, the cowboys with their bluster and horseplay frightened me as a child; it was always a treat to visit my little Indian companions in the homes of their parents. They had a civilization that was in many ways superior to ours. For instance, I never saw an Indian child given corporal punishment. I never heard an Indian child shrill and impudent to its parents. Respect for their elders was inbred in the young Indians; and when a rebuke was administered, it was done in a quiet, instructive way.[6]

In 1881 Dallin went to Boston to study with Truman Bartlett, a sculptor. In 1888 Dallin went to Paris, and in 1889 he completed his clay model, *The Signal of Peace,* the first of the series on the American Indian. *The Signal of Peace,* showing an Indian offering friendship and goodwill to the white man, was exhibited at the 1890 Paris Salon and in 1893 at the Chicago Columbian Exposi–

146 *Appeal to the Great Spirit*, by Cyrus Dallin. Height: 21.5 in. (54.6 cm.). (*Gorham photograph*).

tion. It was installed in Lincoln Park in Chicago in 1894.

In 1898 Dallin, back in Paris after stints in Boston and Philadelphia, sculpted the second of his Indian series, *The Medicine Man*. The statue won a gold medal at the 1900 Paris Exposition and was widely acclaimed. In this sculpture the medicine man warns his people of the coming danger of the white man who was beginning to overrun his lands. The man *and* the horse are vigilant and expectant.

The third sculpture of the series, *The Protest* (1904), shows an angry Indian with a clenched fist, defiant against the onrush of the white man. In the last of the series, *Appeal to the Great Spirit* (1909), the Indian is defeated, and he can only appeal to his God for help (Fig. 146). The original casting of *Appeal to the Great Spirit* is in front of the Museum of Fine Arts in Boston.

Although Dallin's saga specifically illustrated the poignant downfall of the American Indian, his work has a universal quality that has appealed to generations of thoughtful people. Dallin's Indian is defeated but he remains a proud and disturbing figure—a figure that still prods and pricks our conscience.

In 1916 Dallin made an agreement with the Gorham Company to produce in collector's sizes the four statues of his Indian Epic series plus two other Indian equestrian sculptures, *The Scout* and *On the Warpath*. Over a four-year period Dallin and the Gorham workers produced seven master patterns for sculptures. The patterns were made in pieces, the horse loose from the base, and the other parts, such as the arms and horsetails, detached but precisely positioned by means of Roman joints. Bronzes were cast from the master patterns until Dallin's death in 1944. After that they were stored until 1977, when an agreement was made with Lawrence Dallin and Ruth M. Dallin, Cyrus Dallin's heirs, to complete the edition of Dallin's seven equestrian statues:

The Signal of Peace, 32 in. (81.5 cm.). Signed and dated: © C. E. Dallin 1890. Inscribed on rear of base: Gorham Founders QBMV (sequence numbers). Edition: 40, Nos. 1–4 cast between 1921–1944.

The Medicine Man, 16 in. (40.5 cm.). Signed and dated: C. E. Dallin 1899 ©. Inscribed on rear of base: Gorham Founders QALG (sequence number). Edition 41, Nos. 1–5 cast between 1918–1944.

The Protest, 20.5 in. (52 cm.). Signed: C. E. Dallin ©. Inscribed on rear of base: Gorham Founders QALF (sequence numbers). Edition: 46, Nos. 1–10 cast between 1918–1947.

Appeal to the Great Spirit, 21.5 in. (54.5 cm.). Signed and dated: © C. E. Dallin 1913. Inscribed on rear of base: Gorham Founders QPN (sequence numbers). Edition 143, Nos. 1–107 cast between 1916–1944.

The Scout, 36 in. (91.5 cm.). Signed and dated: C. E. D. 1910. On side of base: Copyright 1912 C. E. Dallin. Inscribed on rear of base: Gorham Founders QALH (sequence number). Edition: 43, nos. 1–7 cast between 1916–1944.

The Scout, 22 in. (56 cm.). Signed and dated: C. E. D. 1910. Inscribed on rear of base: Gorham Founders Q488 (sequence number). Edition: 80, Nos. 1–44 cast between 1917–1945

On the Warpath, 22.5 in. (57 cm.). Signed: C. E. Dallin. Inscribed on rear of base: Gorham Founders Q490 (sequence numbers). Edition: 53, nos. 1–17 cast between 1817–1947.[7]

In the Gorham brochure, *The Epic of the Indian,* it is stated that all of these bronzes, whether made during Dallin's lifetime or after his death, are original bronzes: "It should be emphasized that these are *not* recasts or casts from unidentifiable plasters. These are original bronzes, cast from Dallin's master patterns which have remained in Gorham's possession, under the specific authorization of the heirs."

Copies and Originals

What is an original bronze? Unfortunately, there is no easy answer to this seemingly simple question. If an artist makes the model or pattern, casts the bronze, does his own chasing, and applies the final patina, there would be no question that the finished bronze sculpture could be called *the* original. However, the artist is seldom involved in all of these steps in making a bronze. The artist usually makes the original model or pattern himself, whether in clay, wax, plaster, or other material, although, for large pieces, assistants are often employed. It is more or less standard procedure for the artist also to oversee the making of a large, important work. He might supervise the making of the mold, he might specify the composition of the bronze metal to be used, and he probably would be present at the actual casting. After the gates and other extraneous metal are removed, he might either chase the bronze himself or give detailed instructions for chasing. The artist might also do the final finishing of the bronze himself.

This kind of careful, detailed supervision is usually limited to the larger, one–of–a–kind pieces. For smaller pieces, the artist usually supplies the pattern or mold and leaves the rest up to the foundry, except perhaps designating the final finish, such as the light blue–greens Harriet Frishmuth specified for many of her bronzes.

When there are many copies of a piece made over a span of years, it is obvious that the artist has little control of the making of the bronze. It is a matter of the skill and knowledge of the foundry craftsmen and the integrity of the foundry itself. Where such objects are made from the artist's original master pattern, it is usual to call them original bronzes.

What about bronzes made after an artist's death? If they are made by the same foundry that made them during the artist's lifetime, from the original master pattern, following standard practices, the final product may be indistinguishable from earlier castings. In addition, some bronzes, such as Gorham's equestrian series by Dallin, are made under specific standards agreed on with the heirs of the artist. Can such sculptures legitimately be called original bronzes? Perhaps the word original is the problem. In this day of "limited editions" of "original" prints or plates that may run into the tens of thousands, the meaning of the word *original* has become a bit nebulous. No doubt the only true original is the bronze master pattern from whence all the legitimate bronzes were made.

Usually bronzes made during an artist's lifetime command more money than those made later, even though the artist may not have had anything to do with the making of any of the bronzes. In those cases where posthumous bronzes are the only ones that exist, such as those of Rodin and Degas, the point becomes academic.

What about copies? Copies can be made from a bronze by using an "original" as a pattern. There is one way to tell whether this has been done. The copies are slightly smaller than the original; there is a slight shrinkage in the making process. The shrinkage is about 0.015 inches per inch of the original. For example, a copy of a bronze with a height of thirty inches would be about 29 9/16 inches high. Of course, the shrinkage is proportionally the same in all directions —height, length, and width.

A copy is always a copy. Whether a copy is a fake is a matter of intent. Unfortunately, many copies end up being passed off as the real thing, thus becoming fakes.[8]

A. Sterling Calder (1870–1945) was trained as an academic sculptor, but about 1910 he became interested in modern art and his figures became simpler and more

147 Sioux Brave, "Our American Stoic." (Copyright 1912 by A. Sterling Calder.) Height: 29 in. (73.7 *cm.*). *(Gorham photograph).*

abstract with less emphasis on detail. His Sioux brave, "Our American Stoic," in Figure 147, copyright in 1912, shows the beginnings of his new style.

Sterling Calder was completely eclipsed by the fame of his son, Alexander Calder, whose mobiles and stabiles have been given a very high place in the art world of the twentieth century.

Edward Clark Potter (1857–1923), whose sculpture *Dante* is illustrated in Figure 148 is mainly known for his collaborations with Daniel Chester French on several equestrian statues around the turn of the century. French would model the rider and Potter the horse. French, being the designer, got the recognition. Potter did several equestrians on his own: *General McClelland,* in Fairmount Park, Philadelphia, *General Kearny,* in Washington, D.C., and *General Custer,* Monroe, Michigan.

Harriet Frishmuth's *The Joy of the Waters* in Figure 149 depicts a young girl dancing with joyous abandon. She seems to be absolutely unselfconscious. The work, done in the 1920s, was modeled from a dancer named Desha, whose father was a political exile from Yugoslavia. Loring Holmes Dodd, who knew Miss Frishmuth personally,

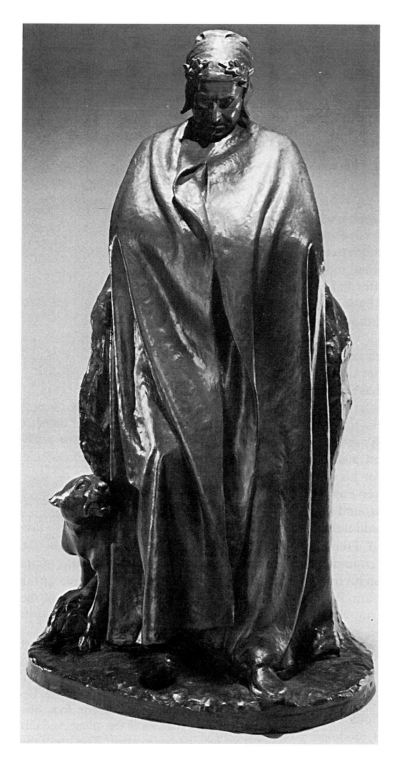

148 *Dante* by Edward Clark Potter. Height: 24 1/2 in. (62.2 cm.). *(Museum of Fine Arts, Boston).*

149 Bronze fountain sculpture, *The Joy of the Waters*, by Harriet Frishmuth. Total height: 63 1/2 in. (161 cm.). *(Gorham photograph).*

tells in his book *Golden Moments in American Sculpture* of the inspiration for the sculpture in Figure 149:

> Oddly, Desha, posing for Miss Frishmuth, dances always to the music of the Victrola. It's the challenging task of the sculptor to record these lightning–swift changes of the dance.
>
> "How would you feel," she once asked Desha, if water were, unexpectedly, to bubble up beneath your feet?"
>
> "Like this," was the quick response. Up went both arms. Up went one foot. She balanced on the toes of the other. And this is the familiar piece called "The Joy of the Waters." It was immediately purchased by a Washington collector with the understanding that no replica of it should be sold in the city.[9]

Harriet Frishmuth was born in Philadelphia and grew up in France where her mother intended her to be a pianist. She apparently loathed the instrument. Her real interest was art and early on she started modeling in clay. She studied with Rodin and Bourdelle, who had been Rodin's pupil. Back in America she studied at the Art Student's League in New York under Gutzon Borglum and Herman McNeil. There were anatomy lessons at the College of Physicians and Surgeons. When Loring Dodd quizzed her about whether she had not been a little faint at her first dissection, she replied: "Oh no. There have been so many physicians and surgeons in my family for generations, dissection must be in my blood. My first 'stiff' did not bother me at all."[10]

Harriet Frishmuth was awarded a prize in the Panama–Pacific Exposition in 1915 and received a number of prestigious awards in the 1920s. Many American museums acquired her works. She was one of the most successful of the artists who designed bronzes for Gorham. She made sculptures in a variety of sizes and subjects, fountains, and a couple of automobile–hood ornaments (Fig. 284, Chapter 13).

After World War II, Harriet Frishmuth's reputation went into eclipse. The huge survey book, *Sculpture in America,* by Wayne Craven (1968), does not even mention her name. Frishmuth's work has a light, decorative, Art Deco quality that no doubt seemed unimportant. However, her reputation is coming back. Her large sculpture, *The Vine* (not illustrated), was conspicuously placed in the Englehard Courtyard of the new American Wing of the Metropolitan Museum of Art in New York when it reopened in 1180. Her pieces are easy to like. They may not have the high seriousness of a Rodin, or the daring of a Brancusi or a David Smith, but they do ha–

ve a quiet integrity, a sense of joy and movement which is at times quite irresistible.

Anna Vaughn Hyatt Huntington (1876–1973) was a prolific and successful sculptor who specialized in animals. Even her very small sculptures, such as the *Jaguar Looking Up* in Figure 150 or her 3 1/4 inch *Rolling Bear* (not illustrated) have a sense of power and grace, and a kind of monumentality that is all out of proportion to the actual size of the pieces.

150 *Jaguar Looking Up* by Anna Vaughn Hyatt Huntington. Height: 8 5/8 in. (22 cm.). *(The Newark Museum).*

Mrs. Huntington's most famous work was *Joan of Arc,* which was acclaimed as one of the great works of art of its time when it was unveiled on Riverside Drive at Ninety–fourth Street in New York in 1915. Replicas were erected in Blois, France, and Gloucester, Massachussetts. Gorham offered two smaller bronze versions of *Joan of Arc*—fifteen inches high and fifty–one inches high.

Architectural Bronzes

Some of the finest work done by Gorham in bronze were the doors, railings, and so on, that copiously adorned many of the public and private structures of America of the first third of the twentieth century.

The detail and finish make such pieces as the Doerschuck mausoleum door in Figure 151 technical tours de force of the first order.

The 1905 Gorham building at Fifth Avenue and Thirty–sixth Street in New York, designed by Stanford White, was a veritable showcase for Gorham's architectural bronzes (Fig. 237, Chapter 11). An advertisement in *The New York Architect* of November 1908 shows a photograph of the bronze canopy at the Thirty–sixth Street entrance of the Gorham building. The caption reads:

The absolute reproduction in bronze of the plastic models as approved by Mr. White, was made possible only by

GORHAM PATENT PROCESS CASTING

The finished ornamental portions of this work were left exactly as taken from the moulds, thereby securing a distinctive art value on the canopies, entrances, frieze ornament, balconies, elevator and window fronts, stairways and grills which were modelled, manufactured and installed by

THE GORHAM COMPANY
ARCHITECTURAL BRONZE
FIFTH AVENUE
NEW YORK

The mere listing of the uses of bronze in the Gorham building makes one realize how much bronze ornamentation was employed in these Beaux Arts structures. Obviously, there is much less bronze in today's buildings, and what bronze is used is generally not ornamented.

Bookends and Ashtrays

Gorham made a variety of small, functional bronzes such as bookends (Fig. 152), door knockers, ashtrays (Fig. 153), lamp bases and automobile–hood ornaments (Fig. 284, Chapter 13). Some of these pieces were signed by the artist, such as the elephant bookends by the Gorham designer Bernard Johnson. Others were unsigned. All usually have the characteristic Gorham marks (see Appendix I).

151 Bronze door of Doerschuck mausoleum. Height: 80 in. (203 cm.). *(Gorham photograph)*.

152

153 Bronze ashtrays. Triangular one at left was made
in 1907. Width: 4 3/4 in. (12.1 cm.). Mark: No. 34,
Q98. Right, with frogs, made in 1922. Width: 5 in.
(12.7 cm.). Mark: No 35, 536. (Courtesy R. O.
Cragin).

152 Elephant bookends by Bernard Johnson. Height:
6 1/4 in. (12.3 cm.). (Gorham collection).

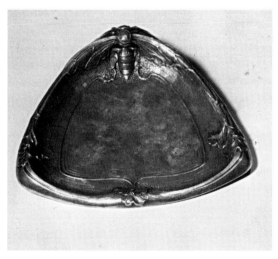

153

153

CHAPTER 9

Presentation Pieces

The sixty–year period, 1850–1910, was the era of great silver presentation pieces. The quality, the size, and the ambition of many of these trophies make them among the most interesting and important of all the objects made by Gorham.

Presentation pieces can be considered both for their association interest, and from a formal point of view as works of art. The variety of forms and techniques employed were extensive. There is no question that by modern standards some of these pieces are wild, sometimes bizarre, but they are seldom dull. One has only to compare them with the usual plain two–handled cup of today to realize how much we have lost. Many are, of course, not great works of art, and some celebrate forgotten people and events, but most evoke a sense of nostalgia for the past; many are fascinating objects.

The earliest known presentation piece associated with Gorham was probably not even made by them. The fine footed Rococo tray or waiter in Figure 154, which was accompanied by six goblets and two pitchers, is clearly marked "J. Gorham & Son." However, it was made in 1845, five years before Gorham attempted to make hol–

154 Footed tray given to Henry Bowen Anthony, editor of the *Providence Journal,* in 1845. The engraving was by George W. Babcock. Length over handles: 27 5/8 in. (70.2 cm.). Mark on handle: PURE SILVER COIN/J. GORHAM & SON. *(Courtesy The Providence Journal).*

low–ware pieces of any size. Probably Jabez Gorham either purchased these pieces or had them made, possibly in New York, and then stamped them with his own mark. This was a common practice in the middle of the nineteenth century.

The tray is engraved with the arms of the State of Rhode Island. The inscription reads:

TO

HENRY BOWEN ANTHONY
Editor of the
PROVIDENCE JOURNAL,
Presented by
CITIZENS of RHODE ISLAND
To testify
The estimation of the valuable service
rendered by that paper
in the cause of
LAW & ORDER
During the Insurrection against the
Government of Rhode Island
A.D. 1842

The tray commemorated an interesting and important event in Rhode Island history, Dorr's Rebellion or the Dorr War.[1] In 1840 Rhode Island still maintained an archaic form of government in which a relatively small part of the population controlled the state. Suffrage was restricted to owners of $134 worth of real estate or property rented at a somewhat smaller sum, and to their eldest sons. Over half the adult male population was not able to vote. Some nineteen towns, with a total of only 3500 voters, elected over half the legislature and controlled the state with a population of 108,000. The Landholder's Party ruled Rhode Island with an iron hand. Thomas Dorr, a young Providence lawyer, took up the cause of the unenfranchised citizens in 1834. In 1841 Dorr organized the reform People's Party. A party convention was held in October 1941. It adopted a new constitution permitting landless men to vote, and submitted it to a referendum of all adult male citizens. It received about 14,000 votes, including 4900 cast by voters qualified under the old constitution, with less than 100 opposed. The People's Party held an election in March 1842 in which Thomas Dorr was elected governor. He was inaugurated on May 3, 1842, by his supporters at Providence, where they had a majority. Meanwhile, at Newport, the regularly elected assembly met and inaugurated its own state

officers, passed resolutions declaring an insurrection existed, and authorized wholesale arrests of the insurgents. Both sides appealed to President John Tyler for support. Dorr went to Washington to plead his cause personally, but the president could not see that federal intervention was necessary.

Dorr took matters into his own hands. On May 17–18 he led an unsuccessful attack on the Providence arsenal, and again faced the state militia at Chepachet in June, but his followers had shrunk to about fifty and they refused to fight. Dorr fled to Connecticut and soon announced the disbanding of his movement. In October–November 1842 the Landholder's Party framed a new constitution, extending suffrage nearly equivalent to Dorr's demands.

Dorr gave himself up in Providence on October 31, 1843. He was tried in the state supreme court for treason. Sentenced to solitary confinement at hard labor for life, he was freed after a year in prison when public opinion forced the legislature to pass a general amnesty. Eventually Dorr was completely cleared by the court.

One of the few calm heads in the crisis in 1842 was Henry B. Anthony, editor of the *Providence Journal*. Intellectually he supported Dorr and said so, but he also said that law and order must be maintained, that a lawless insurrection must not be allowed to go on. His strong, reasonable position made him unpopular with both sides for a while, but he stuck by his guns.

Thinking citizens of Providence were so impressed with Henry Anthony's courageous stand that they had made for him the tray in Figure 154 and goblets and pitchers.[2] The tray, four of the goblets, and a pitcher, are now the property of the *Providence Journal,* where they are on display.

One of the first important testimonial objects actually made by Gorham was a thirty–eight–inch salver, or tray, weighing 319 ounces, presented to Commodore Matthew Perry (whose treaty had opened up Japan in 1854) by the State of Rhode Island in 1855 (not illustrated). Gorham featured a drawing of the Perry salver in their advertisements of the time with a quote from the *Providence Journal*. "This salver was designed, modeled and made in every particular in the establishment of Messrs, Gorham & Company, and there is no doubt that it has the heaviest border ever manufactured in this country."

Figure 155 is a goblet given to Samuel Lilly, who was on his way to Calcutta to be consul general to British India. The goblet is carefully chased in geometric and naturalistic motifs.

The final completion of the Atlantic cable in 1866 was widely hailed in the United States and England, and the engineer who supervised the laying of the cable, Cyrus W. Field, became a kind of folk hero. The 1866 celebrations were the second time around for Field. In 1858 he finished laying a cable from England to America, after four unsuccessful attempts in 1857–58. Field received a hero's welcome in New York. The cable was operated for a month and then it broke down. It was only in 1866 that England and America were finally connected with a satisfactory cable.

The three pieces in Figures 156, 157, and 158 were given to Cyrus Field in 1866 by George Peabody. Peabody, a financier and philanthropist, was well known in the United States and England, and had founded, among others, museums of archaeology and ethnology at Harvard and Yale. A public funeral in Westminster Abbey was given him when he died in England in 1869; his remains were returned to the United States by the British ship of war *Monarch,* and were buried with honors at South Danvers, Massachusetts, which was later renamed Peabody.

The rather chaste Renaissance Revival vegetable dish in Figure 156 has oval medallions with modeled heads of Cyrus Field and George Peabody on one side and an engraved inscription opposite. The handles have cast classical heads.

The kettle and stand in Figure 157 is more eclectic, fitting into the High Victorian style. It has Renaissance Revival medallions and cast masks, classical Greek–key borders, Neo–Grec ornamentation on the stand, and Rococo naturalistic grapevine decorations around the top.

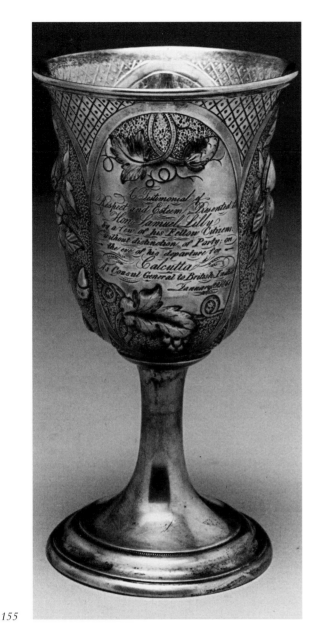

155

155 Goblet, chased and engraved with the inscription: "A Testimonial of/Respect and Esteem, Presented to/Hon. Samuel Lilly/by a few of his Fellow Citizens,/without distinction of Party; on/the eve of his departure for/Calcutta/As Consul General to British India/January 29, 1861." Height: 7 1/2 in. (19.1 cm.). Mark: No. 13/COIN/8. *(The National Museum of American History, Smithsonian Institution).*

156 Vegetable dish with medallions of Cyrus W. Field and George Peabody. Inscription on opposite side: "George Peabody/to/Cyrus W. Field/In testimony and commemoration/of an act of very high/commercial intregrity and honor/ New York 24 Nov. 1866." Mark: 220/ lion–anchor– G. *(Museum of the City of New York).*

15

157

158

The fruit stand or centerpiece in Figure 158 has been called Renaissance Revival because of the medallions of Field and Peabody on the base and the winged putti on the handles.[3] However, this fruit stand is stylistically quite eclectic. The draped female figure is a classical device as is the globe with its ring of zodiac signs. There are four different die–rolled borders used on the piece—the interlocking guilloche band around the bowl on top, the lambrequin and tassel band just above the draped body, the band of beading below the globe, and the band of naturalistic leaves and fruit interspersed between human heads on the base.

The two–handled, hand–hammered loving cup in Figure 159 shows an engraving of the brig *General Armstrong* blasting a British ship at Fayal in the Azores in 1814. Why this cup was presented in 1882, sixty–six years after the event took place, is not clear. Another question

157 Kettle and stand presented to Cyrus W. Field by George Peabody in 1866. Height: 16 1/2 in. (41.9 cm.). Mark: STARR & MARCUS/ lion–anchor–G/390. *(Museum of the City of New York)*.

158 Fruit dish or centerpiece presented to Cyrus W. Field by George Peabody in 1866. Cast figures, globe, and medallions; die–rolled borders. Height: 16 3/4 in. (42.5 cm.). Mark: lion–anchor–G/164. *(Museum of the City of New York)*.

133

159 Two–handled, hand–hammered loving cup. Engraved on reverse: "In commemoration/of the/gallant conduct of Lieutenant/ Frederick A. Worth/of the private armed brig/ Genl. Armstrong/at Fayal 26th of Sept. 1814./New York 1882." Height: 13 3/4 in. (34.9 cm.). Mark: No. 20. *(Museum of the City of New York).*

about this cup is its mark (No. 12, Appendix). The Union Square in the mark seems to indicate it was made at Gorham's New York shop. Mark No. 12 includes both the letters H and I. If these were date letters, dates of 1875 and 1876 would be indicated. However, as noted in Chapter 6, hammered surfaces were not used at Gorham until 1877 or 1878. This suggests that H and I in the mark are part of the design pattern code. The loving cup was probably made in 1882.

Naturalism or rustication, the use of motifs from nature, such as twigs, leaves, and flowers, flourished in the middle of the nineteenth century. Figure 160 is a brilliant example of naturalistic details used to frame academic scenes from three Wagnerian operas. Even the naturalistic forms have taken on a realistic, academic, Beaux Arts look. The naturalism of the 1850s was more stylized. The three–handled cup with the operatic scenes

was presented to Anton Seidl, conductor of German opera at the Metropolitan Opera from 1885 to 1891. In 1891 German opera was temporarily dropped at the Met. In that year Seidel became conductor of the New York Philharmonic, a post he held until his death in 1898. In 1895–97 he again conducted German opera at the Metropolitan Opera.

The flask in Figure 161 was one of a number which Alex R. Shephard had made for his friends. Governor Shephard had left Washington, D.C., to run the silver mine at Batopilas, southeastern Chihuahua state, Mexico, in the western ranges of the Sierra Madre. The etching on the flask is a scene of the large mining enterprise set against rugged mountains, with a number of shacks and a great variety of cacti in the foreground. A bas–relief saguaro cactus trails up each edge of the flask, emerging from other bas–relief cacti. The top of the lid of the flask is engraved "Batopilas," in the same ornate and twisting lettering.

The large and elaborate memorial vase in Figure 162 was presented to Mrs. Samuel S. Cox by members of the Life–Saving Service of the United States in honor of the outstanding work of her husband, who as a congressman was a strong supporter of the service. Mr. Cox served as congressman for twenty years, first from Ohio and then from New York State. He died in New York City in 1889. Two years later General Superintendent S. I. Kimball, in behalf of a committee representing the service, presented the vase to Mrs. Cox. The presentation took place at Mrs. Cox's home in Washington, D.C., on December 12, 1891.[4]

The vase is two feet tall and weighs almost eight pounds. The design was suggested by a committee from the Life–Saving Service. The chasing was supposed to have been the work of one man, but unfortunately, we do not know his name.

The central image on the front of the vase is a scene of lifesavers at work. A rope has been secured between the wrecked vessel and the shore, and one by one the passengers are pulled ashore over and through the towering, thrashing waves. This was a scene repeated hundreds of times off the coast of America in the eighteenth and nineteenth centuries, particularly off such dangerous areas as Cape Cod, the south shore of Nantucket, and Cape Hatteras. The vase is covered with marine symbolism. On the base, above a band of acorn clusters and leaves, are dolphins sporting in the billowing waves. There are seashells and starfish and seaweed, and bands of rope and marine chain. Handles at the sides are cast mermaids, who, with bowed heads and curved bodies, hold in their upraised hands sea plants

160 Three–handled loving cup, repoussé chased with scenes from operas, cast handles in the form of branches. Scene in photograph from *Die Meistersinger*. The other two sides have scenes from *Lohengrin* and *Siegfried*. Engraved on base "Anton Seidl from his New York Admirers Feb 25th 1887." Height: 11 1/2 in. (29.2 cm.). Mark: lion–anchor–G/STERLING/(date mark for 1887). *(Museum of the City of NewYork, Gift of Mrs.Anton Seidl).*

161 Flask with etched view of Batopilas silver mine in Chihuahua state, Mexico. On reverse is donor's portrait with script signature "Alex R. Shephard." Engraved below: "To/General/Philip H. Sheridan/1888." Height: 7 3/4 in. (19.7 cm.). Mark: lion–anchor–G/ Sterling 157 (date mark for 1888). *(The National Museum of American History, Smithsonian Institution).*

160

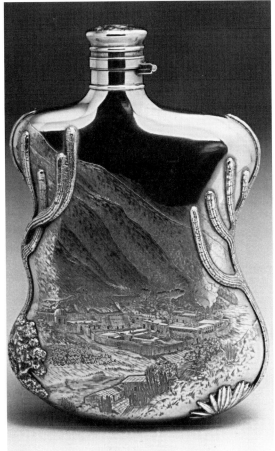

1

growing from the neck of the vase. On the back side is a lifebuoy crossed with a boat hook and oar ornament, and the following inscription:

This Memorial Vase is presented to Mrs. Samuel S. Cox by members of the Life-Saving Service of the United States in Grateful Remembrance of the tireless and successful efforts of her distinguished husband The Honorable Samuel Sullivan Cox to promote the interests and advance the efficiency and glory of the Life-Saving Service.

He was its early and constant friend; its fearless and faithful champion.

I have spent the best part of my life in the public service; most of it has been like writing in water. The reminiscenses of past wrangling and political strife seems to me like nebulae of the past, without form and almost void. But what little I have accomplished in connection with this Life–Saving Service is compensation "sweeter than the honey in the honeycomb." It is its own exceeding great reward.

From speech in the House of Representatives. April 24, 1888.

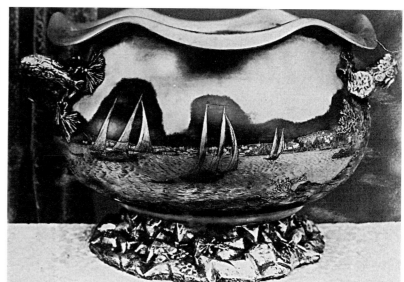

162

162 Memorial vase presented to Mrs. Samuel S. Cox in 1891 by the Life–Saving Service of the United States. Height: 23 5/8 in. (60 cm.). Mark: lion–anchor–G/2465. *(The National Museum of American History, Smithsonian Institution).*

163 Ladies Yacht Prize. Engraved inscription on reverse side: "Presented by the/Ladies Yacht Club/Burlington/Vermont." *(Gorham photograph).*

164 Boston Athletic Club Amateur Championship Cup, PR. 1890. *(Gorham photograph).*

Not all the yachting trophies were for highly publicized ocean races. The delightful Ladies Yacht Prize in Figure 163 with its rustic pine–bough handles and rocky base depicts a realistic view of what appears to be a leisurely race on Lake Champlain, off Burlington, Vermont. The etcher seems to have worked from a photograph since the buildings and the shoreline are depicted with great accuracy.

165 Waiter presented to Washington Augustus Roebling, the builder of the Brooklyn Bridge, and his wife on their twenty–fifth wedding anniversary in 1890. Size 26 x 27 in. (66 x 68.6 cm.). (*Gorham photograph*).

The Boston Athletic Club Amateur Championship Cup of New England for Ten Mile Running in Figure 164 is elegantly simple. The sparse silver spiked running shoe conveys vividly the nature of the event.

The waiter in Figure 165 is etched with a picture of the Brooklyn Bridge and "1865–Roebling–1860" for the twenty–fifth wedding anniversary of Washington Augustus Roebling and his wife. Roebling as a young engineer of thirty–one had to take over the entire direction of the building of the Brooklyn Bridge when his father John Roebling, the chief engineer, had unexpectedly died in 1869. This was by far the largest suspension bridge ever attempted at that date, and he felt the responsibility so strongly and worked so exhaustively that his health broke down, though he continued the supervision from his bedroom until the bridge was completed in 1883.

The flag–holder memento in Figure 166 was a souvenir of a dinner held to honor General Benjamin Harrison on April 3, 1896. On the back of the flag holder is the name F. D. Grant. Frederick Dent Grant was the eldest son of General Ulysses S. Grant. When the dinner was held in 1896 he was police commissioner of New York. In the nineteenth century it was not unusual for guests at important dinner parties to receive silver sou-

166 Flag–holder memento. Engraved "COL. F.D. GRANT./ Our institutions of which/this flag is an emblem are/free institutions." On reverse: Dinner/to/ General Benjamin Harrison/April 3rd/1896/A.W.S." Height: 2 5/8 in. (6.7 cm.). Mark: lion–anchor–G/ STERLING/M. (*The National Museum of American History, Smithsonian Institution*).

167 Love cup made in 1898. Engraved "TOWN TOPICS CUP/
PRESENTED TO THE/HAGUE ROWING ASSOCIATION/AS A PRIZE/
LAUNCH RACES/ 1898." and "WON BY/ 1898. HARRY W. WATRRUS.
LAUNCH BETH" Height: 8 1/2 in. (21.6 cm.). Mark: lion–
anchor–G/STERLING/ A820/8PINT. (Courtesy L. D. Watrous).

168 Pitcher made in 1890. On front, below two enamel flags (American Yacht Club, New York) and a private signal, is the name SENTINEL. On opposite side is the inscription "Presented/to/Charles Fletcher/by/E. Milner, L. R. Peck/ S. W. Kilvert, L. H. Humphries/1890." Height: 11 in. (27.9 cm.). Mark: lion–anchor–G/1831/STERLING. (Private collection).

169 Silver scroll container and mahogany box presented to Mrs. Potter Palmer, Chairman of the National Peace Jubilee Benefit Committee, in 1898. Length of silver container: 151 G/1 C in (39.0 cm.). Mark: SPAULDING & CO/lion–anchor– G/STERLING/8002. (Chicago Historical Society).

168

169

venir mementos, sometimes in the form of name cards.

The love cup in Figure 167 brings back memories of a gentler, more genteel age. The acid–etched scene on the cup, depicting an awning–covered steam launch on Lake George, New York, with wooded hills in the background, was probably taken from a contemporary photograph.

The elegantly dressed people in the launch seem to be posing for the photographer. The launch is obviously not racing furiously across the lake. The cup has naturalistic cast handles. The cast leaf–and–branch decorations around the top are applied, the leaves around the bottom are engraved.

The yachting presentation pitcher in Figure 168 is

GORHAM SILVER

decorated with dolphins, lobsters, seaweed, large chased shells, enameled flags, and the yacht. The die–rolled border of anchors and tridents was a favorite ornament for sailing and yachting trophies.

Figure 169 illustrates a silver scroll container and its silver–ornamented mahogany box for a scroll given to Mrs. Potter Palmer, the rich Chicago socialite, for her services as chairman of the National Peace Jubilee Benefit Committee in 1898. (This was before the days of "chairlady," or "chairperson," or "chair.") The festooned silver scroll holder, with its patriotic eagle, was very much in the Colonial Revival style.

The grandest and certainly the largest of Gorham's presentation pieces is the eight–foot–four–inch loving cup made for Admiral George Dewey in 1899 from 70,000 silver dimes.

In 1898 Dewey had become a national hero. When news of the outbreak of the Spanish–American War reached him he was in Hong Kong as commander of the Asiatic squadron. He was ordered to attack the Spanish squadron in Manila Bay. Dewey had six warships of advanced design, but they were outnumbered by the Spanish squadron and outgunned by Spanish shore batteries around Manila Bay. Nevertheless, Dewey brought his force into the bay under cover of darkness on April 30, slipped past Spanish batteries on Corregidor, and at dawn on May 1 engaged the Spanish squadron, which he entirely destroyed without a single fatal casualty to his own command. Fifteen weeks later Manila fell.

In May of 1899, in anticipation of Admiral Dewey's return home, the *New York Journal* initiated a plan for a silver presentation cup. They suggested that everyone send a dime to the paper for the trophy. The dimes poured in. The *Journal* published the names of school children and the names of the famous who had contributed their dimes. It was a marvelous publicity stunt for the paper. Within five months 70,000 dimes had been donated. Gorham was given the job of making the huge cup. Under the direction of William C. Codman it was finished in four months (Fig. 170).

Sharon Darling has given an excellent description of the cup:

Crowned by a splendid figure of Victory, the cup is ovoid in shape, with three handles and an ornate base.

On the detachable cover, decorated with the prows of three gun boats, Victory nestles an oval colored portrait of the hero, while holding aloft a wreath of laurel (now missing) in the act of crowning the victor. Below, an ornamental border is composed of dimes overlapping one another like the scales of a fish.

170 The Admiral George Dewey loving cup, made from 70,000 silver dimes. Height: 100 in. (254 cm.). *(Chicago Historical Society).*

140

The body of the cup displays three carefully drawn relief panels, reproducing the battle of Manila Bay, the Admiral's home in Montpelier, Vermont, and the enthusiastic reception at Grant's tomb upon his arrival in New York City Three large eagles, their wings raised in token of Dewey's triumph, perch upon red, white and blue enamel shields on the three handles.

The three cornered base is decorated with three dolphins, their heads forming the feet of the base and their bodies and tails arching gracefully toward the center. At center front is engraved "The Dewey Loving Cup presented to the Conquering Admiral by seventy thousand American Citizens as a tribute of their gratitude."

The cup stands upon a round silver pedestal with rough textured body thirty inches in diameter. Its simple decoration includes a cable border, a silver laurel wreath, and a band of oak leaves. Impressed on its underside are the familiar Gorham hallmarks and "Sterling."

The oak platform was built to house a splendid book with thick silver covers identified as "The Dewey Memorial Volume, wherein is set forth the names of seventy thousand American citizens whose contributions made possible the Living Testimonial of which this is a part." Inside the book are newspaper clippings containing the lists of contributors. Originally, a panel opening in the round silver pedestal was to contain the book.[5]

The remarkable inkstand in Figure 171 was made in 1898. The Gorham records indicate it was made for H.S., and cost $1000.

Battleship Silver

The custom of presenting a piece of silver at the launching of a new ship has a long history in the United States Navy. Sometimes, this was even extended to the ship's

builder, as was the case with Edmund Hartt, builder of the frigate *Boston,* who was presented with a tea set made by Paul Revere. As a result of this custom, ships of the United States Navy have been recipients of a vast array of silver, ranging from single pieces to services of hundreds of pieces. The Naval Supply Systems Command of the Department of the Navy keeps extensive records of silver owned by the Navy, some of which dates back to the nineteenth century.

The donors have been private individuals, cities, or states. The city of Albany, for example, presented silver to the cruiser U.S.S. *Albany,* and the state of New Jersey, to the battleship U.S.S. *New Jersey.* In the 1960s the State of Massachusetts presented a silver service to the aircraft carrier U.S.S. *John F. Kennedy,* in honor of the late president.[6]

The silver services are kept on board ship except in times of actual combat when they are usually left ashore for safekeeping. The silver not only has an ornamental role, it is often used at shipboard receptions and other formal occasions.

Although many ships have been supplied with silver services, some have not. The navy seems rather touchy on this point. They emphasize that all such services are *given* to the navy, *not* purchased at the taxpayers' expense.

The fact that some ships did not have their own services seems to have been a problem to some commanding officers:

United States Battle Fleet Battleship
Divisions U.S.S. West Virginia

Enroute San Francisco,
Calif. 19 June, 1929.

171 Inkstand made in 1898 for H.S. Length: 24 in. (61 cm.). Height: 9 3/4 in. (24.8 cm.). No. 7126. *(Gorham photograph).*

From: Commanding Officer
To: The Secretary of the Navy.
Via: Commander BATTLESHIP DIVISIONS, BATTLE FLEET.

SUBJECT: Silver Service for U.S.S. WEST VIRGINIA

1. This ship was not presented a silver service by its name state, as is usually the custom upon commissioning. This omission has been a handicap as well as a humiliation on occasions of entertainment when high officials or notable guests were present. This situation is not unusual since the WEST VIRGINIA is the flagship of the battleships and the latest of the type. It has been repeatedly necessary in the past to borrow from other ships which, of course, have their own names on the silver pieces.

2. It is requested that one of the silver services turned in by a decommissioned ship be reconditioned and marked for this ship.

E. T. CONSTIEN.

Apparently the U.S.S. *West Virginia* never did receive a silver service. In 1968 the Governor, Hulett C. Smith, wrote to West Virginia Senator Jennings Randolph about a service:

State of West Virginia
OFFICE OF THE GOVERNOR
Charleston 25305

June 28, 1968

Honorable Jennings Randolph United States Senator Senate Office Building Washington, D.C.

Dear Jennings:

Mary Alice and I were recently in Columbia, South Carolina, visiting with Governor and Mrs. McNair.

While there, we noticed that the Mansion was graced with the silver service from the USS South Carolina. On inquiry, we learned that it had been obtained for the State several years ago when the USS South Carolina was decommissioned.

We have been trying to find out what happened to the service that was a part of the USS West Virginia. Could you inquire of the Department of Defense or the Secretary of the Navy as to what disposition was made of this silver service? It might be that it is in storage somewhere and

could be obtained for the Mansion.

I certainly think it would be a needed addition and a treasure that we ought to try to preserve in West Virginia.

With best wishes,

Sincerely,
Hulett C. Smith
Governor

The Department of the Navy had to inform Senator Randolph and Governor Smith that the U.S.S. *West Virginia* never had a silver service.

Gorham started making silver services for United States warships in the 1890s. Since that time, they have made more such services than any other silversmithing firm. The latest of these services, was made for the U.S.S. *Long Beach* in 1961 (Chapter 14), bringing the total to sixty–one.

The services of the 1890s and early 1900s were flamboyant and filled with patriotic symbols. The great tureen of the U.S.S. *Minneapolis* service (Fig. 172) has a flag–draped view of Minnehaha Falls, eagles on the handles, dolphin feet, and dolphins on the lid handle. Stylistically many of these pieces are a mishmash. The objective seems to have been to load the pieces with detail, some of which didn't fit too well. However, some pieces are very colorful. The waiter in Figure 173, made for the U.S.S. *New Orleans* in 1899, has vivid scenes of the Mississippi riverfront and moss–hung trees. By 1911, when the silver for the U.S.S. *Utah* was made, the services had become larger and the designs simpler, and perhaps less interesting (Fig. 174). As usual the punch bowl of the Utah service was the largest piece of the service. Some of these punch bowls were huge, of several gallons capacity.

The battleship and cruiser services have had a varied history. Only a few of them are still at sea. Most have been retired to statehouses, governors' mansions, and state historical societies. The service of the U.S.S. *Rhode Island* was in the statehouse in Providence when it was stolen in the 1970s. It was rescued just as it was ready for melting. It was somewhat banged up in this mishap, and was restored by the Gorham Company before it was returned to the statehouse, where security has been considerably tightened.

The following list of Gorham services made for United States naval vessels was compiled with the help of Commander G. P. Beamer of the Naval Supply Systems Com–

142

172

172 Tureen and stand made for the U.S.S. *Minneapolis* in 1895. The tureen has a capacity of six quarts. *(Gorham photograph).*

173 Waiter made for the U.S.S. *New Orleans* in 1899. Length: 24 in. (61 cm.). *(Gorham photograph).*

173

mand of the Department of the Navy:

Vessel	Date
U.S.S. *Albany*	1903
U.S.S. *Arkansas*	1916
U.S.S. *Brooklyn*	1896
U.S.S. *Charleston*	1906
U.S.S. *Chattanooga*	1907

U.S.S. *Chicago*	1945
U.S.S. *Cincinnati*	1895
U.S.S. *Delaware*	1909
U.S.S. *Denver*	1903
U.S.S. *Detroit*	1892
U.S.S. *Florida*	1911
U.S.S. *Georgia*	1907

174 Silver service, "Presented to the U.S.S. *Utah* by the School Children and People of the State of Utah, 1911." *(Gorham photograph).*

U.S.S. *Helena*	1896	U.S.S. *Oklahoma*	1914
U.S.S. *Idaho*	1911	U.S.S. *Olympia*	1899
U.S.S. *Illinois*	1909	U.S.S. *Oregon*	1897
U.S.S. *Indiana*	1899	U.S.S. *Pennsylvania*	1903
U.S.S. *Iowa*	1896	U.S.S. *Providence*	1944
U.S.S. *Kansas*	1905	U.S.S. *Raleigh*	1896
U.S.S. *Kentucky*	1899	U.S.S. *Rhode Island*	1907
U.S.S. *Little Rock*	1945	U.S.S. *Salem*	1949
U.S.S. *Long Beach* (cruiser)	1961	U.S.S. *Salt Lake City*	1929
U.S.S. *Los Angeles*	1952	U.S.S. *South Carolina*	1910
U.S.S. *Maine*	1891	U.S.S. *South Dakota*	1904
U.S.S. *Marietta*	1899	U.S.S. *Scout Salem*	1908
U.S.S. *Milwaukee*	1905	U.S.S. *St. Louis* (cruiser)	1909
U.S.S. *Minneapolis*	1895	U.S.S. *Spokane*	1945
U.S.S. *Missouri*	1905	U.S.S. *Tacoma*	1904
U.S.S. *Mobile*	1947	U.S.S. *Toledo*	1947
U.S.S. *Montgomery*	1893	U.S.S. *Texas*	1914
U.S.S. *Nashville*	1896	U.S.S. *Utah*	1911
U.S.S. *Nebraska*	1905	U.S.S. *Vermont*	1906
U.S.S. *Nevada*	1915	U.S.S. *Vincennes* (cruiser)	1937
U.S.S. *New Orleans*	1899	U.S.S. *Wichita* (cruiser)	1939
U.S.S. *Newport*	1897	U.S.S. *Wilmington*	1897
U.S.S. *North Dakota*	1910	U.S.S. *Wisconsin*	1901
U.S.S. *Ohio*	1905	U.S.S. *Wyoming*	1912

175 Motorboat trophy made in 1911, modeled by E. E. Codman. Eight enameled flags on base and four on boat. Height: 11.5 in. (29.2 cm.). (*Gorham photograph*).

176 Carnegie Steel Safety Trophy made in 1929, sterling and bronze. Height: 28 in. (71 cm.). (*Gorham photograph*).

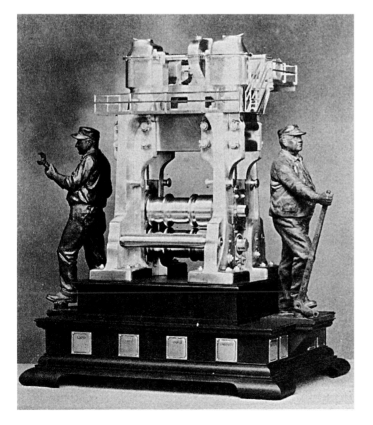

The motorboat trophy in Figure 175 was made in 1911. It was modeled by E. E. Codman. The circular panels on the base are enameled.

The Carnegie Steel Safety Trophy in Figure 176, made in 1929, has a model of a two–high rolling mill in sterling and two figures in bronze—a mechanic with a wrench on the left and a roller on the right. The roller was the most important and highest paid man in a steel finishing mill. With his levers, he engineered the hot steel through the rolls with the finesse of a surgeon.

CHAPTER 10

Souvenir Spoons

In the book *Souvenir Spoons of America,* published for Gorham in 1891, the new craze for souvenir spoons is described in this whimsical paragraph:

> The breath of another fad pervades the atmosphere. The active and unsatiated American public, ever seeking for variety, have something new to chatter about and interest or bore their intimates. The panorama of novelty has been turned, and the fad of souvenir spoons is now reigning. From Maine to California, from Minnesota to Florida, the cry is for souvenir spoons. People visiting a locality, people who have visited a locality, people who would like to visit a locality, people who want to say they have visited a locality, people who think it is the proper thing, the *recherché* thing to have been a traveller, people who want others to remember that they have travelled, people who really believe that they have travelled, people generally of a self-conscious or sentimental disposition, in fact, almost everyone wants souvenir spoons.[1]

In the 1890s and early years of the twentieth century thousands of souvenir spoons were made by dozens of United States manufacturers, in sterling and in silver plate. Gorham, as the largest maker of sterling flatwares, with its extensive design and manufacturing capabilities, was able to dominate the souvenir spoon market almost from the beginning. They probably made more than a thousand different kinds of souvenir spoons. (I am considering the various spoon forms—tea, coffee, orange, etc.—as variants of one spoon design.) To this must be added

many hundreds of regular–line Gorham spoons engraved as souvenirs. If we were to consider the variants as *different* spoons, and add the engraved examples, the total would run into many thousands.

Today the collecting of souvenir spoons is widespread. At the time of the writing of this book many are available in antique shops and flea markets. People often collect in categories: cities, states, regions, Indians, advertising spoons, expositions, etc., etc. There were so many spoons made that it would be almost impossible to have any kind of a definitive collection. Discoveries are continually being made. There is the powerful lure of finding something new for the advanced collector. There are thousands of souvenir spoon collectors in the United States, a passionate, fiercely competitive group. That the interest in souvenir spoons attracts a large public is shown by the number of books[2] and articles in the field. This chapter examines souvenir spoons from several points of view: as examples of a social phenomenon—a popular art for the people; how the spoons were made, how Gorham marked them, and a comparison of some of their shapes and forms. I do not plan to deal with prices, degrees of rarity, detailed historical backgrounds of events depicted on individual spoons, or the iconography of the various spoon designs. These are the very points usually stressed by most books on souvenir spoons. Part of the fun of collecting is to research one's own collection, and souvenir spoons give ample opportunities for such research.

Early Souvenir Spoons

In view of the dominant position of Gorham in the souvenir spoon field it would seem to be a matter of poetic justice to find that they may also have made some of the *earliest* spoons of this type in America.

The beautifully crafted serving or tablespoon in Figure 177, with its engraved inscription "RI State Fair 1852" on the top of the handle (Fig. 178), appears to be, at the time of this writing (1981), one of the earliest known American souvenir spoons.[3] As was noted in Chapter 4, the Rhode Island state fairs of the early 1850s were important showcases of Gorham's work. The state fair commemorated by the spoon in Figure 177 was held in September 1852, just a few weeks after the Gorham name had been changed from Gorham & Thurber to Gorham & Company. This means that the mark on the spoon (mark No.6) is the earliest version of a Gorham &

Co. mark. The "Bushnell" engraved on the front of the spoon handle was for Henry C. Bushnell, who joined the firm Gorham & Thurber in 1850. In 1852 Bushnell became foreman of the spoon department of the newly named Gorham & Company. He held the same job for forty–eight years, retiring in 1900, at the age of seventy–six.

Another Gorham spoon, engraved "EXPOSITION 1876" was described in the September–October 1979 issue of *The Magazine Silver*.[4] The 1876 spoon is a salt spoon with ivy–leaf decoration in the rustic taste so popular at the time.

In the 1880s the interest in spoon collecting was growing. Gorham designed a number of spoons for this market, often in sets of twelve. The *Nuremburg* spoons consisted of twelve different figural handles of German peasants, burghers, and nobles in characteristic costumes (see the knife handles in Fig. 122). A set of *Old Paris* coffee spoons featured eighteenth–century French motifs ranging from a sailing vessel to a king's crown. Sets of Apostle spoons (Fig. 179) were popular and the oversized Evan–

178

177

177 Serving or tablespoon made by Gorham & Co. in 1852. Engraved on front, "Bushnell"; on back, "RI/State Fair/ 1852" (Fig. 178). Length: 8 11/16 in. (22.1 cm.). Mark: No. 6. *(Gorham collection).*

178 Engraved inscription on top back of handle of spoon in Figure 177.

179 Apostle spoon, St. John, made by Gorham about 1901. Inscribed, reverse of medallion, "1876/1901." Length: 8 1/2 in. (21.6 cm.). Mark: lion–anchor–G. *(Courtesy David H. Wood).*

gelist spoons were introduced to round out the line. Later, floral spoons were issued in several designs. There were months, or birthday, sets—January to December.

Although such spoons were (and still are) widely collected, they are not usually classified as souvenir spoons. The first of the true Gorham souvenir spoons seem to have been made in 1890.

In 1890 the spoon fad was snowballing. "The Woman's Hour" column of the *Commercial Advertiser* (New York) of January 24, 1891, talked about it in an article titled "The Mania For Spoons." It was described as "A Collecting Fad Which Has Become Popular—Silver Souvenirs of Widely Separated Places and People—Ancient and Modern Treasures Which Adorn Fashionable Boards." The article noted that "Mrs. Edward Burnette, the only daughter of James Russell Lowell, is possessed of many highly interesting old spoons." "Mrs. Andrew Carnegie has several spoons, both English and Continental, of considerable antiquity." The insinuation was that soon everyone would be hooked: "Of the woman who has not yet been bitten with the spoon-collecting mania you can safely say that—she will be soon."

Women were not only collecting spoons, they were setting their tables with them, mixing spoons of all kinds: "The present fad is to set out one's board with odd spoons altogether, and to quicken the flagging chat with silver souvenirs of as many cities, as many widely removed quarters of the globe and the epochs of as many mouldering kings and ancient patrons of art as one's purse or one's luck or one's travel will provide."[5]

The Introduction to *Souvenir Spoons of America* (1891) documents the steps that led to the souvenir spoon craze:

About three years ago M. W. Galt, Bros. & Co., Washington, produced a copyrighted design of a Washington spoon, depicting a head of the father of his country on the top of the shank. The firm are thus entitled to the pride of being the originators of the fad in this country from a commercial standpoint. It may be said that the Rogers & Hamilton Co., Waterbury, Conn., made a plated souvenir spoon for the Washington Centennial in 1889. During last summer, Daniel Low, Salem, Mass., took a trip to Europe, and made a collection of spoons as others had done before. Upon his return he conceived the idea of getting out a spoon, for Salem the home of witchcraft, and succeeded in producing the now celebrated Witch spoon. Over seven thousand of them have been sold, and their circulation has undoubtedly been an item in the creation of the demand for spoons representing other cities. The time was ripe when Daniel Low began, but his enterprise gave impetus to the fashion. The fad spread throughout Eastern States, silversmiths at Boston, Lynn, New Bedford, Haverhill, Plymouth and at

other places, devised spoons for their several places. The fashion was then taken up in New York, and thence spread to every corner of the country."[6]

Gorham's Souvenir Spoons

The above account suggests that the success of Daniel Low's first Salem witch spoon, which was made by the Durgin Company of Concord, New Hampshire (Durgin was later merged into the Gorham Company), was the one single event that sparked Gorham's entry into the souvenir spoon business. The first Durgin witch spoons were made in 1890, although some of the Durgin spoons were issued with the mark "PAT, MCH.3, 91 STERLING D. LOW , which indicates the date of the design patent.[7]

The year 1890 must have been a year of frantic activity at Gorham. It was a particularly propitious time for Gorham to enter such a fast-growing market as souvenir spoons. The company had moved to their new building in Elmwood, where their new facilities for flatware production were unparalleled anywhere in the world. Gorham had to have moved fast to produce as many spoon designs as they did in such a short time. They were able to announce in a March 25, 1891, advertisement that: "In answer to the demand, we have produced for the trade an unusually large number of odd and peculiar spoons, suitable as mementoes of places and events, which have met with marked approval."[8]

If the company was able to say they had produced "an unusually large number" by March 1891, it meant that they had been working on souvenir spoons for at least a year—probably since the first part of 1890. Even this would have been a prodigious task, taking into consideration the time needed to design and either cut the dies for the die-struck examples, or do the modeling for the cast examples.

In 1891 Gorham mounted a major marketing effort. The objective was simple: to capture as large a share as possible of the souvenir spoon market. They advertised heavily and there was obviously a strong push by the company salesmen. In 1891 Gorham had a large direct sales force that could almost literally blanket the country. The dozens of exclusive deals with jewelers throughout the country is evidence of widespread activity. Examples: *Old Orchard* spoon, made for Geo. E. Twambley, Saco, Maine; the Ouray spoon, made for C. E. Rose, Ouray, Colorado; the Coal Breaker spoon, made for W. H. Mortimer, Pottsville, Pennsylvania; the Lincoln spoon, made for J. B. Trickey & Co., Lincoln, Nebraska. Well over one hundred such deals were consummated by the end of 1891.

Gorham issued two major publications in 1891 to advertise their souvenir spoons: *Souvenir Spoons of America,* published for Gorham by the Jewelers' Circular Publishing Co., and *Souvenir Spoons,* compiled by George B. James, Jr. The former contained pictures and descriptions of about 180 spoons, while James's book pictured over 200 spoons marketed by Gorham and affiliated jewelers all over the United States. The James book also contained descriptions of Gorham's regular flatware patterns such as *Cluny, Colonial, Medici,* and *St. Cloud.* There were advertisements of various suppliers and agents. J. R. Tennant, 140 West Twenty–third Street, New York, stated: "SOUVENIR SPOONS. It will save you time, trouble and expense if you send your orders for Souvenir Spoons to me. I have the agency for every spoon in America."[9]

How Souvenir Spoons Were Made

First came the concept. Ideas seemed to have come from everywhere, from jewelers and silverware dealers, from salesmen, and of course from the Gorham design department. Many of the designs from the field were sketches, sometimes they were mere ideas. The design department researched the ideas, studied drawings and photographs of the subject, and finally came up with a finished design. Detailed drawings were made of the front and back of the spoon.

Once the drawings were approved the spoons were made using standard production procedures. Models were made of the spoons in order to fully develop the design in three dimensions. Only then was the design ready for the crucial step of making the actual dies or casting patterns.

For spoons that were to be stamped (Fig. 184, for example), the next step was to cut the back and front dies that were to be used in the drop presses for making the actual spoons. The direct cutting of patterns in steel involves a high order of craftsmanship. The difficulty of cutting highly detailed patterns for such surfaces as spoon bowls should not be underestimated.

Since so many patterns were cut in a relatively short time it was necessary for Gorham to subcontract a lot of their die–cutting. A full page advertisement in *Souvenir Spoons* (p. 217) reads in part:

CONRAD EGGE
MEDAL AND GENERAL DIE SINKER,
SEAL ENGRAVER AND LETTER CUTTER
97 OLIVER STREET
BOSTON, MASS.

A large percentage of the illustrated foregoing Souvenir Spoons having been struck from dies of my manufacture. I take occasion to present, through this medium, my establishment to the combined Jewelry and Silverware trade of the country for the execution of original designs in the line of Souvenir Spoons.

The finished dies were used in Gorham's regular flatware drop presses. There were four steps in the making process:

1. Correctly sized spoon blanks were stamped in the drop press.
2. Rough edges were filed or ground off.
3. The front of the handle was oxidized to sharpen the design.
4. The spoon was given final light polishing.

The writer of *Souvenir Spoons of America* noted (p. 78): "the die work, being of the highest character, reproduces all the details contained in original conceptions, and the subjects embodied in each souvenir are the most salient features of the spoons. *The beautiful oxidation of the fronts lends richness and art to the ensemble.*" (My italics). I have noted several times in this book the fact that dark oxidized backgrounds on ornamented silver surfaces were customary in the nineteenth century. These backgrounds are part of the design and *should not be removed.* Don't overpolish. Never use a buffing wheel on such surfaces.

Two different casting methods were employed by Gorham in making souvenir spoons:

1. Sand casting.
2. Lost–wax casting.

In both cases the first step was to fabricate by hand a metal model of the spoon. This model was then used to make a master casting pattern in bronze. The bronze master pattern was carefully chased and hand finished. This bronze master pattern was then used in the subsequent manufacture of all silver spoons. (If the volume of production was high, more than one master casting pattern was made.)

SAND CASTING: Most of the simpler souvenir spoons, such as the Actress spoons in Figure 188, were made by sand casting. The master pattern (or patterns) with connecting gates was packed between two layers of fine French casting sand. The layers were then separated, the pattern removed, and the two halves pinned together. Molten silver filled the space left by the pattern. After cooling, the casting was taken out of the sand, and the gates cut off. Rough edges were polished and the spoons were then finished in the same way as the die–struck examples.

LOST–WAX PROCESS: Spoons with complex, three–dimensional designs (Fig. 203), particularly those designs with undercutting, were made by the lost–wax process. (The lost–wax process for bronzes is described in Chapter 8.) The usual practice was to make several spoons at a time—up to a dozen. The master bronze pattern was first copied in wax by the use of two–section molds. The wax replicas were then modeled with tools to the degree of finish required in the casting. The finished wax spoon forms, with connecting gates, were then covered with a "mother shell" of damp clay, the interior of which took a negative impression of the wax surface. When the whole mass was heated, the wax melted and ran out of vents provided for the purpose (the "lost" wax). The space which it had previously occupied was then filled with molten silver. After cooling, the casting was broken out. The gates and vents were removed and rough edges smoothed. This was followed by oxidation and light polishing.[10]

A particular handle design was often used with different bowl designs to create "new" spoons. The interchangeability of parts in the making of souvenir spoons obviously saved time and money and enabled Gorham to greatly increase its output of new spoons in a time like 1890 and 1891 when there was a rush to get a lot of different spoons on the market. Figure 181 shows five different bowls all using the same cast Indian–with–arrow handle. Figure 184 shows four of the Columbian Exposition spoons, all with the same die–struck handle. Bowls were also interchangeable. The bowl with the rocky seascape is used with an Indian in Figure 181 (No. 2), and with a bather in Figure 206 (No. 2).

The Spoons

Most of the spoons illustrated in this chapter are from the collection of several hundred souvenir spoons owned by the Gorham Company. Since it is possible to illustrate only a sampling of a hundred or so spoons, I thought I should be candid about how the selections were made. I consciously chose examples that delight the eye; that picture famous people or places; and that make, as a group, interesting design statements. Finally, a couple of spoons are illustrated which I found amusing, if not downright funny, although I know they were not meant to be.

Figure 180 illustrates two sizes (tea and coffee) of the most famous of all souvenir spoons, the Salem Witch

spoon, second version, first made in 1890 or 1891. The spoon, which shows all the paraphernalia of witchcraft—the witch, the broom, the cat, the rope, the new moon—was no doubt designed at Gorham. The Gorham spoon is much more interesting and more inventive than Durgin's "first version."

The Witch spoon was available in a number of sizes and forms. The following list is from *Souvenir Spoons* (p. 12):

Price List

Tea Spoon $3.00 with gold bowl $3.50
Orange Spoon 3.25 with gold bowl $3.50
Coffee Spoon 1.75 with gold bowl 2.00
Bonbon Spoon 3.25 with gold bowl 3.75
Sugar Spoon 3.50 with gold bowl 4.00
Sardine Fork 3.50 with gold tines 4.00
Paper Knife 3.50 large size 4.00

Indians were among the most popular of souvenir spoon motifs. Occasionally however, the juxtaposition

180 Salem Witch spoons. *Left*: teaspoon. Length: 5 1/2 in. (14.9 cm.). On front of handle, "SALEM 1692." Mark: STERLING. *Right*: coffee spoon. Length: 4 1/8 in. (10.5 cm.). On front of handle, "SALEM 1692. Mark: lion–anchor–G/STERLING/DANIEL LOW. *(Gorham collection)*.

PLATE I   Mixed-metal and silver berry bowl. In the Japanese taste; of circular form with spot-hammered surface, with raised bronze loop handles continuing around the foot rim and bound by silver wire, the body applied with water lilies with gold-sheathed buds, with applied die-rolled border around rim, the interior gilt. 1879
Height to bowl rim: 3 5/8 in. (9.2 cm.), Length over handles: 11 in. (27.9 cm.), Mark: B47

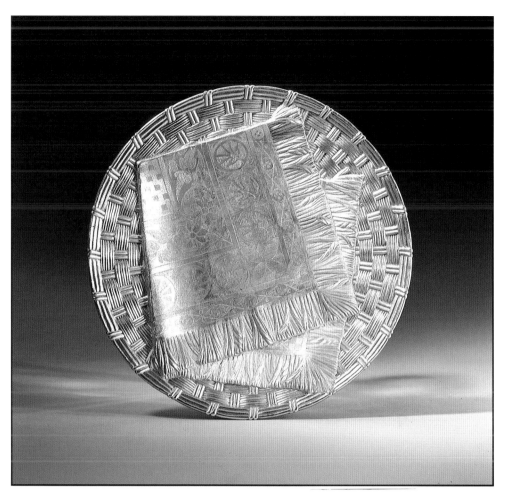

PLATE III   Parcel-gilt silver fruit plate. In the Russian taste; of circular form, the field finely chased with basketweave design centering a fringed damask napkin with gilt borders, on circular foot, engraved on base with inscription *Clara from F. F. C. June 7th 1881.* 1881
Diameter: 10 in. (25.4 cm.), Mark: Z312

PLATE II   (left) Silver-mounted iron tea caddy. Of oval form with fluted base, the sides applied with a silver dragon, fan, and the initials A.R., further inset with a panel depicting a sculptor carving a demon mask, the slip-on cover surmounted by an applied silver crab and carved with stylized scrolls. 1883
Height: 6 1/4 in.(15.9 cm.), Mark: W27. See illustration p. 80

(right) Silver-mounted copper tray. In the Japanese taste; of oval form, the surface hammered into bark texture, the sides raised and rolled over, applied with copper plum blossoms and twigs, silver pine branches, and a Japanese figure riding the back of a yak and playing the flute. 1883
Length: 9 1/4 in. (23.5 cm.), Mark: Y59

(top) Silver-mounted ivory loving cup. In the Japanese taste; of cylindrical form, with scalloped silver rim at base, the sides applied with a bird, palm fronds, a spider, a dragon and a later shield, the handles with silver joins, one also applied with a bug, with glass bottom. 1883
Height: 5 5/8 in. (14.3 cm.), Mark: P/7. See illustrations 87 & 89 p. 79

PLATE IV   (left) Mixed-metal and silver bowl. In the Japanese taste; of circular form with spot-hammered surface, on spreading base, the sides applied with copper grape vines suspending copper grapes and gilt leaves, also applied with a copper butterfly, swallows in flight, and shore birds by a marsh, the rim slightly convex. 1882
Height: 2 1/2 in. (6.4 cm.), Diameter: 6 5/8 in. (16.8 cm.), Mark: 1847

(right) Silver-mounted copper tea caddy. In the Japanese taste; of ginger-jar form, the spot-hammered copper surface applied with branches with silver leaves and flowers, a silver bird and moth, the slip-on cover applied with a silver lizard. 1882
Height: 4 1/4 in. (10.5 cm.), Mark: Y160

PLATE V   Five-piece silver tea and coffee service. In the Persian taste; comprising coffee pot, teapot, sugar bowl and cover, cream jug and waste bowl; each repoussé and chased with flowering fruit branches, the rim die-rolled with geometric decoration, the elephant's-head handles with ivory insulators, the spouts chased with flutes and flowers, the hammered hinged domed covers with reeded rectangular finials, each engraved on base *William and Clara Bryce from Mary Hemenway March 1st 1882*. 1881
Height of coffee pot: 7 1/2 in. (19 cm.), Mark: 1670

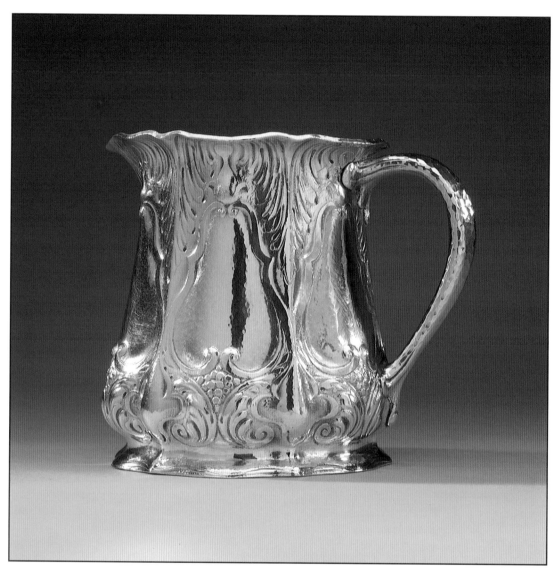

PLATE VI   Martelé silver pitcher. Of shaped baluster form on circular undulating base, with spot-hammered
                  surface and handle, the body chased with panels of strapwork and leaves, with flaring undulating
                  rim. Designed in 1897 by William C. Codman
                  Height: 6 1/4 in. (15.7 cm.), Weight: 29oz. 10dwt., Mark: 9458 in oval
                  See illustration p. 188

PLATE VII   Martelé silver flagon (Martelé Tankard). In the Art Nouveau taste; of cylindrical form, with spreading base and scalloped border, with repoussé foliage, rising to diagonal sweeping ribs, the handle issuing from a leaf, with chased
foliate decoration, with similar vines and leaves at the shoulder, with undulating rim to fit the shaped domed cover
and lipped spout, with rolling thumbpiece. Designed by William C. Codman for the Paris exposition of 1900.
Height: 15 5/8 in. (39.7 cm.), Mark: 4294

PLATE VIII   Silver coffee pot. Athenic pattern; of shaped baluster form on molded base, the body repoussé, chased and engraved with strapwork and flowers, with curving ivory handle and undulating rim, the hinged domed cover with ivory baluster finial. 1902
Height: 10 3/4 in. (27 cm.), Mark: A2836

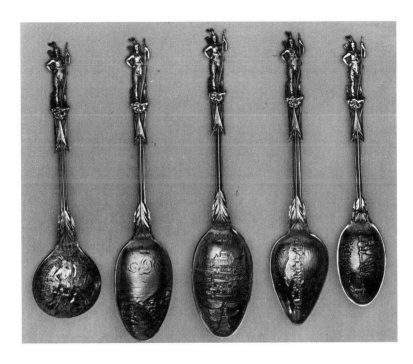

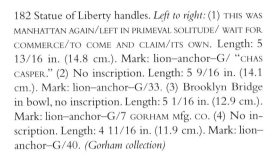

181 Indian handles. *Left to right*: (1) SARATOGA SPRINGS. Length: 5 1/8 in. (13 cm.). Mark: lion–anchor–G. (2) Rocky sea coast (no inscription). Length: 5 5/8 in. (14.3 cm.). Mark: lion–anchor–G/STERLING. (3) "PAXINOSA INN/ LAFAYETTE COLLEGE." Length: 5 3/4 in. (14.6 cm.). Mark: lion–anchor–G/STERLING. (4) "BAR HARBOR" Length: 5 3/8 in. (13.7 cm.). Mark: lion–anchor–G/STERLING. (5) "CHICAGO," Length: 5 in. (12.7 cm.). No mark. *(Gorham collection).*

182 Statue of Liberty handles. *Left to right:* (1) THIS WAS MANHATTAN AGAIN/LEFT IN PRIMEVAL SOLITUDE/ WAIT FOR COMMERCE/TO COME AND CLAIM/ITS OWN. Length: 5 13/16 in. (14.8 cm.). Mark: lion–anchor–G/ "CHAS CASPER." (2) No inscription. Length: 5 9/16 in. (14.1 cm.). Mark: lion–anchor–G/33. (3) Brooklyn Bridge in bowl, no inscription. Length: 5 1/16 in. (12.9 cm.). Mark: lion–anchor–G/7 GORHAM MFG. CO. (4) No inscription. Length: 4 11/16 in. (11.9 cm.). Mark: lion–anchor–G/40. *(Gorham collection)*

of an Indian–brave finial with such bowls as Paxinosa Inn in Figure 181 seems inappropriate. One suspects this was purely an arbitrary selection by the customer. The Statue of Liberty spoons in Figure 182 were certainly made with New York City visitors in mind. Replicas of the great statue of Bartholdi of *Liberty Enlightening the World* were widely used on souvenir spoons. Many versions, by many makers, were made of the bronze lady and her torch.

Many souvenir spoons made use of borrowed design ideas. The four spoons in Figure 183 have handle outlines based on Gorham's *St. Cloud* pattern. It was obviously a device to save design time and tooling costs. Another somewhat related example is the use of the same die–struck handles on a series of related bowls in the Columbian Exposition spoons with their identical handles and different bowls, illustrating the principal buildings of the fair (Fig. 184).

The 1893 Chicago Columbian Exposition represented the high noon of the souvenir spoon day. Dozens of spoons were made specifically for the fair. Gorham made, in addition to the fair building series in Figure 184, a number of serving pieces illustrating what they called "The Story of Columbus in Pictures of Silver." Fourteen notable events in the life of the great navigator were used to make handle illustrations for serving pieces, which ranged from knives and forks to ladles and salt

183 *St. Cloud* handles. *Left to right*: (1) "1777/ISRAEL PUTNAM/ 1843." Length: 5 15/16 in. (15.1 cm.). Mark: lion–anchor–G/E. SCHALL HARTFORD/PAT. 1891. (2) "RED JACKET." Length: 5 7/8 in. (14.9 cm.). Mark: lion–anchor–G. (3) Racetrack scene in bowl. On handle, "ROCHESTER/ MINN." Length: 5 7/8 in. (14.9 cm.). Mark: lion–anchor–G. (4) "RICHFIELD SPRING/ N.Y." Length: 5 3/4 in. (14.6 cm.). Mark: lion–anchor–G. *(Gorham collection)*.

184 Columbian Exposition spoons. *Left to right*: (1) "LIBERAL ARTS BUILDING, CHICAGO 1893." (2) "HORTICULTURE HALL, CHICAGO 1893." (3) "ELECTRICITY BUILDING, CHICAGO 1893." (4) "FORESTRY BUILDING, CHICAGO 1893." Length of all spoons: 5 1/2 in. (14 cm.) Mark on all spoons: lion–anchor–G/STERLING/SPAULDING & CO. *(Gorham collection)*.

spoons. There was a total of sixty–six different pieces. Although drawings of these pieces are in the Gorham files, no actual serving pieces were located.

The graves of Generals Ulysses S. Grant and Robert E. Lee illustrated on the spoon bowls in Figure 185 are somber reminders of the Civil War.

Fraternal orders—the Elks and the Masons—are fea–tured on the spoons in Figure 186.

The spoons featuring American actresses and actors in Figures 187 and 188 were made for the Actors Fund Fair which was held at New York's Madison Square Garden, May 2–7, 1892. The booths at the fair were manned by well–known actresses. Souvenir spoon sales were brisk. One published account noted that $600 worth of spoons were sold at the silver booth within twenty minutes after the fair opened. The six–day event

185   186   187

185 Grant and Lee. *Left*: GRANT'S TOMB/NEW YORK. Length: 5 7/8 in. (14.9 cm.). Mark: lion–anchor–G. *Right*: "GEN R. E. LEE/1807/LEXINGTON, VA." Length: 5 7/8 in. (14.9 cm.). Mark: lion–anchor–G. *(Gorham collection)*.

186 Fraternal orders. *Left*: "B.P.O.E." (Brotherhood of Protective Order of Elks). Length: 5 5/8 in. (14.3 cm.). Mark: lion–anchor–G. *Right*: Masonic spoon, "SAGINAW." Length: 5 7/8 in. (14.9 cm.). Mark: lion–anchor–G. *(Gorham collection)*.

187 Actor's Fund spoon. On back, "ACTORS FUND FAIR/MAY 2nd to 7th 1892." On bowl, "PARK THEATER/NEW YORK." Front, top to bottom, "CUSHMAN/ANDERSON/MORRIS/ETHEL/LOTTA." On back, "FORREST/BOOTH/DAVENPORT/JEFFERSON/FLORENCE." Length: 5 7/8 in. (14.9 cm.). Mark: lion–anchor–G. *(Gorham collection)*

raised $186,500 for the Actors Fund "ensuring the perpetuity of its work of mercy and charity."[11]

The attractive Catskill landscape spoons in Figure 189, with their pseudo–Chinese calligraphy, are paired with the industrial landscape of the Coal Breaker spoon in Figure 190. As with so many other spoons in James's

Souvenir Spoons, the Coal Breaker spoon advertisement (p. 93) makes no mention of Gorham; only the local jeweler, in this case, W. H. Mortimer, Pottsville, Pennsylvania.

Figures 191, 192, and 193 feature more Indians. In Figure 191 the figure on the left holds a handgun in his right hand, while the Indian on the right has a spear in his left hand. Both Indians seem to have been made from the same basic casting pattern. The handles and the bowls of the spoons in Figure 192 are vigorously modeled. Figure 193 features busts of Indians. There seems to have been an attempt at portraiture on the two spoons on the right—Montezuma and Ouray, Colorado.

With Gorham having its factory at Providence, Rhode Island, it is only natural that a considerable number of souvenir spoons were made for places in the state of Rhode Island. Figure 194 shows four Rhode Island seal spoons for New port, Narragansett, Providence (showing Roger Williams's arrival), and Jamestown. There were many others.

Figure 195 shows spoons for three cities: Detroit, Chicago, and Washington. Figure 196 is a small but robust spoon with the White House depicted in the bowl. Figure 197 shows the state seals of Pennsylvania, Maine, and New York.

188

189

190

The hollow–handled cheese knife in Figure 198 was based on a design patented by Gorham (W. C. Codman, Pat. No. 27,588, dated August 31, 1897). The patent was directly assigned to Greenleaf and Crosby of Jacksonville, Florida. The design features a coat of arms on one side and a sally–port or gate on the other, the whole being decorated with oranges and orange leaves.

188 Actress spoons. *Left to right*: (1) "SARAH BERNHARDT." (2) "ANNIE RUSSEL." (3) "ROSE COGHLAN." (4) "FANNY DAVENPORT." (5) "AGNES BOOTH." (6) "MADGE KENDALL." (7) "MAY ROBSON." (8) "EFFIE SHANNON." (9) "MAUDE HARRISON." (10) "ROSINA VOKES." (11) "HELOISE MODJESKA." (12) "GEORGIA CAYVAN." (13) "LILLIAN RUSSELL." (14) "MARIE BURROUGHS." (15) "SYDNEY ARMSTRONG." Length: 4 1/2 in. (11.4 cm.). Mark: lion–anchor–G. *(Gorham collection)*.

189 Catskill spoons. *Left*: Orange spoon, "CATSKILL MOUNTAINS." Length: 5 13/16 in. (14.8 cm.). Mark: 692 Pat. 1892/ lion–anchor–G. *Right*: "CATSKILL MOUNTAINS." On banner, "KAATERSKILL FALLS." Length: 5 15/16 in. (15.1 cm.). Mark: lion–anchor–G. 693 PAT. 1892. *(Gorham collection)*.

190 Coal Breaker spoon. Length: 6 in. (15.2 cm.). Mark: lion–anchor–G. *(Gorham collection)*.

191 Indian chiefs. *Left*: SEAL OF THE CITY OF/ PITTSBURGH. Length: 4 15/16 in. (12.5 cm.). No mark. *Right*: on barrel in bowl, "B&CO/ PADUCAH"; on handle, "PADUCAH." Length: 4 5/8 in. (11.7 cm.). No mark. *(Gorham collection)*.

191

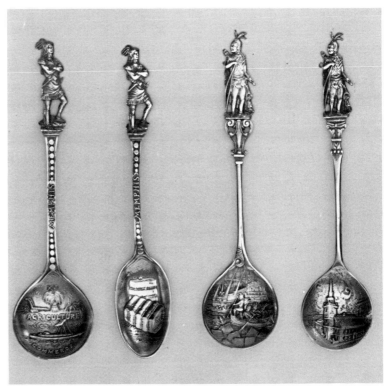

192

193

192 More Indians. *Left to right*: (1) In bowl, "AGRICULTURE/ COMMERCE"; on handle, "MEMPHIS." Length: 5 3/16 in. (13.2 cm.). Mark: lion–anchor–G. (2) "MEMPHIS." Length: 5 in. (12.7 cm.). (3) Boston Tea Party. Length: 5 in. (12.7 cm.). Mark: lion–anchor–G. (4) Old South Meeting House. Length: 5 in. (12.7 cm.). Mark: lion–anchor–G. *(Gorham collection).*

193 Indian busts. *Left to right*: (1) "SARATOGA SPRINGS." Length: 5 1/2 in. (14 cm.). Mark: lion–anchor–G. (2) Orange spoon, no inscription. Length: 5 5/8 in. (14.3 cm.). Mark: lion– anchor–G. (3) "SAN MIGUEL CHAPEL SANTA FE/NM/ BATTLE OF CHRISTIANITY IN AMERICA/1550. On handle, MONTEZUMA." Length: 5 13/16 in. (14.8 cm.). Mark: lion–anchor–G. (4) "OURAY COLORADO." Length: 5 7/8 in. (14.9 cm.). Mark: lion–anchor–G. *(Gorham collection).*

194 Rhode Island spoons. *Left to right*: (1) "THE/LIME-ROCKS/NEWPORT/R.I." Length: 5 1/4 in. (13.3 cm.). Mark: lion–anchor–G. (2) "NARRAGANSETT/PIER/RHODE ISLAND." Length: 5 1/4 in. (13.3 cm.). Mark: lion–anchor–G. (3) "WHAT CHEER/1636." Length: 5 1/5 in. (13 cm.). Mark: lion–anchor–G. (4) "THE DUMPLINGS/JAMESTOWN/R.I." Length: 5 7/8 in. (14.9 cm.). Mark: lion–anchor–G/H.A. HEATH & CO. (*Gorham collection*)

195 Cities. *Left to right*: (1) "CITY OF DETROIT/ MICHIGAN." Length: 6 in. (15.2 cm.). Mark: lion–anchor–G. (2) "CITY OF CHICAGO/ INCORPORATED 4th MARCH 1837." (Note face at tip of bowl.) Mark: lion–anchor–G. (3) "WASHINGTON." Length: 5 5/8 in. (14.3 cm.) Mark: lion–anchor–G. (*Gorham collection*).

196 "PRESIDENTS MANSION." Length: 4 7/8 in. (12.4 cm.). Mark: lion–anchor–G. (*Gorham collection*).

197 State seals. *Left to right*: (1) Independence Hall, state seal of Pennsylvania. Length: 5 in. (12.7 cm.). Mark: lion–anchor–G. (2) "BAR HARBOR," state seal of Maine. Length: 5 1/4 in. (13.3 cm.). Mark: lion–anchor–G. (3) "GENESEE FALLS," state seal of New York. Length: 5 1/4 in. (13.3 cm.). Mark: lion–anchor–G. (4) "PORTLAND," state seal of Maine. Length: 5 3/4 in. (14.6 cm.). Mark: lion–anchor–G. (*Gorham collection*)

198 Cheese knife, hollow sterling handle, electroplated blade. Engraved on blade, "ST AUGUSTINE/FLORIDA." Stamped on opposite side of blade, "GREENLEAF & CROSBY CO./FLORIDA." Length: 8 1/2 in. (21.6 cm.). Mark: lion–anchor–G/STERLING (*private collection*).

199 The sea. *Left*: Battle of Lake Erie. Length: 6 1/8 in. (15.6 cm.). Mark: lion–anchor–G. *Right*: Whaling City (New Bedford). Length: 5 3/8 in. (13.7 cm.). (*Gorham collection*).

200 The souvenir spoon as sculpture. *Left to right*: (1) "HOTEL BON AIR/AUGUSTA, GA." Length: 5 5/16 in. (13.5 cm.). Mark: lion–anchor–G/STERLING. (2) 1861. Length: 5 7/8 in (14.9 cm.). Mark: lion–anchor–G. (3) On bowl, "SAVANNAH, GA/CITY HALL"; on back, "MONUMENT/TO/GEN GREENE/OF/RHODE ISLAND." Length: 4 15/16 in. (12.5 cm.). (4) "NASSAU HALL/PRINCETON." Length: 4 13/16 in. (12.2 cm.). (*Gorham collection*).

196

197

198

199

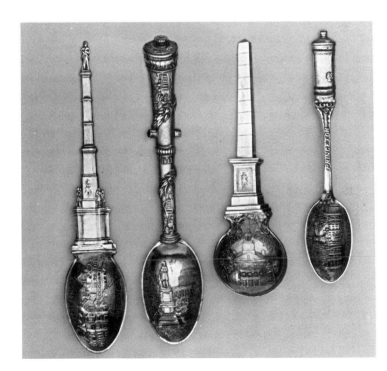

200

201

202

201 Sculptured portrait heads. *Left to right*: (1) Robert Ingersoll, "REASON/LIBERTY." Length: 5 7/8 in. (14.9 cm.). Mark: lion–anchor–G/PAT. 1892. (2) On back, "REV. R. W. BEECHER"; in bowl, "CITY OF CHURCHES." Length: 6 in. (15.2 cm.). (3) "1706 B. FRANKLIN 1790." Length: 6 in. (15.2 cm.). (4) "COL./DRAKE/FIRST OIL WELL." Length: 5 13/16 in. (14.8 cm.). (*Gorham collection*).

202 Pine cones and nutmeg. *Left to right*: (1) "WAUPACA." Length: 5 5/16 in. (13.5 cm.). Mark: lion–anchor–G/STERLING. (2) "CITY OF BANGOR/ INCORPORATED/FEB 12/ 1831." On handle, "CHAMPLAIN AND DUMONTS 1605." Length: 5 1/4 in. (13.3 cm.). Mark: lion–anchor–G/STERLING. (3) "LAKEWOOD." Length: 5 3/8 in. (13.7 cm.). Mark: lion–anchor–G/STERLING. (4) "CONNECTICUTENSIS/SIGILLUM REIPUBLICAE". Length: 4 3/4 in. (12.1 cm.). Mark: lion–anchor–G/STERLING. (*Gorham collection*).

Figure 199 illustrates two beautifully modeled spoons with thoroughly marine motifs. The Battle of Lake Erie spoon on the left has the sailor finial perched on a twisted rope handle with anchor. The whaling spoon on the right features a whaling bark in full sail, an old–fashioned harpoon, and the sperm whale churning in the spoon bowl.

Figures 200 through 204 suggest that souvenir spoons can function as sculpture. With most of these spoons we think much less of their original function as spoons than how they work as art. In fact, purely as spoons some of these examples would be almost useless.

Perhaps the most obvious examples of souvenir spoons as sculpture are Nos. 1 and 3 of Figure 200, where actual architectural elements, such as outdoor monuments, are used as elements in the spoon design. In the same way the portrait busts, copied from sculptured heads, are used as finials in Figure 201.

The nature–handled spoons in Figure 202 are related to the flower spoons that were so popular in the 1890s

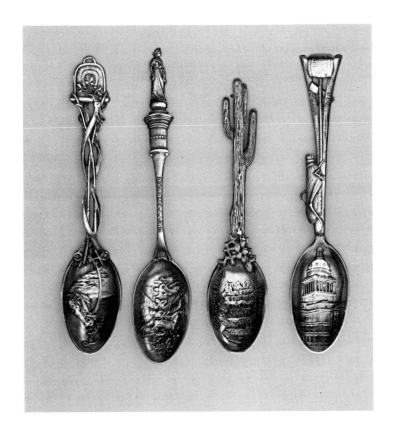

203 *Left to right*: (1) "ROCHESTER/MINN." Length: 5 5/8 in. (14.3 cm.). Mark: lion–anchor–G. (2) "GETTYSBURG." Length: 6 in. (15.2 cm.). Mark: lion–anchor–G. (3) CASA GRANDE RUINS/ARIZONA. Length: 5 1/4 in. (13.3 cm.). Mark: lion–anchor–G. (4) "LINCOLN/NEB." Length: 5 7/8 in. (14.8 cm.). Mark: lion–anchor–G. (*Gorham collection*).

204 *Left to right*: (1) "OLD/ORCHARD/BEACH." Length: 5 5/8 in. (14.3 cm.). (2) "U.S.A./SPRINFIELD MASS." Length: 5 5/8 in. (14.3 cm.). (3) "HUTCHINSON/KANSAS." On barrels, "SALT." Length: 5 3/4 in. (14.6 cm.). (4) "BETHLEHEM PA/FIRST HOUSE 1741." Length: 5 1/5 in. (13 cm.). (*Gorham collection*).

and early 1900s. Some of the most interesting and inventive of all Gorham souvenir spoons are the examples in Figures 203 and 204. Whimsy is a good word for such delightful spoons as the Rochester, Minnesota, spoon, with its tangle of "leather" lines leading to the stirrup–tipped handle; the cactus–handle Casa Grande Ruins spoon; or the trumpet–handle Bethlehem, Pennsylvania, spoon announcing the dawn of a new day.

There were a number of spoons commemorating the great Chicago Fire of 1871 and the Phoenix–like rising of the city out of the ashes. The little spoon in Figure 205 certainly deals with the symbolism of this tragic event, but somehow one feels that the sculptor got a bit carried away with his scantily clad, voluptuous lady. He created her in the great Chicago Exposition cheesecake tradition that was so ably carried on in the Chicago World's Fair of 1934, when the author, a high–school boy from West Virginia, watched Sally Rand dance gracefully across a dimly lit stage in swirls of shimmering, diaphanous fans.

The bathing beauties in Figure 206 must be taken more seriously. The anonymous author of *Souvenir Spoons of America* informs us that: "The handle of the spoon, as seen in the illustration, is modelled after the celebrated statue by Tabacchi, of Rome, The Bather, which during

205 Cheesecake and the Chicago fire. The "I MUST" spoon, "1871" front and back. Length: 5 in. (12.7 cm.). Mark: JOHN LARSON & CO/lion–anchor–G. (*Gorham collection*).

206 Bathing beauties. *Left to right*: (1) "GLENWOOD SPRINGS COLO." Length: 4 3/4 in. (12.1 cm.). Mark: lion–anchor. G. (2) No inscription. Length: 5 13/16 in. (14.8 cm.). Mark: lion–anchor–G. (3) "GLENWOOD SPRINGS COLO." Length: 5 3/4 in. (14.6 cm.). Mark: lion–anchor–G. (*Gorham collection*).

the past fifteen years has been reproduced a thousand–fold. The miniature is perfectly executed and artistically finished in high relief" [p. 40]. Not that one doesn't believe the author, but one wonders whether Mr. Tabacchi's statue really looked like that. Did his lady wear that bathing suit?

Some of the most interesting of the souvenir spoons are the enameled examples in Figure 207. Because of the additional time and expense involved in the making of such spoons they are relatively scarce. Far fewer of them were made.

At the beginning of this chapter the engraving of ordinary spoons to make souvenirs was mentioned. Figure 208 show four standard Gorham pattern spoons so engraved. The engraving could have been done by Gorham in Providence on order, or a local engraver could have done the work. The knowledge of engraving, like so many other silver–making skills, was much more widespread the turn of the century than it is now.

The last souvenir spoon shown is the "Gorham spoon"

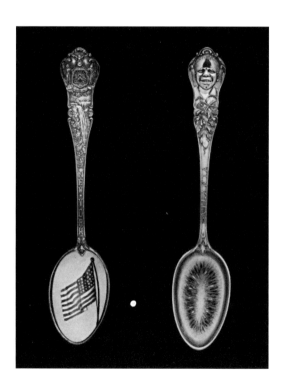

207 Enameled bowls. *Left*: "NEW YORK." Mark: lion–anchor–G/H 943 STERLING. *Right*: "ATLANTA." Mark: lion–anchor–G/STERLING/CHARLES W. CRANKSHAW 1896. (*Margaret Woodbury Strong Museum, Rochester, N.Y.*).

in Figure 209, which pictures the new plant in Elmwood in the bowl, and the company seal with the Gorham mark as the handle. James noted that this spoon was "presented to visitors to their factory in Elmwood, in the city of Providence, R.I."

The decade of the 1890s was the heyday of souvenir spoons. Most of Gorham's spoons were made in the first half of that decade. By 1905 Gorham had started to sell dies for some of their spoons. The craze had spent itself. Souvenir spoons were a truly popular art form. Most of the forms were quite different from the Academic and Art Nouveau forms of Gorham's more sophisticated silverwares of the 1890s. However, it was not necessarily a case of high versus low art. Souvenir spoons cannot be relegated to low art. Many were beautifully designed and crafted. It was just the fact that style was not a primary concern of souvenir spoons. They were celebrations of people and places and events.

The collecting of souvenir spoons in the 1890s was part of the Colonial Revival movement. There was a new interest in the country's past—the romance of history. People became more and more interested in the monuments of the past at the very time when these monuments started to disappear. The American Indians were never more romantic than when most of them had been killed off; Grant and Lee were universally mourned— after they were dead. But one must not be too cynical. Perhaps we should not take souvenir spoons *that* seriously. Accept them for what they are. Interesting, sometimes fascinating, reminders of our past.

208 Souvenir spoons made by engraving the bowls of regular Gorham patterns. *Left to right:* (1) *New Plymouth*, engraved "CITY HALL/MILWAUKEE WIS." On back, "1900." (2) *Fleury*, engraved "HIGH SCHOOL/LANCASTER, WIS." (3) *Strasbourg,* engraved "LIBERTY STATUE/NEW YORK." (4) *Wyndham*, engraved "LANCASTER/WIS." (*Private collection*).

209 The "Gorham spoon." Length: 5 7/8 in. (14.9 cm.). Mark: lion–anchor–G/STERLING. (*Courtesy Donna H. I Felger*).

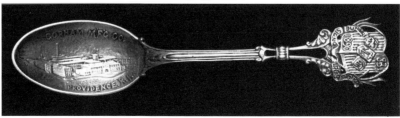

CHAPTER 11

Holbrook and Codman

The twenty–five–year period from 1890 to 1915, a time of great growth and real artistic achievement for Gorham, was dominated by two men, Edward Holbrook and William Christmas Codman. Holbrook was the entrepreneur, the salesman, the natural born leader. In the early 1900s he gained control, through a holding company, the Silversmiths Company, of a number of American silver manufacturers. By 1913 the Silversmiths Company had the folowing holdings:

Gorham Manufacturing Co., Providence, R.I.
William B. Durgin Co., Concord, N.H.
Whiting Manufacturing Co., New York, N.Y.
William B. Kerr, Newark, N.Y.
Roger Williams Silver Co., Providence, R.I.
The Mauser Manufacturing Co., Mt. Vernon, NJ.
Hayes & McFarland, New York, N.Y.

Edward Holbrook was indeed the John D. Rockfeller of the silver industry (Fig. 210).

If Holbrook dominated the management of Gorham, his designer, William C. Codman, certainly dominated the artistic direction of the company. Holbrook and Codman were proud and ambitious men and their whole efforts were geared toward making Gorham preeminent in the field of fine silverwares. The great international expositions were their principal promotional vehicles. Gorham had done well in the Philadelphia Centennial and the 1889 Paris Exposition, but Holbrook, being a realist, knew that his rival, Tiffany & Co., probably had a greater reputation in the United States, and certainly in Europe. He meant to change that.

Holbrook knew, of course, that the international expositions were mainly showcases, but he also was quite aware that reputations were made and lost at these expositions, and that winning top prizes *did* have a sizable commercial impact.

New Plant at Elmwood

As we have seen from the entries from Mr. Crins's diaries quoted in Chapter 7, the decision to build a new manufacturing plant was made soon after Edward Holbrook gained control of the company. The situation at the plant in downtown Providence had become difficult. The old rabbit warren of a building complex on Steeple Street had become jammed and there was no more room to expand (Fig. 138, Chapter 7). A move to a new site had become imperative.

The thirteen–acre site in the Elmwood section of Providence was deemed an ideal location. It was on the edge of the city, easily accessible by road and railroad.

210 Edward Holbrook, from a photograph of about 1910. (*Gorham collection*).

The plant, which was finished in 1890, was the most modern and efficient in the world for the making of silverwares and bronzes. The well-lit buildings, which were laid out with great care, occupied about six acres of the building site (Fig. 211). The complex had its own independent water supply, its own fire department, its own "electric light plant," its own photographic studio, and a building for making the wood cases for silverwares. The establishment was completely integrated, from sterling–alloy melting facilities, to the great pressroom for stamping flatware and hollow ware (Fig. 212).

The center building housed the offices, designing rooms, library, and museum. The museum contained plaster casts and examples of American and European silver, both original pieces and electrotype reproductions. (Apparently, much of the museum material was sold or discarded before World War II.)

211 Architect's drawing of the new Gorham plant in the Elmwood section of Providence, Rhode Island, about 1890. (*Gorham collection*).

212 Pressroom at the Gorham plant, about 1890. *(Gorham photograph)*.

William C. Codman

The new plant solved most of the company's production difficulties, but Holbrook was faced with a tough organizational problem. A new chief designer was needed. George Wilkinson, who was functioning as both superintendent and chief designer, was no longer very active in the latter capacity. When the new plant was finished in 1890 he was seventy–one and not in very good health. Antoine Heller obviously was not considered for the top job. His niche was design, modeling, and die–cuttings.

In 1891 Holbrook hired William Christmas Codman, a fifty–two–year–old Englishman, as Gorham's chief designer (Fig. 213). Codman, who *was* born on Christmas Day (1839), showed an early talent for painting and drawing. He studied art in Norwich, England. His first job in the art world involved three seasons decorating the nave of Ely Cathedral, a beautiful old structure at the Isle of Ely in Cambridgeshire, which was begun by the Normans in 1081. The restoration of the Ely Cathedral was under the direction of Sir Gilbert Scott, a famous Victorian architect. T. Gambier Parry was the artist who was in charge of the painting of the Ely Cathedral nave, with young Codman acting as his assistant.[1]

213 William Christmas Codman, from a photograph of about 1895. *(Gorham collection)*.

William Codman worked as an ecclesiastical designer, making designs for Scott and later for Elkington, the well–known Birmingham silver maker. Codman, working for Scott, designed works for Westminster Abbey, All Saint's, and St. Mary's. He designed lighting fixtures for the Luxembourg Cathedral; the Communion plate for the See of Liverpool and the Memorial Chapel in Delhi, India; stained–glass windows in the Ottawa, Canada, Cathedral; and candelabra for St. Paul's in London.

Although Codman was known in England as an ecclesiastical designer working in the Gothic style (Fig. 214), he was also involved in furniture making. One of the well–known suites of late Victorian furniture was the one made in 1884–1887 for the music room of the New York house of Henry Gurdon Morguard, designed by Sir Lawrence Alma–Tadema, the English painter. The suite was described in J. Moyr Smith's *Ornamental Interiors* in 1887:

> …The furniture made by Messrs. Johnstone, Norman & Co. [London], it is of the most costly materials and exquisite design.
> …The designs of these veritable works of art in furniture has been done by Mr. Alma–Tadema and have been admirably worked out under his superintendence by Mr. W. C. Codman. To find furniture of equal beauty and intelligence of design and equal choiceness of material and workmanship, we should have to combine the palmy days of Greek art with the luxury of the Roman Empire at its best period of taste (pp. 95–96).[2]

The Alma–Tadema furniture made use of contrasting woods, cedar and ebony, inlaid with ivory, mother–of–pearl, and abalone shell. Codman was to use similar materials and a related design approach in the writing table and chair he made for Gorham in 1903 (Fig. 219).

Silver for the Columbian Exposition

Much of William Codman's time during his first two years with Gorham must have been spent in planning and designing works for the Columbian Exposition in Chicago. Originally, there had been talk of celebrating the four–hundreth anniversary of Columbus's voyage with a fair in New York. In fact, Gorham made a contribution in 1888 for a study proposal for a New York fair. The Chicago Columbian Exposition was originally scheduled for 1892, but it was 1893 before it finally opened.

Gorham planned a major exhibit for Chicago. The pieces Codman designed were intricate, sometimes flamboyant examples of Acadamic design. There was more

214 Portion of a drawing of the plan for a chandelier to hold thirteen candles, by William C. Codman, ca. 1885. (William Codman, *An Illustrated History of Silverware Design* [Providence: The Gorham Co., 1930], p. 20).

than a hint of what was called in the Introduction of this book the Exposition style.

The two pieces illustrated in Figures 215 and 216 are not the most extreme examples of the silver Codman designed for the Columbian Exposition. Other pieces were fancier, less restrained, and more overblown. The ewer tray with its bucolic cherub themes in Figure 215 is a detailed, beautifully crafted piece. The two–handled vase in Figure 216 is one of the most interesting pieces designed by Codman for Chicago. Although the chased ornament has clear Rococo origins, and the naturalistic leaves, tendrils, and fruit clusters hark back to High Victorian designs, this vase is very much of its time. The undulating body and the swirling freedom of the decorations forecast Codman's Art Nouveau designs. The vase is a key transition piece in Codman's work. Up to this time all of Codman's work that we know of was that of a traditional Victorian designer steeped in the styles of the past—styles which he used quite unselfconsciously.

215 Ewer tray, designed by William C. Codman for the 1893 Chicago Columbian Exposition. Diameter: 12 1/8 in. (30.8 cm.). *(Gorham photograph)*.

There is no indication that Codman was influenced by Japanese art. We have no record that he was in any way involved in the Aesthetic movement in England in the 1870s and 1880s. It was only after he came to America that his work began to change and evolve toward the new art of the time, Art Nouveau. Chapter 12, "Martelé," documents this side of Codman's work after 1893.

Some of the most florid pieces shown at Chicago were enameled and jeweled ewers and trays with enameled paintings of Venus in her shell and Fragonard dancers. The pieces of silver were made in Providence and the enameling was done in New York by G. de Festetics, a "collaborateur" of the Gorham Company who had been trained in Europe.[3]

The piece de resistance of the Gorham exhibit at Chicago in 1893 was the lifesized solid silver casting of *Christopher Columbus* modeled by Frederic Auguste Bartholdi (1834–1904) in Paris (Fig. 217). Bartholdi's most famous work, *Liberty Enlightening the World,* popularly known as the Statue of Liberty, had been erected on Bedloe's Island in New York harbor a few years before, in 1886.

The solid silver *Columbus* contained 30,000 troy oun-

216 Two–handled vase made about 1892. *(Gorham photograph)*.

217 Life–sized silver *Christopher Columbus*, modeled by Frederic Auguste Bartholdi, exhibited at the 1893 Chicago Columbian Exposition. Weight 30,000 troy ounces. *(Gorham photograph)*.

ces—a ton—of sterling. It was celebrated as the largest silver sculpture in the world. It was apparently melted down early in this century, but there *were* bronze casts made of it.

The Gorham exhibit at the 1893 Columbian Exposition was well received. The company was awarded fifty–five medals and the critics were kind. *The New York Times* of September 20, 1893, had a long, glowing, three–columned account of the Gorham exhibit. The official French government report on the Columbian Exposition, published in 1894, compared the Gorham and Tiffany exhibits:

The two great American Silversmiths have very different styles. Tiffany is the silversmith–jeweler, with whom silver is only a pretext for jewels and enamel work Gorham is the silversmith proper—the great manufacturer who produces silverware for daily use, and who throws every day on the American market, millions of table services—in silver and plated ware— but who owes to the mechanical processes and complete equipment of which he has the use, the means of doing well and economically work to satisfy his customers. At the same time, he is able to produce artistic and decorative work, calling for the highest skilled and careful hand labor.[4]

The French report praised the Gorham exhibit, but it chided the company for including the Century Vase at Chicago after it had been shown at Philadelphia in 1876

218 Centerpiece with detachable vase, made in 1903 for the St. Louis Exposition. Height: 17 3/4 in. (45 cm.). Width: 23 1/2 in. (59.7 cm.). Mark: lion–anchor–G/FCT/SL. (*Gorham collection*).

219 Lady's writing table and chair designed by William. C. Codman, made in 1903. Length of table: 50 in. (127 cm.). Depth: 28 in. (71.1 cm.). Total height: 50 in. (127 cm.). *(Museum of Art, Rhode Island School of Design)*.

and Paris in 1889. Gorham never exhibited the Century Vase again.

Although Chicago represented the high point of Academic style for Gorham, they continued making fine examples in the style for quite a few years. The large centerpiece in Figure 218 combines the Academic style with Art Nouveau.

One of William C. Codman's great tour–de–force designs in the Academic style (with bits of Art Nouveau flourishes) is the spectacular inlaid–ebony lady's writing table and chair made in 1903 (Fig. 219). No doubt Codman's experience in working on the Alma–Tadema furniture, mentioned earlier, inspired him to make his own designs.

The ebony table has ornamental mountings of silver, and inlays of silver, ivory, redwood, boxwood, and mother–of–pearl. The mirror on top of the table and the gallery at back are silver, ornamented with poppies and morning glories. Around the top is a band of thuya wood. The top and sides are decorated with lilies, wild roses, chrysanthemums, and pine cones. The chair is made of ebony, with silver mountings and ivory moldings. The cover of the seat is leather, handwrought, carved, and embossed.

The following statistics may be noted on the writing table and chair:

	Table	Chair
Sterling Silver	661 ounces	99 ounces
Silversmithing	1695 hours	558 hours
Chasing	2709 hours	850 hours
Modeling	12 weeks	7 weeks
Inlaying Cost	$3700	

The writing table, which bears Codman's signature, and the chair were first shown at the St. Louis Exposition in 1904 where they were awarded a gold medal. They were also exhibited at the Panama–Pacific International Exposition in San Francisco in 1915.

The price set on them was $25,000. They were purchased for a Lady Esther, in whose English drawing room they remained for a number of years. Lady Esther's maiden name was Antoinette Heckscher and her father was August Heckscher, a well–known American financier.

In 1954 the writing table and chair turned up at Christie's in London. It was purchased for $3500 by Mr. & Mrs. Frederick B. Thurber of Providence, descendants of John Gorham's partner, Gorham Thurber, and given to the Rhode Island School of Design.

Chantilly

On July 30, 1895 William Codman was granted a design patent for a new flatware pattern which was named *Chantilly,* for the old town of the same name twenty–five miles northeast of Paris. *Chantilly* was a pretty pattern, but certainly not very daring in its design. Its overlapping scrolls discreetly surround plain surfaces which are topped by a fleur–de–lis (Fig. 220). The most interesting thing about *Chantilly* is its popularity. It is the most popular sterling flatware pattern made in the twentieth century by any firm. Even today, over eight decades after it was first issued, it continues to be Gorham's best–selling sterling flatware pattern.

Why? Many people have tried to answer that question without much success. A common answer is that *Chantilly* is not too fancy and not too plain. It is not flashy in design, and it is not flashy in its finish. The standard finish for the handle of *Chantilly* pieces is a mat, satin surface called a butler finish. The handles are oxidized to emphasize the pattern.

William Codman designed over fifty flatware patterns during his twenty–three years at Gorham, but none of them have had the staying power of *Chantilly*.

220 *Chantilly* salad fork and spoon. Engraved MLB. Length: 83/4 in. (22.2 cm.). Mark: PAT. 1895/lion–anchor–G/STERLING. (*Courtesy Mona Sawyer*)

Colonial Revival Silver

The Colonial Revival style really came into its own in the first years of this century, becoming the dominant style in Gorham hollow ware, a position it has maintained to this day. Since Colonial Revival is a kind of watered–down version of "Early American" styles it has always been slightly suspect. It has usually been treated unkindly by critics, being dismissed as pop culture. The problem is that it is, and has been for the last eighty years or so, the single most popular and enduring style in American silver.

As noted in the Introduction, the style was already called *Colonial* at the beginning of this century. Although John Holbrook's speech, parts of which were quoted, said the style derived from American and English eighteenth– and early nineteenth–century silver, the following quotation from a piece of Gorham promotional literature on their Louis XVI silver (ca. 1912) includes French silver as a source of *Colonial*:

221

LOUIS XVI

With the accession of Louis XVI and Marie Antoinette, came a complete revolution in the world of art.

The marked characteristic of the style is a well defined return to more symmetrical and more classic forms. Another point of interest for us in America in the Louis XVI period is the fact that this style, transmitted through England in the time of the Georges, gave rise to our own Colonial, than which no style better adapted to our own home needs has been developed. One of its main elements of strength lies in the fact that it is in such exquisite taste, when executed, one never tires of it, as one often does of the more elaborately ornamented or over–ornamented style. It is good to live with, in everyday homes, and its refined beauty is beyond reproach.

The evidence of the Gorham catalogs of the first decade of the twentieth century suggests that the relatively plain Colonial Revival silver was fast replacing the more ornamental styles of the past. Some of the expensive tea and coffee services were still made in a variety of Academic styles, but such Colonial Revival pieces as the vegetable dish in Figure 221 and the salt and pepper in Figure 222 were the norm for this period. Figure 223 is a particularly attractive Colonial Revival jar, in which the green glass lining was blown into the silver bottle frame. The bottom of the silver frame is open to expose the glass.

222

Novelties and Children's Silver

Many delightful and interesting novelties and gadgets were made by Gorham during this period. In 1897 the company advertised widely to the trade that they were introducing a sterling postal scale (Fig. 224). The minature 3 1/2–inch patented scale was "warranted absolutely accurate." The sterling string holder in Figure 225 was made about 1895.

Children's silver, ranging from spoons to complete sets, obviously received a lot of design attention by Gorham. There were bowls, plates, cups, napkin rings, rattles, and flatware. Some of these sets are almost regal in their splendor; almost all were well designed. The crisply crafted plate and bowl in Figure 226 has a die–rolled border of vignettes of the farm, the household, and fairy tale.

Medals and Coins

Gorham made a number of medals during the last quarter of the nineteenth century and the first quarter of the

223

221 Vegetable dish made about 1905. Length: 11 1/16 in. (28 cm.). Mark: 306/STERLING/500/lion–anchor–G/5. *(The Margaret Woodbury Strong Museum)*.

222 Salt and pepper, dated 1908. Height: 5 1/4 in. (13.3 cm.). Mark: lion–anchor–G/STERLING, NDR. *(Gorham collection)*.

223 Green glass bottle with silver frame, ca. 1908. Height: 5 1/2 in. (14 cm.). *(Gorham collection)*.

224

225

224 Postal scale made about 1897. Engraved on top A.M.W. Height: 3 1/2 in. (10.9 cm.). Mark: lion–anchor–G/sterling/ B398/ PAT. APLD. FOR (*Margaret Woodbury Strong Museum*).

225 String holder made in 1895. Height: 3 3/4 in. (9.5 cm.). Mark: lion–anchor–G/10/sterling/ plus date mark for 1895. (*Burt collection*).

226 Child's bowl and plate made in 1900. Engraved on plate:"Virginia McKenny/from Grandfather and Grandmother/ McKenny /June 20th 1900." On bowl: "Baptized, August 26th 1900/by/The Reverend William B. Bodine D.D./St. James Chapel/ Elleron, New Jersey" plus same inscription as on the plate. Mark: lion–anchor–G/sterling/110 (bowl), 111 (plate). (*The National Museum of American History, Smithsonian Institution*).

present century. Three are illustrated in Figure 227. The Columbus celebration medal at the top was designed by Charles Frederick Naegele. The die was cut by Antoine Heller. The medal was made in gold ($150), silver ($5), bronze ($1), white metal (25 cents).

The Columbus medal shows the great navigator clean–shaven, surrounded by the ocean. On the margin, with their masts pointing toward the center, are representations of the *Santa Maria*, the *Pinta*, and the *Niña*. The reverse side of the Columbus medal bears the inscription:

October XII /MCCCXCII/ to /COMMEMORATE THE FOUR/ HUNDREDTH ANNIVERSARY OF/THE DISCOVERY OF AMERICA BY/CHRISTOPHER COLOMBUS/BY AUTHORITY OF THE/COMMITTEE OF ONE/HUNDRED CITIZENS/OF NEW YORK/OCTOBER XII/ MDCCCXCII/PAT'D 1893

The so–called Bryan dollars are among the best known of the Gorham medals or tokens.[5] In 1896 and 1900 William Jennings Bryan ran for the presidency on a platform of "free silver," demanding the free coinage of silver by the United States at a ratio of sixteen–to–one of silver to gold. The opposition, headed by William McKinley, attacked Bryan's position as being fiscally unsound. McKinley won in both 1896 and 1900.

Bryan's free–silver stance was satirized by silver tokens issued by Gorham (and others) in both 1896 and 1900 in which they literally put enough silver to make a coin equivalent to one gold dollar, which was bulky and unwieldy (Fig. 227, middle and bottom). The idea was to show how absurd Bryan's ideas were.

The Bryan "dollar" in the middle of Figure 227 has an inscription on the cartwheel:

SIZE OF GOVERNMENT DOLLAR
CONTAINING 412 1/2 GRAINS OF SILVER
900/1000 FINE.

On the reverse:

A GOVERNMENT DOLLAR
CONTAINS/412 1/2 GRAINS/COIN SILVER
900/1000 FINE/THIS PIECE CONTAINS
823 GRAINS COIN SILVER/IN VALUE
THE EQUIVALENT OF/ONE GOLD
DOLLAR/SEPT. 16TH 1896./GORHAM
MFG. CO., SILVERSMITHS

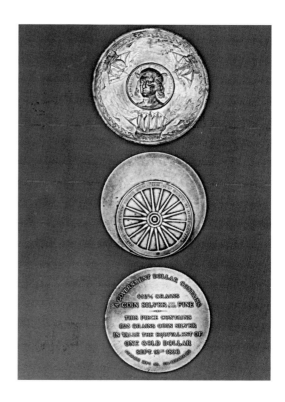

227 *Top*: The Columbian celebration medal, patented in 1893, in white metal. Diameter: 4 1/4 in. (5.7 cm.). *Middle*: Bryan "dollar," 1896. Diameter: 2 1/16 in. (5.2 cm.). *Bottom*: Bryan "dollar," 1896. Diameter: 2 1/16 in. (5.2 cm.).

The Bryan "dollar" at the bottom of Figure 227 has the same inscription as the reverse of the token in the middle. The reverse side of the token at the bottom of Figure 227 is blank.

There was a story about Gorham's Bryan tokens in a Providence paper in September 1896 saying they could be purchased for one dollar each. Sales were *too* good. A. B. Burdick, of Daniels, Cornell & Co. immediately placed an order and got this response:

Providence, Oct. 3, 1896

Messrs. Daniels, Cornell & Co.:
Gentlemen—

Your letter, with cheque for $25 for twenty–five of the silver tokens, is received. It makes us smile. We will not promise to send anymore. You can readily see that in putting 823 grains instead of 412 1/2, or in other words a dollar's worth of bullion in cash, we don't get a cent for our work. We only intended to make a limited number to illustrate and show what an "honest dollar" would be. The newspaper notice has stirred up a hornet's nest for us and we could sell a million at one dollar each, but where would we be?

Yours truly,
Gorham Manufacturing Co.
J. F. P. Lawton, Secretary

Gorham minted a few coins for foreign governments. In 1917 the company minted five- ten- and twenty-para coins for Serbia, and in 1919 five- and ten-centavos coins for Ecuador.

The rectangular "medal" or plaque in Figure 228 pictures the Gorham plant in about 1910 after the new wing to the south had been added. This medal was made in bronze and silver-plated bronze. It was designed and modeled by Edwin E. Codman, a son of William Christmas Codman.

229 Cut-glass bowl with sterling rim, made about 1900. Diameter: 9 in. (22.9 cm.). Mark on rim: lion–anchor–G/ STERLING D957. Glass has mark of L. Strauss & Sons, New York, N.Y. *(Private collection)*

228 Bronze plaque or medal, silver–plated, with view of Gorham plant, about 1910. Signed at lower right, "E. E. CODMAN SC. "Size: 11 5/16 in. x 3 1/2 in. (4.9 x 8.9 cm.)

Glass and Ceramics

Glass and ceramics were combined with silver in a number of ways by Gorham designers. The oldest method was the simple mounting of a piece of glass with a silver ornament, thus forming a clasping framework or mount. The cut-glass bowl in Figure 229, made about 1900, has a silver rim with a die-rolled border. The glass bowl was made by L. Strauss & Sons of New York City. The silver rim not only serves as a decorative element on the bowl, it also has the very practical function of strength-

ening the bowl and protecting the edge. The raw glass rims of most cut-glass bowls are their most vulnerable part.

The handsome carafe in Figure 230, made in 1904, has a silver neck chased with a stylized floral design mounted onto an intaglio-engraved glass bowl. The lobed glass base is unmarked. It could have been made by Dorflinger, Steuben, or Webb. T. G. Hawkes & Co. has also been suggested as a maker, but most of their glass of this period is marked.[6]

Another method of combining glass and silver, which was first employed by Gorham about 1892, involved blowing glass into a silver framework. These frameworks with glass consisted of small forms such as the bottle in Figure 223, up to a large vase made for the 1893 Columbian Exposition, with glass bulging from the interstices of the silver frame (not illustrated).

A third method, silver deposit, was used with both glass and ceramics. Since glass and ceramics are nonconductors of electricity they cannot normally be electroplated. The articles are transformed into electrical conductors by coating them completely with a composition containing graphite or similar conductive substance, then immersing them in a plating bath where the entire surface of the object is plated with silver. The design is then painted on top of the silver surface with a nonconductive "resist" varnish (Fig. 231). It is then placed in the plating bath under opposite conditions, with the plating current reversed. The silver, except those parts

230 Intaglio cut–glass carafe with sterling neck. Height: 9 3/4 in. (24.8 cm.). Mark: lion–anchor–G/STERLING 11 plus date mark for 1904. *(Private collection)*.

231 Making silver–deposit wares. Artist painting nonconductive "resist" varnish on a silver–coated bottle, ca. 1892. (Plate III, *Woman's Work at the Gorham Manufacturing Company Silversrmiths*).

232 Rookwood vase made in 1892 with silver–deposit decoration. The vase is signed A.V.B. (Artus van Briggle) plus 763SB on bottom. (*Mead Art Museum, Amherst College*).

of the surface covered by the nonconductive varnish, is redissolved from the piece, leaving the design intact. The varnish is removed from the design by an organic solvent, leaving the silver in the desired configuration on the surface of the glass or ceramic.

A number of pieces of Rookwood pottery were decorated with silver deposit for Gorham's exhibit at Chicago in 1893. The Rookwood Pottery had been founded in Cincinnati, Ohio, in 1880 by Maria Longworth Nichols to "give employment to the idle rich." What

started almost as a hobby quickly became a commercial and artistic success. By the 1890s Rookwood pottery was well known in America and Europe, the firm having won a gold medal at the 1889 Paris Exposition.[7]

The Rookwood vase in Figure 232, decorated with rococo silver–deposit decorations, was made in 1892. The vase is signed A.V.B. for Artus van Briggle. The body is fluted, the glaze is the standard Rookwood brown, with holly leaves and berry decorations. The silver–deposit overlay frames the decoration on the vase.

The silver itself does not appear to be marked. A possible reason for this is the danger of damaging the vase if a mark is struck onto the silver. The design of the silver overlay is so similar to photographs of many other pieces in the Gorham files as to make an attribution to Gorham reasonably certain.

Figure 233 pictures a dark olive–green bottle with a silver overlay, made about 1905.

Art Nouveau and Athenic

The Martelé line of handmade silver, described in the next chapter, constituted the great body of Art Nouveau work made by Gorham. However, there were sterling pieces made throughout the 1897–1915 period in the Art Nouveau style. The leaf–shaped bonbon dish (one of a pair) in Figure 234 is related to motifs found in Japanese paintings and wood–block prints. The decorations on some of these pieces in the Japanese style are quite scholarly, including specimens of Japanese calligraphy. The "Japanese" pieces are very much in the Beaux Arts tradition, except that the inspiration came from the art of Japan, rather than Europe.

In about 1901 Gorham introduced a new line called Athenic. Many of the Athenic pieces involved combinations of sterling with copper, glass, and ivory. The styles of Athenic ranged from Art Nouveau to Academic. The Athenic line was designed as an Art line in sterling to complement Martelé. Although there was much handwork involved in the making of some of the pieces, the machine was used wherever possible. The bodies of pieces were usually made on a spinning lathe rather than by hammering from a flat piece of silver as with Martelé.

There were some first–rate pieces in the Athenic line. The bold and surging lines, the jaunty curve of the colored ivory handle on the pot gives the black–coffee service in Figure 235 a great vitality and verve. The cigar box in Figure 236 with its elegant framework tracery of silver represents the second period of Gorham's copper objects. These later copper pieces are not usually hammered, and the colors are not as varied as those obtained in the copper pieces of the 1880s. The decorative emphasis in the later pieces, such as the box in Figure 236, was more on the design of the slim strips of silver set off against the copper backgrounds. Many of the later copper pieces are in the Art Nouveau style.

233 Silver deposit on dark olive–green glass bottle. Initials JSH for John S. Holbrook. Height: 9 in. (22.9 cm.). Mark: lion–anchor–G/POL. Mold signature on bottom of glass bottle: P. DAWSON/DUFFTOWN–GLENLIVET. *(Gorham collection)*.

234 Bonbon dish (one of a pair) made ca. 1900. Length: 8 in. (20.3 cm.). Mark: lion–anchor–G/STERLING/104. *(Chrysler Museum at Norfolk)*.

235 Athenic black–coffee set and tray. Length of tray: 14 in. (35.6 cm.). Coffeepot No. 2361. *(Gorham photograph).*

236 Athenic copper and silver cigar box made in 1901. Length: 8 in. (20.3 cm.). *(Museum of Art, Rhode Island School of Design).*

The Gorham Building

Gorham's new offfice building at Thirty–sixth Street and Fifth Avenue in New York was completed in 1905 (Fig. 237). It was designed by Stanford White of the prestigious firm McKim, Mead & White. White considered it one of his best designs. It had a kind of logical purity that reflected White's careful, meticulous design approach. Although it was in the Florentine Renaissance style, it was a modern, functional building. As noted in Chapter 8, the building made extensive use of bronze, both inside and outside.

The Gorham building was not only a showpiece for the company, it was also a symbol of Edward Holbrook's power. It was during this time that he was consolidating his dominant position in the silver industry, acquiring control over the companies listed at the beginning of this chapter.

Holbrook's drive to form a kind of trust in the fine silverwares business in America was remarkably successful, but he did have *one* failure, which understandably was not headlined by Gorham publicists of the time. This was the unsuccessful attempt to take over Reed &. Barton, the long–established silverwares and britannia

237 The Gorham building at Fifth Avenue and Thirty–sixth Street in New York, finished in 1905. Designed by Stanford White of the firm McKim, Mead & White. *(Gorham photograph).*

company of Taunton, Massachusetts.[8]

In 1907, a disgruntled group of Reed & Barton stock-holders, headed by George Hale Brabrook, offered 3530 shares of the company stock to Edward Holbrook. This represented about 47 percent of the total number of Reed & Barton shares. Brabrook had been defacto general manager of Reed & Barton during the later years of Henry Reed's life. Reed had controlled Reed & Barton for more than half a century. When Reed died he left his shares to his daughters, with his son–in–law, William B. H. Dowse, a Boston lawyer, designated as trustee of the estate. Within a week Dowse was appointed to the board of trustees and named president of the company.

One of Dowse's first acts as president of Reed & Barton was to relieve George Brabrook of his control of finances, sales, and manufacturing, leaving him only with the nominal title of treasurer.

With this background it is perhaps understandable why Brabrook eventually sold out to the competition. On January 10, 1907, Edward Holbrook, through the Silversmiths Company's subsidiary, the Silverwares Stock

Co., acquired the 3530 shares of Reed & Barton stock for $ 535,000.

Dowse was furious. He fired Brabrook and his associates from the Reed & Barton board and he declared war on Holbrook and the Silversmiths Company. He would not give them information on Reed & Barton's operations, refused to see their representatives, and drastically limited stock dividends.

In 1908 the Silversmiths Company brought suit against Reed & Barton to gain access to company records. Holbrook's strategy was to show that Reed & Barton needed new capital, which would force unissued Reed & Barton treasury stock on the market. It was a struggle for control. As the suit progressed, it became clear that Dowse was a very astute lawyer. On February 8, 1910, the suit was dismissed.

The Silversmiths Company found itself in possession of a substantial block of Reed & Barton stock which was relatively unprofitable because of Dowse's control of dividends. They had no option but to sell out to Dowse. The eventual settlement price was $792,750.

238 The company car, about 1900. Right, J. F. P. Lawton, secretary of Gorham since 1865. Left, his son, Fred Lawton, superintendent. (Gorham photograph).

CHAPTER 12

Martelé

In the 1880s and early 1890s the English Arts and Crafts movement received wide publicity in both England and America, and it was changing ideas as to how objects should be made.[1] There was a reaction against the cheap, shoddy designs that were flooding the market—of everything from furniture to ceramics, to wallpaper, to silver, particularly electroplated silver. The machine was named the culprit. There was a growing nostalgia for the long-lost world of the medieval guilds, where well–trained craftsmen working in small shops patiently made useful objects by hand—completely by hand. It was felt that men working in this happy milieu would surely make objects that were useful, well made, and beautiful.

The Arts and Crafts Movement

John Ruskin (1819–1900) is usually given credit for formulating, in the 1840s and the 1850s, many of the ideas that were to lead, two generations later, to the Arts and Crafts movement.[2] His ideas are also one of the important intellectual sources of Art Nouveau, although the actual roots of the Art Nouveau movement go back to such diverse sources as Japanese prints and decorative arts,[3] French Rococo, and the drawings of William Blake. William Morris (1834–1896), the English painter,

craftsman, writer, and lecturer, was the chief propagandist for Ruskin's idea that true art was the expression of man's pleasure in his work, that the right attitudes and skills would produce objects that would be both beautiful and useful. Morris is considered the real founder of the Arts and Crafts movement in England.

In the 1880s and early 1890s England was a hotbed of new ideas and new experiments in the arts. The ideas ranged from the practical idealism of people like the architect–craftsmen–designers Arthur Mackmurdo and Charles Ashbee on the one hand, to Oscar Wilde and Aubrey Beardsley, the consummate aesthetes, on the other.

Arthur Heygate Mackmurdo (1851–1942) was a key figure in the English Arts and Crafts movement. About 1881 he founded the Century Guild of Arts and Crafts, a group of artists–craftsmen. The journal of the Century Guild, *The Hobby House,* gave wide publicity to the new movement. In 1883 Mackmurdo produced a book, *Wren's City Churches,* with a famous woodcut title page which Nikolaus Pevsner called "the earliest work of Art Nouveau in existence."[4]

Charles Robert Ashbee (1863–1942) was well known as a craftsman and spokesman for the Arts and Crafts movement in both England and America. He visited the United States a number of times and was a friend of

Frank Lloyd Wright. In 1888 Ashbee founded, in London, a guild and crafts school which flourished for two decades before petering out around 1910. The original notice stated the objectives of the school:

> The Guild and School of Handicraft has for its object the application of art and industry. It is a Co–operative Society of Workmen, working out original designs, either of their own or such as be submitted to them from without. In connection with, and dependent on it, is a School of about one hundred working men and boys. Its effort is to apply the Guild System of Mediaeval Italy to modern industrial needs, and to the movement for Technical Education.[5]

Ashbee was a hardworking idealist. He reiterated the old complaint of artists working in the so–called minor arts— that painters received all the glory: "Under modern conditions of art, picture–painting is forced into artificial prominence, and the constructional and decorative arts, the real background, have as yet no right recognition among us."[6] Even when the guild became financially successful in the 1900–1905 era from the sales of their handmade wares, Ashbee steadfastly maintained it was not a business. "The Guild is a protest against modern business methods, against the trade point of view, against the commercial spirit."

In a few years, however, Ashbee saw his guild collapse and, in his 1911 book, *Should We Stop Teaching Art,* he made it clear that artists would have to learn to live with the machine.

The wonderfully colorful, and eventually terribly sad, life of the writer–lecturer–gadfly Oscar Wilde (1854–1900) is part of the folklore of the fin de siecle. Oscar Wilde *was* the supercilious dandy, and his success *was* accompanied by scandal, but his ideas about art for art's sake had a powerful influence on the intellectual world of his time. The epitome of this influence was the artistry of Aubrey Beardsley (1872–1898), the brilliant, "decadent" artist, whose career was as spectacular as it was brief. *The Yellow Book,* the classic showpiece of Beardsley's work, ran as a quarterly for thirteen issues, from April, 1894, to April, 1897. One year later he was dead, at the age of twenty–six.

William Codman was certainly familiar with the ideas of all of these men. He might have known Charles Ashbee personally. They shared so many ideas and interests.

The intellectual climate that fostered the Arts and Crafts movement in England had considerable influence on Codman's work at Gorham. It is fair to say that Codman's Art Nouveau silverwares designed for Gorham came straight out of the English Arts and Crafts move–ment and should be considered, if not a part of, at least an extension of that movement.

Martelé the Name

In 1896 Gorham initiated a revolutionary new program to produce a line of handmade silverwares. When examples of these wares were first shown by Gorham at the Waldorf Astoria Hotel in New York in November 1897, the line was not named. The published account of the Waldorf exhibit spoke only of "hand wrought silver."[7] An 1899 article on Gorham's new handmade wares used the name *martelé* (the French word for hammered or hand–hammered; not capitalized).[8] When the line was finally introduced commercially in 1900 it was called Martelé. From that time onward Gorham used the name Martelé for their entire handmade line, including the sterling pieces made in 1897 and the .950 fine pieces made in 1898 and 1899. Almost none of these earlier pieces is marked with the word Martelé. (See Appendix I, "Marks," for a discussion of the Martelé marks.)

The 1900 Paris Exposition had been picked as the introductory showcase for the new line. It is possible that the name Martelé was specifically adopted with the Paris Exposition in mind. In 1900 Paris was the style and art capital of the Western world; the French set the standards. The name Martelé was meant to have an aura of style, quality, and exclusivity.

Martelé and the Arts and Crafts Movement

It is not clear from the Gorham record whose idea it was to go into a line of handmade silverwares. William Codman and Edward Holbrook are given joint credit. A Gorham publication written fo the 1900 Paris Exposition noted:

> For years now this gradual development in art, guided and directed by Mr. William C. Codman, a true master of design in metal, who, with Mr. Holbrook, first conceived its possibility, has been allowed to take its own course; it has been nourished but not forced—and the result is shown in the present exhibit.[9]

The direction Gorham was to take, a direction toward expensive, prestigious, handmade silverwares was, as mentioned above, a direct outgrowth of the English Arts and Crafts movement. There was a great interest in the movement in America. Providence itself is the location of a landmark Arts and Crafts building, the Fleur de Lys Studio, built in 1885 by a group called the Art Work–

ers' Guild.[10]

In retrospect, the introduction of a major line of hand-made silverwares by Gorham at this time might seem an odd direction for the company to take. We have seen how the steam–powered drop press revolutionized flat-ware manufacture and how the new factory in Elmwood was the most effficient and modern in the world. Gorham's highly mechanized methods of silvermaking had made fine silverware affordable to great numbers of people.

Gorham was quite conscious of this contradiction. The Paris Exposition publication stated:

> The nineteenth century, especially in America, has been characterized by the enormous mechanical production of articles of one sort or another, many of them largely mer-etricious, and having neither the design nor the workman-ship that would permit them to stand as works of art. But the *abuse,* not the *use,* of machinery is responsible for this.[11]

This same publication contained an essay titled, "An Artistic Experiment," by Horace Townsend, which spelled out the philosophic and practical base of Gorham's Martelé:

> There is no art in which the hammer plays so important a part as that of the silversmith, for there is no metal which lends itself more readily to the influence of the simple ham-mer than silver. Even gold, though scientifically more mal-leable, does not compare with silver in this respect. Almost from prehistoric times this has been recognized, and Pliny mentions that in his time silver was worked more than gold by the aid of the simple hammer, just in proportion as the silvermakers of all ages have forsaken the hammer in favor of the chisel or the mould of the caster, so has the artistic excellence of the work produced declined. There is an adjunct to the hammer, however, among the silversmith's tools, which after all relies for the effect it produces upon the hammer itself; this is the chasing tool, which is essen-tially merely a punch of varying shape and size with which the surface of the metal is modelled under the influence of percussion.

This description of the power of the hammer was fol-lowed by three principles on which Martelé was based:

> These were the facts, then, which the Managers of the Gorham Company fully recognized when they decided upon their new departure and which they determined to adopt as their most artistic principle. The hammer, they determined, should reign supreme. Secondly, they laid it down as an axiom that the designer and the craftsman, if they could not actually be united in the same individual,

should be at all events brought into such close connection that the resultant effect should be practically the same.

> There was yet a third guiding principle to be borne in mind. The work they produced should be of its own cen-tury. Beautiful as is the work of the "Little Masters" of the past it yet speaks in a dead and forgotten tongue. The de-signer of today, if he is a true artist, must create and not copy. This is the result which those who had led in the modern revival of the sister arts had taught, and it was felt to be time for the silversmith in his turn to teach it through the agency of the works he should produce.[12]

Josef Hoffmann, working in Vienna in the first years of this century, used the same kind of language in de-scribing the rationale of the Wiener Werkstatte, even though stylistically their work had little in common with Gorham's Martelé. Hoffmann wrote:

THE WORK PROGRAM OF THE
WIENER WERKSTÄTTE 1903

> The boundless evil caused by shoddy mass–produced goods and by the uncritical imitation of earlier styles, is like a tidal wave sweeping across the world. We have been cut adrift from the culture of our forefathers and are cast hither and thither by a thousand desires and considerations. The machine has largely replaced the hand and the busi-nessman has supplanted the craftsman. To attempt to stem this torrent would seem like madness.

> Yet for all that we have founded our workshop. Our aim is to create an island of tranquility in our own country, which, amid the joyful hum of arts and crafts, would be welcome to anyone who professes faith in Ruskin and Morris. We are calling for all those who regard culture in this sense as valuable and we hope that the errors we are bound to commit will not dissuade our friends from lend-ing their support…[13]

Gorham's entry into a line of handmade silverwares placed them squarely in the forefront of the Arts and Crafts movement in America. Arts and Crafts societies were formed in both Boston and Chicago in 1897, the year Gorham started making Martelé, and the stated pur-poses of these societies were strikingly similar to those of Gorham. In fact, Gorham was represented in the Arts and Crafts exhibition which opened at Copley Hall in Boston on April 3, 1897, an exhibit which led directly to the forming of the Society of Arts and Crafts in Bos-ton. The Boston group had its organizational meeting on October 13, 1897. Professor Charles Eliot Norton was elected president. Professor Norton outlined the aims of the society:

The Society of Arts and Crafts is incorporated for the purpose of promoting artistic work in all branches of handicraft. It hopes to bring designers and workmen into mutually helpful relations, and to encourage workmen to execute designs of their own. It endeavors to stimulate in workmen an appreciation of the dignity and value of good design; to counteract the popular impatience of Law and Form, and the desire for over–ornamentation and specious originality. It will insist upon the regard for the relation between the form of an object and its use, and of harmony and fitness in decoration put upon it.[11]

The *making* of Martelé wares was wholly in the Arts and Crafts tradition. The concepts of handmaking objects from flat pieces of silver using only hammers and chasing tools, of the designers working hand in hand with the craftsmen, of leaving hammer marks in the finished piece to indicate clearly it was handmade are all basic Arts and Crafts precepts.

It was in the matter of *style* that Gorham parted company with most of the other American makers of Arts and Craft silver vares of the 1890s and early 1900s Gorham took a stand against the styles of the past. When they said their new work was to be "of its own century," they meant *now*, 1900. The work was to be in the style of the time—"modern art"—and the modern art of 1900 was Art Nouveau.

The allegiance to Art Nouveau, truly the *new* art of 1900, for Gorham's hand made wares contrasted with the handmade silver of their contemporaries, mos of whom made conservative, plain, traditional pieces. Colonial Revival was the dominant style.

Most of Gorham's contemporaries making Arts and Crafts silver were small firms. They simply couldn't afford to be avant–garde. Most of their customers preferred earlier, simpler forms and the makers supplied the demand.[15] The craftsmanship could be impeccable, but the forms were a return to a simpler past.

The period of the early 1900s was one of the high points in the Colonial Revival movement. There was a conscious revival of both early American styles *and* early American silversmithing methods and techniques. This widespread interest in the past on both the part of the craftsmen and the buying public is undoubtedly one of the main reasons why so little Art Nouveau silver was made by the smaller Arts and Crafts shops at the turn of the century in America.

The Alloys Used in Martelé

Three different alloys were used in the making of Gorham's Martelé silverwares of the 1897–1912 period:

Year	Silver Alloy
1897	.925 fine (sterling)
1898–1904	.950 fine
1905–1912	.9584 fine

In 1897 the first item was recorded in the first Martelé plant record book. It was a love cup (No. 8454) entered in the book on March 11, 1897. It was made of sterling. Some 343 entries (representing perhaps 400 individual pieces of silver) were made in the Martelé book in 1897. Apparently almost all pieces of Martelé made in 1897 were made in sterling.

At the beginning of 1898 the alloy for making Martelé was changed from sterling, .925 fine, to a .950 fine composition. The .950 fine alloy was used until the end of 1904.

The change from sterling to the .950 fine composition resulted in a softer, more ductile alloy. The change was made primarily to improve costs. Although the new .950 alloy was slightly more expensive because of its higher silver content, it was much easier to work and the time required to make a piece of silverware could be cut down. The overall cost of the finished piece would be less.

Figure 239 shows the variations of properties of silver–copper alloys with varying percentages of the two metals. Note that the hardness falls off sharply as the percentage of silver increases, while the percent elongation, which is a measure of ductility, increases dramati-

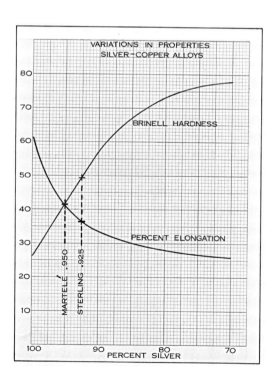

cally. The increase in silver from sterling, .925 fine, to the Martelé alloy, .950 fine, results in an alloy about 16 percent softer and 20 percent more ductile, which is proportionally easier to work. Present–day Gorham silversmiths estimate that the use of this softer alloy would result in perhaps a 10– to 12–percent savings in the making time of a large piece of silver. This would mean that a piece that would have taken say 200 hours to make in sterling, could be made in the .950 Martelé alloy in 175 to 180 hours, a saving of two or three days work.

There is one disadvantage in the use of the .950 fine silver alloy. Because it is softer the surface is not as durable as sterling. Repeated polishing can cause a loss of detail and the use of a buffing wheel could be disastrous.

In 1905 the composition of the Martelé alloy was changed again. The change was announced in a brief interoffffice memorandum from F. E. Lawton, the Gorham superintendent, dated December 31, 1904: "Commencing January 2, 1905, the standard of our Martelé will be .959 fine, instead of .950, as heretofore."

When pieces with the alloy were actually made they were marked .9584 instead of .959 as stated in Lawton's memorandum. The .9584 figure obviously reflected a *standard* rather than an *analysis*. It is not feasible under normal plant operating conditions to control a silver alloy composition to the fourth decimal place. This very point was investigated a few years ago in the Winterthur laboratories. Six pieces of Gorham Martelé silver with the .9584 figure in the mark were analyzed by means of x–ray fluorcscent spectroscopy. The analyses showed that, although some pieces were close to the .9584 figure (none had this *exact* composition), others contained up to one percent more silver.[16]

The main reason for adopting the .9584 standard in 1905 was almost certainly to make the Martelé alloy conform to the English Britannia standard.[17] The Britannia standard was originally used in England for wrought silverwares between March 27, 1697, and June I, 1720. The standard was adopted to prevent the use of coins, which were of sterling quality, in the making of silverware. Sterling was defined as a composition containing 11 1/10 troy ounces of fine silver per 12 ounces of alloy (i.e., .925 fine), while the britannia metal contained 11 1/2 troy ounces of fine silver per 12 ounces of alloy, or .95833 fine. Gorham rounded off the latter figure to .9584. Although the Britannia standard ceased to be compulsory in 1720, it remained an optional standard and has been used up to the present time. The most famous English silversmith of the first half of the eigh–teenth century, Paul de Lamerie, continued to work with

the Britannia standard long after 1720. It was not until 1732 that he entered a sterling standard mark at Goldsmiths' Hall.

The mark for Britannia standard is a figure of Britannia. Incidentally, the Britannia standard should not be confused with britannia metal. The latter is a white-metal alloy of tin, copper, and antimony that was often used as a base for electroplating in the nineteenth century.

The Making of Martelé

In 1896 Gorham initiated a "school" to train silversmiths to make silver hollow wares directly from flat sheets of silver, using only the simplest of hand tools. The eighteenth–century practice of hand raising a form from a flat piece of silver was new to many of Gorham's silversmiths. Horace Townsend wrote in his afore–mentioned essay: "Workmen had to be trained and taught to forget much which had taken a lifetime to learn, while the artistic temperament, which luckily goes hand–in–hand with skilled craftsmanship, had to be fostered and encouraged" (p. 34)

Codman's concept was quite revolutionary for a commercial silverwares producer. For more than a half century silversmiths had been using mechanical aids such as spinning lathes and stamping presses to make objects. Hand labor was kept at a minimum. The craftsmen worked from detailed, full–scale drawings prepared by the design department. These conventional plant working drawings, which gave the silversmith little leeway, show precise information for the maker as to dimensions, details of parts; and the types of castings and borders to be used. Chasing and engraving details were usually indicated in separate fullscale drawings.

Codman, adopting the Arts and Crafts philosophy, insisted that the designer become closely involved in the making process, while at the same time the silversmith was to become involved in the design process. A study of the Martelé drawings and photographs of the finished pieces based on these drawings shows clearly the importance of this relationship between the designers and the silversmiths.

In some cases the designer made the most cursory of sketches for a piece. Sometimes the drawings were not even in the same scale as the finished pieces. Figure 240 shows one of the more informal of the Martelé drawings. This sketch, which was little more than an idea, gave the silversmith very little to work with. The silversmith had to produce an object in the round from these few lines. The finished piece made from this sketch (Fig. 241) shows that the silversmith followed the outlines rather faithfully.

The drawing in Figure 240 was probably made by Codman himself. It was his practice to make rough sketches which were developed further by the designers working for him. In the case of this drawing it appears that it was the actual one used by the silversmith.

Most of the drawings for Martelé were more finished than the sketch in Figure 240. Some were even finished, detailed watercolors, such as the drawing for a bowl in Figure 242. A comparison of the drawings and photographs of the finished objects indicates that decorative details were frequently altered, and occasionally completely changed. (However, the finished bowl, not illustrated, made from the drawing in Figure 242 is quite faithful to the drawing itself.)

We know from the plant records that at least two different craftsmen worked on each piece of Martelé. The silversmith made the basic shape and the chaser applied any called–for decorations. When the Martelé program started in 1897, silversmiths were paid forty–five cents per hour and chasers forty cents per hour. In 1900 the silversmiths were still making forty–five cents per hour while the chasers' wage had increased to fifty cents an hour, which suggests that chasers who could do the Martelé work were perhaps in short supply.

The normal procedure was for the designer to draw the chasing designs directly on the body made by the silversmith, before starting the actual chasing. There was the feeling that this direct drawing on the object resulted in ornamentation that was an integral part of the object rather than something added to it.

The finished Martelé piece was hand polished and marked with marking punches. The pieces were not buffed on a wheel. No mechanical finishing of any kind was used. The idea was to leave the finished object the way it was when it came from the craftsman working directly with the metal. They were truly handmade objects.

William Codman, as art director, set the general tone of the Martelé designs. It is not possible to tell from any

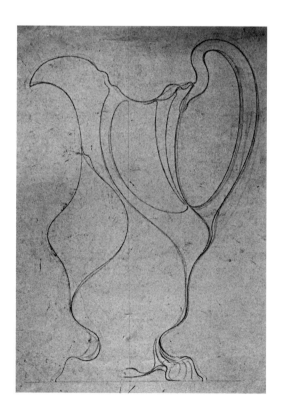

240 Drawing for Martelé pitcher in Figure 241. (*Gorham collection*).

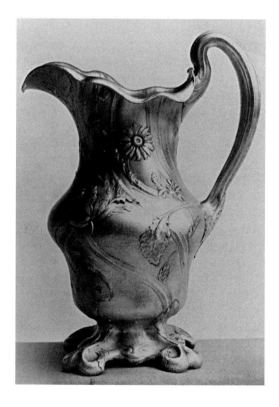

241 Martelé pitcher made in 1905. Height: 16 1/4 in. (41.3 cm.). Marked HKF (*Gorham photograph*).

242 Watercolor drawing for Martelé bowl, 1904. *(Gorham collection).*

243 Martelé drawing with William C. Codman's comments. *(Gorham collection).*

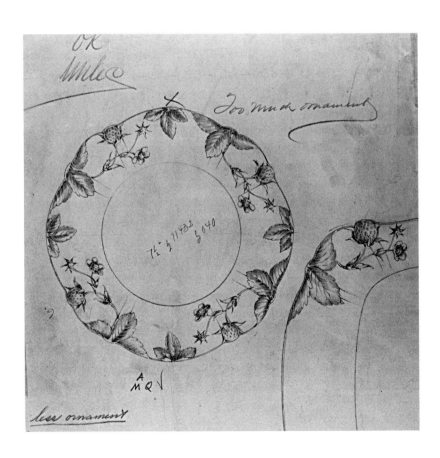

of the Gorham records which pieces he may have designed himself. There are a number of Martelé pieces with an engraved signature "W. C. Codman" (Fig. 246), which suggests that these particular pieces may have been designed by Codman himself, but this cannot be corroborated from the Gorham records.

The drawings for Martelé are in several different styles, indicating that a number of designers worked on the line. A particularly interesting example of a drawing of a designer working under Codman is shown in Figure 243. It has an "OK WCC" penciled in the upper left corner of the drawing plus the comments "Too much ornament" and "less ornament." The photograph of the piece as made (not illustrated) indicates the design *was* simplified.

It is of course obvious that Codman could not have designed all, or even many, of the 4800–or–so pieces of Martelé made in the 1897–1912 period, but the stamp of his genius is on almost all of the pieces.

Hammered Finishes

There was no uniform surface of Martelé pieces. Hammer marks were sometimes left conspicuously in a piece, while others have most of the hammer marks planished smooth. In a few cases the hammer marks were part of the design of a piece. In the fish dish in Figure 252 the hammer marks in the bottom simulate water, completing and tying together the whole marine theme of the piece. The handle of the cup in Figure 247 is hammered in much the same manner as the silver in the Japanese style of the 1870s and 1880s.

Most Martelé pieces were finished so that only faint bits of the hammering marks were left in the surface. The Gorham advertising literature spoke of the "soft mist texture." It is a surface that glows and shimmers in changing lights. It is a delicate and somewhat fragile surface, one that can be damaged or ruined by a bufffing wheel or prolonged overzealous polishing.

Oxidation

Almost all Martelé pieces were originally oxidized to bring out the details of the chasing more clearly. The oxidation process makes use of sulfides which oxidize the surface of the silver, resulting in the deposition of a black silver sulfide coating. Originally, liver of sulfur was universally employed, this chemical being a crude mixture of potassium polysulfides and thiosulfate. The photographs of the Martelé pieces, when new, show that such chased details as leaf and flower patterns are clearly

outlined with the black oxidation product. Today most of these black deposits are gone. Without the black outlining, the chased details are less distinct. Forms tend to melt into the surface of the pieces.

Some of the surface oxidation has probably been lost as a result of repeated polishing. The black silver sulfide oxidized surfaces are rather fragile. However, one suspects a lot of oxidation has been removed simply because of a misunderstanding of the intentions of the makers of Martelé. Mistaking the oxidation product for tarnish, the black surfaces have simply been scrubbed off. Some Martelé pieces are so skinned that a bufffing wheel must have been used to remove the black deposit. A warning note: The utmost caution should be taken in polishing Martelé. Use only the mildest polishes—never use a bufffing wheel.

The Beginnings of Codman's Art Nouveau Designs

In the early 1890s some of William Codman's designs began to display shapes and forms that were to appear time and again in his Art Nouveau silver: low bowls with easy, sensuous curves, undulating out–turned rims, bases of four arched feet, and sensuous, nature–based chased decorations. Many of Codman's pieces of the early 1890s were academic in design, loaded with detail. But the forms of some of these, with their soft curves, were not at all academic. Strip off the academic details from these pieces and they would look Art Nouveau.

There was a side of Codman's sensibility that loved traditional forms and traditional decorative details, and until about 1894 traditional ideas formed his entire work. Codman was a typical Victorian designer. The idea of working with styles of the past so dominated the thought of the time that it would never have occurred to him to work in any other way.

The 1893 Chicago Exposition marked the high point of Codman's academic designs. In a way, the great out-pouring of designs for Chicago, with their complexity and virtuosity, seemed to allow Codman to get these ideas out of his system. It was almost as if he was trying to prove a point. The Chicago Exposition was the first real showcase of his work in America. Academic, Beaux Arts design was in the air. Codman set out to prove he was a master of the style.

The 1893 Columbian Exposition marked a turning point in William Codman's career as a designer. Although academic design continued to be a strong element in Gorham silver right up to World War I, there is every indication that after 1893 Codman's interests and sympathies were more and more captured by Art

Nouveau and the ideas of the Arts and Crafts movement.

Design Sources

William Codman's *forms* seemed to have developed naturally out of his own work. There was a certain English solidness (and occasionally stolidness) in his silverware designs. The pieces were masculine in feel, even when he was dealing with such thoroughly feminine forms as the dressing table in Figure 256.

It would appear that stylistically Codman was mostly influenced by his contemporaries. The Art Nouveau vocabulary of decorative devices—the whiplash line, undulating curves, women's hair flowing in the wind, mermaids emerging from the water, waves, flowers, and flower forms—were all commonly used motifs in the new art of the 1890s. It is hard to trace the sources of any specific motifs in Codman's work. In fact, it has often been noted by writers in the field that designers everywhere began to use many of the Art Nouveau decorative details almost simultaneously.

Codman would have kept close tabs with what was going on in England and the Continent from Holbrook's annual visits and through the art journals. The Gorham library still has long runs of such periodicals as *The International Studio, The Art Amateur, Art et Décoration,* and so on, which regularly reported on the new works of the Art Nouveau movement.

There was one design source that Codman apparently did *not* use. That was the work of English and French metalsmiths of the 1890s. The photographs of many of these wares are still in the Gorham files. They bear little resemblance to Codman's Martelé designs. There are photographs of French bronzes with such decorative devices as mermaidlike figures riding on waves, but the vaguely related designs by Codman are earlier and far more subtle in execution.

William Codman's Art Nouveau style was fully formed by 1898. It was a characteristic style which, although it was related to European Art Nouveau in many of its decorative details, was very much his own. It resulted in a body of silverwares which represented the culmination of his life's work. This work is certainly one of the important manifestations of Art Nouveau in America.

The large vase in Figure 244, made in 1894, is one of the earliest of Codman's designs which is clearly in the Art Nouveau manner. The undulating leaf forms recall Japanese precursors, although the realistically chased flower and the tall vase shape are completely Western.

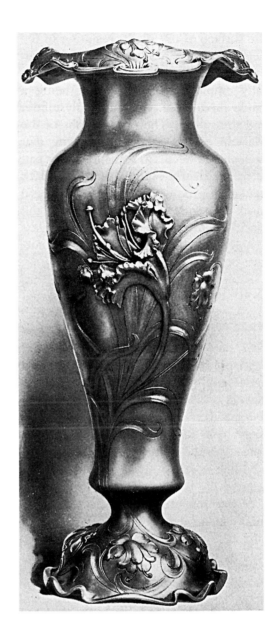

244 Sterling silver vase made in 1894. Height: 17 in. (43.2 cm.). (*Gorham photograph*).

Handwrought Silver

As mentioned earlier, the first piece of handmade silver (which was later to be called Martelé) was a sterling love cup, entered in the plant account book on March 11, 1897. In March 1897 about twenty-five pieces were finished, including cups, child's cups, berry bowls, plates, olive dishes, pitchers, and a jardiniere. It is assumed that some of these newly finished pieces were the ones shown at the Boston Arts and Crafts exhibition in April 1897. The second showing of Gorham's handmade silverwares

245 Martelé berry bowl in sterling, made in 1897. Diameter: 8 3/4 in. (22.2 cm.). *(Burt collection).*

was in New York at the Waldorf Hotel in November, 1897. The exhibition, obviously engineered by Edward Holbrook, opened with a private preview for the press, which was followed the next day with a showing for "a selected group of artists, architects and collectors." It was then opened to the public for a week.

A glowing account of the Waldorf exhibit, in the November 17, 1897, *Jeweler's Circular,* entitled "Rare and Unique Exhibit of Works of Hand Wrought Silver," described several pieces in some detail. It noted that "while the designs are generally of one man, W. C. Codman, Art Director of the Gorham Manufacturing Co.'s designing department, the articles themselves were wrought under his direction by different skilled silver workers, and show to a considerable extent the individuality of the makers."

246

247

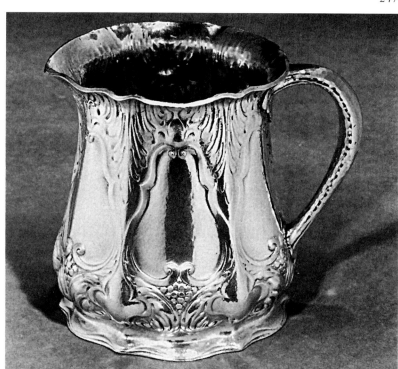

246 Gorham mark, plus retailer's mark of Bailey, Banks & Biddle, engraved signatures "W. C. Codman" and " F.A. Jordan," on bowl in Figure 245.

247 Martelé love–cup, pitcher in sterling made in 1897. Height: 6 3/16 in. (15.7 cm.). Mark: No. 37. *(Private collection).* See Plate VI.

There is no record of any pieces being sold from either the Boston or the New York Waldorf exhibitions. Later Gorham publications suggest that nothing was offered for sale until late in 1899 or in 1900.

Two pieces made in 1897 are illustrated. The berry bowl in Figure 245 was entered into the plant records on October 2, 1897, as a "fruit dish." The photographic record named it a "berry bowl." Although the bowl is somewhat conventionally chased with strawberry plants and strawberries, the undulating out–turned lip and the organic–formed foot are in the Art Nouveau manner. Faint hammer marks were left on the surface.

The berry bowl was retailed by Bailey, Banks & Biddle of Philadelphia (Fig. 246). Engraved on the base are the signatures "W. C. Codman" and "F. A. Jordan." The latter name could not be identified from the Gorham records.

The small love–cup pitcher in Figure 247, made in 1897, is an example of how Codman interpreted the Arts and Crafts philosophy in silver. The piece is not highly finished either in its silversmithing or in its chasing. The chasing is an integral part of the piece; it is not a decorative design added to the piece as an afterthought. The lip flares out slightly, leaving the undecorated, raw edge of the original flat piece of silver very much in evidence. The body retains light hammer marks, while those on the handle are more pronounced. It is related

to the hammering that was on Gorham's silver in the Japanese style of the 1870s and 1880s. In fact, it could have been done by one of the older Gorham craftsmen who had worked on the earlier wares.

The large tureen in Figure 248, made in 1898, is a very typical piece of Martelé. The undulating base, the generous, flowing body chased with flowers, the handles with the extra curve, the undulating turned–back lip with its unfinished edge, the top neatly fitting into the wavy lip, arching up to the pert bow handle—all are devices used over and over in Martelé. The lightly hammered surface has a soft glow.

The tureen in Figure 248 is part of what Gorham called their No. A9511 line, which included a tea and coffee service, gravy boats, meat and entree dishes, salad bowls, vases, candelabra, centerpieces, etc., a total of twenty–five pieces in a coordinated design pattern. Pieces for the No. A9511 line were made in 1897 and 1898.

Apparently only one set of flatware was made in Martelé. The pieces of this set, which are quite plain, are not in the Art Nouveau style. They have rather heavy initials in the handle as their main decorative element. There were a number of Martelé ladles and other serving pieces made. Figure 249 shows spoons from two children's sets. The spoon on the left was made to accompany a porringer, while the one on the right went with a cup, bowl, and plate.

248 Martelé soup tureen with lid, made in 1898. Height: 9 1/8 in. (23.2 cm.), width 15 in. (38.1 cm.). *(Private collection)*.

189

249 Martelé spoons from children's sets, made in 1898. (*Gorham photograph*).

250 Martelé five–light candelabrum (one of a pair), made in 1900. Height: 25 1/4 in. (64.1 cm.). Mark: 9527 plus date mark for 1900. (*Private collection*).

The large five–light candelabrum in Figure 250 was entered into the plant accounts on July 27, 1900, although the number 9527 suggests it may have been designed in 1897. It was part of the Fleur–de–lis line. A photograph unfortunately does not give a real feeling of the monumental quality of such pieces of Martelé. This candelabrum contains 157 ounces of silver and soars over two feet in height without candles. It reminds us of the elegance that must have been displayed when pieces of silver of this size and ambition graced a dining–room table. The design is beautifully balanced, from the typical undulating base with arched feet, richly chased with plant forms, to the arched stems holding the softly curving candle holders.

There was a phenomenal amount of work involved in the making of such large pieces of Martelé. The plant account record indicates that 209 hours, a month's work, was involved in the making of one of the candelabrum, and the chasing another 185 hours. To this must be added the design time, finishing, and so on. It took more than four months to design and make this pair of candelabra. The price was $1200 each, $2400 for the pair.

A number of pieces of Martelé were made in gold. Among the more unusual items are the 18–karat–gold umbrella handles in Figure 251. The motif of the head of a lovely young girl with her hair blowing easily in the wind was a favorite European Art Nouveau device which Codman adopted for a rather mundane object, an umbrella, turning it into a marvelously elegant work of art.

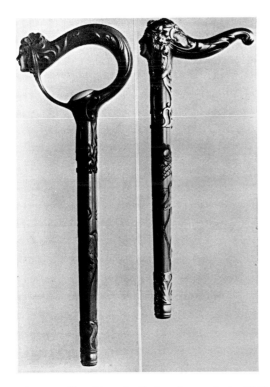

251 Martelé gold umbrella handles made in 1900.
(Gorham photograph).

Martelé Pieces Made for the 1900 Paris Exposition

Planning for the great Paris International Exposition of 1900, the *Exposition Universelle,* had been under way in Paris for four years. In 1898 Gorham initiated plans to participate. They decided to enter a major exhibit and to feature their new line of handmade silverwares. The Paris Exposition was to be the introductory international showcase for Martelé.

Why Gorham chose to wait three years before offering Martelé for sale generally is not clear. The company had been making Martelé since early in 1897, and a thousand or more pieces had been finished by 1900. Gorham filed the application for the trademark used on Martelé on November 22, 1899. An article on Martelé appeared in the December, 1899, issue of *House Beautiful,* referring to pieces of Martelé at Spaulding and Co. in Chicago.

Spaulding introduced Martelé to the buying public in this country in their Chicago store and later in Paris at their store at 36 Avenue de l'Opera. The Spaulding company had been incorporated in 1888 in Chicago. Two Chicagoans, H. A. Spaulding. and L. J. Leiter each subscribed to 31 percent of the shares, and Edward Hol-

brook 31 percent. The remaining shares were owned by three other individuals. Holbrook soon gained working control of Spaulding. It was for many years known as Spaulding–Gorham. One of the earliest advertisements on Martelé appeared in *Harper's Magazine* for April, 1900, which read:

Martelé is the most
Exclusive Silverware for
Wedding Gifts

The few examples of the new and exquisite *Martelé* that the Gorham Company, Silversmiths, have been able to produce, up to the present time for the consideration of discriminating art lovers, have emphasized anew the value of individuality in all worthy art work. Each piece is the product of an artist trained in the Gorham Company's own school of design, established four years ago with the express purpose of reviving the best traditions and restoring the spirit of healthy competition that underlay the beautiful work of mediaeval metal–workers and goldsmiths. *Martelé,* as its name indicates, cannot be imitated successfully by any of the inferior and purely mechanical methods that are too often used in an attempt to trade upon the ideas of really creative artists.

Gorham Company
Silversmiths
Broadway and Nineteenth Street

The statement in the advertisement that the Gorham Company had only been able to produce a "few examples of the new and exquisite Martelé" was, of course, advertising license. As mentioned above, over a thousand pieces of Martelé had been made by that time.

Some of the best and most ambitious pieces of Martelé were made for the Paris Exposition. Many of these pieces are illustrated in one or more of the publications Gorham put out for the exposition. One book, titled *The Gorham Manufacturing Company, Silversmiths,* was published in both an English and French edition. Parts of this book were quoted earlier in this chapter. A more general catalog, prepared for the trade in this country, illustrated both Martelé and the company's regular lines of flatware and hollow ware.

Six of the more interesting pieces of Martelé made for the Paris Exposition are discussed and illustrated in following pages.

Among the first pieces actually made for Paris is the fish dish in Figure 252 which was entered in the plant account book on May 2, 1898. The marine theme of the tray is carried into the bottom where elongated hammer marks simulate ripples of the sea. The lobster and

252 Martelé fish dish made in 1898. Length: 22 in. (55.9 cm.). No. *360. (Gorham photograph)*

crabs are a bit out of scale with the fishermen (children?) handling the nets on the border. The whole border is a series of heaving, turning waves.

One of the more unusual works of Martelé made for the Paris Exposition is the chalice and paten in Figure 253. The paten is of 18–karat gold, with an inset enameled silver plaque. The chalice base was made of .950 fine silver, the bowl of 18–karat gold. The records do not tell what kind of jewels (cost, $566.75) were used in the chalice. The two pieces had a retail value of $3500.

The patern is an attractive, but quite conventional, enameled dish. At first glance the chalice is also conventional in its design. One remembers the quote that William Codman, the designer, was "a master of the Gothic genre." However, when we look more closely at the chalice we realize it is a rich, complex example of high Art Nouveau, an incredibly sensual object.

Several liqueur sets were made with Martelé silver stands fitted with Tiffany Favrile glass. The Gorham plant records on such items usually have a note to the effect that Tiffany glass was used. The liqueur set in Figure 254, made for the Paris Exposition, had a stoppered bottle and six glasses, all with applied lily–pad decorations. The motifs on the silver stand of grapes, grape leaves, and tendrils are conventional for punch bowls and other pieces associated with wine. Note how the tendril motif is carried into the glass holders of the stand.

William Codman and Louis Comfort Tiffany probably knew each other. They certainly knew each other's work. The Morse Gallery of Art in Winter Park, Florida, owns a Gorham Martelé water pitcher made in 1905 (not illustrated) which is engraved on the bottom with the inscription "I.S.G. to L.C.T./Laurelton Hall." Di-

rectly above the inscription is engraved "W. C. Codman." The pitcher was given by Mrs. Isabella Stewart Gardner of Boston to Louis Comfort Tiffany for his newly completed house, Laurelton Hall, at Oyster Bay, Long Island.

Gorham Records on Martelé

The tankard in Plate VII is also shown in Figure 255 to illustrate the kinds of records kept by the Gorham Company on their Martelé pieces. There are two kinds of documentation: photographs of the pieces when they were made, and plant cost records. The original caption on the photograph of the tankard in Figure 255 gives us several pieces of information. The oval line surrounding the number 4294 indicates that the piece was a "special," that is, a one–of–a–kind piece. The A– prefix of the number indicates the piece was made of silver. (The prefix 0– indicated silver electroplated objects.) The name Tankard indicates the form. The form as shown in the photograph might suggest a flagon, but one suspects that the company may have felt that a tankard was a more salable form than a flagon. The word Martelé is of course the name of Gorham's line of handmade silverwares. Gorham did not register Martelé as a trademark. The United States trademark (No. 33,903, Registered Dec. 19, 1899), usually associated with Martelé—the spread eagle centered over the regular lion–anchor–G Gorham mark (Mark No. 38)—makes no mention of the word Martelé. Martelé is an *arbitrary* term for Gorham's handmade silverwares of the 1897–1912 period. The fleur–de–lis in the caption indicates the tankard was specifically made for the 1900 Paris Exposition.

253 Martelé silver chalice, with 18–karat–gold bowl, inset with semiprecious stones, and 18–karat–gold enameled paten, made for the 1900 Paris Exposition. Height of chalice: 12 1/2 in. (31.8 cm.). Diameter of paten: 6 3/4 in. (17.1 cm.). *(Gorham photograph)*.

253

254 Martelé liqueur set, with Tiffany glass, made in 1900. No. 3355. *(Gorham photograph)*.

254

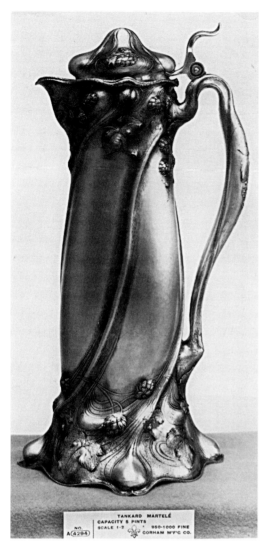

255 Original Martelé file photograph of tankard in Plate VII.

The plant cost record gives the following information on the tankard:

Date Finished	March 15, 1900
Silver Composition	.950 fine
Record Number	4294
Form	Tankard
Weight	77.75 troy ounces

Cost of .950 fine alloy	$ 71.10
Making(65 hrs @.45)	29.25
Chasing (68 hrs @.50)	34.00
Oxidized Finish	1.50
Casting	.17
Guilding (inside)	8.00
Overhead and Profit	$ 95.98

NET	$ 240.00
Retail Price	$ 480.00

It has been estimated that if the tankard were to be made today (1981) it would have to have a retail price of at least $15,000. And that figure is based on the doubtful assumption that silversmiths and chasers who could do work of such quality could be found.

From a formal point of view, the design of the tankard in Plate VII is quite successful. The typical Art Nouveau chased areas around the bottom and the top are held together by the powerful diagonal ribs that sweep dramatically up the body of the piece. The tankard shows Codman's mastery of the Art Nouveau vocabulary. Some of the details are closely related to English and French Art Nouveau but the overall design is very much Codman's own.

The three–handled love cup in Plate VIII, with its applied enameled flowers and leaves and the gently swaying chased flower forms is one of the most attractive of the Martelé pieces. There were only a relatively few pieces of enameled Martelé made. The chased curves of the flower stems are related to examples of Japanese art, but the literal rendering of the enameled flowers is Western.

The remarkable toilet table and mirror with stool in Figure 256 was the largest and most valuable Martelé work made for the Paris Exposition. In the French edition of the book titled *The Gorham Manufacturing Co. Orfèvres* a photograph of the toilet table and stool was featured as a frontispiece with the caption "Service de Toilette, *Martelé,* 'Matin et Soir'." The toilet table was finished on December 11, 1899. It involved a total of 2332 hours in its making. The table weighed 1080 troy ounces (about 75 pounds), while the bench weighed 173 troy ounces. The net cost of the two pieces was just under $10,000, which meant they would have had a retail price of about $20,000.

The voluptuous mirror and its base is in the Art Nouveau style, but the table itself is a bit more restrained in a French Rococo manner. The back legs of the table have Queen Anne–like pad feet while the front feet of the table and all four feet of the bench are claw-and–ball. The naturalistic crook of the legs above the claw–and–ball feet is quite different from anything in eighteenth–century American furniture, and reflects Codman's English background.

Gorham's exhibit at the 1900 Paris Exposition was a success. The Gorham Manufacturing Co. won the grand prix and gold medal for their silverwares and Edward Holbrook was made a Chevalier of the Legion of Honor of France. If Gorham's exhibit did not attract as much attention as S. Bing's Art Nouveau pavilion or Loie Fuller's dancing, it was still well received. Certainly the sil-

256 Martelé lady's toilet set, consisting of dressing table and stool, made in 1899. (*Gorham photograph*).

versmiths from all over Europe took a long look at Gorham's Martelé. It was the outstanding silverware in the Art Nouveau style at the exposition. Holbrook and Codman must have felt that their exhibit was a triumph.

Martelé 1900–1912

From a silversmithing point of view the large tea and coffee services are among the great achievements of Martelé. To hand raise and coordinate the designs of all the pieces of these large sets was a formidable task. The design of the individual pieces and their relationship to the whole had to be carefully worked out. If the individual pieces seemed *too* busy the effect of the set when assembled could be a bit overwhelming. One of the finest of the Martelé services is the one in Figure 257. En suite with this six–piece service and tray is a small three–piece black–coffee set and tray in the same design (not illustrated) and the water pitcher in Figure 258, making a total of twelve pieces in all. This spectacular service, which was retailed by Spaulding & Co. of Chicago, was a twenty–fifth wedding anniversary gift.

257 Martelé tea and coffee service made in 1900. Height of coffeepot: 10 1/8 in. (25.6 cm.). Length of tray: 27 5/8 in. (70.2 cm.). Inscription on bottom: "Charles Henry Aldrich/ Helen Urania Roberts/1875 October Thirteenth 1900." Mark: No. 39. *(Art Institute of Chicago).*

258 Martelé pitcher made in 1900. Engraved on bottom: "Charles Henry Aldrich/Helen Urania Roberts/ 1875 October Thirteenth 1900." Height: 8 1/2 in. (21.6 cm.). Mark: No. 39. *(Art Institute of Chicago).*

Because of the height of the shakers in Figure 259(5 3/8 inches) one would tend to call them casters. However, the plant records designate them "pepper and salt." They were finished on June 14, 1901.

The pitcher and tray in Figure 260 are chased with dandelion motifs. The undulating chased sides of the tray are so typical of Codman's work that one could call it a trademark. The contour of the handle of the pitcher is also a typical Codman form.

The photographic records show that there was an almost exact duplicate (No. 8213) made of the pitcher and tray in Figure 260. The only difference is a slight rearrangement of the chased motifs.

Figure 261 illustrates a punch bowl and ladle made for the St. Louis Exposition in 1904. Figure 262 shows a detail of the ladle handle.

Gorham participated in all of the great international expositions of the time. In Turin, Italy, in 1902 the company won a gold medal for their exhibit which featured Martelé. There were apparently no pieces made specifically for the Turin Exposition.

259 Martelé salt and pepper made in 1901. Height: 5 3/8 in. (13.6 cm.). *(Private collection)*.

260 Martelé pitcher and stand made in 1902. Engraved initials HKMcC. Height of pitcher: 9 3/4 in. (24.7 cm.). Mark: No. 39 (8212) plus THEODORE B. STARR/NEW YORK. *(Burt collection)*.

261 Martelé punch bowl with plateau and ladle, made in 1904. Height with plateau: 13 5/8 in. (34.6 cm.). Mark for St. Louis Exposition. *(Private collection)*.

262 Handle of ladle in Figure 261.

261

262

263 Martelé centerpiece made in 1904 for the St. Louis Exposition. *(The Chrysler Museum, Norfolk, Virginia).*

264 Martelé three–handled loving cup made in 1905 Height: 6 1/2 in. (16.5 cm.). Marked uᴴᴛ. *(Gorham photograph).*

There were a number of pieces made for the St. Louis Fair in 1904 where Gorham had a large exhibit showing a complete cross section of their wares. Pieces made for the St. Louis Exposition are marked with a small letter s superimposed over the capital letter L.

Gorham completely dominated the prizes at St. Louis. They won the grand prizes for silverware and goldware, jewelry, bronze work, leather work, and for "Applied Arts, Fine Arts Gallery" for the lady's writing table and chair in Figure 219. In addition, Edward Holbrook and William C. Codman were personally awarded grand prizes and five gold medals were given to their collaborators.

The centerpiece in Figure 263, which was made for the St. Louis Exposition, shows a kind of virtuosity in metal forming. The metal seems so stretched as to appear paper–thin. The piece appears almost to float in space. The centerpiece contrasts with the chunky, solid punch bowl in Figure 261.

There were more pieces of Martelé made in 1905 than in any other year. There is a considerable range in design of the pieces made in 1905, which suggests Codman was giving much more leeway to the designers working under him. Some of the 1905 designs are quite atypical and show little or none of Codman's influence.

The loving cup in Figure 264, with its sturdy but vo–

265 Martelé vase. Height: 15 1/2 in. (39.4 cm.). Mark:
No. 40, G^{H}H (*Gorham collection*).

more related to Scandanavian Art Deco silver of the 1930s than it does to turn–of–the–century Art Nouveau. The code letters (H over GH) suggests it could have been made in 1905.

Another variation of Martelé design is the chocolate set in Figure 266 with the repeated rhythms of the chocolate and hot milk pots. The set has an almost Oriental splendor. The strong diagonal chased forms, the lovely sprays of flowers, and the jaunty turned–back finials all lend a sense of fantasy to this delightful set.

The chunky black–coffee set in Figure 267 is a bit more reserved than most of the Martelé sets of this kind. A favorite form was the Turkish pot with its slimy tall, curving spout and its delicate handle. There must have been a lot of black coffee served at the beginning of the twentieth century, because these little three–piece sets (often with tray) are relatively common.

The loving cup in Figure 268, with its chaste and reticent flower decorations, illustrates the kind of design that became more popular at the end of the Martelé period. The wonderful tension of the earlier high Art Nouveau pieces is gone. The design is relaxed—pretty—but the vitality, is not there.

After 1905 there seemed to be a drop-off in energy in Martelé. The latter pieces tend to be plainer. One senses that the Art Nouveau movement had lost its vigor. Certainly this seems to be true for many of the Martelé pieces made after 1905.

There were a few pieces of Martelé made throughout the 1897–1912 period that were essentially undecorated. The pitcher in Figure 269, with its simple flowing lines is a good example of the type.

The production of Martelé pieces fell off drastically after 1909. Less than a dozen pieces were made in each of the years 1910 and 1911. There were about four–dozen pieces made in 1912, the last year of regular production of Martelé. There were a few special–order pieces of Martelé made after 1912. A couple–of–dozen commissioned pieces were made in the 1920s. The latest piece that can be located from the Gorham files is a very plain, undistinguished vase made in 1930.

There is at least one exception, and a major one, to the statement above that the energy level of Martelé fell off after 1905. That is the large, three–handled prize cup in Figure 270. This cup was made in 1914, Codman's last year at Gorham. One likes to think that this was an old man's wonderful last fling. He designed an object that summed up everything he knew about the art of silversmithing, an object pulsing with joyous vitality. William Christmas Codman didn't end *his* career at Gorham with a whimper!

luptuous form, its sharply chased naturalistic flowers and leaves around the base, and the plain hammered body, makes a strong contrast with the wispy curves of the centerpiece in Figure 263. If the centerpiece seems to float, the loving cup is planted down solidly. The loving cup has a plain, unadorned turned–out lip—the Arts and Crafts touch.

The tall, graceful vase in Figure 265 is a true anomaly among Martelé designs. It is symmetrical and relatively unadorned, and what ornament it does have seems much

266 Martelé chocolate set—chocolate pot, hot milk pot, sugar, and tray, made in 1905. Height of chocolate pot: 9 7/8 in. (5 cm.). *(Gorham photograph).*

267 Martelé black–coffee set made in 1905. Height of coffeepot: 10 15/16 in. (27.8 cm.). Mark: No. 40. *(Private collection).*

268 Martelé three–handled loving cup made in 1905. Height: 7 1/4 in. (18.4 cm.). Marked vᴴv. (*Gorham photograph*).

269 Martelé pitcher made in 1906. Height: 6 3/4 in. (17.1 cm.). (*Gorham photograph*).

The following list of the types of Martelé pieces made was compiled from the Gorham photographic records. (The plant cost records are too incomplete to use for such a compilation.) A few pieces of Martelé not identified in the photographic records can be identified from the plant cost records. There are also a couple of pieces of silver, with Martelé marks that appear quite legitimate, that cannot be identified from either the photographic records or the plant cost records at Gorham.

The list includes a number of items which consist of two or more pieces of silver, so a pure tabulation of the number of *items* (about 2800) does not indicate the number of *pieces* made. For what it is worth, it is estimated that the total number of *pieces* of Martelé made was about 4800.

TYPES OF MARTELÉ

	Number of Items
1. Bowls and centerpieces (including bon bon, olive, fruit and salad dishes, and compotiers)	697
2. Vases	231
3. Pitchers (about half with trays)	214
4. Waiters and trays	198
5. Loving cups	180
6. Candlesticks (including chamber sticks and snuffers)	91
7. Black coffee sets (2–5 pieces, some with trays)	89
8. Tea sets (up to 7 pieces, some with trays)	86
9. Child's bowl and plate sets (some with knife, fork, and spoon)	83
10. Entrée and service plates	78
11. Child's cups	76
12. Black coffee pots	57
13. Punch bowls (many with ladles)	48
14. Sauceboats and trays	33
15. Bread trays	31
16. Children's flatware sets	30
17. Fish dishes and fish dish sets	30
18. Porringers	29
19. Tankards	29
20. Ice cream sets (2–3 pieces)	28
21. Ink bottles and stands	25
22. Tête–à–tête sets (usually 4 pieces)	23
23. Meat dishes	22
24. Ewers	18
25. Tea caddies	18
26. Napkin rings	17
27. Kettles	15
28. Cigar lighters	13
29. Vegetable dishes	13

270 Martelé prize cup made in 1914. Height: 18 3/4 in. (47.6 cm.). Mark: No 40 plus JME. (*The Newark Museum*).

30. Mirrors	12	81. Flatware set	1
31. Sugars and creamers	12	82. Glove stretcher	1
32. Asparagus dishes	11	83. Goblet	1
33. Brushes	11	84. Grape dish	1
34. Candelabra	10	85. Hairpin tray	1
35. Fish knives and forks	10	86. Lamp	1
36. Pen holders and trays	9	87. Lavatory set (12 pieces)	1
37. Jewel boxes	8	88. Razor strop	1
38. Chocolate pots and sets	7		
39. Salad forks and spoons	7		
40. Smokers sets	7		
41. Tureens	7		
42. Glass and silver cruet sets	6		
43. Paper racks	6		
44. Scissors	6		
45. Combs	5		
46. Paper knives	5		
47. Baskets (with handles)	4		
48. Calendars	4		
49. Chafing dishes	4		
50. Chafing–dish fork and spoon sets	4		
51. Child's single plates	4		
52. Cigar and cigarette vases	4		
53. Claret bottles and sets	4		
54. Fern dishes	4		
55. Liquor sets with Favrile glass	4		
56. Picture frames	4		
57. Terrapin sets	4		
58. Toilet sets	4		
59. Bells	3		
60. Glove hooks	3		
61. Ice cream servers and forks	3		
62. Letter clips	3		
63. Matchbox holders	3		
64. Mucilage pots	3		
65. Nail files and polishers	3		
66. Toddy kettles	3		
67. Blotters	2		
68. Bottle stands	2		
69. Coffee spoons	2		
70. Condiment sets	2		
71. Desk pad sets	2		
72. Hot milk pots	2		
73. Reading glasses	2		
74. Salts and peppers	2		
75. Buttonhook	1		
76. Bill file	1		
77. Curling lamp	1		
78. Dressing table and bench	1		
79. Eraser (silver handled)	1		
80. Flacon (no lid)	1		

William Codman's Achievement

William Codman retired in 1914 at the age of seventy–five. He returned to England to live and died at his home in Woking, Surrey, in 1921.

Codman's twenty–three–year career at Gorham was remarkable on several levels. The sheer volume of his output was impressive. He obtained fifty–five flatware design patents. One of these, *Chantilly*, is by far the most popular sterling flatware pattern ever designed. The out-pouring of designs for the 1893 Chicago Exposition helped establish Gorham as the number one silvermaker in the world. The Martelé exhibits at Paris, Turin, and St. Louis gave Gorham and Codman international recognition.

I obtained a kind of personal glimpse of William Codman from a man who actually worked with him at Gorham. Mr. F. Russell Woodward, retired chief designer of Gorham, worked in the design department under Codman for five years, from 1909 to 1914. When I asked Mr. Woodward what kind of a man Codman was, he said, "Wonderful man. A great artist. The best." I asked whether Codman really designed all those Martelé pieces. "Most of them," he said. "Mr. Codman would hand a sketch to one of his men—sometimes it was a tiny, rough drawing—and the designer was allowed to develop the design in his own way. But it was still Codman's idea."[18]

William Codman carried on the Gorham tradition of having both a commercial line of silverwares and an art line. His commercial silver designs were highly successful. His art designs—Martelé—gave Gorham a permanent place in the history of the American decorative arts. As more is known of the quality and originality of William Christmas Codman's best work, his importance will be acknowledged.

CHAPTER 13

Art Deco

The period of World War I and its aftermath was a troublesome time for Gorham. At the outbreak of the war some of the company's facilities were directed toward making munitions, principally for France and Russia; and upon this country's entrance into the conflict in 1917, more than two–dozen contracts were secured for supplying materials needed in the war effort. During this time sales of silverwares and bronzes decreased substantially.

On May 19, 1919, Edward Holbrook died, in his seventieth year. He was succeeded as president of Gorham by his son, John Holbrook, who had been a vice–president since 1906. Unfortunately, John was a failure as president. Perhaps he had been too long in the shadow of a strong and domineering father. Perhaps he did not have the incentive. (John Holbrook was wealthy in his own right.) The company's designs had begun to lag behind their competitors. It was said that William C. Codman's and Edward Holbrook's venture into hand-made Martelé wares had been carried too far. Martelé had given Gorham prestige and standing but there was a feeling that their regular lines had been neglected. Whether this was true is hard to say. Art Nouveau, as a vital style, had been long dead when Codman retired in 1914 and nothing had yet come along to take its place.

William Codman, who succeeded his father, William C., as chief designer of the company in 1914, was not of the same caliber as his father. He was well trained in academic styles, but public taste was turning away from these styles to simpler "modern" forms.

The year 1920 was said to have been the poorest in the company's history. The managment of the company seems to have been in chaos. Between June 23 and July 16, 1920, John Holbrook acted as chairman, with Harry A. Macfarland serving briefly as president. Holbrook was then again president until April, 1921, at which time Franklin A. Taylor became president and chief executive officer. Possibly because of the unsettled times and the condition of the company, Taylor made drastic changes in the company's traditional marketing policies. This involved jobbing the line through wholesalers instead of selling solely to and through retail establishments. It did not work; sales suffered drastically. Taylor resigned on May 23, 1923. For a two–year period the company had no president. Henry J. Fuller, as chairman of the board, ran the company and reorganized the business.

In the reorganization, there was considerable retrenchment and consolidation. The holding company, The Silversmiths Company, was purchased by Gorham Manufacturing Company, and the subsidiary companies, which had operated independently since before World War I, were merged. Whiting moved to Providence in 1924, Kerr in 1927, and Durgin in 1931.

Edmund C. Mayo, an experienced executive, was hired in 1923. Within two years he became president and chief executive officer of Gorham. Mayo was a good manager. He strengthened the marketing efforts of the company, and set up budgetary and inventory control systems.

One of the effects of Mayo's leadership was the delegation of design to a position, if not secondary, at least subordinate to production and marketing. Part of this was undoubtedly due to William Codman, who stayed on as chief designer until the thirties. One has only to read Codman's book *An Illustrated History of Silverware Design* (1930) to realize how strongly committed he was to the styles of the past, and how little empathy he had with contemporary design. Two paragraphs from the book summarize his position:

Recently a style so called "Modern" has been introduced to the public, but it does not appear to have made much headway; and it only remains to be said that the fashion worthy of a place in succession to the best of the Georgian and Colonial periods has yet to be devised.[1]

If we see elements of the Greek, the Gothic, or more of the Italian Renaissance in our silverware, let us be thankful our designers have the good sense to value the best in the past and the courage to show us that they can use the past in new ways.[2]

That Edmund Mayo may not have been completely sympathetic with Codman's ideas is indicated by the hiring of Erik Magnussen, a Danish silversmith, who worked as a designer–silversmith for Gorham, independently of Codman, from 1925 to 1929. More on Magnussen later.

In 1928 the Alvin Silver Company was acquired and it maintained its own separate product identity and its own sales force.

In 1929 the Gorham company's New York City retail store at Fifth Avenue and Forty–seventh Street merged with Black, Starr & Frost, the new store being known as Black, Starr & Frost–Gorham, and later as Black, Starr & Gorham.

In 1931 the McChesney Company was purchased and moved to Providence.

Academic Design and Colonial Revival

Even a casual perusal of the Gorham silver catalogs of the 1920s shows that the dominant styles were Colonial Revival and Academic. In William Codman's book, *An Illustrated History of Silverware Design,* mentioned above, he discusses the historical silver styles and shows examples of how Gorham interpreted these styles. The section on the Italian Renaissance illustrates a Florentine black coffee and stand by his father, William C. Codman, which is covered with detail. A later coffee service, designed in the 1920s, is called Florenz. It is simpler in shape and ornamentation. If one did not have Codman's book as a reference, one might call the Florenz set Colonial Revival. This seems to have been a pattern. The earlier versions (1885–1915) of the Academic styles are more detailed, and appear to be more historically correct, at least in spirit, than the watered–down versions of these styles in the 1920s Academic designs of Gorham.

In every case the designs of the younger Codman, whether Louis XIV, Louis XV (he called it a "debased" period), Louis XVI, Elizabethan and Jacobean, Georgian, or Colonial, were simplified, stylized, derivations of the historical styles. Almost all of these 1920s interpretations have today a Colonial Revival look about them. Possibly part of this is because the earlier historical periods mentioned above do not seem to interest many designers today. Also the fact that in the very act of simplification the end result is a series of designs that look more and more like each other as time passes, rather than looking like the styles they were supposed to have been copying.

The coffeepot in Figure 271, made in 1918, was the kind of Academic object that William Codman espoused, a piece that was beautifully crafted, but whose design elements came out of older pieces of English and French silver. The handle and spout derived from eighteenth–century examples and the chasing on the body from the eighteenth and nineteenth centuries. The coffeepot is one of the very few pieces of Gorham silver, or American silver for that matter, that is completely signed. On the bottom of the pot are the usual Gorham marks, plus engraved: "Designed by F. Stark/Hand Wrought by W. Arnold/Chased by Eugene Kauer/1918." These men obviously took great pride in their work.

In about 1920 William Codman designed a coffee service called *Colonial* which featured clean, undecorated,

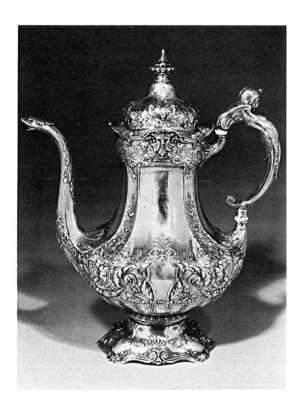

271 Coffeepot made in 1918. Engraved on bottom:"Designed by F. Stark/Hand Wrought by W. Arnold/Chased by Eugene Kauer/ 1918. " Height: 12 1/4 in. (31.1 cm.). Mark: lion–anchor–G/STERLING/LUA. (*Gorham collection*).

squarish, footed shapes (Fig. 272). Another similar pattern, *Fairfax*, was designed by Durgin in the 1920s and still remains a part of the Gorham line. The *Fairfax* pattern is slightly more angular than *Colonial*. Instead of the corners of the square bodies being rounded off, they are flattened, resulting in octagonal bodies. The finials and handles are similar. Both *Colonial* and *Fairfax* are reticent, carefully designed *interpretations* of earlier silver. Although they can clearly be classified as Colonial Revival, they have the look of the 1920s. Colonial Revival was never a static or homogeneous style. There was a constant reinterpretation of past styles.

Erik Magnussen

In 1925 a well–known Danish silversmith, Erik Magnussen, was hired as a Gorham designer. His employment record card designated his occupation as "Designer (Special work)." Apparently he was hired by the new president, Edmund Mayo, and he seems to have worked completely independently from William Codman, the chief designer. Magnussen was a modernist and his work was very different from the academic, traditionalist approach of Codman. The photograph of him working in his rather elegant studio (Fig. 273) is in contrast to all other photographs of the Gorham designing room from the late nineteenth century on, which always show the designers working together in the large designing room. The individual designers had their own

272 *Colonial* coffee service, designed by William Codman about 1920. (*Gorham photograph*).

273 Erik Magnussen, Danish silversmith, who worked at Gorham from 1925 to 1929. *(Gorham photograph).*

specific areas with partitions but they were always in the same general area. Magnussen was obviously treated differently, as an important person.

One can hardly believe that William Codman could have been very happy with the arrangement. He doesn't mention Magnussen at all in his *History of Silverware Design,* which was written in 1929 while Magnussen was still at Gorham. He did not illustrate any of Magnussen's work, and makes only the one previously mentioned disparaging remark about the "Modern" style.

Erik Magnussen, who was born in Denmark May 14, 1884, came to silversmithing at a very interesting time in the history of the art form. In the early 1900s two of the most avant–garde groups in Europe were beginning to work in silver—the Danish group revolving around Georg Jensen, and the Wiener Werkstatte in Vienna, with Josef Hoffmann and others. Both groups

worked in modern styles which would later be classified as Art Deco. The Art Deco movement itself received its first large public showing in Paris in 1925 in the Exposition des Arts Décoratifs et Industriels Modernes. The stylized forms of Art Deco had a great diversity, from objects with soft, curving forms to harsh, geometric forms that came out of Cubism. In this country we often associate Art Deco with the Chrysler building and the Radio City Music Hall in New York, and the movie sets of the 1920s and the 1930s. In the decorative arts the movement was probably most influential in France. The furniture of Emile–Jacques Ruhlmann, Paul Vera, Jules Leleux, and others, the Deco rugs, lamps, and so on, completely took over the fashionable interior.

Magnussen grew up in an intellectual household. His mother was Hedwig Charlotte Claudine Sommer and his father was the writer Johannes Julius Claudi Magnussen. From 1898 to 1901 Magnussen was apprenticed at Winkel & Magnussen (his uncle's art gallery). He studied sculpture with Stephan Sindig about 1901,

274 Five–piece tea and coffee service designed and made by Erik Magnussen in 1926. Hammered silver, ivory insulators and finials. Height of coffeepot: 7 1/4 in. (32.9 cm.). *(Gorham photograph)*.

and he worked as a chaser with the silversmith Viggo Hansen in 1902. From 1907 to 1909 he worked as a chaser with Otto Rohloff in Berlin. From 1909 Magnussen had his own workshop in Denmark.

Before he came to Gorham in 1925 Magnussen's work was widely exhibited, He exhibited at the Danish Museum of Decorative Art, Copenhagen, in 1901, 1904, and 1907; he had special exhibitions at Winkel & Magnussen from 1901; Berlin, 1910 and 1911; Charlottenborg and Copenhagen, 1919; Salon d'Automne, Paris, 1922; and Rio de Janeiro, 1922 (together with the jeweler to the Royal Danish Court, Peter Hertz).

In his early years Magnussen belonged artistically to the same group in Denmark as Georg Jensen and Mogens Ballin. He made hollow ware and jewelry. The jewelry often made use of animal and insect forms in combination with colored stones. The Danish Museum of Decorative Art purchased a large brooch with a grasshopper as its main motif.

One of the first items Magnussen designed at Gorham was the tea and coffee service in Figure 274, made in 1926. The full, rounded bodies and lids are hand hammered in the Arts and Crafts tradition. Ivory insulators manner. The ball–shaped forms of the service contrast with the geometric parallel lines used on the necks, the on the handles and finials are rounded in a decorative

handles, and the rim of the tray. The set has a solid, heavy, modern look quite different from the Academic and Colonial Revival tea and coffee services that dominated Gorham's line at that time.

In 1927 Magnussen made a number of pieces that were much more radical than the service in Figure 274. Figure 275 shows a remarkable coffee set which was radical from a formal point of view and radical in its use of color. The forms are broken down into a series of irregular triangles. Flat, shiny silver areas are contrasted with triangles of gilt and oxidized brown. This kind of geometric abstraction not only comes out of Cubism, with its splintering of forms into facets, but also from Constructivism, which made use of geometric forms, sometimes simple and squared off, sometimes complex and angular. There are parallels in European painting ranging from the early Cubism of Braque, Picasso, and Juan Gris, to the abstractions of Kasimir Malevich and Piet Mondrian, and in America the paintings of Stuart Davis and Charles Shaw.

The tray for the "Cubic" service in Figure 276 was, according to the plant records, "fire gilded." This would indicate that gold was applied to the surface by the old,

275 Three–piece "Cubic" coffee set designed and made by Erik Magnussen
in 1927. Sterling with panels of gilt and liver–colored oxidation. Height of
coffee pot: 9 1/2 in. (24.1 cm.). Mark: No. 26. Serving fork and spoon,
parcel–gilt and oxidized panels. Length of fork: 10 3/8 in. (26.3 cm.).
Mark: No. 26. (*Gorham collection*).

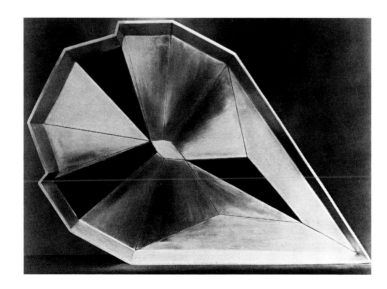

276 "Cubic" tray designed and made by Erik Magnussen in
1927, fire–gilt and oxidized panels. Size: 13 1/4 x 21 1/2 in.
(33.7 x 54.6 cm.). (*Gorham photograph*).

277

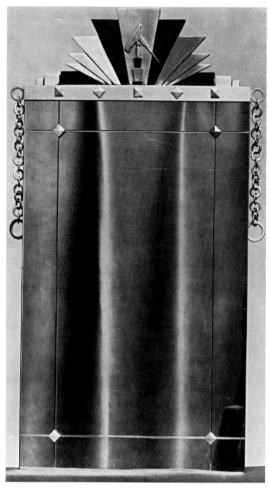

279

278

277 "Manhattan" serving pieces designed by Erik Magnussen in 1927. *Left:* Berry spoon. Length: 9 7/8 in. (25.1 cm.), *Center:* Serving spoon. Height: 9 3/8 in. (23.8 cm.). *Right:* Serving fork. Length: 9 1/4 in. (23.5 cm.). *(Gorham photograph.)*

278 *Manhattan*, by Charles Shaw (1896–1974), ca. 1930. Oil on canvas, 24 1/2 x 16 in. (61.6 x 40.6 cm.). *(Photograph courtesy Washburn Gallery, New York).*

279 Mirror, sterling, enameled and parcel gilt, and glass. Designed by Erik Magnussen in 1927. Height: 38 1/4 in. (97.2 cm.). *(Gorham photograph).*

280 "Ornament" designed and made by Erik Magnussen in 1928. Hammered silver with agate set in finial, green copper base. (*Gorham photograph*).

281 Centerpiece with ebony finial, made in 1928. Height: 11 3/4 in. (29.8 cm.). (*Gorham photograph*).

outlawed mercury–amalgam process. The process had been outlawed because the mercury–gold amalgam, on heating, gave off poisonous fumes of mercury. It is said to have given richer and more varied shades of gold than is obtained by the gold electroplating process where gold is deposited electrolytically in a plating bath. The "Cubic" service was designed *and* executed by Magnussen (see mark No. 26). The service was exhibited a number of times and was pictured in *The New York Times*, where it was named "The Lights and Shadows of Manhattan."

The serving pieces in Figure 275 are in the same style as the "Cubic" coffee set, with facets of silver, gilt silver, and oxidized brown, and ivory tips on the handles.

The oxidized and partially gilt handles of the serving pieces in Figure 277, called Manhattan, are more geometric, and, in a way, more realistic than the serving pieces in Figure 275. These pieces of silver have a striking resemblance to some of the paintings and shaped constructions of Charles Shaw (1896–1974), an avant–garde New York artist who had lived and studied in Paris in the 1920s. Figure 278 is an oil painted by Charles Shaw about 1930, also titled *Manhattan*. Both Magnussen and Shaw showed their love of the New York skyline in

282

283

284

a surprisingly similar way; Magnussen in silver and Shaw in painting.

The silver crest of the mirror in Figure 279 is partially gilt and oxidized in the manner of the "Cubic" coffee set, but the stylized bird and the sterling chains hanging at the sides add new notes that would have made the mirror at home in the campiest of the movie sets of the time.

Magnussen produced some work that was stylistically related to contemporary Danish silver. His pieces often incorporated ivory and semiprecious stones such as lapis lazuli, turquoise, amethyst, and agate. Exotic woods such as ebony, horse, and cocabola were incorporated into designs. The "ornament" in Figure 280 with agates in the finial, a hand–hammered body, and a green copper base, is mounted with six stylized cast animals.

The centerpiece with an ebony finial in Figure 281, with its evenly spaced lines dividing the piece like a cake, is simpler than the candlesticks in Figure 282 with their complex base–supports of silver and turquoise.

In addition to hollow ware and flatware of the type shown, Magnussen designed the sleek sailboat in silver in Figure 283.

Magnussen left Gorham on the first of October 1929. In 1932 he had a workshop in Chicago, and from 1932 to 1938 he worked in Los Angeles. In 1939 he returned to Denmark, where he died on February 24, 1961.

282 Pair of candlesticks designed by Erik Magnussen, ca. 1928. Blue turquoise spheres in ring base. Height: 13 3/4 in. (34.9 cm.). Mark: GORHAM/EM/lion–anchor–G/STERLING/45. (Gorham collection).

283 Sterling sailboat designed by Erik Magnussen in 1927. Height: 15 in. (38.1 cm.). (Gorham photograph).

284 Bronze auto mount modeled by Harriet Frishmuth in 1923. Length: 8 in. (20.3 cm.). (Gorham photograph).

Harriet Frishmuth's bronze sculptures were discussed in Chapter 8. Although her larger sculptures are sometimes stylized, they are quite realistic, reflecting her academic training. However, in the 1920s Miss Frishmuth designed two bronze auto mounts for Gorham in the Deco tradition. One of these, "Speed" (not illustrated), is shown in Gorham's *Famous Small Bronzes.* "Speed" is a dashing winged figure with outstretched hands, atop a ball. The caption in Gorham's book indicates the thinking that went into the design:

> Decorating the radiator of fine automobiles with figures in the feeling of forward motion is a sculptural activity bounded by definite considerations. Such pieces as this must be designed so that their lines create an effect of motion. At the same time they must assume a pleasing impression from every possible angle. Note the streamlined hair and wings; the lines diverging like ripples from the point where the outstretched hands cut the air; the happy and united composition of the whole figure [p. 23].

The other of Harriet Frishmuth's auto mounts is shown in Figure 284. This small sculpture shows the nongeometric side of Art Deco.

Frishmuth's auto mounts were made in bronze with bronze finishes and were treated as sculpture. When the bronzes were meant to be used on an automobile they were silver plated. The bronze in Figure 284 is an eight-inch length, while "Speed" was available in six- and twelve-inch lengths.

The most famous automobile race in the United States, the Indianapolis 500, celebrates its winners with a mammoth five-foot-seven-inch Deco trophy made by Gorham in 1935 (Fig. 285). The trophy was designed by Robert J. Hill. The squares of the trophy echo the squares of the flag held by the nude classical figure on top. Sculptured portrait heads of the winners are in squares above the squares showing names and dates. Each year's winner receives a small version to keep.

285 Borg–Warner Trophy for the Indianapolis 500–mile auto race, made in 1935. Height: Trophy, 51 in. (129.5 cm.), marble base, 16 in. (40.6 cm.). *(Gorham photograph)*.

CHAPTER 14

After World War II

World War II forced drastic changes in Gorham's operations. A government order in December 1941 prohibited the use of copper and its alloys in making civilian goods, so the company ceased the manufacture of bronze and brass goods, and all plated wares. From 1943 to 1945 a War Production Board order limited the use of silver during each quarter to 12 1/2 percent of the amount consumed in 1941.

The company's bronze division converted 100 percent to war work, and the personnel of the silver division were transferred to war work at such a rate that, by 1943, the number of production workers in silverware had shrunk to about 160. As early as June 1, 1942, the Company's customers were placed under a strict rationing program. Toiletware and most church goods were discontinued. Hollow–ware production was cut 70 percent. Sterling flatware production was limited to six–piece place settings in the thirteen most popular patterns.

More than thirty kinds of war material were manufactured, as diverse and as foreign to Gorham's normal goods as small arms parts, 40mm steel cartridge cases, tank bearings, and torpedo components. The company and its employees were three times honored with the Army–Navy Award for High Achievement in Production of War Materials.[1]

A Safe Haven—
Merger with Textron

In 1967, one hundred and thirty–six years after its founding, Gorham was merged with the Providence–based conglomerate, Textron. Gorham had approached Textron as a "safe haven" under the threat of an unfriendly takeover.

In the late 1950s and early 1960s Gorham had embarked on an acquisition program which was designed both to expand their present lines and to diversify them into new businesses. Silverware acquisitions included Quaker Silver Co. (1959), Friedman Silver Co. (1960), and Graff, Washbourne & Dunn (1961). In 1960 the Rabun Bronze Foundry of California was acquired to strengthen the bronze division on the West Coast. Diversification acquisitions included the Eaton Paper Co. of Pittsfield, Massachusetts (1959), Pickard & Burns Inc., an electronic research and development firm of Waltham, Massachusetts, the Camp Manufacturing Co. (1965), and the Adpress Co. (1965). Gorham was on the way to becoming a small conglomerate itself.

In the middle 1960s Gorham became one of those cash–rich companies whose book value was higher than their quoted stock price on the American exchange. Part of this was due to increased silver prices which increased the value of their inventories. The company became a prime target for a takeover. They received—and turned away—feelers from a number of large companies. One of these was from Textron. Rupert Thompson, then head of Textron (Textron's founder, Royal Little, had left the management of Textron several years earlier), is quoted as saying to Burrill Getman, Gorham's president, "If you ever need a safe haven from a takeover, come to us."[2]

Some weeks later it happened. A new outside member of the Gorham board, a Mr. Thomas Wyman, brought to the company an offer from a large national firm of $60 cash per share of Gorham stock, then selling for about $40. This was at a board meeting on Friday of the July Fourth long weekend, 1967. It was considered an unfriendly takeover bid, and the Gorham board agreed to approach Textron immediately. Thompson and his associate at Textron, G. William Miller, moved fast. By the following Wednesday an announcement was made of Gorham's acquisition by Textron. Shareholders approved the deal in September in which each Gorham share was exchanged for Textron stock worth about $73 at that time.

Silverware

There were no marked style changes in Gorham's silver after World War II. The great upheavals in American painting in the 1950s and 1960s, Abstract Expressionism, Minimalism, and Pop Art, movements that gave American art a worldwide fame, seemed to have had little effect on the decorative arts objects made by commercial firms in America.

Gorham's silver forms tended to become more clean–cut, and such "modern" designs as the flatware pattern *Golden Snowflake* (Fig. 286) were popular. *Golden Snowflake* was part of a series called *Thread of Gold* which featured tips of 18–karat gold and gilt details, such as the engraved snowflakes on the handles.

In the 1960s there was an increased interest in heavy, fancy flatware patterns. Older Gorham flatware patterns such as *Chantilly* (1895), *Buttercup* (1899), and other nineteenth–and early twentieth–century patterns, not only remained popular but in some cases increased in popularity.

The latest of the Gorham silver battleship services was made in 1961 for the Cruiser U.S.S. *Long Beach*. The *Long Beach* was the first atomic–powered cruiser of the United States Navy. It was commissioned at the South Boston Annex of the Boston Naval Shipyard, Boston,

286 *Golden Snowflake* pattern, 18–karat–gold tips at ends of handles, snowflakes gilt. Designed in 1952 by J. Russell Price. *(Gorham photograph)*.

Massachusetts, on Saturday afternoon, September 9, 1961. The citizens of Long Beach, California, ordered a silver service from Gorham for the commissioning. The service, designed by Richard Huggins, was deemed appropriate for the atomic age. The finials of the coffee service in Figure 287 are atomic models with depictions of electron paths. The odd, sticklike legs give the pieces of the tea set an other–worldly look; they almost seem like creatures from another planet. The punch bowl and tray in Figure 288 are designed in the same manner. Possibly unconsciously, the designer of the *Long Beach* service was following a well–established Gorham tradition for ship silver that seemed to demand a certain flamboyance, as if these services should be "different" and larger than life.

Trophies and presentation silver had been an important part of Gorham's output from the earliest days. The sleek trophy in Figure 289, with a standing bear holding an oar, is inscribed:

287 Coffee service, made in 1961 for the U.S.S. *Long Beach*. Height of coffeepot: 11 7/8 in. (30.2 cm.). (*Gorham_photograph*).

288 Punch bowl, tray, and ladle made for the U.S.S. *Long Beach* in 1961. Width of punch bowl over handles: 19 7/8 in. (50.5 cm.). Length of tray: 28 in. (71 cm.). (*Gorham photograph*).

WALTER J. STEIN TROPHY
Presented annually to the winner of the
Harvard, Brown and Rutgers
Rowing Competition
1964

On the base is engraved a series of rowing sculls and the inscription:

In 1857, Rowing was officially recognized at Brown University becoming the first inter–collegiate sport at Brown. The first inter–collegiate rowing meet was held between Harvard–Yale and Brown at Worcester, July 26, 1859.

In 1964 J. Russell Price designed a punch bowl, tray, goblets, and ladle for presentation to Shah Reza Pahlavi and Empress Farah of Iran. The punch bowl of the service featured portrait heads of the shah and his empress, surrounded by the flora and fauna of Iran (Fig. 290). The base of the punch bowl is mounted with a row of red and green stones.

Figure 291 shows Gorham's President's Cup for Outstanding Sales Contribution designed by Burr Sebring in 1979. The sculptured figure on top is Vulcan, a scaled–down model of the 7 1/2–foot bronze Vulcan, by M. Raggi, which was placed in front of the Gorham building in Providence in 1894.

289 Walter J. Stein trophy for Harvard, Brown, and Rutgers rowing competition, 1964. Height to tip of oar: 21 in. (53.3 cm.). *(Gorham photograph)*.

290 Punch bowl made for the shah and empress of Iran in 1964. Height: 11 1/4 in. (28.6 cm.). *(Gorham photograph)*.

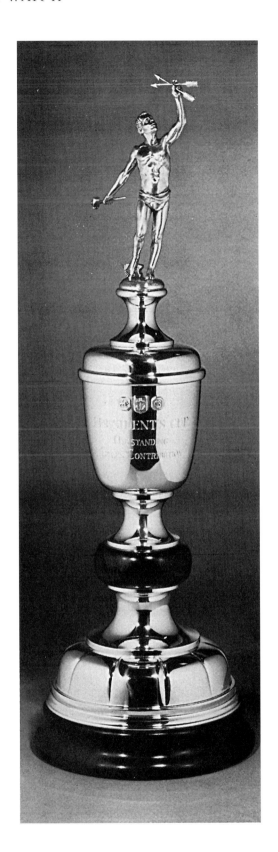

291 The Gorham President's Cup, 1979. Sterling and rosewood. Height: 20 3/4 in. (52.7 cm.). *(Gorham photograph)*.

292 Bronze eagle, modeled by Douglas Corsini in 1976. Wing span: five feet. *(Gorham photograph).*

Gorham's bronze business has changed considerably since the 1920s. Bronze dedication tablets for buildings and memorial plaques for cemeteries are now the main business of the bronze division. The interest in Art bronzes is not as great as it was in the twenties and thirties. Production is limited to such works as the Dallin Indian series (Chapter 8) and an occasional bronze such as the large Corsini eagle in Figure 292. Douglas Corsini, born in 1945, is a Providence–based sculptor, trained at the Art Institute of Boston and the Boston Museum School of Fine Arts. He spent time in Florence, Italy. The eagle in Figure 292, with a five–foot wingspan, was modeled in 1976.

The 1970s have seen a considerable diversification of Gorham's lines. The company has gone into chinaware and crystal, collectibles, including all kinds of items incorporating Norman Rockwell's paintings, giftwares, and jewelry. Stainless steel and pewter flatware patterns have been added to the traditional sterling and electroplated wares. New hollow-ware pieces have been made in pewter and brass. Although the pewter coffee service in Figure 293 (the design is called *Octette*) is based on Geor–

293

293 *Octette* coffee set, designed by Burr Sebring in 1973. *(Gorham photograph).*

294 Handwrought coffeepot, made by Burr Sebring in 1965. Height: 9 1/2 in. (24.1 cm.). *(Gorham photograph).*

294

295 Enameled gold chain and pendant made for Brown University in 1965. On the back of the pendant is a Latin inscription which translates: "To Brown University, now completing its second century, During the presidency of Barnaby Conrad Keeney, This interlaced chain and its pendant Have been given by a most illustrious, former leader, 1965." (*Gorham photograph*).

gian silver forms, it has a clean, contemporary look which reflects the modern predilections of Burr Sebring, the designer. *Octette* is evidence of the continuing popularity of the Colonial Revival style. Sebring is an accomplished silversmith in his own right, as exemplified by the sleek hand–raised coffeepot made in 1965 (Fig. 294). Gorham has long had close ties with such Rhode Island institutions as Brown University. It was noted early in this book (Chapter 3) that in the 1850s Commencement Day at Brown was one of the four holidays Gorham granted its employees, along with Thanksgiving, Christmas, and the Fourth of July. In 1965 Gorham made an exceptionally fine ceremonial gold chain and pendant for Brown University (Fig. 295), which the president of Brown wears at the opening convocation of the school year in September and at commencement exercises.

Gorham celebrated its one–hundred–and–fiftieth birthday in 1981. The first edition of this book was not written for the anniversary, but it is perhaps fitting that the manuscript was completed in that anniversary year.

Notes

1. Introduction

1. See, for example, Simon Jervis, *High Victorian Design* (Ottawa: National Gallery of Canada for the Corporation of the National Museums of Canada, 1974); Berry B. Tracy, et al, *19th–Century Amerieca: Furniture and Other Decorative Arts* (New York: The Metropolitan Museum of Art, 1970); Marvin D. Schwartz, *Collectors' Guide to Antique American Silver* (New York: Doubleday & Co., 1975); Patricia Wardle, *Victorian Silver and Silver–Plate* (New York: Thomas Nelson and Sons, 1963); Graham Hood, *American Silver: A History of Style, 1650–1900* (New York: Praeger Publishers, 1971).

2. The copy of Owen Jones's *Grammar of Ornament* in the Gorham library is a magnificent elephant folio copy "With 100 Folio Plates" in full color (21 5/4 x 14 1/2in.). (London: Day and Son, 1856).

3. Nikolaus Pevsner, *Studies in Art, Architecture and Design* (London: Thomas and Hudson, 1968), Vol. 2, p. 54.

4. Ad Reinhardt's observation was also used in our book: Charles H. Carpenter, Jr., with Mary Grace Carpenter, *Tiffany Silver* (New York: Dodd, Mead & Co., 1978), p. xvi.

5. Kenneth L. Ames, "What is the Neo-Grec?" *Nineteenth Century*, Vol. 2, No. 2, Summer 1976, pp. 13-21.

6. For examples of the English silver, see John Culme, *Nineteenth Century Silver* (London: Country Life Books, 1977); Patrica Wardle, *Victorian Silver and Silver–Plate* (New York: Thomas Nelson and Sons, 1963); and *The Crystal Palace Exhibition, Illustrated Catalogue*, (New York: Dover Publications, Inc., 1970).

7. John S. Holbrook, "The Art of the Silversmith and Its Development" (New York: Privately printed for the Gorham Co., no date), pp. 16–18.

8. *Jewelers' Circular and Horological Review, Oct.* 1878, p. 184.

9. The first two paragraphs of this description of Art Deco is an edited quote from *Tiffany Silver, p.* 268.

10. See *Tiffany Silver,* Chapter 12, "The Making of Tiffany Silver," pp. 222–242, for a description of silver manufacturing methods of the 1870s. Gorham's practices and equipment were similar to Tiffany's at the time, with the exception of flatware manufacture. Tiffany was still using spoon and fork rolls in the 1870s, while Gorham had been using drop presses since the 1850s. We know of cases where craftsmen worked for both companies at different times in their careers. There appears to have been few trade secrets.

11. John Ruskin, *The Seven Lamps of Architecture,* Library Edition, Vol. VIII, p. 218.

12. Jorge Luis Borges, "Kafka and His Precursors," in *Labyrinths* (New York: New Directions, 1964), p. 201.

13. *The Statistical History of the United States from Colonial Times to the Present* (Stamford, Conn.: Fairfield Publishers, 1962), pp. 90–92.

14. Ibid., p. 371.

2. The Beginnings

1. *Rhode Island Tercentenary Celebration, a Catalog of an Exhibition of Paintings by Gilbert Stuart, Furniture by the Goddards and Townsends* (Providence: Art Museum, Rhode Island School of Design, 1936), p. 19.

2. Ralph E. Carpenter, Jr., *The Arts and Crafts of Newport, Rhode Island* (Newport: The Preservation Society of Newport County, 1954), pp. 155–198.

3. Alice Morse Earle, *In Old Narragansett* (New York: Charles Scribner's Sons, 1898), p. vi.

4. William Davis Miller, *The Silversmiths of Little Rest* (Kingston, R.I.: Privately printed, 1928), pp. xi–xii.

5. Kathryn C. Buhler and Graham Hood, *American Silver, Garvin and Other Collections in the Yale University Art Gallery* (New Haven: Yale University Press, 1970), Vol. 1, p. 289.

6. Kathryn C. Buhler, *American Silver, 1655–1825, in the Museum of Fine Arts, Boston* (Greenwich, Conn.: New York Graphic Society, 1972), p. 564.

7. William Davis Miller, *The Silversmiths of Little Rest*, p. 4.

8. Ibid., p. 7.

9. Ibid., p. 7 and Kenneth Scott, *Counterfeiting in Colonial Rhode Island* (Providence: The Rhode Island Historical Society, 1960), pp. 55–56.

10. Henry N. Flynt and Martha Gandy Fales, *The Heritage Foundation Collection of Silver* (Old Deerfield, Mass.: The Heritage Foundation, 1968), p. 203.

11. Lewis W. Clarke, "Ye Ancient Jewelers of Providence," *The Manufacturing Jeweler*, January 1894, pp. 12–16.

12. *Mechanics' Festival and Historical Sketches* (Providence: 1860), p. 104.

13. Gilbert S. Suzawa, "Seril Dodge: Real Jewelry Industry Pioneer?" *URI Alumni Quarterly*, Summer 1979, pp. 26–28. The possibility that the Dodges may have been using the well–known "close–plating" process should not be discounted. This involved the covering of small metal objects with silver foil and borax and heating to red–heat to fuse the metals. (Michael Snodin and Gail Belden, *Collecting for Tomorrow, Spoons* [Radnor, Pa., Chilton Book Co., 1976], p. 20.)

14. Henry S. Gorham, *The Gorham Family in Rhode Island* (Boston: David Clapp & Son, 1900).

15. From a copy of a letter addressed to Lewis W. Clarke dated New York, January 13, 1894.

16. The obituary of William Hadwin, *Nantucket Weekly Mirror*, March 29, 1862.

17. Flynt and Fales, *The Heritage Foundation Collection of Silver*, p. 283.

18. William Hadwin obituary.

19. "Among the Workers in Silver," *Atlantic Monthly*, December 1867, p. 731.

20. Gorham files.

3. Coin Silver Spoons

1. Much of the historical material in Chapter 3 is from the Gorham manuscript files. Most valuable was a hand–written notebook account of the early days of the company written by John Gorham in 1893. Although this account was apparently never finished and has some obvious inaccuracies, it supplies unique material on Gorham in the 1840s and 1850s.

The first page of John Gorham's account starts:

New York, July 1893

To My Boys Charlie & Jabez—

Your mother asks me to note down an account of my beginnings in the silver business,—what led me to it, and some of my early experiences in it. She thinks it will interest you as this business occupied nearly forty of the best years of my life, and has long been known as the Gorham Manufacturing Company.

To begin with, my father Jabez Gorham was a manufacturer of fine gold jewelry…

2. Edwin T. Freidley, ed., *Leading Pursuits and Leading Men* (Philadelphia: Edward Young, 1856), p. 397.

3. From a letter in the Gorham files dated New York, January 13, 1894, from John Gorham to Lewis W. Clarke, editor of *The Manufacturing Jeweler*, supplying material used in an article "Silvermaking in America, Part II, Gorham Mfg. Co.–History and Development," *The Manufacturing Jeweler*, June 6, 1894, pp. 2–3.

4. These notes on Henry Webster's career after leaving Gorham in 1852 are from the Gorham files ("Historical Notes"). They are at a slight variance with the account in Dorothy T. Rainwater's *Encyclopedia of American Silver Manufacturers* (New York: Crown Publishers, Inc., 1975), p. 92, which says Webster's new firm was called Webster & Knowles.

5. Jabez Gorham married again on April 16, 1822. His second wife was Lydia Dexter, daughter of Lewis and Lydia (Comstock) Dexter. She was born in Smithfield, Rhode Island (no date). She died September 4, 1873. Children of Jabez and Lydia were: Benjamin, b. Feb. 2, 1823, d. Dec. 5, 1823; Amey, b. May 7, 1824, d. Jan. 30, 1864; Susan, b. July 3, 1825, d. Feb. 1, 1898; Charles Field, b. Mar. 5, 1834, d. Aug. 16, 1906. Data from: *The Gorham Family in Rhode Island, Notes on the Providence Line* (Boston: David Clapp & Son, 1900) and Brenner, *Rhode Island Genealogy–Biography*, Vol. II (pp. 942–944).

6. Henry C. Bushnell, *Recollections of the Early History of the Gorham Company* (unpublished manuscript), p. 1.

7. Michael Gibney obtained the first United States design patent for a flatware pattern: Design Patent No. 26, Dec. 4, 1844. See Dorothy T. Rainwater and Donna H. Felger *American Spoons* (Hanover, Pa.: Everybody's Press, 1977) pp. 12–13.

8. John Gorham's *Notebook*, p. 7.

9. *Vital Records of Nantucket, Massachusetts, to the Year 1850* (Boston: New England Genealogical Society, 1927), Vol. III., p. 144.

10. Deborah Dependahl Waters, "From Pure Coin, The Manufacture of American Silver Flatware, 1800–1860." *Winterthur Portfolio* 12, ed. I. M. G. Quimby, 1977, p. 19.

11. Henry C. Bushnell, *Recollections*, p. 1.

12. "Among the Workers in Silver," *Atlantic Monthly,* December 1867, pp. 438–439.

13. "Silver and Silver Plate," *Harper's New Monthly Magazine,* No. CCXX, Vol. XXXVII, September 1868, pp. 438–439.

14. Deborah Dependahl Waters, "From Pure Coin . . . ," p. 20.

15. The analytical method is described in Victor F. Hanson, "Quantitative Elemental Analyses of Art Objects by Energy–Dispersive X–Ray Fluorescence Spectroscopy," *Applied Spectroscopy, Vol.* 27, No. 5, 1973, pp. 309–333.

16. These data were based on "Winterthur Report A.L. 915–Revised," dated Feb. 21, 1980, and A.L. 954, Jan. 10, 1980. The analytical technique used was energy dispersive x–ray fluorescence, a truly nondestructive analytical method. The x–rays employed are weak and do not alter the object in any way. The Winterthur report indicated the percentages of fifteen different elements in each spoon, but it was judged that the four elements shown on the table—silver, copper, gold, tin—were of the most significance. Victor F. Hanson and Maruta Skelton were most helpful in interpreting the data.

17. Victor F. Hanson provided the following note: "Due to differences in the melting temperatures of silver (960.5°C) and copper (1083°C), there is a copper enrichment at the chilled faces of the casting in contact with the mold and a higher silver content at the top. These differences persist through the rolling and forging operation and appear on the opposite sides of the finished piece, be it a fork, spoon, or coin."

18. For an account of eighteenth–century spoonmaking methods see Henry J. Kaufman, *The Colonial Silversmith, His Techniques and His Products* (New York: Galahad Books, 1969), pp. 51–55. Dorothy T. Rainwater, in her book *Encyclopedia of American Silver Manufacturers* (New York: Crown, 1975), p. 152, quotes an 1848 description of spoon making in Hartford, Connecticut.

19. *Harper's New Monthly Magazine,* September 1868, p. 437.

20. Henry C. Bushnell, *Recollections,* p. 2.

4. *John Gorham: The Expansionist*

1. In June 1850 the employees of Gorham & Thurber were: H. L. Webster, Charles Cabot, Owen Salisbury, James Salisbury, James Furlong, John Robinson, George Dean, Henry Bushnell, Charles Pennell, Giles Manchester, Charles Godfrey, Isaiah Gothran, Charles Gallagher, and Felix McCabe. (Data from the large historical chart of the company's history, ca. 1909).

2. John Gorham's *Notebook*, p. 11.

3. From a letter in the files of the Art Institute of Chicago.

4. *Tiffany Silver,* Figure 4, p. 10.

5. Sotheby Parke Bernet Sale No. 696, January 20, 1979, No. 284.

6. Katharine Morrison McClinton, *Collecting American 19th Century Silver* (New York: Bonanza Books, 1968), p. 49.

7. Carey T. Mackie, H. Parrott Bacot, and Charles L. Mackie, *Crescent City Silver* (New Orleans: The Historic New Orleans Collection and the Anglo–American Art Museum, Louisana State University, 1980), Figure 44, p. 43.

8. *Providence Journal*, September 19, 1850, p. 2.

9. *Providence Journal,* September 13, 1851, p. 2.

10. *Tiffany Silver*, p. 233.

11. John Gorham's *Notebook,* pp. 23–24.

12. Ibid., pp. 24–25.

13. T.K. Terry and Trevor I. Williams, *A Short History of Technology* (New York and Oxford: Oxford University Press, 1961), pp. 352–353.

14. Justin G. Turner and Linda Levitt Turner, *Mary Todd Lincoln, Her Life and Letter,* (New York: Alfred A. Knopf, 1972).

15. Ibid., p. 615.

16. Ibid., p. 88.

17. Ibid., p. 505.

18. Ibid., p. 611.

19. Ibid., pp. 615–616.

20. "Silver and Silver Plate," *Harper's New Monthly Magazine,* September 1868, p. 443.

21. John William Tucker began business in San Francisco as J. W. Tucker & Co., Importing Jeweler, in August 1850. See Edgar W. Morse, *San Franciseo Silver Ware* (San Francisco: Argentum Antiques, Ltd., 1977), a two–page listing.

22. George C. Shreve had been in San Francisco since 1852.

5. *The Post–Civil War Years*

1. John Culme, *Nineteenth Century Silver* (London: Country Life Books, 1977), p. 206.

2. Ibid., p. 208.

3. Nikolaus Pevsner, *Studies in Art, Architecture and Design* (New York: Walker & Co., 1948), Vol. 2, p. 52.

4. Dorothy T. Rainwater, *Encyclopedia of American Silver Manufacturers,* (New York: Crown Publishers, Inc., 1975), pp. 122–123.

5. *Tiffany Silver,* pp. 56–67 and 100–101.

6. Gorham historical files.

7. John Culme, *Nineteenth Century Silver;* pp. 25 and 66

8. *Jewelers' Circular,* December 15, 1874, p. 194.

9. *Jewelers' Circular,* December 15, 1874, p. 193.

10. John Y. Simon, ed., *The Personal Memoirs of Julia Dent Grant* (New York: G. P. Putnam's Sons, 1975), p. 189.

11. Esther Singleton, *The Story of the White House* (New York: McClure Co., 1907), p. 178.

12. Letter from Richard Nixon dated January 16, 1981.

13. Gorham records.

14. Alexander Farnum, *The Century Vase* (Providence: Livermore & Knight, 187G), pp. 7–8.

15. Ibid., p. 10.

16. *Tiffany Silver,* pp. 32–36.

17. For a historical and technical discussion of electroplated silvers, see Dorothy T. and H. Ivan Rainwater, *American*

Silverplate (Hanover, Pa.: Thomas Nelson, Inc. and Everybody's Press, 1968).

18. *Harper's New Monthly Magazine,* September 1868, p. 446.

19. Ibid., p. 448.

20. Ibid., pp. 445–446.

6. Innovation and Fantasy

1. See Frank Whitford, Japanese *Prints and Western Painters* (New York: Macmillan Publishing Co., 1977); and Gabriel Weisberg, Phillip O. Cote, Gerald Needham, Martin Eidelberg, and William R. Johnston, *Japonisme, Japanese Influence on French Art, 1854–1910*, published jointly by the Cleveland Museum of Art, the Rutgers University Art Gallery, and the Walters Art Gallery, 1975; Siegfried Wichmann, *Japonisme: The Japanese Influence on Western Art in the Nineteenth and Twentieth Centuries* (New York: Crown Publishers, 1981); Yamada, Chisaburoh, et. al., eds., *Japonisme in Art: An International Symposium* (New York: Kodansha International, 1981).

2. The Japanese books from the Gorham Library were identified by Money L. Hickman of the Museum of Fine Arts, Boston.

3. A complete set of the *Manga* (a word that literally means " sketches," "cartoons," "studies") consisted of fifteen volumes. Hokusai's *Manga* was a wide–ranging view of Japanese things and Japanese life.

4. H. Russell Robinson, *Japanese Arms and Armor,* (New York: Crown Publishers, 1969), Plates 86 and 87.

5. Edwin O. Reischauer, *The Japanese* (Cambridge, Mass.: Harvard University Press, 1977), p. 57.

6. *Tiffany Silver*, p. 190.

7. Pairpoint wrote a scrics of articles on "Art Work and Silver" that appeared in the Jewelers' Circular and Horological Review from September 1879 through March 1880.

8. This diary of a silversmith who worked at Tiffany & Co. in the 1876–1883 period was found in the Gorham files, indicating he may have come to Gorham in 1883. The silversmith's name is not in the diary, and so far he has not been identified. A number of entries indicate he was the principal assistant to Edward C. Moore, Tiffany's chief designer. The diary is a rich and articulate accounting of a great period in American silver making. The author of this book hopes in the future to publish an annotated version of the diary.

9. Tiffany Silver, p. 189.

10. Graham Hughes, Modern Silver (New York: Crown, 1967), pp. 146–147.

11. An edited quote from Frank Archibald Turk, *Japanese Objects D'Art* (New York: Sterling Publishing Co., 1963), p. 93.

12. Herbert Maryon, *Metalwork and Enamelling* (New York: Dover Publications, 1971), pp. 264-265.

13. George E. Gee, *The Silversmiths' Handbook* (London: Crosby Lockwood & Co., 1885), p. 140.

14. See Elizabeth Aslin, *The Aesthetic Movement: Prelude to Art Nouveau* (London: Elik Books, Ltd., 1969).

15. John Culme, *Nineteenth Century Silver* (London: Country Life Books, 1977), p. 211.

7. Antoine Heller and the New Academy

1. There is no evidence that Heller actually attended the École.

2. Richard Guy Wilson, Dianne H. Pilgrim, and Richard N. Murray, *The American Renaissance, 1876–1917* (New York: The Brooklyn Museum, 1979), pp. 56–61.

3. From a sixteen—page typescript in the Gorham files entitled "History of Gorham Mfg. Co., 1878 to 1935" by William Codman, p. 2

4. *Tiffany Silver*, pp. 112–113.

5. "History of Gorham Mfg. Co. 1878 to 1935," p. 2.

6. Soup tureens in the form of sea turtles are illustrated in Charles James Jackson, *History of English Plate* (London: Country Life and B. T. Batsford, 1911), Vol. II, p. 817, Fig. 1056; and Frederick Bradbury, *History of Old Sheffield Plate* (London: Macmillan and Co., Ltd., 1912), p. 389.

7. Both the dates of Heinzelman's birth and death in Townsend's account differ from the dates on the shield in Figure 135. Since there are other errors in Townsend (edited out in the text), I believe the dates on the shield (1837–1900) are probably correct.

8. Horace Townsend, *Nicholas Heinzelman, The Man and the Artist* (New York: The Gorham Co., For Private Circulation, 1918).

9. The surviving diaries of William Crins cover the years 1888, 1889, and 1894 through 1900. The diaries were made available through the courtesy of Mr. Charles Chapin, Mr. Crin's great–grandson.

8. The Bronzes

1. A gating system consists of three parts: (1) the down *sprue* into which the molten bronze is poured, (2) the *runner*, through which the hot metal flows to the (3) *ingates* (there are usually more than one), which deliver the molten bronze to the casting space. The *vent* (or *vents*) allows air, steam, and hot gases to be displaced by the molten metal. The *riser* is used as a reservoir of hot metal to "feed" the casting as it cools and contracts.

2. See Jean de Marco "Bronzes and Their Patinas," *National Sculpture Review*, Spring 1972, pp. 23–25, and Summer 1972, pp. 25–26.

3. The information on Houdon's *George Washington* and the 1856 Hubard copies is mainly from an undated typescript document prepared for the 56th Congress of the United States, concerning the acquisition of a statue of Washington for the Capitol Rotunda. A copy of the typescript was furnished by the Architect of the Capitol, Washington.

4. The information on the "Independent Man" was abstracted from an article on the sculpture by Ralph W.

Hiatt and Cliff Kite in the *Gorham Perspective,* November 1976.

5. "Remember Those Who Go Down to the Sea in Ships," *The Foundry,* April 1, 1927.

6. Patricia Janis Broder, *Bronzes of the American West* (New York: Harry N. Abrams, 1974), p. 93. Much of the information on Dallin's life was abstracted from Ms. Broder's book. Also useful were Loring Holmes Dodd, *Golden Moments in American Sculpture* (Cambridge, Mass.: Dresser, Chapman & Grimes, 1967), pp. 33–37; and Wayne Craven, *Sculpture in America* (New York: Thomas Y. Crowell Co., 1968), pp. 527–531.

7. These data on the Dallin bronzes are from an illustrated Gorham brochure, "The Epic of the Indian," ca. 1980, pp. 8–9.

8. "A Statement of Standards for Sculptural Reproduction and Preventative Measures to Combat Unethical Casting in Bronze," *Art Journal,* Fall 1974. This committee report discusses bronze copies, or *surmoulage,* and makes the following statement: "In our opinion a bronze from a finished bronze, *unless under the direct supervision of the artist,* even when not prohibited by law and authorized by the artist's heirs or executors, is a counterfeit, as it imitates, resembles, has the appearance or is a copy of the original, with or without implying deceit."

9. *Golden Moments in American Sculpture,* pp. 4950.

10. Ibid., p. 48.

9. Presentation Pieces

1. Entries on "Dorr, Thomas Wilson" and "Dorr's Rebellion" in *Encyclopedia Americana* (1965), Vol. 9, p. 268; Arthur May Mowry, *The Dorr War* (Providence: 1901).

2. *Providence Journal,* July 11, 1845, p. 2.

3. Berry B. Tracy, et al., *19th–Century America: Furniture and Other Decorative Arts* (New York: The Metropolitan Museum of Art, 1970), No. 181.

4. Margaret Brown Klaphthor, *Presentation Pieces in the Museum of History and Technology* (Washington, D.C.: Smithsonian Institution, 1965), pp. 98–99.

5. Sharon S. Darling, "Admiral Dewey's Loving Cup," *The Magazine Silver,* January–February 1976, pp. 10–12.

6. Frank J. Petramalo, "Navy Presentation Silver," *Navy Supply Corps Newsletter,* June 1969, pp. 48–49.

10. Souvenir Spoons

1. *Souvenir Spoons of America,* "Published for Gorham Mfg. Co. by the Jewelers' Circular Publishing Co," 1891 (no author), p. 3.

2. The most comprehensive book on American souvenir spoons is Dorothy T. Rainwater and Donna H. Felger, *American Spoons, Souvenir and Historical* (Hanover, Pa.: Everybody's Press, Inc., 1977). Others include Albert Stutzenberger, *American Historical Spoons* (Rutland, Vt.: Charles E. Tuttle Co., 1971), and three books privately printed by Anton Hardt: *Souvenir Spoons of the 90s* (1962), *Adventuring Further in Souvenir Spoons* (1971), and *New Discoveries in Historical Spoons* (1979). Two books which were published for Gorham in 1891 were most useful in writing this chapter: *Souvenir Spoons of America,* op. cit., and *Souvenir Spoons,* compiled by George B. James, Jr. (Boston, Mass.: A. W. Fuller & Co., 1891).

3. Charles H. Carpenter, Jr., "An Early Souvenir Spoon," *The Magazine Silver,* May–June, 1980, pp. 12–13.

4. Anton Hardt, "Earliest Souvenir Spoon Discovered," *The Magazine Silver,* September–October 1979.

5. "The Mania for Spoons" in "The Woman's Hour" column of the *Commercial Advertiser* (New Yol c), January 24, 1891.

6. *Souvenir Spoons of America,* p. 4.

7. Rainwater and Felger, *American Spoons, Souvenir and Historical,* p. 15.

8. From an advertisement in *The Jeweler's Circular,* March 25, 1891, as quoted in Anton Hardt, *Adventuring Further in Souvenir Spoons* (New York: Greenwich Press, 1971), p. 9.

9. James, *Souvenir Spoons,* p. 223.

10. The lost–wax process is still used at Gorham to make small pieces and parts. See Douglas Ash, *Dictionary of British Antique Silver* (London: Pelham Books, 1972), p. 51.

11. Gertrude Schmidt, "Fifteen Famous Actresses and Their Souvenir Spoons, 1892," *The Spinning Wheel,* October 1964, p. 8.

11. Holbrook and Codman

1. Most of the information on William C. Codman's English background comes from the Gorham files. Most useful was an unpublished typescript, ca. 1935, "History of the Gorham Company Since 1878," written by William Codman, the son of William Christmas Codman, and a newspaper clipping of W. C. Codman's obituary dated Dec. 8, 1921.

2. *The Magazine Antiques,* September 1980, p. 450.

3. From a clipping in the Gorham file "The Gorham Exhibit," *The Providence Sunday Journal,* April 23, 1893.

4. A quote from a typescript of a report by the French Ministry of Commerce, "International Exposition of Chicago, 1893, Committee 24, Jewelry, Gold & Silverware," p. 2. The report was published under the direction of M. Camille Krantz, Commissioner General of the French Government (Paris: National Press, 1894).

5. Farran Zerbe, "Bryan Money, Tokens of the Presidential Campaigns of 1896 and 1900–Comparative and Satirical." *The Numismatist,* Vol. XXXIX, July 1926, No. 7 pp. 313–320.

6. From a letter dated June 3, 1981, from Jane Shadel Spillman, Curator, American Glass, the Corning Museum of Glass.

7. Martin Eidelberg, "Art Pottery," in Robert Judson Clark, ed., *The Arts and Crafts Movement in America* (Princeton: Princeton University Press, 1972), p. 119.

8. George Sweet Gibb, *The Whitesmiths of Taunton, A History of Reed & Barton, 1824–1943* (Cambridge, Mass.: Harvard University Press, 1943), pp. 308–314.

12. Martelé

1. The literature of the British Arts and Crafts movement is extensive. See Gillian Naylor, *The Arts and Crafts Movement: A Study of its Sources, Ideals and Influence on Design Theory* (Cambridge, Mass.: The MIT Press, 1971); Elizabeth Aslin, *The Aesthetic Movement* (New York: Frederick A. Praeger, 1969); and E. P. Thomas, *William Morris and the Romantic Revolt* (London: Lawrence and Wilshart, Ltd., 1955). A useful work on the movement in America is Robert J. Clark, ed., *The Arts and Crafts Movement in America, 1876–1916* (Princeton: Princeton University Press, 1972).
2. John Ruskin's long and influential career as a writer, art critic, and social reformer need not be recounted here. His great works on architecture, *The Seven Lamps of Architecture* (1849) and *The Stones of Venice* (3 vols., 1851–1853), and such essays as "Work," published in *The Crown of Wild Olive,* have had a continuing influence on Western thought.
3. The author is particularly interested in Japanese influences on Western metalworks. See *Tiffany Silver,* Chapter 10, "The Japanese and Other Exotic Influences," and my article in *Connoisseur,* January 1979, "Tiffany Silver in the Japanese Style," and Chapter 5 in this book. A forthcoming article, tentatively titled "Japanese Influences on American Metalworks of the 19th and Early 20th Centuries," will explore the Japanese influences on American silver of the 1870s and 1880s, and a variety of metalworks of the Art Nouveau and Arts and Crafts movement.
4. *Art Encyclopedia,* McGraw–Hill, Vol. I, p. 811.
5. Gillian Naylor, *The Arts and Crafts Movement* (London: Studio Vista, 1971), p. 154.
6. Ibid., p. 155.
7. *The Jewelers' Circular,* Nov. 17, 1897, p. 16.
8. Charlotte Moffit, "New Designs in Silver," *House Beautiful,* December 1899, p. 56.
9. *The Gorham Manufacturing Company, Silversmiths* (New York: Cheltenham Press, 1900), p. 16.
10. Edgar Kaufmann, Jr., "Some American Architectural Ornament of the Arts and Crafts Era," *Journal of the Society of Architectural Historians,* XXIV (December 1965), pp. 285–91.
11. *The Gorham Manufacturing Company, Silversmiths,* p. 14.
12. Ibid., pp. 32–34.
13. Christian Meyer, *Josef Hoffmann, Architect and Designer, 1870–1956* (Vienna: Galerie Metropol, 1981), pp. 8–9.
14. Allen H. Eaton, *Handicrafts of New England* (New York: Harper & Brothers, 1949), p. 283.
15. See Margaretta Gebelein Leighton, *George Christian Gebelein, Boston Silversmith, 1878–1945* (Boston: Privately printed, 1976).

16. A report from the analytical laboratory of the Winterthur Museum, "Request No. 372," September 12, 1975, by Karen Papanchado.
17. Douglas Ash, *Dictionary of British Antique Silver* (London: Pelham Books, Ltd., 1972), pp. 38–39. Also private correspondence with Susan M. Hare, Librarian, Goldsmiths' Hall, London.
18. I interviewed Mr. Woodward on October 30, 1980, at a nursing home in Attleboro, Massachusetts. He informed me he was ninety—three years old. He was bright and articulate.

13 Art Deco

1. William Codman, *An Illustrated History of Silverware Design* (Providence: The Gorham Co., 1930), p. 72.
2. Ibid., p. 76.
3. The information on Erik Magnussen's European background was kindly furnished by Flemming Eskildsen of Georg Jensen, Copenhagen. His sources included *Dansk Kunsthandvaerkerleksikon,* Rhodes, 1979; *Weilbachs Kunstnerleksikon,* Aschehoug Forlag, 1947.
4. Katharine Morrison McClinton, *Art Deco, A Guide For Collectors* (New York: Charles N. Potter, 1972), pp. 1360.
5. Gorham files, no date.,
6. Letter from Flemming Eskildsen of Georg Jensen, Copenhagen, dated April 2, 1981.
7. *Famous Small Bronzes* (New York: The Gorham Co., 1928), p. 23.

14. After World War II

1. J. Warren Thomas, *A Brief History of Gorham* (an unpublished manuscript, 1978), p. 27.
2. Robert S. Eisenhauer, *Textron . . . From the Beginning,* (Privately published by Textron, 1979), p. 98.
3. I am grateful to Mr. Erskine N. White, Jr., for his help in reconstructing these events. Mr. White was executive vice president of Gorham in 1967, becoming president in 1968. In 1969 Mr. White was transferred to Textron, where he afterwards became executive vice president.

APPENDIX I

Gorham Marks

This section strives to give a reasonably comprehensive sampling of Gorham marks from the beginning of the company in 1831, with emphasis on the marks of the nineteenth century. A number of variants are shown, but no attempt is made to show all known marks. From 1831 to 1868 the marks give an indication of a time period rather than an indication of an actual year. In 1868 Gorham initiated a system of date letters and symbols to indicate the specific year in which a piece was made.

Flatware, 1831–1865

The marks on the Gorham pieces of the 1831–1852 period are typical of the coin silver era. The marks stamped on flatware may record up to three kinds of information: The maker's name, the place of manufacture, and the words COIN or PURE COIN. From 1855 the patent date may be included on those patterns which had been protected by a United States design patent.

1831–1837, Gorham & Webster:

1.

1837–1841, Gorham, Webster & Price:

2

1841–1849, J. Gorham & Son:

3.

4.

1850–1852, Gorham & Thurber:

5.

1852–1865, Gorham & Co.:

6. 1852

7. 1852–ca. 1855

8 Patented 1855. Mark *on Josephine* teaspoon in Figure 33, Chapter 4. A number of Gorham spoons of the 1850s have no Gorham marks, only the patent date and COIN:

9. Patented 1861

Lion-Anchor-G

The traditional three-symbol mark of a lion, an anchor, and G has been associated with silver made by the Gorham companies since the middle of the nineteenth century. The lion was meant to represent silver (coin silver before 1868 and sterling after that date), the anchor was the symbol for Rhode Island, and the G for Gorham. Up to the middle of the 1860s the lion in the mark usually faced *left*. Flatware and small pieces of hollow ware of the 1850–1865 period occasionally made use of a lion that appears to be standing straight up on its rear haunches. From 1865 onward the lion faces *right*.

It is not known when the lion-anchor-G mark was first used. The mark was not registered at the United States Patent Office until December 19, 1899 (No. 33,902). The trademark statement said, "This mark has been continuously used by the said corporation since about January 1, 1853."

Circumstantial evidence suggests that the lion-anchor-G mark *may* have first been used in the 1840s. The butter knife in Figure 25 engraved "J. M. & S. G. Bunker" was supposed to have been part of the wedding silver of James M. Bunker and Sarah G. Folger when they were married in Nantucket on February 10, 1848.

The only mark on the butter knife is a lion anchor-G:

10.

A child's knife with a similar mark in the Gorham collection is engraved with an 1848 birthday. The knife is accompanied by a letter (written in the twentieth century) saying it had been presented soon after the birth in 1848.

The problem is that, although these engraved inscriptions suggest dates in the 1840s, it cannot be proven that either of the knives were actually *made* then. If a piece were known with both the lion-anchor-G mark *and* the mark J. GORHAM & SON it would prove a pre-1850 dating for the former. At the time of the writing of this book no pieces of Gorham silver have been located with either the mark of J. Gorham & Son (1841-1849) or the mark of Gorham & Thurber (1850-1852) *and* the lion-anchor-G. Thus, there is no solid evidence that the lion-anchor-G mark was used before about 1853.

Hollow Ware, 1850–1868

1850–1852, Gorham & Thurber:

11.

1852–1865, Gorham & Co.:

12. Ca. 1855

13. Ca. 1856

14. Ca. 1859. Mark on the Lincoln tea and coffee service in Figure 43, Chapter 4.

15. Ca. 1863-1865 (lion facing right).

16. Ca. 1863–1865 (lion facing right).

1865–1868, Gorham Manufacturing Co.:

17. 1867 (Fig. 24)

Pattern Numbers

Several of the above hollow-ware marks have pattern numbers in the mark. These pattern numbers have only a limited value for identification purposes. Pattern numbers seemed to have been assigned arbitrarily by Gorham in the nineteenth century. They were not used sequentially, and the same number can be used on different objects. For example, a specific number may be used on all the pieces of a tea and coffee service, on a pitcher, on a candlestick, and so on.

The Gorham records can sometimes be used to date specific pieces made before 1868, but this must be done on a case by case basis. Even when this laborious procedure is followed and a date is found in the records, it is usually only an indication when the design was first made. For example, there are other tea sets in the Lincoln pattern No. 30 (mark no. 14) which were made after 1859.

Date Marks

In 1868 Gorham adopted the English sterling standard of 92.5 percent silver alloy. The word STER-LING was usually part of the mark stamped on a piece. Also in 1868 Gorham adopted a system of date-letters and symbols. The letter A represented 1868, B 1869, and so on to Q for 1884. From 1885 onward a different symbol was used for each year:

A.	1868		(symbol)	1903
B.	1869		(symbol)	1904
C.	1870		(symbol)	1905
D.	1871		(symbol)	1906
E.	1872		(symbol)	1907
F.	1873		(symbol)	1908
G.	1874		(symbol)	1909
H.	1875		(symbol)	1910
I.	1876		(symbol)	1911
J.	1877		(symbol)	1912
K.	1878		(symbol)	1913
L.	1879		(symbol)	1914
M.	1880		(symbol)	1915
N.	1881		(symbol)	1916
O.	1882		(symbol)	1917
P.	1883		(symbol)	1918
Q.	1884		(symbol)	1919
(symbol)	1885		(symbol)	1920
(symbol)	1886		(symbol)	1921
(symbol)	1887		(symbol)	1922
(symbol)	1888		(symbol)	1923
(symbol)	1889		(symbol)	1924
(symbol)	1890		(symbol)	1925
(symbol)	1891		(symbol)	1926
(symbol)	1892		(symbol)	1927
(symbol)	1893		(symbol)	1928
(symbol)	1894		(symbol)	1929
(symbol)	1895		(symbol)	1930
(symbol)	1896		(symbol)	1931
(symbol)	1897		(symbol)	1932
(symbol)	1898		(symbol)	1933
(symbol)	1899			
(symbol)	1900			
(symbol)	1901			
(symbol)	1902			

During 1933 year marks were discontinued.

January 1941 year marking was resumed on Sterling Holloware except lower priced items.

(symbol) **1941**

The square frame indicates the decade of the 40's. The numeral indicates the year of the decade.

(symbol) **1950**

(symbol) **1951**

The pentagon indicates the decade of the 50's

The numeral indicates the year of the decade.

(symbol) **1960**

(symbol) **1961**

The hexagon indicates the decade of the 60's.

The numeral indicates the year of the decade.

The heptagon was used for the 1970s, and the octagon for the 1980s.

Sterling Marks Since 1868

18. 1869

19. 1875

20. Ca. 1875–1885. It is thought that pieces marked UNION SQUARE were actually made at the small shop Gorham operated in New York at this time.

21. 1896

Sterling Flatware Items Were Sold in Different Weights

In the late nineteenth and early twentieth centuries some flatware items were made in as many as five different weights. It was normal practice to stamp symbols for the weight used on the pieces, with the exception of regular weights, which were not marked:

Average Weights of Chantilly *Teaspoons*

Weight	Symbol	Troy ounces per dozen
Trade	T	9
Extra	E	10
Regular		*12*
Heavy	H	14
Massive	M	15

22. 1907. Mark of Trade (T) on souvenir spoon in Figure 208:

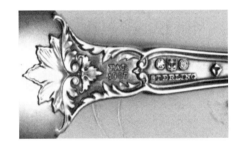

Special and Mixed Metal Pieces

23. 1879. Mark on bowl in Plate I. The EX at the top of the mark may represent Extra or Experimental.

24. 1882. The mark STERLING & OTHER METALS is on the bowl in Plate IV.

Marks of Erik Magnussen, 1925-1929

25.

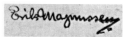

26.

Electroplate Marks

Gorham's electroplated wares in the nineteenth century were usually marked with an anchor on a shield. The words SILVER SOLDERED on a mark indicates only the fact that hard silver solder was used in the making of the piece. It was a circumspect way of indicating that a piece was made of silver plate rather than sterling. Very few nineteenth-century manufacturers used the straight-forward mark ELECTROPLATED on their wares. The usual mark was SILVER SOLDERED or EP, or no mark at all.

27. 1875. The first digit in the pattern number, O, signifies an electroplated item. (A in a pattern num–ber indicates sterling.)

28. 1882

A number of different electroplate marks have been used in the twentieth century, including EPNS, for electroplated nickel silver. Two marks of the 1920S were:

29.

30

Gold

31.

Copper

32. 1882. The prefix Y is for copper. This mark is on the tea caddy in Plate IV right.

Bronze

33. 1906 (Fig. 140).

34. 1907

35. 1922

Athenis

36. 1901 to about 1915

Martelé

As noted in Chapter 12, Gorham adopted the word Martelé in about 1900 as their name for their handmade line, the first pieces of which were made in 1897. The word Martelé is not part of the mark of most pieces made before 1900. The word Martelé is also not mentioned in the Gorham trademark registered on December 19, 1899 (No. 33,903). The trademark shown in the registration document is similar to No. 38 below. The mark consists of the traditional lion-anchor-G with a spread-winged eagle centered over the anchor.

Many Martelé pieces include code numbers or letters as part of the mark. Occasionally these numbers or letters are separated from the Gorham mark and are stamped on another part of the piece.

The casual and sometimes irregular markings on pre–1900 Martelé pieces has made it difficult to identify them without resorting to the Gorham Co. records. The Martelé records, as mentioned in Chapter 12, include four plant account books titled "Martelé," and the Martelé photographic records.

The following are typical marks on Martelé pieces of the 1897–1912 period:

37. 1897. Mark on love–cup pitcher in Figure 247.

38. 1900. Mark on tankard in Plate VII.

39. 1900. Mark on tea and coffee service in Figure 257.

40. 1905. Mark on coffee set in Figure 267.

The following chart, prepared from data in the Gorham records, gives the number- or letter-code ranges for Martelé pieces made in the years 1897 to 1912. This chart is meant to be used as a general guide. It cannot be considered definitive since an occasional piece does not fit exactly into the sequence of numbers or letters.

Martelé Codes by Year

Year	Number or Letter Code		
1897	8454 to 9941	1906	J L / K K to P K
1898	9942 to 9999 / 1 to 1437	1907	L N / P O to S H
1899	1407 to 2344	1908	N R / U V to R R
1900	2506 to 5511 / CG to FR	1909	R S / W R to Z S
1901	4737 to 4744 / FA to BKR	1910	U W / G P to I X
1902	AIF to DGK	1911	W Z / D K to M A
1903	DEO to EUG	1912	Z Z / N W to L C
1904	F G / Y S to V B		
1905	H J / B C to K L		

APPENDIX II

Gorham Sterling Flatware Patterns

The 315 sterling flatware patterns in this appendix cover the period from 1831 to the date of the new edition of this book (1997). The pattern name and the date the pattern was introduced are shown below each pattern. Because of space limitations, the handles only of the patterns are illustrated.

Great efforts were made to make an accurate, definitive listing of all of the company's standard flatware patterns. However, the listing cannot be considered complete. There are too many variations of the standard patterns made by the use of engraving, chasing, etching, hammering, applique, and gold plating. In 1927 a new version of the *Mothers* pattern came out which added a rattail to the back of the pattern. A number of the variants are shown, but it would be almost impossible to show them all. Private patterns and those made on a special order basis are not included.

A number of patterns, such *as Japanese, Mythologique,* and *Old Masters,* have different handles for different types of pieces. Only one piece of each of these patterns is illustrated. At least three sterling patterns, *Roman, Regent,* and *Kings,* were also made in electroplate.

It proved impractical to include in this list the flatware patterns of those companies merged into Gorham in the twentieth century. However, two Durgin patterns, *Fairfax* and *Hunt Club,* and Whiting's *Cinderella,*

are included since they have come to be considered as Gorham patterns, being items in Gorham's line and made with Gorham marks.

Identification of flatware patterns can sometimes be confusing because throughout the company's history different names were used for the same pattern, and sometimes the same name was used for different patterns. The name problem is complicated even further when we learn that such patterns as *Gorham Plain* were promoted in different localities by names chosen by the local dealer. *Gorham Plain* was sold in Providence, Rhode Island, as *Old Kingston;* in Burlington, Vermont, as *Ethan Allen;* in Milwaukee, Wisconsin, as *Marquette;* in Philadelphia, Pennsylvania, as *Sweet Briar,* and so on.

The preparation of the following listing involved an updating and revision of standard company lists, and also published lists, such as the one *in Jewelers' Circular Keystone Sterling Flatware Pattern Index* (Radnor, Pa.: Chilton Co., 1970), pp. 29–51. Pre–1850 patterns were completely realigned after studying known marked pieces and bills of sale of the time (Chapter 3). A search of flatware design patents in the United States Patent Office (there were almost a hundred flatware design patents issued to Gorham by 1915) necessitated the revision of many introduction dates. The patent date, when available, was used as the introduction date. The Gorham catalogs of the 1880s and 1890s were helpful in identifying the date when patterns of this period were introduced.

The following abbreviations are used in the flatware captions:

Appl. for Applied
ca. for circa
Eng. for Engraved
Engl. for English
Hmrd. for Hammered

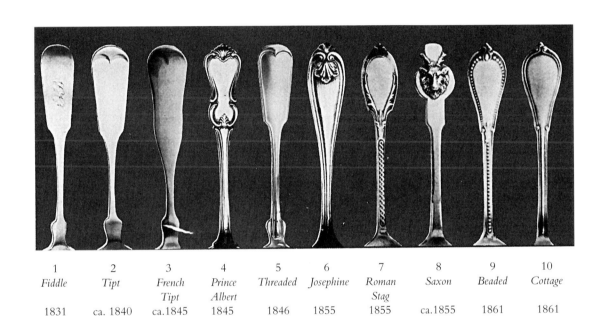

1	2	3	4	5	6	7	8	9	10
Fiddle	Tipt	French Tipt	Prince Albert	Threaded	Josephine	Roman Stag	Saxon	Beaded	Cottage
1831	ca. 1840	ca.1845	1845	1846	1855	1855	ca.1855	1861	1861

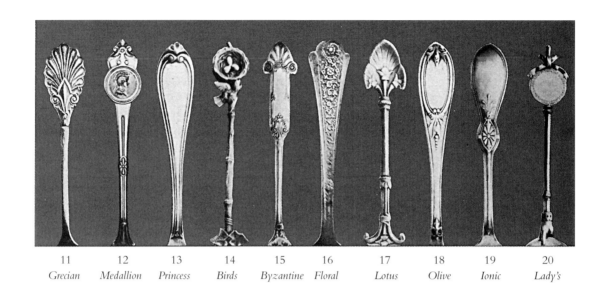

11	12	13	14	15	16	17	18	19	20
Grecian	*Medallion*	*Princess*	*Birds Nest*	*Byzantine*	*Floral*	*Lotus*	*Olive*	*Ionic*	*Lady's*
1861	1864	ca. 1865	ca. 1865	ca.1865	ca.1865	ca.1865	ca.1865	1868	1868

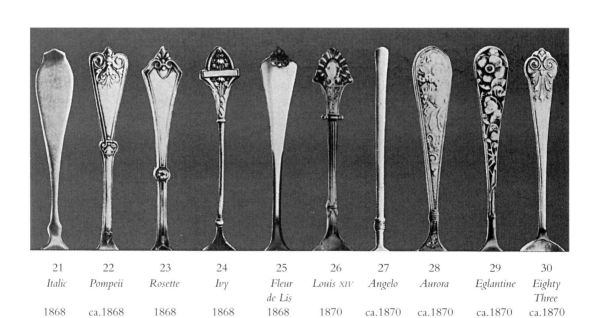

21	22	23	24	25	26	27	28	29	30
Italic	*Pompeii*	*Rosette*	*Ivy*	*Fleur de Lis*	*Louis XIV*	*Angelo*	*Aurora*	*Eglantine*	*Eighty Three*
1868	ca.1868	1868	1868	1868	1870	ca.1870	ca.1870	ca.1870	ca.1870

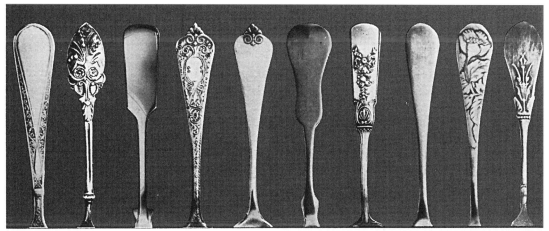

31	32	33	34	35	36	37	38	39	40
Eva	*Lily*	*Old En-glish Tipt*	*Queen Anne*	*Queens*	*Fiddle*	*H. 83*	*Knicker-bocker Plain*	*Knicker-bocker Etched*	*New Tipt*
ca.1870	1870	ca.1870	ca.1870	ca.1870	ca.1870	ca.1870	ca. 1870	ca. 1870	1871

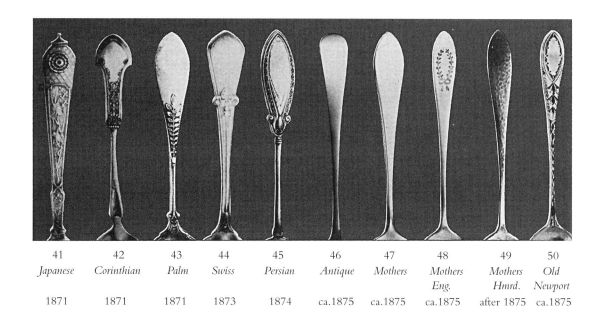

41	42	43	44	45	46	47	48	49	50
Japanese	*Corinthian*	*Palm*	*Swiss*	*Persian*	*Antique*	*Mothers*	*Mothers Eng.*	*Mothers Hmrd.*	*Old Newport*
1871	1871	1871	1873	1874	ca.1875	ca.1875	ca.1875	after 1875	ca.1875

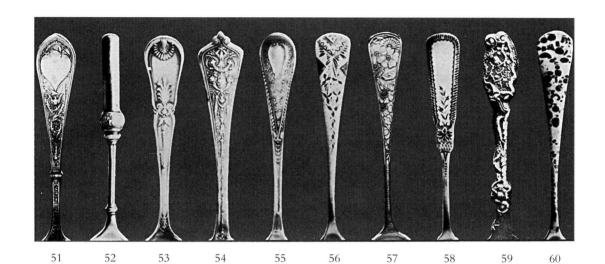

51	52	53	54	55	56	57	58	59	60
Raphael	*Dowager*	*Kings I*	*Lady Washington*	*Hindostanee*	*Diana*	*Delhi*	*Daisy*	*Hizen*	*Cairo*
ca.1875	ca.1875	1876	1876	1878	1880	ca.1880	ca.1880	ca.1880	ca.1880

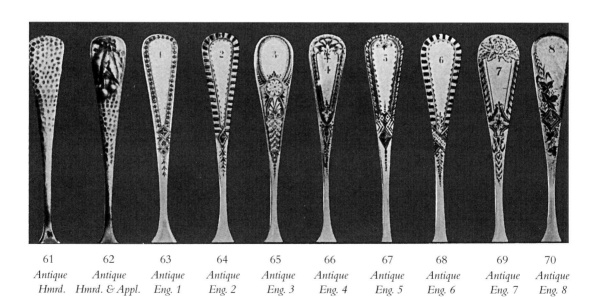

61	62	63	64	65	66	67	68	69	70
Antique Hmrd.	*Antique Hmrd. & Appl.*	*Antique Eng. 1*	*Antique Eng. 2*	*Antique Eng. 3*	*Antique Eng. 4*	*Antique Eng. 5*	*Antique Eng. 6*	*Antique Eng. 7*	*Antique Eng. 8*
1880	1880	1880	1880	1880	1880	1880	1880	1880	1880

71	72	73	74	75	76	77	78	79	80
Antique	*Antique*	*Antique*	*Antique*	*Gilpen*	*Gorham*	*Grape*	*Hamburg*	*London*	*Marigold*
Eng. 9	*Eng. 10*	*Eng. 11*	*Eng. 12*						
1880	1880	1880	1880	ca.1880	ca.1880	ca.1880	ca.1880	ca.1880	ca.1880

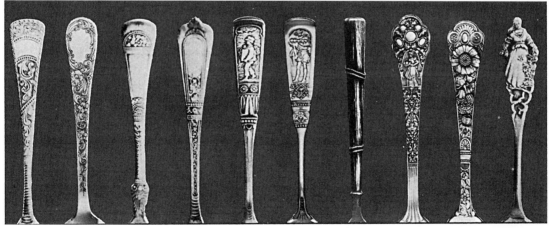

81	82	83	84	85	86	87	88	89	90
Tudor	*Huguenot*	*Empress*	*Domestic*	*Piper*	*Fontaine-*	*Bamboo*	*Medici, Old*	*Cluny*	*Nuremburg*
	Eng.				*bleau*				
ca.1880	1880	1881	1881	1882	1882	1882	ca.1883	ca.1883	ca.1884

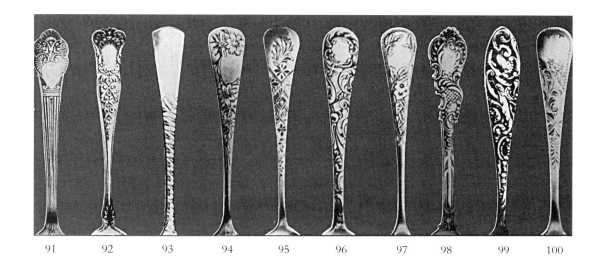

91	92	93	94	95	96	97	98	99	100
Milan	*Maryland*	*Colonial*	*Chrysan-themum*	*Acanthus*	*Berlin*	*Clematis*	*Dresden*	*French*	*Hawthorne*
1884	1885	1885	ca.1885	ca.1885	ca. 1885	ca.1885	ca.1885	ca.1885	ca.1885

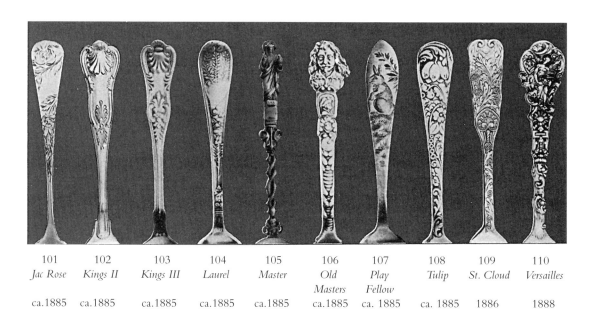

101	102	103	104	105	106	107	108	109	110
Jac Rose	*Kings II*	*Kings III*	*Laurel*	*Master*	*Old Masters*	*Play Fellow*	*Tulip*	*St. Cloud*	*Versailles*
ca.1885	ca.1885	ca.1885	ca.1885	ca.1885	ca.1885	ca. 1885	ca. 1885	1886	1888

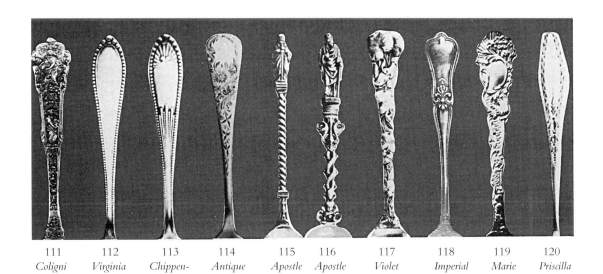

111	112	113	114	115	116	117	118	119	120
Coligni	*Virginia*	*Chippen-dale*	*Antique Eng. 15*	*Apostle Small*	*Apostle Large*	*Violet*	*Imperial*	*Marie Antoinette*	*Priscilla*
1889	1890	1890	ca.1890	ca 1890	ca.1890	ca.1890	1891	1891	1892

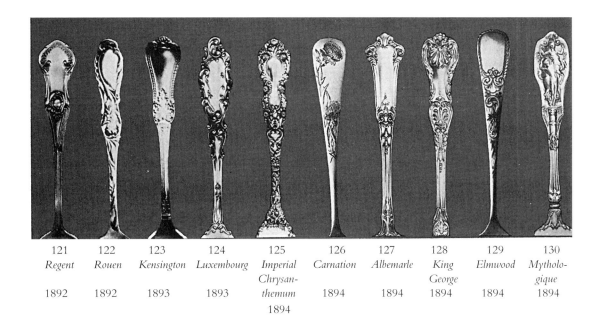

121	122	123	124	125	126	127	128	129	130
Regent	*Rouen*	*Kensington*	*Luxembourg*	*Imperial Chrysan-themum*	*Carnation*	*Albemarle*	*King George*	*Elmwood*	*Mytholo-gique*
1892	1892	1893	1893	1894	1894	1894	1894	1894	1894

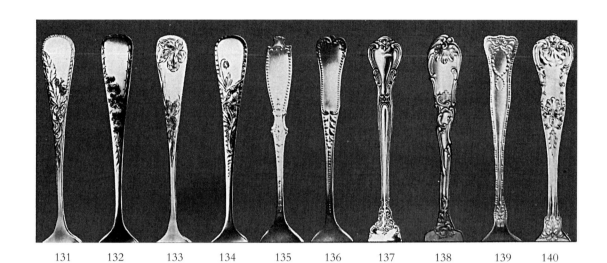

131	132	133	134	135	136	137	138	139	140
Oak &	*Cherry*	*Orchid*	*Poppy*	*Bedford*	*Bristol*	*Chantilly*	*Hanover*	*New*	*New*
Acorn	*Blossom*							*Empire*	*Queens*
1894	1894	1894	1894	1895	1895	1895	1895	1895	1895

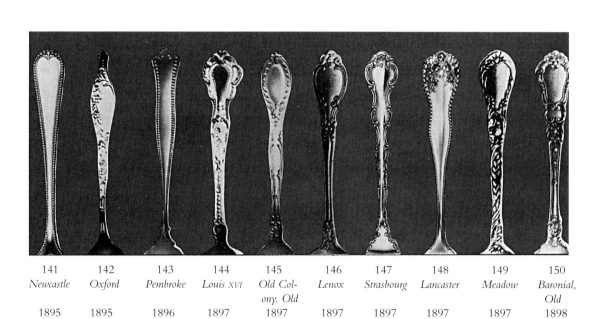

141	142	143	144	145	146	147	148	149	150
Newcastle	*Oxford*	*Pembroke*	*Louis XVI*	*Old Col-*	*Lenox*	*Strasbourg*	*Lancaster*	*Meadow*	*Baronial,*
				ony. Old					*Old*
1895	1895	1896	1897	1897	1897	1897	1897	1897	1898

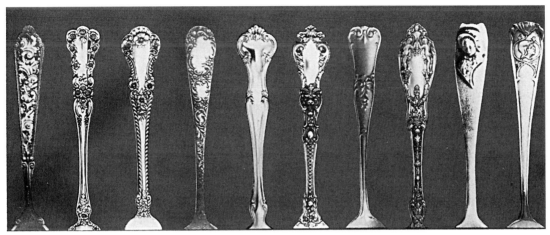

151	152	153	154	155	156	157	158	159	160
Scandina-	*Buttercup*	*Cambridge*	*Douglas*	*Cromwell*	*Henry II*	*New*	*Paris*	*H. 108*	*H. 109*
vian						*Plymouth*			
1898	1899	1899	1899	1900	1900	1900	1900	1900	ca. 1900

161	162	163	164	165	166	167	168	169	170
H. 200	*H. 252*	*H. 316*	*H. 385*	*H. 443*	*H. 451*	*Florence*	*Florentine*	*Marguerite*	*Patrician*
ca.1900	ca.1900	ca.1900	ca.1900	ca.1900	ca.1900	1901	1901	1901	1902

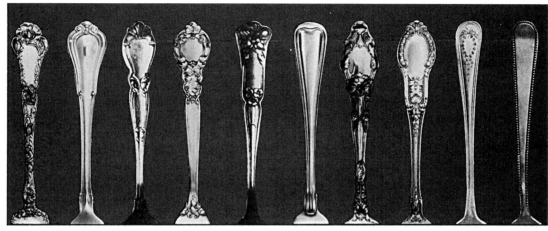

171	172	173	174	175	176	177	178	179	180
Poppy	*Norfolk (Villa, Nolfolk)*	*Portland*	*Royal Oak*	*Atlanta*	*Old French*	*Virginiana*	*Tuileries*	*Jefferson*	*Martha Washington*
1902	1903	1904	1904	1904	1904	1905	1906	1907	1907

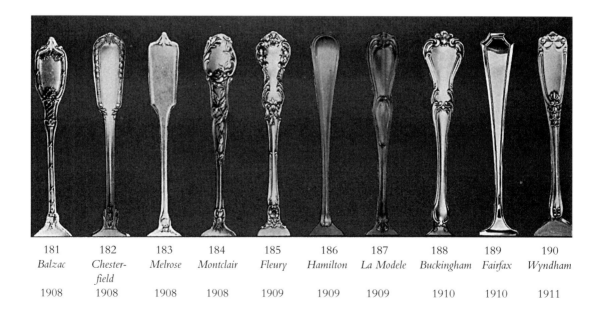

181	182	183	184	185	186	187	188	189	190
Balzac	*Chester-field*	*Melrose*	*Montclair*	*Fleury*	*Hamilton*	*La Modele*	*Buckingham*	*Fairfax*	*Wyndham*
1908	1908	1908	1908	1909	1909	1909	1910	1910	1911

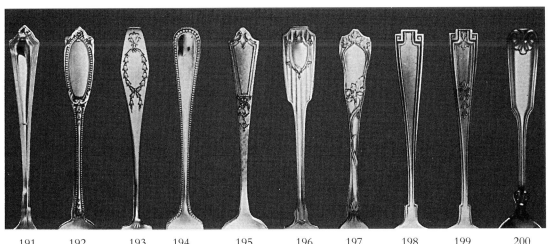

191	192	193	194	195	196	197	198	199	200
Plymouth	*Chelmsford*	*Wreath*	*Old Dominion*	*Pattern A*	*Spotswood*	*Vine*	*Etruscan*	*Etruscan Eng.*	*Hampton*
1911	1911	1911	1911	1912	1912	1912	1913	1913	1913

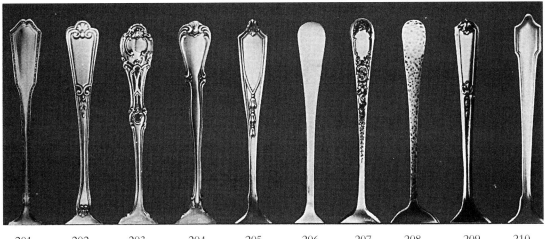

201	202	203	204	205	206	207	208	209	210
Roanoke	*Farnham*	*Hardwick*	*Hazelmere*	*Beverly*	*Covington*	*Covington Eng.*	*Covington Hmrd.*	*Guilford*	*Marion*
1913	1913	1913	1913	1914	1914	1914	1914	1914	1914

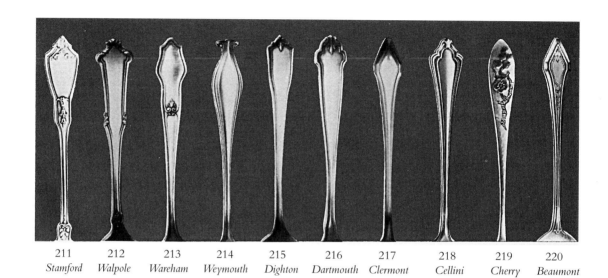

211	212	213	214	215	216	217	218	219	220
Stamford	*Walpole*	*Wareham*	*Weymouth*	*Dighton*	*Dartmouth*	*Clermont*	*Cellini*	*Cherry Blossom*	*Beaumont*
1914	1914	1914	1914	1914	1914	1915	1915	1915	1915

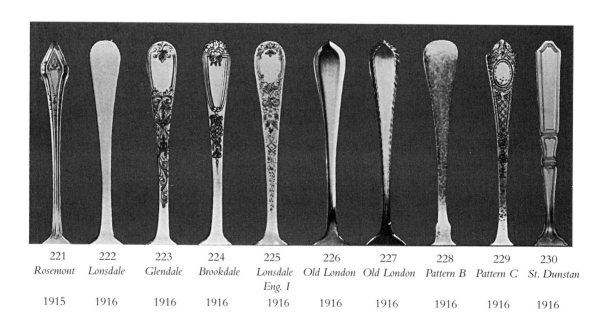

221	222	223	224	225	226	227	228	229	230
Rosemont	*Lonsdale*	*Glendale*	*Brookdale*	*Lonsdale Eng. I*	*Old London*	*Old London*	*Pattern B*	*Pattern C*	*St. Dunstan*
1915	1916	1916	1916	1916	1916	1916	1916	1916	1916

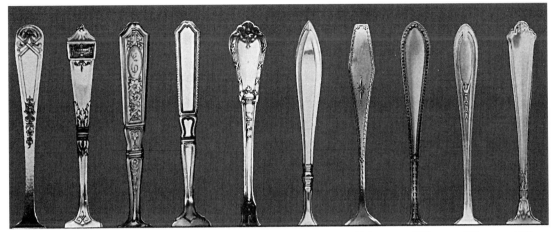

231	232	233	234	235	236	237	238	239	240
Somerset	*Lansdowne*	*St. Dunstan Chased*	*St. Dunstan Eng.*	*Touraine*	*Portsmouth*	*Swansea*	*Edgeworth*	*Fanshawe*	*Griswold*
1916	1917	1917	1917	1917	1918	1919	1922	1922	1922

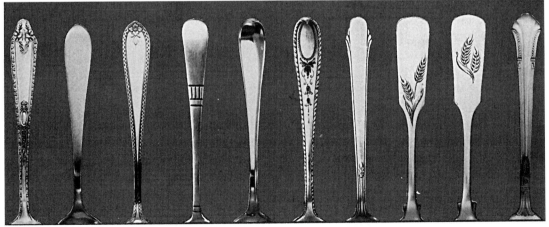

241	242	243	244	245	246	247	248	249	250
Cinderella	*Old Colony*	*Old Colony Eng.*	*Modern American*	*Dolly Madison*	*Dolly Madison Eng.*	*Hunt Club*	*Old Engl. Tipt, Eng. Wheat A*	*Old Engl. Tipt, Eng. Wheat B*	*Shamrock V*
1925	1926	1927	1928	1929	1929	1930	1931	1931	1931

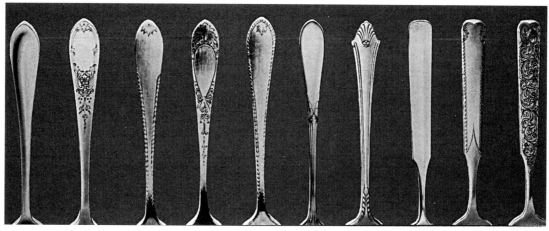

251	252	253	254	255	256	257	258	259	260
Gorham Plain	*Gorham Plain Chased (Winthrop)*	*Gorham Plain Eng. A*	*Gorham Plain Eng. B*	*Gorham Plain Eng. C*	*Rose Marie*	*Late Georgian*	*Christina*	*Christina Eng. Feather Edge*	*Christina Eng. Old English Scroll*
1933	1933	1933	1933	1933	1933	1934	1935	1935	1935

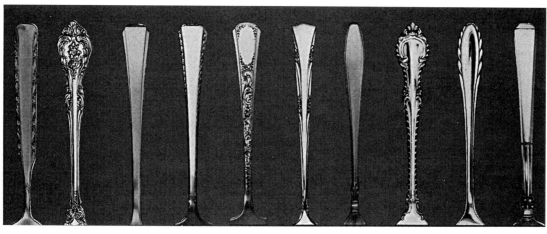

261	262	263	264	265	266	267	268	269	270
Eventide	*King Edward*	*Governor's Lady*	*Governor's Lady Eng. A*	*Governor's Lady Eng. B*	*Greenbrier*	*Nocturne*	*English Gadroon*	*Lyric*	*Epic*
1936	1936	1937	1937	1937	1938	1938	1939	1940	1941

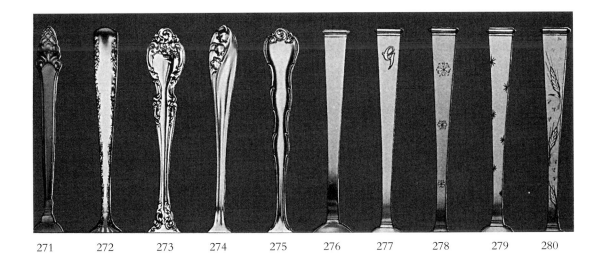

271	272	273	274	275	276	277	278	279	280
Sovereign, Old	*Camellia*	*Melrose*	*Lily of the Valley*	*Rondo*	*Gold Tip*	*Gold Cipher*	*Golden Snowflake*	*Golden Stardust*	*Golden Wheat*
1941	1942	1948	1950	1951	1952	1952	1952	1952	1952

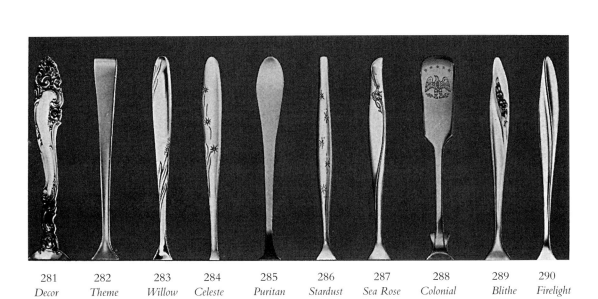

281	282	283	284	285	286	287	288	289	290
Decor	*Theme*	*Willow*	*Celeste*	*Puritan*	*Stardust*	*Sea Rose*	*Colonial Eagle*	*Blithe Spirit*	*Firelight*
1953	1954	1954	1956	1956	1957	1958	1959	1959	1959

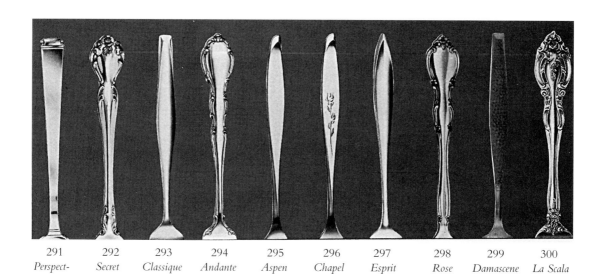

291	292	293	294	295	296	297	298	299	300
Perspect-ive	*Secret Garden*	*Classique*	*Andante*	*Aspen*	*Chapel Rose*	*Esprit*	*Rose Tiara*	*Damascene*	*La Scala*
1959	1959	1961	1963	1963	1963	1963	1963	1964	1964

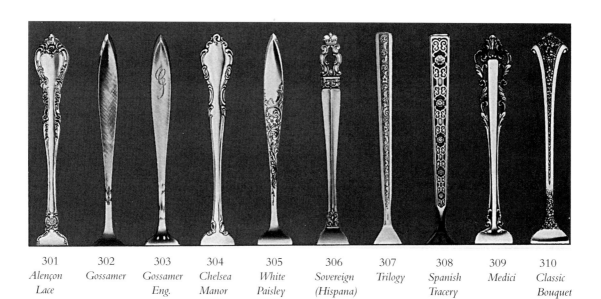

301	302	303	304	305	306	307	308	309	310
Alençon Lace	*Gossamer*	*Gossamer Eng.*	*Chelsea Manor*	*White Paisley*	*Sovereign (Hispana)*	*Trilogy*	*Spanish Tracery*	*Medici*	*Classic Bouquet*
1965	1965	1965	1966	1966	1968	1969	1970	1971	1972

311	312	313
Baronial	Crown Baroque	Golden Scroll
1972	1975	1978

314	315
Sea Sculpture	Townsend
1985	1987

A Partial List
of Well-Known Bronzes
Cast by Gorham

Location	Art Bronze	Sculptor
Arlington, Va.	General Kearney	E. C. Potter
Arlington, Va.	Victory Figure	Augustus St.-Gaudens
Athens, Ga.	Spanish War Soldier	T.A.R. Kitson
Billings, Mont.	Bill Hart and Horse	C. C. Christadoro
Baltimore, Md.	Samuel Tattersall	Edward Berge
Baltimore, Mc.	Francis Scott Key Memorial	Charles H. Niehaus
Blois, France	Jeanne D'Arc	Anna Hyatt Huntington
Boston, Mass.	General Kosciusko	T. A. R. Kitson
Boston, Mass.	Shaw Memorial	Augustus St.-Gaudens
Boston, Mass.	Doors—Salada Tea Bldg.	John Wilson
Boston, Mass.	Guardian Angel Statue	T. A. R. Kitson
Boston, Mass.	Phillips Brooks Statue	Augustus St.-Gaudens
Brewster, N.Y.	Memorial Monument	Chester Beach
Brockton, Mass.	Vision Harriet	W. Frishmuth
Brooklyn, N.Y.	World War Statue	Anton Schaaf
Brooklyn, N.Y.	Bailey Memorial	Eugene Savage
Brooklyn, N.Y.	Lafayette Memorial	Daniel Chester French
Buenos Aires, Arg.	El Cid	Anna Hyatt Huntington
Buffalo, N.Y.	Fillmore Statue	Bryant Baker
Buffalo, N.Y.	Lincoln Statue	Bryant Baker
Carisle, Pa.	Molly Pitcher	J. Otto Schweizer
Charlotte, N.C.	The Flyer Memorial	Gutzon Borglum
Charlottesville, Va.	George Rogers Clark Memorial	Robert Aitken
Chicago, Ill.	Marquette Memorial	Herman A. MacNeil
Chicago, Ill.	Groups—Elk Building	A. A. Weinman
Chicago. Ill.	Lincoln Memorial	Augustus St.-Gaudens

Location	Art Bronze	Sculptor
Chicago, Ill.	Alexander Hamilton	Bela L. Pratt
Cleveland, Ohio	Lincoln	Max Kalish
Cleveland, Ohio	Chief Justice Marshall	Herbert Adams
Clinton. N.Y.	Alexander Hamilton	George T. Brewster
Columbus, Ohio	Washington	Houdon
Denver, Colo.	The Christ	Harriet W. Frishmuth
Denver, Colo.	Elk Statue	Eli Harvey
Detroit, Mich	Until the Dawn	Bruce Saville
Eddystone, Pa.	Baldwin	Herbert Adams
East Tarvas, Mich.	Logging Group	Robert Aitken
Eugene, Ore	Pioneer	A. P. Proctor
Fitchburg, Mass.	War Memorial	Herbert Adams
Galveston, Texas	The Lost Cause	Amateis
Gettysburg, Pa.	General Howard	Robert Aitken
Gloucester, Mass.	The Gloucester Fisherman	Leonard Craske
Grand Rapids, Mich.	Spanish War Soldier	T. A. R. Kitson
Iceland	Lief Ericson	A. Stirling Calder
Kansas City, Mo.	The Scout	C. E. Dallin
Kansas City, Mo.	General Jackson	Charles Keck
Lexington, Ky.	Seated Figure	Augustus Lukeman
Libertyville, Ill.	Female Figure	Herbert Adams
London, Eng.	Lincoln	Augustus St.-Gaudens
Louisville, Ky.	General Castleman	R. Hinton Perry
Manchester, N.H.	Spanish War Veteran	T. A. R. Kitson
Malden, Mass.	Soldier's Memorial	Bela L. Pratt
Marshalltown, Iowa	Elk Statue	Eli Harvey
Memphis, Tenn.	Snowden Memorial	William Couper
Meriden, Conn.	War Memorial	A. B. Cianfarani
Millford, Mass.	General Draper— Equestrian	Daniel Chester French
Milwaukee, Wis.	Wolcott—Equestrian	F. H. Packer
Mohawk Trail, Mass.	Elk Statue	Eli Harvey
Newark, NJ.	Seated Lincoln	Gutzon Borglum
New Bedford, Mass.	The Whaleman	Bela L. Pratt
Newport News, Va.	Doors—The Mariner's Museum	Herbert Adams
New York, N.Y.	Bronx War Memorial	Belle Kinney and L. F. Scholz
New York, N.Y.	Doors—Academy Of Science and Letters	Herbert Adams
New York, N.Y.	Roosevelt Group	James E. Fraser
New York, N.Y.	Doors—Indian Museum	Berthold Nebel
New York, N.Y.	Doors—Maison Français Rockefeller Center	Alfred Janniot
New York, N.Y.	Doors—British Empire Bldg. Rockefeller Center	Carl Paul Jennewein
New York, N.Y.	Jeanne D'Arc	Anna Hyatt Huntington
New York, N.Y.	General Sherman	Augustus St.-Gaudens
Omaha, Neb.	Elk Statue	Eli Harvey
Ottawa, Can.	Baldwin & La Fontain	Waller S. Allward
Palm Beach, Fla	Actaeon & Diana	Paul Manship

Location Art Bronze Sculptor

Location	Art Bronze	Sculptor
Pawtucket, R. I.	Soldier's Memorial	W. Granville Hastings
Philadelphia, Pa.	Amazon	August Kiss
Philadelphia, Pa.	General Hancock	J. Q. A. Ward
Philadelphia, Pa.	Nicholson	J. Otto Schweizer
Philadelphia, Pa.	General McClellan	E. C. Potter
Pittsburgh, Pa.	Westinghouse Memorial	D. C. French & P. Fjeide
Plymouth, Mass.	Massasoit	C. E. Dallin
Plymouth, N.H.	Boy Scout	George H. Borst
Portland, Me.	Longfellow	William Couper
Portland, Me.	Spanish War Soldier	T. A. R. Kitson
Providence, R.I	Oliver Hazard Perry	William Walcutt
Providence, R.I.	Brown Bear	Eli Harvey
Providence, R.I.	Columbus	Bartholdi
Providence, R.I.	Bajnotti Fountain	Enid Yandell
Providence, R.I.	Vulcan	M. Raggi
Providence, R.I.	The Falconer	H. H. Kitson
Richmond, Va.	Maury Statue	F. W. Sievers
Richmond, Va.	General " Stonewall" Jackson	F W Sievers
San Gabriel, Cal.	Washington	Houdon
San Francisco, Cal.	Fireman Monument	Haig Patigian
San Francisco, Cal.	El Cid	Anna Hyatt Huntington
Riverside, Conn.	Vine	Harriet W. Frishmuth
Saratoga Springs, N.Y.	Spencer Trask Memorial	Daniel Chester French
Seattle. Wash.	Chief Seattle	James Wehn
Smithfield, N.C.	World War Soldier	T. A. R. Kitson
St. Augustine, Fla.	Ponce De Leon	H. W. Miller
St. Louis, Mo.	La Clede	George J. Zolney
St. Louis, Mo.	Alma Mater	C. E. Dallin
Syracuse, N.Y.	Spanish War Soldier	T. A. R. Kitson
Tarrytown, N.Y.	Rip Van Winkle Memorial	Daniel Chester French
Terre Haute, Ind.	Elk Statue	Eli Harvey
Toledo, Ohio	Elk Statue	Eli Harvey
Toronto, Can.	Peace Walter	S. Allward
Utica, N.Y.	Vice-President Sherman	George T. Brewster
Valley Forge, Pa.	General Von Steuben	J. Otto Schweizer
Vicksburg, Miss.	General Tilghman—Equestrian	F. William Sievers
Vicksburg, Miss.	General Steel	T. E. Elwell
Vicksburg, Miss	General McClernand Equestrian	E. C. Potter
Washington, D.C.	Red Cross Nurse	R. Tait McKenzie
Washington, D.C.	John Paul Jones	C. H. Niehaus
Washington, D.C.	General Phillip Sheridan Equestrian	Gutzon Borglum
Washington, D.C.	Washington	Houdon
West Haven, Conn.	War Memorial	Anton Schaaf
Wichita Falls, Texas	Spanish War Soldier	T. A. R. Kitson
Wilmington, Del.	Caesar Rodney—Equestrian	James E. Kelly
Wilmington, N.C.	Davis Memorial	F. H. Packer
Winchester, Mass.	War Memorial	Herbert Adams
Worcester. Mass	General Devens—Equestrian	D. C. French & E. C. Potter

APPENDIX IV

Gorham Presidents
1865–1994

John Gorham	1865–1878
William H. Crins	1878–1894
Edward Holbrook	1894–1919
John S. Holbrook	1919–1920
Harry A. Macfarland	1920–
John S. Holbrook	1920–1921
Franklin A. Taylor	1921–1923★
Edmund C. Mayo	1925–1959
Wilbur H. Norton	1959–1963
Burrill M. Getman	1963–1968
Erskine N. White, Jr.	1968–1969
Walter J. Robbie	1969–1977
Frank E. Grzelecki	1977–1983
James W. Thomas	1983-1988
Brian O' Malley	1988-1989
Richard Ryan, Jr.	1989-1991
James Solomon	1991-1994

★During an interim period from May 1923 to April 1925 Gorham had no president. During this time Henry J. Fuller, chairman of the board, acted as chief executive officer.

Gorham Source Material

The Gorham records are varied and extensive. The historical records include material dating back to the early part of the nineteenth century. Plant records date back to the 1850s and photographic records date from the 1870s.

Plant Records

Record books with dates of manufacture, weights, prices, and time records of various operations. Time cards, with the same kinds of information as in the plant record books. Early plant records are located at the John Hay Library of Brown University, Providence, R.I.

Historical Records

The Gorham records contain several unpublished historical documents which were useful in the writing of this book, such as John Gorham's account of the early years of the company. There are many early letters, such as Jabez Gorham's 1819 letters, and the letters to John Gorham written in 1852 and 1860 while he was in Europe (Chapter 4). There are commercial records, such as bills of sale, and scrapbooks of clippings.

Photographic Records

Starting in the 1870s a photographic record was made of ev-
ery hollow-ware and flatware form made by the company. There are still many hundreds of thousands of photographs in the various Gorham files.

Drawings

Pre–1890 working drawings are preserved on microfilm. Many of the original drawings since 1890 are on file.

Die Vaults

The die vaults contain many thousands of dies for flatware, hollow ware, ornamental castings, decorative borders, and medals.

Library

The Gorham library contains an extensive collection of books on the decorative arts, long runs of magazines, and Gorham catalogs and promotional literature (Chapter 4).

Silver Collection

The Gorham collection includes early spoons and miscellaneous objects such as Jabez Gorham's water jug (Fig. 51). There are a number of reproductions of pieces of the company's nineteenth century silver. The Furber collection (Chapter 5) is an important body of the best of Gorham silver of the 1870s. The silver collection is now located in the Museum of Art, Rhode Island School of Art, Providence.

Bibliography

Ames, Kenneth L., "What is the Neo-Grec?" *Nineteenth Century*, Vol. 2, No. 2, Summer 1976, pp. 13–21.

"Among the Workers in Silver," *Atlantic Monthly*, December 1867.

Ash, Douglas, *Dictionary of British Antique Silver* (London: Pelham Books, 1972).

Aslin, Elizabeth, *The Aesthetic Movement: Prelude to Art Nouveau* (London: Elik Books, Ltd., 1969).

"A Statement of Standards for Sculptural Reproduction and Preventative Measures to Combat Unethical Casting in Bronze," *Art Journal,* Fall 1974.

Barber, Edwin Adee; Lockwood, Luke Vincent; and French, Hollis, *The Ceramic, Furniture, and Silver Collectors' Glossary* (New York: Da Capo Press, 1976).

Bigelow, Francis Hill, *Historic Silver of the Colonies and Its Makers* (New York: Macmillan Co., 1917).

Borges, Jorge Luis, *Labyrinths* (New York: New Directions, 1964).

Bradbury, Frederick, *History of Old Sheffield Plate* (London: Macmillan Co., 1912).

Broder, Patricia Janis, *Bronzes of the American West* (New York: Harry N. Abrams, 1974).

Buhler, Kathryn C., *American Silver, 1655–1825, in the Museum of Fine Arts, Boston* (Greenwich, Conn.: New York Graphic Society, 1972).

Buhler, Kathryn C., and Hood, Graham, *American Silver, Garvin and Other Collections in the Yale University Art Gallery* (New Haven: Yale University Press, 1970).

Butler, Joseph T., *American Antiques, 1800–1900, A Collector's History and Guide* (New York: Odyssey Press, 1965).

Butts, Allison, ed., *Silver: Economics, Metallurgy and Uses* (New York: Van Nostrand & Co., 1967).

Carpenter, Charles H., Jr., "An Early Souvenir Spoon," *The Magazine Silver*, May-June, 1980, pp. 12–13.

Carpenter, Charles H., Jr., "Tiffany Silver in the Japanese Style," *Connoisseur,* January 1979, pp. 42–47.

Carpenter, Charles H., Jr., with Carpenter, Mary Grace, *Tiffany Silver* (Dodd, Mead & Co., 1978).

Carpenter, Ralph E., Jr., *The Arts and Crafts of Newport, Rhode Island* (Newport: The Preservation Society of Newport County, 1954).

Clark, Robert J., ed., *The Arts and Crafts Movement in America, 1876–1916* (Princeton: Princeton University Press, 1972).

Clarke, Lewis W., "Ye Ancient Jewelers of Providence," *The Manufacturing Jeweler,* January 1894, pp. 12–16.

Codman, William, *An Illustrated History of Silverware Design* (Providence: The Gorham Co., 1930).

Codman, William, "History of Gorham Mfg. Co., 1878–1935" (a sixteen-page typescript in the Gorham files).

Craven, Wayne, *Sculpture in America* (New York: Thomas Y. Crowell Co., 1968).

Crystal Palace Exhibition, Illustrated Catalogue, (New York: Dover Publications, 1970).

Culme, John, *Nineteenth-Century Silver* (London: Country Life Books, 1977).

Culme, John, and Strang, John G., *Antique Silver and Silver Collecting* (London: Hamlyn Publishing Group Ltd., 1973).

Darling, Sharon S., "Admiral Dewey's Loving Cup," *The Magazine Silver,* January–February 1976, pp. 10–12.

Darling, Sharon S., *Chicago Metalsmiths* (Chicago: Chicago

Historical Society, 1977).

Dansk Kunsthandvaerkerleksikon, Rhodos, 1979.

de Marco, Jean, "Bronzes and Their Patinas," *National Sculpture Review,* Spring 1972, pp. 23–25, and Summer 1972, pp. 25–26.

Dodd, Loring Holmes, *Golden Moments in American Sculpture* (Cambridge, Mass.: Dresser, Chapman & Grimes, 1967).

Earle, Alice Morse, *In Old Narragansett* (New York: Charles Scribner's Sons, 1898).

Eaton, Allen H., *Handicrafts in New England* (New York: Harper & Brothers, 1949).

Eisenhauer, Robert S., *Textron . . . From the Beginning* (Privately published by Textron, 1979).

Fales, Martha Gandy, *Early American Silver for the Cautious Collector* (New York: E. P. Dutton, 1973).

Famous Small Bronzes (New York: The Gorham Co., 1928).

Farnum, Alexander, *The Century Vase* (Providence: Livermore & Knight, 1876).

Flynt, Henry N., and Fales, Martha Gandy, *The Heritage Foundation Collection of Silver* (Old Deerfield, Mass.: Heritage Foundation, 1968).

Freidley, Edwin T., ed., *Leading Pursuits and Leading Men* (Philadelphia: Edward Young, 1856).

Gee, George E., *The Silversmiths' Handbook* (London: Crosby Lockwood & Co., 1885).

Gibb, George Sweet, *The Whitesmiths of Taunton, A History of Reed & Barton, 1824–1943* (Cambridge, Mass.: Harvard University Press, 1943).

Gorham Catalogs and Books. See pages 134–135 for an outline listing of the books and catalogs published by Gorham in the nineteenth and early twentieth centuries.

Gorham, Henry S., *The Gorham Family in Rhode Island* (Boston: David Clapp & Son, 1900).

The Gorham Manufacturing Company, Silversmiths (New York: Cheltenham Press, 1900).

Hadwin, William, obituary, *Nantucket Weekly Mirror,* March 29, 1862.

Hanson, Victor F., "Quantitative Elemental Analyses of Art Objects by Energy-Dispersive X-Ray Fluorescence Spectroscopy," *Applied Spectroscopy,* Vol. 27, No. 5, 1973, pp. 309–333.

Hardt, Anton, "Earliest Souvenir Spoon Discovered," *The Magazine Silver,* September–October, 1979.

Hardt, Anton, *Adventuring Further in Souvenir Spoons* (New York: Greenwich Press, 1971).

Hardt, Anton, *New Discoveries in Historical Spoons* (New York: Greenwich Press, 1979).

Hardt, Anton, *Souvenir Spoons of the 90s* (New York: Greenwich Press, 1962).

Hiatt, Ralph W., and Kite, Cliff, "The Independent Man," *Gorham Perspective,* November 1976.

Holbrook, John S., *The Art of the Silversmith and Its Development* (New York: The Gorham Co., no date).

Holland, Margaret, *Silver, An Illustrated Guide to American and British Silver* (New York: Derby Books, 1973).

Hood, Graham, *American Silver: A History of Style, 1650–1900* (New York: Praeger Publishers, 1971).

Honour, Hugh, *Goldsmiths and Silversmiths* (New York: G. P. Putman's Sons, 1971).

Howard, Montague, *Old London Silver, Its History, Its Makers and Its Marks* (New York: Charles Scribner's Sons, 1971).

Hughes, Bernard, and Hughes, Therle, *Three Centuries of English Domestic Silver, 1500–1820* (New York: Wilfred Funk, 1952).

Hughes, Graham, *Modern Silver Throughout the World, 1880–1967* (New York: Crown Publishers, 1967).

Hulme, F. Edward, *A Series of Sketches From Nature of Plant Forms* (London: Day and Son, 1868).

Jackson, Charles James, *History of English Plate* (London: Country Life and B. T. Batsford, 1911).

James, George B., *Souvenir Spoons* (Boston: A. W. Fuller & Co., 1891).

Jervis, Simon, *High Victorian Design* (Ottawa: National Gallery of Canada, 1974).

Jewelers' Circular, 1873–1900.

Jewelers' Circular Keystone Flatware Pattern Index (Radnor, Pa.: Chilton Co., 1970).

Jones, Owen, *Grammar of Ornament* (London: Day and Son, 1856).

Kauffman, Henry J., *The Colonial Silversmith, His Techniques and His Products* (New York: Galahad Books, 1969).

Kaufmann, Edgar, Jr., "Some American Architectural Ornament of the Arts and Crafts Era," *Journal of the Society of Architectural Historians, XXIV* (Dec. 1965), pp. 285–291.

Klapthor, Margaret Brown, *Presentation Pieces in the Museum of History and Technology, Smithsonian Institution* (Washington, D.C.: Smithsonian Institution, 1965).

Krantz, M. Camille, Report of the French Ministry of Commerce: "International Exposition of Chicago, 1893, Committee 24, Jewelry, Gold and Silverware" (Paris: National Press, 1894).

Lancaster, Clay, *The Japanese Influence in America* (New York: Walter H. Rawls, 1963).

Lassen, Erik, *Georg Jensen Silversmithy, 77 Artists, 75 Years* (Washington, D.C.: Smithsonian Institution Press, 1980).

Leighton, Margaretta Gebelein, *George Christian Gebelein, Boston Silversmith, 1878–1945* (Boston: Privately printed, 1976).

Link, Eva M., *The Book of Silver,* translated from the German by Francisca Garvie (New York: Praeger Publishers, 1973).

Mackie, Carey T.; Bacot, H. Parrott; and Mackie, Charles L., *Crescent City Silver* (New Orleans: The Historical New Orleans Collection and the Anglo–American Art Museum, Louisiana State University, 1980).

McClinton, Katharine Morrison, *Art Deco, A Guide For Collectors* (New York: Clarkson N. Potter, 1972).

McClinton, Katharine Morrison, *Collecting American 19th Century Silver* (New York: Charles Scribner's Sons, 1968).

Maryon, Herbert, *Metalwork and Enamelling* (New York: Dover Publications, 1971).

Mechanic's Festival and Historical Sketches (Providence: 1860).

Miller, William Davis, *The Silversmiths of Little Rest* (Kingston, R.I.: Privately printed, 1928).

Moffit, Charlotte, "New Designs in Silver," *House Beautiful,*

December 1899.

Morse, Edgar W., *San Francisco Silver Ware* (San Francisco: Argentum Antiques, Ltd., 1977), a two-page listing.

Mowry, Arthur May, *The Dorr War* (Providence, R.I., 1901).

Naylor, Gillian, *The Arts and Crafts Movement: A Study of Its Sources, Ideals and Influence on Design Theory* (Cambridge: The MIT Press, 1971).

Pairpoint, Thomas, "Art Work and Silver," a series of articles, *Jewelers' Circular*, September 1879 through March 1880.

Petramalo, Frank J., "Navy Presentation Silver," *Navy Supply Corps Newsletter*, June 1969, pp. 48 49.

Pevsner, Nikolaus, *Studies in Art, Architecture and Design* (London: Thomas 8c Hudson, 1969), Vol 2.

Providence Journal, July 11, 1845, p. 2; September 19, 1850, p. 2; September 13, 1851, p. 2; April 23, 1893.

Rainwater, Dorothy T., *Encyclopedia of American Silver Manufacturers* (New York: Crown Publishers, 1975).

Rainwater, Dorothy T., ed., *Sterling Silver Holloware* (Princeton, N.J.: The Pyne Press, 1973).

Rainwater, Dorothy T., and Felger, Donna H., *American Spoons, Souvenir and Historical* (Hanover, Pa.: Everybody's Press, 1977).

Rainwater, Dorothy T., and Rainwater, H. Ivan, *American Silverplate* (Nashville, Tenn.: Thomas Nelson and Hanover, Pa.: Everybody's Press, 1968).

Reischauer, Edwin O., *The Japanese* (Cambridge: Harvard University Press, 1977).

"Remember Those Who Go Down to the Sea in Ships," *The Foundry*, April 1, 1927.

Rhode Island Tercentenary Celebration, a Catalog of an Exhibition of Paintings by Gilbert Stuart, Furniture by the Goddards and Townsends (Providence: Art Museum, Rhode Island School of Design, 1936).

Robinson, H. Russell, *Japanese Arms and Armor* (New York: Crown Publishers, 1969).

Ruskin, John, *The Crown of Wild Olives* (Philadelphia: Henry Altemus, 1895).

Ruskin, John, *The Seven Lamps of Architecture*, Library Edition, Vol VIII.

Schmidt, Gertrude, "Fifteen Famous Actresses and Their Souvenir Spoons, 1892," *The Spinning Wheel*, October 1964, p. 8.

Schwaru, Marvin D., *Collectors' Guide to Antique American Silver* (New York: Doubleday & Co., 1975).

Scott, Kenneth, *Counterfeiting in Colonial Rhode Island* (Providence: Rhode Island Historical Society, 1960).

"Silver and Silver Plate," *Harper's New Monthly Magazine*, No. CCXX, Vol XXXVII, September 1878.

"Silvermaking in America, Part II, Gorham Mfg. Co.—History and Development," *The Manufacturing Jeweler*, June 6, 1894.

Simon, John Y., ed., *The Personal Memoirs of Julia Dent Grant* (New York: G. P. Putman's Sons, 1975)

Singleton, Esther, *The Story of the White House* (New York: McClure Co., 1907).

Smith, Howard R., *Economic History of the United States* (New York: Ronald Press Co., 1955).

Snodin, Michael, and Belden, Gail, *Collecting for Tomorrow, Spoons* (Radnor, Pa.: Chilton Book Co., 1976).

Souvenir Spoons of America (Published for Gorham Mfg. Co. by the Jeweler's Circular Publishing Co., 1891).

Statistisal History of the United States From Colonial Times to the Present (Stamford, Conn.: Fairfield Publishers, 1962).

Stutzenberger, Albert, *American Historical Spoons* (Rudand, Vt.: Charles E. Tutde Co., 1971).

Suzawa, Gilbert S., "Seril Dodge: Real Jewelery Industry Pioneer?" *URI Alumni Quarterly*, Summer 1979, pp. 26–28.

Terry, T. K., and Williams, Trevor I., *A Short History of Technology* (New York and Oxford: Oxford University Press, 1961).

Thomas, E. P., *William Morris and the Romantic Revolt* (London: Lawrence & Wilshart, Ltd., 1955)

Townsend, Horace, *Nicholas Heinzelman, the Man and the Artist* (New York: The Gorham Co., 1918).

Tracy, Berry B., *A Bicentennial Treasury: American Masterpieces from the Metropolitan* (New York: The Metropolitan Museum, 1976).

Tracy, Berry B., et al., *19th Century America: Furniture and Other Decorative Arts* (New York: The Metropolitan Museum, 1970).

Turk, B. F., *Japanese Objects D'Art* (New York: Sterling Publishing Co., 1963).

Turner, Justin G., and Turner, Linda Levitt, *Mary Todd Lincoln, Her Life and Letters* (New York: Alfred A. Knopf, 1972).

Turner, Noel D., *American Silver Flatware, 1837–1910* (New York: A. S. Barnes and Co., 1972).

Vital Records of Nantucket, Massachusetts, to the Year 1850 (Boston: New England Genealogical Society, 1927), Vol III, p. 144.

Ward, Barbara McLean, and Ward, Gerald W. R., eds., *Silver in American Life* (New York: The American Federation of Arts, 1979).

Wardle, Patricia, *Victorian Silver and Silver–Plate* (New York: Thomas Nelson and Sons, 1963).

Waters, Deborah Dependahl, "From Pure Coin, the Manufacrure of American Silver Flatware, 1800–1860," *Winterthur Portfolio 12*.

Whitford, *Frank, Japanese Prints and Western Painters* (New York: Macmillan Publishing Co., 1977).

Weilbachs Kunstnerleksikon, Aschehoug Forlag, 1947.

Weisberg, Gabriel; Cate, Phillip D.; Needham, Gerald; Eidelberg, Martin; and Johnson, William R., *Japonisme, Japanese Influence on French Art, 1854–1910*, Published jointly by the Cleveland Museum of Art, the Rutgers University Art Gallery, and the Walters Art Gallery, 1975.

Wilson, Richard Guy; Pilgrim, Dianne H.; and Murray, Richard N., *The American Renaissance, 1876–1917* (New York: The Brooklyn Museum, 1979).

Zerbe, Farran, "Bryan Money, Tokens of the Presidential Campaigns of 1896 and 1900—Comparative and Satirical," *The Numismatist*, Vol. XXXIX, July 1926, pp. 313–320

Index